ANALOG ELECTRONICS FOR MICROCOMPUTER SYSTEMS

by

D0869239

Dr. Paul F. Goldsbrough
Dr. Trevor Lund
Dr. John P. Rayner

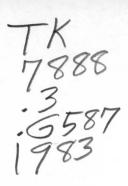

FIRST EDITION
FIRST PRINTING — 1983

International Standard Book Number: 0-672-21821-6
Library of Congress Catalog Card Number: 83-61062

Edited by: *White River Press*
Illustrated by: *Wm. D. Basham*

Printed in the United States of America.

Preface

This book is concerned with the analog electronics required to implement a microcomputer-based instrument or control system. Rapid advances in microcomputer technology have meant that design work can now be done almost entirely at the systems level rather than at the chip level. As a result, there is a strong tendency to overlook the basic electronic principles, both analog and digital, which are necessary for the successful implementation of a design. The complete avoidance of analog electronic principles is particularly common. Our intention with this book is to redress the imbalance by providing the practical analog circuits and the basic theory that are essential in microcomputer design and implementation.

A special feature of this text is that it introduces and explains a broad range of analog electronic topics and principles relevant to microcomputer systems. Existing discussions on most of the topics are scattered through myriad textbooks, application notes, and data books, if they can be found at all! This book divides a microcomputer system into five modules and discusses three in detail: the *analog input subsystem* (Module 1), the *microcomputer subsystem* (Module 2), and the *power subsystem* (Module 3). The purpose and content of each chapter are presented in the *Introduction* (Chapter 1). Key topics include:

- The principles of data acquisition for microcomputer systems, including a design approach for selecting ADCs, sample-and-hold amplifiers, and analog multiplexers.
- Analog signal conditioning and processing.
- Making the microprocessor and its bus system work.
- Designing and/or selecting power supplies and voltage references.

To effectively use this book, the reader should have a fair knowledge of digital electronics and microcomputing. The reader should also understand the principles of basic electronics including Ohm's law, L, R, C, the bipolar and FET transistor as circuit elements, and the basic operational amplifier configurations (inverting, noninverting, differential, and voltage-follower) and their characteristics.

Although the book is broadly based and does not fit neatly into a specific unit or subject in a study program, we believe that it should make an excellent *practical reference textbook.* It identifies and brings together, in a coherent form, a whole range of analog electronic topics relevant to microcomputer system design. It is the kind of text that engineering and science students should read while taking a senior course in digital electronics or microcomputers. The book should also be very useful to the practicing engineer or scientist and the interested hobbyist.

This work would not have been completed without the assistance of many people to whom we are indebted. Specifically, we would like to thank Bev Seagg from Canberra CAE, who patiently and skillfully prepared the manuscript on a word processor from our handwritten drafts and heavy editorial efforts and who, in the process, taught us how to use a WP effectively. Special thanks also to Jon Titus of The Blacksburg Group whose timely encouragement and concern kept the pages coming during some very tough times for us.

One final point. This book covers what we believe to be a fun area in which there is almost unlimited scope for ingenuity and imagination. Since the field is so vast, we can do no more than introduce the basic theory, some of the analog building blocks, and a few circuit ideas with comprehensive design procedures as the starting point for your own creativity. Have fun!

Paul Goldsbrough
Trevor Lund
John Rayner

DEDICATIONS

To Anne, Carl, Georgia, and Glenn with love.
— Paul Goldsbrough

To Marie, Dennis, and Michael.
— Trevor Lund

To the memory of my father, Jack Rayner.
—John Rayner

Contents

Chapter 4

SIGNALS AND NOISE

Chapter 5

ANALOG SIGNAL CONDITIONING

Chapter 6

ANALOG SIGNAL PROCESSING

Chapter 7

ANALOG-TO-DIGITAL CONVERSION

Module 2

THE MICROPROCESSOR SUBSYSTEM

Chapter 8

ELECTRICAL PROPERTIES OF MICROCOMPUTER ICs

Chapter 9

MAKING THE BUS SYSTEM WORK

Chapter 10

MAKING THE MICROPROCESSOR WORK

Module 3

THE POWER SUBSYSTEM

Chapter 11

Chapter 12

APPENDICES

Appendix A

Appendix B

THE THEORY AND DESIGN OF SWITCH-MODE POWER SUPPLIES

Appendix C

DIGITAL IC VOLTAGE AND CURRENT SPECIFICATIONS: DEFINITIONS

The authors currently hold positions in the School of Applied Science at Canberra College of Advanced Education (CCAE), ACT, Australia.

Dr. Paul Goldsbrough, lecturer in electronics at CCAE, teaches digital electronics, microcomputer design and interfacing, and analog electronics. He has specialized in the design and development of microcomputer-based data acquisition and control systems. He is the author of the Sams book *Microcomputer Interfacing Using the 8255 PPI* and has conducted numerous short courses on microcomputer programming and interfacing.

Dr. Trevor Lund, lecturer in electronics, teaches analog electronics, including control theory, at both the graduate and undergraduate levels. He also teaches courses in solid-state physics, a field in which he pursued the early part of his postdoctoral research career in both the USA and the UK. As a visiting fellow in the Department of Behavioral Biology at the Australian National University, he is now helping to develop the instrumentation and control systems needed for behavioral and neurological research.

Dr. John Rayner, senior lecturer in electronics, took his early training in physics and subsequently carried out research in hypersonics and plasma physics at the Australian National University. Transferring to CCAE, he was responsible for establishing the electronics program there. His current areas of interest are analog electronics and telecommunications. His other areas of interest include electromagnetic field theory and magnetohydrodynamics.

Overview

1-1 THE IMPORTANCE OF ANALOG ELECTRONICS IN MICROCOMPUTER SYSTEMS

The electronics industry has experienced three revolutions in the last thirty years. Each has had a profound impact on the industry and its personnel, on the scientific and industrial communities, and on society in general. Before the 1950s, electronics was dominated by the vacuum tube. The development of the bipolar transistor in 1948, however, meant that the fifties were destined to be a decade of profound change, highlighted by a trend towards miniaturization. This trend continued in the sixties with the introduction of the small-scale integration, bipolar integrated circuit. It reached a climax in the seventies with the development of large-scale integration, MOS integrated circuits, exemplified by the 8-bit (1972-73) and later the 16-bit (1978-79) microprocessors.

The consequences of these major developments in large-scale integrated circuits have been widespread and are well known. Two effects are relevant here:

- Component miniaturization.
- Development of a systems approach to electronic design.

These effects are closely related, because component miniaturization has led to the development of integrated circuit subsystems. These subsystems implement operations that previously required a large array of discrete transistors, resistors, and capacitors. The subsystems themselves may now be regarded as the new "components" which can be mixed and matched to form a total system. An example of

11

such a component is the *microcomputer,* which, in the form of the Intel 8051 or 8748 devices or the Motorola 6809, represents the implementation of a complete computer on a single silicon chip. In the early 1950s, the various computer subsystems, including the arithmetic/logic unit (ALU), registers, control, input/output (I/O), and memory, were implemented using transistors. The minicomputer in the 1960s was the result of mixing small-scale integrated circuits and transistors. The systems approach became a practical reality in the early 1970s with the appearance of the *microprocessor* whose registers and control logic were implemented on a single large-scale integrated circuit. With two or three additional integrated circuits, a single-board microcomputer such as Motorola's MEK6800D2 kit was possible.

An important result of component miniaturization and the resultant systems approach to electronic design has been a move away from discrete circuit electronics. This tendency began quite naturally in both analog and digital electronics with the introduction of the operational amplifier (op amp) and the digital integrated circuit (IC). The detailed knowledge of electronics required to get an electronic system up and running has been simplified and reduced. For example, it is no longer necessary to understand the design of an amplifier in detail. Since the op amp is now a basic analog electronic building block, the more important things to understand are its performance characteristics and the methods of configuring it for various applications. This considerable advantage accruing from our developing technology has brought with it hidden but very real problems. In a sense, things are harder today than they were before. We now need an understanding of complete, complex systems that are much more sophisticated than were previously possible. Our attention has moved, in a sense, from the trees to the wood. However, there is still a need for a solid foundation in basic analog and digital electronics principles so that:

- The connections between the "trees" — the advanced IC subsystems — can be understood and effectively designed.
- The total system can be made to function as intended.

The tendency to overlook basic electronics principles is quite common in the application, use, and discussion of microcomputers and microcomputer systems. Textbooks on microcomputers tend to concentrate on the software aspects of microcomputer system design, and the design and implementation of hardware systems and interfaces are gener-

12

ally discussed at the level of block diagrams. Although this approach is a necessary first step, the successful application of microcomputers to real-world tasks requires that the designer come to grips with basic analog and digital principles and techniques in the context of microcomputer systems. Because microcomputers are fundamentally digital subsystems, the basic digital electronics required to design with microcomputers is readily available and has been presented elsewhere.[1] This book presents the practical circuits and basic theory of *analog electronics* which are essential in microcomputer system design and implementation. It also provides the necessary discussion of the interaction of these circuits with the microcomputer and its software.

A block diagram of a typical microcomputer-based instrument incorporating both data acquisition and control is shown in Fig. 1-1 to illustrate the scope of the material that follows. This book is concerned with *data acquisition* and thus deals with the analog electronics of the *analog input* (Module 1), the *microprocessor* (Module 2) and the *power* (Module 3) subsystems. The figure shows their relation to the system control and to the subsystems concerned with *output* and *feedback*. The remainder of this chapter introduces the three microcomputer subsystems discussed in this volume.

1-2 MODULE 1: THE ANALOG INPUT SUBSYSTEM

Because the input and output interfaces are the system blocks in which the analog inputs are conditioned (amplified, offset, etc.) and converted to and from digital form, these two blocks taken together are commonly referred to as the *analog subsystem.* In 1977, this subsystem was discussed in *Electronic Design* in the following terms:

> Analog subsystems are needed to interface microcomputers with the real world of analog signals. In process control, transducers . . . cannot be directly connected to a microcomputer. The interface board for data acquisition must bridge the gap.[2]

The article goes on to describe the commercially available input and output analog signal conditioning boards, their cost/benefit trade-off, and the problems associated with such boards. We will discuss such boards in the chapters on data acquisition (Chapter 2) and analog signal conditioning (Chapter 5). However, the major problem with the commercially available data acquisition interface boards is worth noting at this point. Again, from *Electronic Design:*

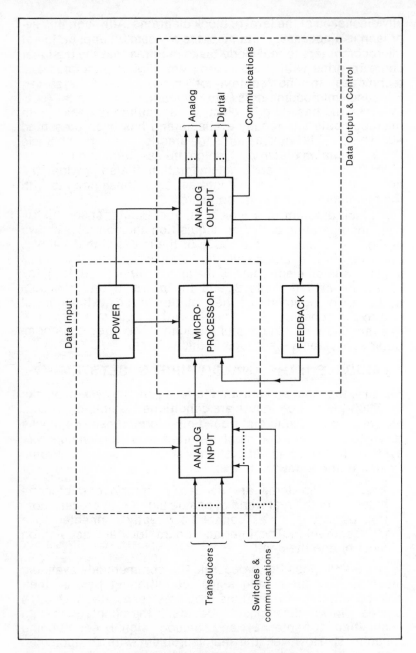

Fig. 1-1. The major data input subsystems of a typical microcomputer-based instrument or control system.

Unless you're using one of the most popular microcomputers — say, from Intel, Motorola, Digital Equipment, Pro-Log or Zilog — you may not be able to buy a ready-made and compatible analog-interface board. And even if you find a compatible board, you may find it doesn't have the specific features you need in your application.[3]

The article also mentions that the channel capacity of such boards — usually sixteen single- or double-ended inputs — may be insufficient for the likely applications. It is more common, we suspect, that the channel capacity is too large for the small user and that the commercial analog interface board represents a costly solution to the analog interfacing task.

For these reasons, it is often more convenient to tailor the analog interface circuits specifically to the characteristics of the transducers being used. Indeed, a primary objective of this book is to introduce the theory and practical circuits that facilitate this task. Thus, Module 1, which describes the analog input subsystem, introduces the basic theory via the principles of data acquisition in microcomputer systems (Chapter 2) and the sources of system noise (Chapter 4). After that, transducers (Chapter 3), analog signal conditioning (Chapter 5), and processing (Chapter 6) are introduced to illustrate the practical implementation of this theory. The module concludes with a discussion of the interface block — the analog-to-digital converter (ADC) between the analog input and microprocessor subsystems (Chapter 7). This chapter emphasizes the analog electronics required to get the ADC to operate satisfactorily and the calibration procedures, both hardware and software, which are necessary for successful data acquisition.

As an example of a small tailored analog input/output subsystem, consider the circuit of Fig. 1-2, which is part of a controller for a chemical reactor. The objective is to control the position of the solenoid valve (ON/OFF) and the state of the vacuum backing pump (ON/OFF), depending on the pressure in the line leading to the chemical reactor. The analog subsystem can be seen to consist of an input section and an output section. As is usually the case, the interfacing of these subsystems to the microprocessor is facilitated by the use of a commercial, digital interface IC. In this case, it is the 8255 parallel peripheral interface (PPI), which connects easily to the data, address, and control buses of the microprocessor. The more demanding design problem is the analog input and output subsystems whose requirements are as follows:

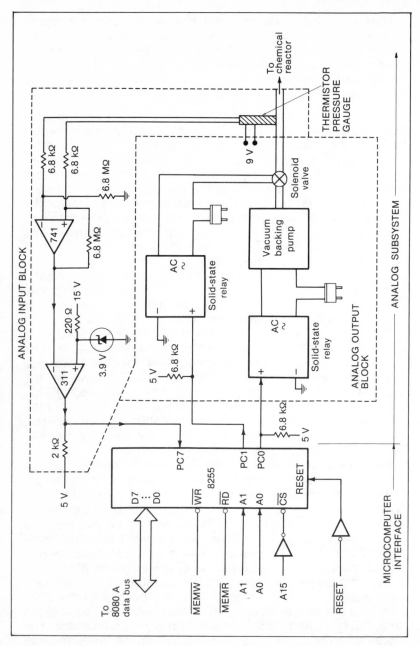

Fig. 1-2. The input and output subsystems for a microcomputer-based chemical reactor controller.

Input Subsystem: Accept from the thermistor pressure transducer a floating analog signal in the range of 120 mV (atmospheric pressure) to about 3–4 mV (0.005 mm of Hg) and produce a logic level input (0–5 V) to the PPI. The logic level is to be an active high signal which is normally low (∼0.4 V) and is switched to a high (∼2 V) when the analog signal is ∼4 mV. As the system is pumped down, the rate of decrease in pressure below 0.01 mm of Hg is very slow. The resulting rate of decrease in the analog output of the transducer below ∼10 mV is ∼0.2 mV per second.

Output Subsystem: The PPI outputs are required to switch two mains-operated devices. The problem is that while the 2-mA current drive capability of the PPI at a high is much higher than normal for a high, it is still inadequate for direct use. Fig. 1-2 shows a working solution that satisfies these requirements for the input and output subsystems.

1-3 MODULE 2: THE MICROPROCESSOR SUBSYSTEM

This module (Chapters 8–10) represents an end point in our discussion of the analog electronics of microcomputer systems, in the sense that the preceding Chapters (2–7) are devoted to the *data input subsystem* which finishes at the *microprocessor subsystem.* However, the microprocessor subsystem, illustrated in Fig. 1-3, is extremely important in its own right since it forms the heart of any microcomputer system. It is a bus-oriented subsystem with data represented in the digital data domain. As a result, the electrical properties and problems of this subsystem are significantly different from those of the data input subsystem which dealt predominately with single-line signal paths. The aim of Chapters 8–10 is to explore the principles and practical considerations essential to the *electronic* design of this subsystem.

To achieve this aim, we need a strong mental picture of the basic blocks which comprise the microprocessor subsystem and of its physical appearance and characteristics. Although our definition is rather arbitrary, we have chosen to consider that the subsystem contains those digital elements needed to access and execute system software and to communicate with user peripherals. A conceptual boundary can be sketched by noting that data remains exclusively within the digital data domain in this subsystem. Thus, although the microprocessor and memory are core blocks, digital arithmetic processors and peripheral controllers are also included. The key characteristic of the subsystem is the bus system, which is essential for

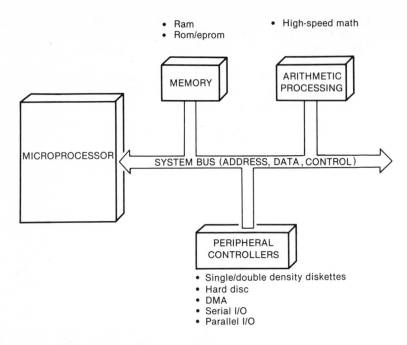

Fig. 1-3. Block diagram of the microprocessor subsystem.

the controlled transfer of digital data and machine code into and out of the microprocessor.

Although the physical implementation of the subsystem varies enormously, it is always centered on the method used to implement the bus system. In some systems, all of the blocks are layed out on a *single printed circuit board* which can be up to 18 × 12 inches and contain perhaps one hundred integrated circuits. An internal bus system of arbitrary definition is then possible, since the subsystem is self-contained. Analog input and output subsystems are also laid out on this type of board so that only plug-type sockets and connectors are needed to attach the necessary input and output devices, such as VDUs, discs, printers, analog inputs and outputs, and so forth. This approach is popular in custom designed microcomputer-based instrument and control systems. An alternate and very popular approach is to use a *backplane bus structure* so that different blocks, including those of the input and output subsystems, can be developed and implemented separately and then interconnected through the backplane. Each printed circuit (PC) board has a gold plated edge connector (Fig. 1-4) to which the address, data, control, and power buses have been wired. The backplane (Fig. 1-5) consists of a number of sockets which are connected in parallel on a PC board. The various blocks needed for a particular system application are then interconnected by inserting the PC boards for each block into the backplane sockets as illustrated in Figs. 1-5 and 1-6. A number of backplane bus structures have been developed, each having a well-defined physical arrangement of address, data, control, and power buses. These include the STD, Intel MULTIBUS® (IEEE-796), and S100 (IEEE-696) buses.

Many books on microcomputers discuss the operation and the *logical* design and interconnection of the blocks shown in Fig. 1-3. The assumption in most of these books is that when the microprocessor, EPROMs, RAMs, and peripheral controller ICs are logically interconnected, the resulting microprocessor subsystem will automatically work. This "black box" approach ignores the electrical characteristics of each element and the electrical problems that can arise, usually at the least expected times and places, when the elements are connected through a common bus structure.

In Module 2, by contrast, we will concentrate on the *electronic engineering aspects* of the design of the microprocessor subsystem. Chapter 8 is devoted to the electrical properties and basic operating principles of the MOS and bipolar integrated circuit (IC) families which together provide virtually all the subsystem components. The characteristic properties of each IC family are introduced to explain their role in this subsystem. The operation of the basic gate in each family is also reviewed to provide insight into the formulation and meaning of their DC and AC electrical specifications. These specifications are essential in Chapter 9, which is devoted to the *electrical* design of the bus system. In this chapter, the reasons for and solutions to such electrical problems as bus loading, timing errors, and improper bus termination are discussed. Key topics include DC current and voltage specifications and the consequent need for pull-up resistors and current/voltage buffering; AC specifications and bus timing; and the transmission line effects that make bus termination necessary. Chapter 10 explains how to get the microprocessor IC to work and includes a comprehensive discussion of clocks, crystals, and reset circuits.

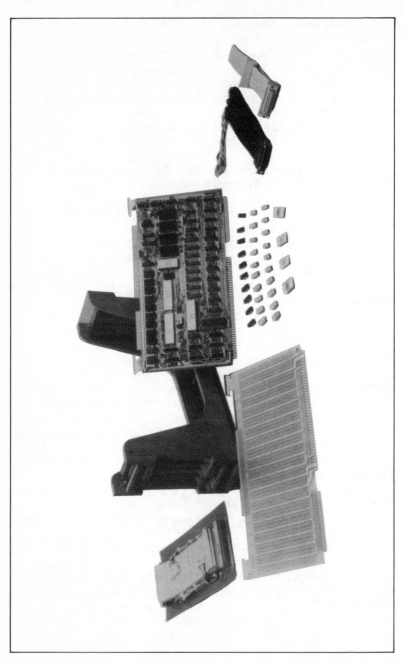

Fig. 1-4. An illustration of the PC boards used with a backplane bus structure.

Fig. 1-5. Backplane shown beneath a card cage for modular PC boards.

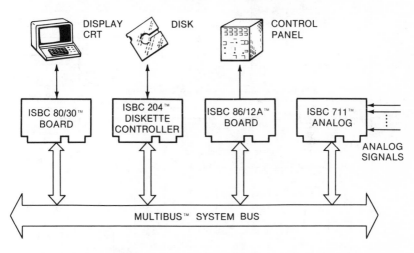

Fig. 1-6. System flexibility can be achieved with a multiboard busing system.

1-4 MODULE 3: THE POWER SUBSYSTEM

The microcomputer subsystem that has received almost no attention in previous books on microcomputers is the *power block.* Fig. 1-7 shows the circuit schematic for the micro-

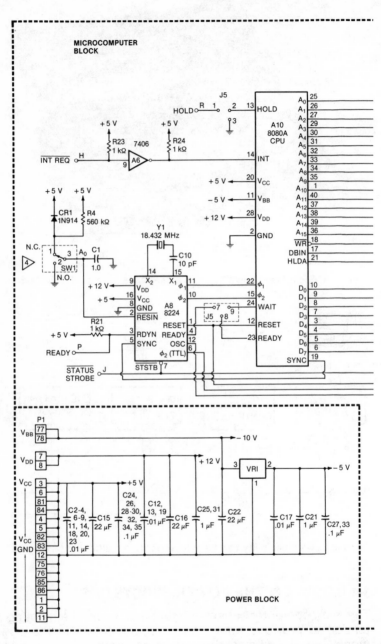

Fig. 1-7. Circuit of the SDK-80

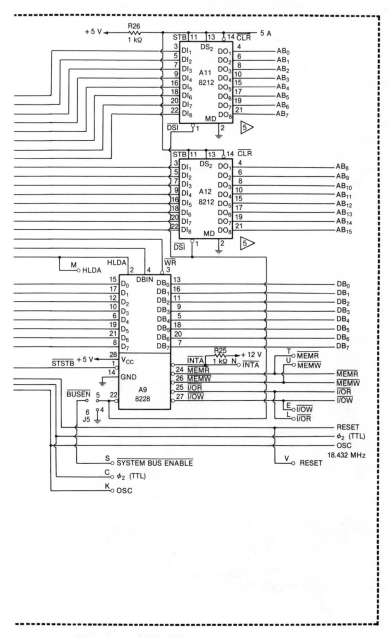

microcomputer. (*Courtesy Intel Corp. Inc.*)

processor portion of Intel's SDK 80 microcomputer, where it can be seen that the user is expected to provide the $+5$-V, $+12$-V and -10-V power supplies. One solution is to purchase a ready-made, packaged power supply, for example, the power module of the Intel ISC 80 Industrial Controller, shown in Fig. 1-8. As with the input and output subsystems, such commercially available solutions may represent a costly overkill. In any case, one must understand the specifications and requirements of power supply subsystems. Since it may be necessary to design and build a power supply before a microcomputer system can be started up, Module 3 is devoted to a discussion of the basic principles of power supply design and specification (Chapter 11). Also included in this module is a related and equally important topic, the generation of stable voltage references (Chapter 12). These are essential for the reliable, accurate, and stable operation of an analog subsystem.

Fig. 1-8. The Intel ICS80 Industrial Controller System.

1-5 REFERENCES

1. P.R. Rony, *Logic and Memory Experiments using TTL Integrated Circuits.* Howard W. Sams & Co., Inc., 1978; P.R. Rony, *Introductory Experiments in Digital Electronics and 8080A Microcomputer Programming and Interfacing,* Howard W. Sams & Co., Inc., 1977.

2. M. Elphick, "Analog Boards for Microcomputers: You Can't Always Get What You Want," *Electronic Design,* 1977, *25:19,* p. 1.

3. Elphick, 1977, pp. 26-32.

MODULE 1

THE ANALOG INPUT SUBSYSTEM

Principles of Data Acquisition for Microcomputer Systems

2-1 INTRODUCTION

Most microcomputer-based instruments and systems interact with the real world and therefore have an *input subsystem* whose inputs can be broadly classified as either *commands* or *data*. Command inputs, which are for system definition and operator input, are commonly implemented using push buttons, switches, or keyboards. These will be discussed in a later chapter. Data inputs may be in the form of either continuous physical variables, such as temperature, pressure, and rate of flow, or discrete events, such as radioactive decay pulses or the set point for a control variable being exceeded. In this chapter, the principles of data acquisition and their implementation in a microcomputer system will be discussed at a systems level, emphasizing the acquisition of continuous physical data. The practical implementation of an analog input subsystem is then presented in Chapters 3 (Transducers), 4 (Signals and Noise), 5 (Analog Signal Conditioning), 6 (Analog Signal Processing), and 7 (Analog-to-Digital Conversion).

2-2 DATA AND ITS REPRESENTATION

Since the input subsystem of a microcomputer-based instrument or control system is primarily concerned with data acquisition and signal conditioning, it helps in understanding the operation of the subsystem to be fully conscious of how a data variable is represented at any point. Once the variable has been transformed into an electrical signal by a transducer, the variable is then represented by some characteristic or property of that signal. Each characteristic or property of the electrical signal is known as a *data domain.*[1] Although the data domain concept can be used to describe any form — electrical or nonelectrical — in which information is represented, our discussion will be limited to the various *electrical* data domains. Three broad classifications can be identified: analog, time, and digital. In each of these broad categories, physical information may be represented in a number of different forms which are summarized in Table 2-1.

Table 2-1. Electrical Data Domains

Classification	Types
ANALOG	Charge, current, voltage, power, resistance, capacitance, inductance
TIME	Frequency, period, rate
DIGITAL	Count, byte or word, serial bit stream, logic one, logic zero

The data acquisition input subsystem shown in Fig. 2-1 uses a series of data domain conversions. Data from the physical data domain (temperature, pressure, etc.) is first transformed into the electrical domain using a transducer. Analog signal conditioning is used to convert the data to an analog voltage, and then an analog-to-digital converter (ADC) transforms the data into the digital domain as a parallel byte or word.

The approach shown in Fig. 2-1 is employed when we need the *values* of the physical variable over their dynamic range. The values are input by the microcomputer as the magnitude of a binary word. If, however, the important information is the occurrence of an *event,* then the sample-and-hold amplifier and the analog-to-digital converter are replaced by a *threshold detector* which determines the occurrence of the event. This type of data acquisition input subsystem was illustrated earlier in Fig. 1-2, where the establishment of vacuum conditions within a reactor was to be sensed. In that figure, IC1 is the analog signal conditioning element and IC2 is the

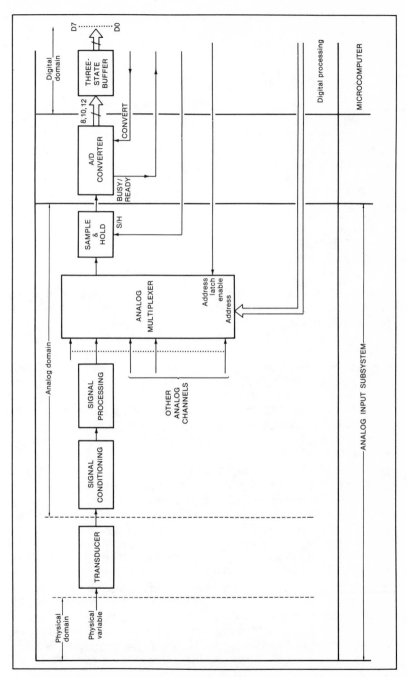

Fig. 2-1. Data acquisition input subsystem and its interface with the microcomputer.

31

threshold detector. The detection threshold is set by the 3.9-V zener diode and the voltage gain of IC1. The event data is input by the microcomputer as a status flag.

2-3 ANALOG SIGNAL CONDITIONING

In Chapter 3, we will see that transducers respond to changes in a physical variable by changing one of the analog data domain variables, which are listed in Table 2-1. Since analog-to-digital converters generally require unipolar input voltage in the range of 0–5 or 0–10 V, the first requirement of the data input subsystem is to convert the transducer's output signal to the voltage domain. Thereafter, the following modifications to the signal are usually essential:

- Voltage amplification
- DC offset
- Bandwidth limiting
- Noise suppression

These modifications are performed in the analog domain by the *amplifier* and *filter* blocks and will be collectively described as *analog signal conditioning.*

Voltage amplification is used to increase the amplitude of low-level signals to a maximum value of 5 or 10 volts, depending on the type of analog-to-digital converter used. Amplification is generally done in a number of stages. Occasionally the transducer output voltage exceeds the maximum value specified for the ADC, in which case voltage attenuation is necessary to adequately condition the signal amplitude.

DC offset of the signal is necessary if the transducer output is nonzero at the minimum specified value of the input physical variable. An example of this occurs with the National Semiconductor absolute pressure transducer, type LX1702A, for which the minimum output voltage is 2.5 V at absolute zero pressure. Another common situation requiring DC offset signal conditioning is where improved resolution is sought by concentrating on or accepting only a small portion of the overall dynamic range of a given input variable. In such cases, the base value of the data input is generally above its minimum value and this produces a nonzero base value for the transducer output. In the case of the LX1702A, the specified input pressure range of 0–15 psi results in a voltage output of 2.5–12.5 V. Within the accuracy of the transducer itself, the resolution of the signal at the ADC may be improved by a factor of two by concentrating, for example, on the 7.5–15 psi pressure range. The transducer output then is 7.5–12.5 V, which requires unity gain and a −7.5-V DC offset to produce an acceptable ADC input voltage range of 0–5 V.

The *signal bandwidth* must be limited by filtering in accordance with the sampling rate that is chosen for the sample-and-hold amplifier. This is essential, because noise outside the bandwidth of interest can appear as low-frequency noise within the signal bandwidth if the signal is sampled at a rate less than twice the maximum signal frequency (f_{MAX}). This effect is known as *aliasing* (see Section 2-6-3) and must be eliminated or at least minimized by suppressing noise above f_{MAX} using a low-pass filter. Sampling and the sample-and-hold amplifier are discussed in Section 2-6.

Noise suppression is an important requirement of the analog signal conditioning modules because noise may degrade considerably the effective minimum system resolution. Bandwidth limiting using low-pass filters is an important method for suppressing noise that is above f_{MAX}. Noise below f_{MAX} can also be removed by low-pass filtering, but some degradation of the signal amplitude and phase must be accepted. A differential amplifier, however, can be used to greatly reduce noise both inside and outside the signal bandwidth. This amplifier is designed to reject noise that appears identically on its two inputs (common-mode noise) while amplifying the signal on one input with respect to the other. Differential amplifiers have a high common-mode rejection ratio and are very effective in suppressing common-mode noise.

2-4 ANALOG SIGNAL PROCESSING

The analog signal conditioning operations described above are those most commonly needed to transform a low-level, noisy signal from the transducer into a relatively "clean" analog signal that can be presented directly to the ADC for digitization. However, there are a number of additional signal modifications that are only occasionally necessary and that usually can be implemented in the analog or digital data domains by the analog input subsystem or the microcomputer, respectively. These modifications will be described as analog or digital *signal processing.* They include the following operations:

- Linearization
- Dynamic range compression or expansion
- Determination of absolute values

33

- Integration/differentiation
- Multiplication
- Addition and subtraction
- Comparison of signal levels

Since this book is principally concerned with the analog electronics of microcomputer-based systems, the analog implementation of these operations will be described in detail in Chapter 6. Comparison of an input signal with some reference level can be regarded as a form of analog signal processing, since a decision must be made. However, the discussion of what is in effect a two-state ADC will be presented in Chapter 7. The factors determining whether signal processing should be implemented in the analog domain, in the digital domain using specialized arithmetic or signal processing digital ICs, or in software are also discussed in Chapter 6. These factors include flexibility, precision, speed, real time implementation, system resource management, and ease of implementation.

2-5 DIGITIZING

Two processes are required to convert an analog, time-varying voltage into the digital data domain, namely, *sampling* and *digitizing.* In principle, both processes are implemented by the analog-to-digital converter. In practice, however, considerable time, ranging from microseconds to milliseconds, is required for the ADC to digitize an analog input. During this time, the analog input voltage must remain stable if an accurate digital representation of the analog input is to be obtained. Let us assume for the moment that any changes in the input signal amplitude are very slow compared to the digitizing time of the ADC, so the input signal is stable for the time required to digitize it. This situation is very common in process control applications where changes in process variables, such as temperature and pressure, are often less than 0.5% per minute. With this assumption, we can focus attention on the digitizing of the analog signal and defer consideration of the sampling process to Section 2-6.

Analog-to-digital conversion or digitizing is a two-step process involving the *quantization* and *coding* of the analog input. Quantization is defined by Zuch as "the process of transforming a continuous analog signal into a set of discrete output states."[2] These output states must then be coded, which involves assigning a binary bit pattern to each output state. The two steps can be seen clearly in the operation of parallel or "flash" ADCs. Here a set of discrete states is generated using a bank of voltage comparators, and the binary code is produced by encoding the outputs of the comparators (see Fig. 2-2A). The sequential nature of these two steps is less obvious in other types of ADCs such as the successive-approximation converter where the processes occur more nearly simultaneously. The transfer function of an ideal 3-bit ADC is shown in Fig. 2-2B and illustrates clearly the two steps involved in digitizing.

It is worth noting briefly here that a threshold detector, which is used for event detection, is also a very simple digitizer. In this case, quantization of a continuously variable analog signal is implemented using *a single detection threshold* to generate *two discrete output states.* These are coded by the threshold detector, at the moment of quantization, as a single binary digit or bit.

The two parameters of an ADC that are important from a systems point of view are its *resolution* and its *conversion time.* The *resolution* (R) of the ADC is important since the system resolution is determined by this parameter. It is usually defined as the analog voltage needed to produce a change in the least significant bit of the ADC. For an *n*-bit ADC, the resolution may be expressed as:

$$R(\text{volts}) = \frac{\text{full scale input voltage}}{(2^n - 1)} \qquad \text{(Eq. 2-1)}$$

or, in terms of a percentage of full scale, as:

$$R(\%) = \left[\frac{1}{(2^n - 1)} \right] \times 100 \qquad \text{(Eq. 2-2)}$$

In many cases, the resolution of an ADC is quoted somewhat loosely as the width, *n,* of the binary word that is generated by the ADC.

The *conversion time* (t_c) of an ADC is the time required, after the application of a convert pulse, for the ADC to quantize the analog input and to provide, at its output, the binary equivalent of the analog input. The maximum permissible conversion time of an ADC in an analog input subsystem is determined, in general, by the requirements of the Sampling Theorem, because the conversion time must be less than the time between samples (see Section 2-6). Thereafter, the choice of an appropriate ADC is a simple trade-off between cost (which can be very high) and performance. For microcomputer systems, cheap ($5–$10), moderately fast (~25-μs) 8-bit ADCs are readily available. These provide approximately 0.4% resolution, which is more than adequate in many systems where the accuracy of the transducers is commonly closer to 1%. If higher system resolution is needed, 10-, 12-, and 16-bit ADCs are available, but these are considerably more expensive. In most microcomputer-based data acquisition and control systems, the choice is made from the 8-, 10-, and 12-bit ADCs, the 10-bit converter being most popular in control situations where improved resolution is required. Table 2-2 shows the relationship between ADC word length and resolution.

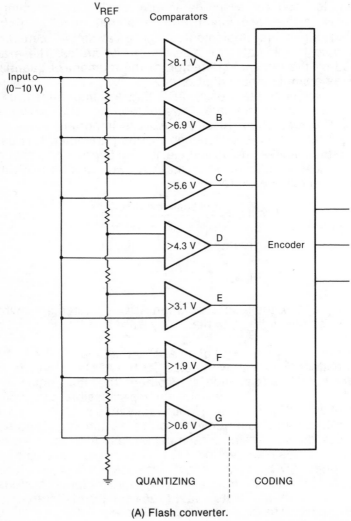

(A) Flash converter.

Fig. 2-2. Quantizing

Table 2-2. ADC Resolution

ADC Word Length (bits)	% Resolution
8	0.39
10	0.098
12	0.024
16	0.0015

2-6 SAMPLING AND THE SAMPLE-AND-HOLD AMPLIFIER

In discussing the process of digitizing, it was assumed that the analog input to the analog-to-digital converter remained stable over a period that was very long compared to the conversion time of the ADC. In this section, we consider the problems associated with digitizing a signal whose variations are significant over the ADC conversion time. Two basic system problems can be identified in the following questions:

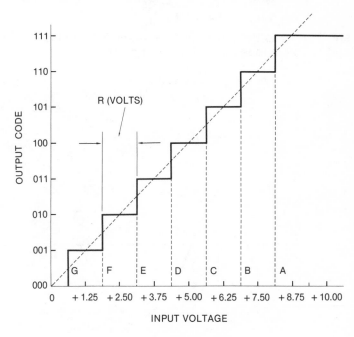

(B) Transfer function.

and coding.

1. What is the maximum time available to sample the input signal before its amplitude changes by half the ADC resolution, introducing an error into the digitized result? This window in time is known as the *system aperture time,* t_{sa}.
2. What sampling rate or time between samples, t_s, is required to ensure that the signal information is fully recovered?

2-6-1 System Aperture Time

The system aperture time is a function of both the ADC resolution, R(volts), and the signal frequency, f. To derive an expression that relates t_{sa} to R(volts) and f, consider a sinusoid of maximum peak-to-peak amplitude, V_p, which is shown in Fig. 2-3. The maximum rate of change in sinusoid voltage occurs at the zero crossing of the signal (point 0 in the figure). If we approximate the signal by the straight line AOB, then from the geometry,

$$\frac{\Delta V}{V_p} \approx \frac{\Delta t}{T/2} = 2f\Delta t \qquad \text{(Eq. 2-3)}$$

where $T = 1/f$ is the period of the sinusoid. Precise analysis using the true shape of the sinusoid gives

$$\frac{\Delta V}{V_p} = \pi f \Delta t. \qquad \text{(Eq. 2-4)}$$

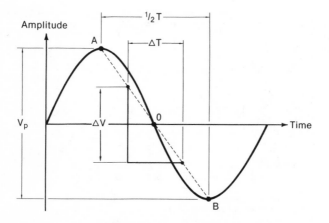

Fig. 2-3. Sinusoid of period T and peak-to-peak amplitude V_p.

Since Δt represents the system aperture time, t_{sa}, when ΔV is equal to R(volts)/2, then Equation 2-4 can be rewritten as

$$t_{sa} \leqslant \frac{R(volts)}{2\pi f V_p}. \qquad \text{(Eq. 2-5)}$$

Using Equation 2-1, Equation 2-5 can also be rewritten as

$$t_{sa} \leqslant \frac{1}{(2^n - 1)2\pi f}. \qquad \text{(Eq. 2-6)}$$

Thus, if a 1-kHz sinusoid is digitized using an 8-bit ADC, then from Equation 2-6,

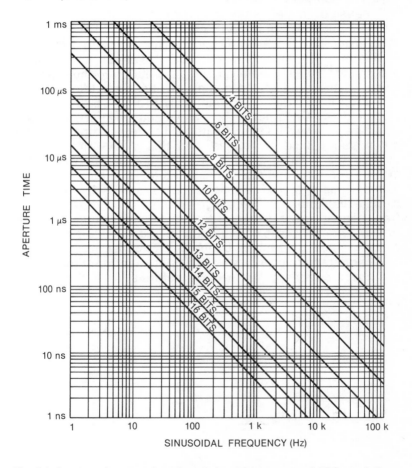

Fig. 2-4. Aperture time as a function of signal frequency and ADC resolution.
(*Courtesy Datel Systems, Inc.*)

$$t_{sa} \leqslant \frac{1}{(2^8 - 1) \cdot 2\pi \cdot 1000} = 0.62\,\mu s.$$

This time is approximately one order of magnitude smaller than the conversion time of a moderately priced ($10–$100) ADC. The system aperture times required for sinusoids with frequencies in the range of 1–100 kHz, and for ADCs with binary outputs ranging from 4–16 bits, are shown in Fig. 2-4. Note that the system aperture time derived in our example is by no means the worst case. Times of about 100 ns are not unreasonable, even for a 10-bit ADC!

2-6-2 The Sample-and-Hold Amplifier

Because of the requirement that sampling of the analog input be completed before the signal changes by R/2 volts, the system aperture times are very short. This means that ADCs of moderate price cannot directly digitize most time-varying analog signals. Fortunately, a simple solution to the problem exists in the form of the sample-and-hold amplifier, whose operation is illustrated schematically in Fig. 2-5. During the sample time, the output of the sample-and-hold (S/H) amplifier accurately follows its input. In its hold state, the amplifier output remains fixed or latched, and this allows the ADC to digitize the sample accurately. The conflict between the system aperture time requirement and the available ADC conversion time can now be resolved. This is done by using the sample-and-hold amplifier's high switching speed — switching from sample to hold mode — to satisfy the system aperture time requirement. The aperture time of a data acquisition subsystem is now determined by the S/H amplifier.

When attempting to relate the system aperture time, t_{sa}, to the specifications given in manufacturers' data sheets, dif-

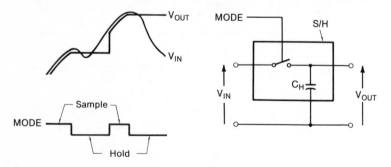

Fig. 2-5. Sample-and-hold amplifier operation. (*Courtesy Blacksburg Group, Inc.*)

ficulties arise because the definitions of the various S/H times seem to vary between manufacturers. However, if we examine the sample-to-hold process in more detail, as illustrated in Fig. 2-6, it appears that the three most commonly quoted times are[3,4]:

t_{ad}, the aperture delay time;
t_u, the aperture uncertainty or jitter; and
t_{set}, the hold mode settling time.

As the figure shows, t_{ad} is the time from the initiation of the hold command to the point where the switch (Fig. 2-5) is effectively open. This, then, is simply a timing offset that can be compensated for by advancing the timing of the hold command. The hold mode settling time, t_{set}, defines the time after the switch has fully opened before the held value settles to within some specified percentage of its final steady-state value — usually half of R(%) of the ADC. *It is therefore safe to issue the start conversion command to the ADC only after a time of* $t_{SH} = t_{ad} + t_{set}$.

The time t_u represents the uncertainty or variation in the aperture delay time. This effect cannot be eliminated and always leads to an error or uncertainty in the held voltage. *It is therefore* t_u *which must satisfy the system aperture time requirement.*

The hold state of the sample-and-hold amplifier is implemented by charging a capacitor during the sample time (Fig. 2-5) and then isolating the capacitor to prevent its discharge during the hold state. This isolation is never complete, and some discharge of the capacitor occurs during the hold time. This discharge results in a *droop* of the amplifier's

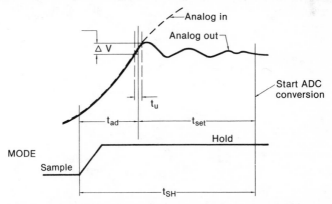

Fig. 2-6. Times associated with the sample-to hold transition.

output, as shown in Fig. 2-7. To avoid an ADC conversion error, the product of the rate of voltage droop (dV/dt) of the S/H amplifier's output and the conversion time, t_c, must be less than half the ADC resolution:

$$\frac{dV}{dt} \cdot t_c \leqslant \frac{R(\text{volts})}{2} \qquad \text{(Eq. 2-7)}$$

Hence, if the ADC conversion time and its resolution are known, together with the input signal's highest frequency of interest, Fig. 2-4 can be used to determine the maximum system aperture time. From there we can determine the aperture uncertainty (t_u) requirement of the sample-and-hold amplifier, and Equation 2-7 can be used to determine its maximum allowable droop rate.

2-6-3 What Sampling Rate?

The *rate* at which an analog signal is sampled is important in determining how well the resulting set of samples represents the original continuous analog signal. The *minimum* sampling rate is specified by the *Sampling Theorem,* which can be stated as follows:

If a signal is band-limited to a maximum frequency, f_m, then it must be sampled at greater than $2f_m$ to ensure that no information is lost during the sampling process.

In practice, care should be taken to avoid a sampling rate

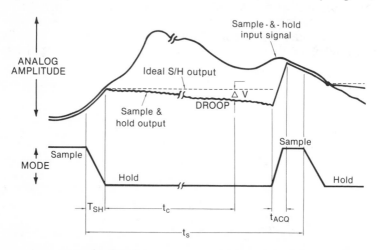

Fig. 2-7. Sample-to-hold time, t_{SH}, droop, and acquisition time, t_{acq}, of a sample-and-hold amplifier (t_{SH} is exaggerated for effect).

close to $2f_m$. Although theoretically no information is lost by sampling a single sinusoid of frequency f_m at a rate just slightly in excess of $2f_m$, the reconstructed form of this sampled waveform will appear to be a very coarse and angular representation of the original. Certainly the frequency f_m is still present, but the reconstruction process required to fully recover the sinusoidal *shape* of the signal is not easy. The theorem is intended to be applied to complex signals of bandwidth f_m. Under the theorem, the shape of the signals is retained if their frequency components near f_m are small in relation to their low-frequency components. Since this cannot be guaranteed, a sample rate of $5f_m$ is usually specified as a more satisfactory practical sampling criterion.

Failure to sample a signal at greater than $2f_m$ results in two types of signal corruption. First, if the sampling rate is f_s, then information contained in frequencies above $f_s/2$ is lost. Consequently, the frequency $f_s/2$ is very special and is called the *Nyquist frequency* f_N. Second, the undersampled frequencies above f_N appear below f_N and act to further distort the original signal. The resulting frequencies below f_N are called *aliases* and the effect is known as *aliasing.* The production of an alias as a result of inadequate sampling is shown in Fig. 2-8. In Fig. 2-8A, the aliasing effect is shown in the time domain. The effect is commonly described as a frequency folding effect since the frequency of the alias can be determined by accurately folding the frequency spectrum of the signal about the Nyquist frequency f_N, as illustrated in Fig. 2-8B. Quantitatively, the alias frequency f_a is determined by the equation

$$f_a = f_s - f_{signal}. \qquad \text{(Eq. 2-8)}$$

Only two solutions exist to the aliasing problem: either increase the sampling rate or reduce the signal bandwidth. In many cases, neither solution will look attractive. Increasing the sampling rate implies a need for a fast (or short) conversion time ADC, and the relationship between ADC speed and cost is closer to an exponential than to a linear function. On the other hand, reducing the signal bandwidth can often mean a loss of critical information. If band-limiting is the only choice because of the prohibitive cost of a faster ADC, then there is really no issue. The only "choice" in this case is between accepting a controlled degradation in the high-frequency response of the system through low-pass filtering or accepting an uncontrolled and less easily identified signal degradation as a result of aliasing.

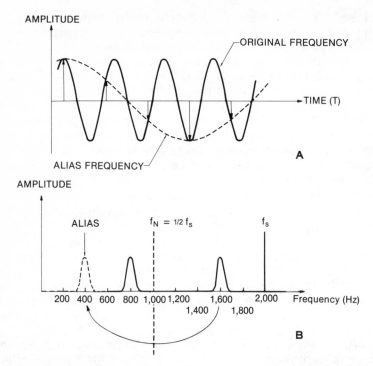

Fig. 2-8. Aliasing shown in the time domain (A) and frequency domain (B).

2-6-4 Timing Considerations

In Sections 2-5 and 2-6, a number of different and possibly confusing time periods have been introduced:

t_c, the ADC conversion time
t_{SH}, the effective hold time of the S/H amplifier
$t_s = 1/f_s$, the time between samples.

These times are illustrated in Fig. 2-7, together with the acquisition time of the sample-and-hold amplifier, t_{acq}. This is the time required by the amplifier for its output to reach a final value (within a specified error range) after the *sample* command has been given. It is primarily a function of the amplifier's output slewing rate and settling time.

From Fig. 2-7, it can be seen that:

$$t_s \geq t_{SH} + t_c + t_{acq}. \qquad \text{(Eq. 2-9)}$$

The effective hold time (t_{SH}) of the S/H amplifier ranges from 150 ns to a few microseconds, depending on the ADC resolution. The minimum sampling time, t_s, is usually determined by the ADC conversion time (t_c) and, to a lesser extent, by the S/H acquisition time (t_{acq}), which ranges from about 1 to 5 microseconds for moderate performance devices.

2-7 ANALOG MULTIPLEXING

The purpose of the analog multiplexer is to combine a set of analog signals in such a way that they can be accessed sequentially and presented in turn to a single S/H amplifier and ADC. In a simple situation, we can assume that each of the input channels needs to be sampled at the same sampling rate f_{s1} so that if there are n channels then the multiplexer needs to run at a rate nf_{s1}. As a result, the effective sampling rate or system acquisition speed (f_s) required at the output of the multiplexer is nf_{s1}, and the time available for the S/H and ADC to complete a conversion (t_s) becomes

$$t_s = \frac{1}{f_s} = \frac{1}{nf_{s1}}. \qquad \text{(Eq. 2-10)}$$

By way of example, if we have a 32-channel system and each channel requires a sampling frequency of 8 kHz, then $f_s = 32 \times 8$ kHz $= 256$ kHz and $t_s = 3.9 \mu$s.

In a more complex system, the sampling rate required for each channel may not be the same. In such situations it is convenient to think of a conceptual hierarchy of multiplexers, arranged in such a way that the effective sampling frequency at each input to a multiplexer is the same. Thus, if we have m channels requiring a low sampling frequency of f_m and n channels requiring a much higher sampling frequency of f_n, then a conceptual arrangement such as that shown in Fig. 2-9 would be appropriate. In this diagram, multiplexer #1 combines the m channels to give an effective output frequency of mf_m. This output provides one input to multiplexer #2, together with the n fast channels, and we must ensure that

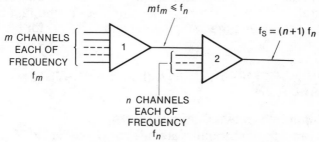

Fig. 2-9. Conceptual analog multiplexer hierarchy.

$$mf_m \leqslant f_n. \qquad \text{(Eq. 2-11)}$$

The effective sampling rate, f_s, at the output of multiplexer #2 therefore becomes $f_s = (n + 1) f_n$ with a corresponding system sampling time, t_s, of

$$t_s = \frac{1}{f_s} = \frac{1}{(n + 1)f_n}. \qquad \text{(Eq. 2-12)}$$

By a simple extension of this idea, multiplexer systems can be designed that combine signals with many different sampling frequencies. This approach is far more efficient in terms of maximizing the available system sampling time, t_s, compared with the use of a single simple multiplexer. A large value for t_s is desirable since it lessens the demands made on the speed of the S/H, ADC, and microprocessor input. To illustrate this point, consider a system consisting of four channels with a sampling frequency of 100 Hz and two channels with a sampling frequency of 1 kHz. If a single simple multiplexer is employed, then $f_s = 6 \times 1$ kHz $= 6$ kHz and $t_s = 166$ μs. However, if two cascaded multiplexers are connected as in Fig. 2-10A, then $f_s = 3 \times 1$ kHz $= 3$ kHz and $t_s = 330$ μs, so that the available sampling/conversion time is increased by a factor of two. Note that, in this example, each of the four slow channels is actually sampled at a rate of 250 Hz, which is considerably more than the minimum requirement of 100 Hz. Thus, some increase in the maximum frequency of each of these channels is possible without changing the value of f_s. Alternatively, the number of 100-Hz channels could be increased to ten without changing the rest of the system.

In practice, cascaded multiplexing can be achieved using a single physical device, provided that the input channels are selected in the correct sequence. Figure 2-10B shows a physical multiplexer which implements our previous example if the timing sequence shown in Fig. 2-10C is employed. This diagram also shows the relationship between the output sample duration, t_s; the time between samples for the fast channels, t_{s0} and t_{s1}; and the sample intervals t_{s2}, t_{s3} . . . for the slow channels.

2-8 MICROCOMPUTER/DATA INPUT SUBSYSTEM INTERACTION

2-8-1 Input Subsystem Configurations

The analog input subsystem shown earlier in Fig. 2-1

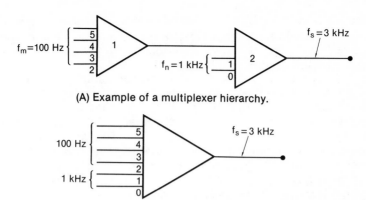

(A) Example of a multiplexer hierarchy.

(B) Implementation of (A) using a single physical multiplexer.

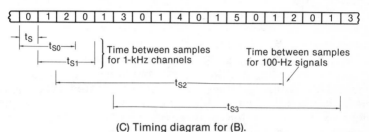

(C) Timing diagram for (B).

Fig. 2-10. Cascaded multiplexing.

represents probably the most common arrangement of the analog signal conditioning, analog multiplexer, sample-and-hold, and ADC blocks. There are many variations on this basic theme however. The subsystem in Fig. 2-1 has been described in *Electronic Design*[5] as a "multiplexed random channel addressing" configuration and it is characterized by the multiplexing of high-level ($\sim$1 volt) analog signals. The advantage of this approach is that the sample-and-hold amplifier and the ADC (generally the most costly single module in the subsystem) are shared by the input channels through multiplexing. In addition, the signal conditioning for each channel can be tailored to suit the characteristics of the various types of transducers that may be employed in a total system.

If the transducers are identical—a bank of temperature transducers, for example—then it is not necessary to use a bank of identical signal conditioning modules. In this case, the multiplexer can be placed *before* the analog signal conditioning module in Fig. 2-1. A single analog signal conditioning module is now shared, along with the sample-and-hold

47

amplifier and ADC, by the transducers. Because of the difficulty in switching low-level signals, this approach is better suited to situations in which transducers with high-level outputs are being used.

The use of a common analog signal conditioning path by transducers having different full-scale output levels and signal bandwidths is more difficult, but it is possible with today's components. The essential requirement is that both the gain of the main voltage amplifier and the bandwidth of the low-pass filter be digitally programmable. The problem is that, because only a limited range of discrete gains and bandwidths is possible, considerable thought is needed to design a general-purpose analog signal conditioning line capable of accommodating the requirements of all the different transducers. The advantage is clearly the reduced component count. It is now quite common to provide programmable gain amplifiers in analog input subsystems that are marketed specifically for microcomputer systems.

At the other extreme, and less common, is the configuration in which no analog multiplexer is used and an ADC is provided for each channel. Although low-cost integrated-circuit ADCs have reduced the cost of this configuration, it still represents a very expensive option and is used only in circumstances demanding maximum system data acquisition speed.

In Fig. 2-1, the transducers are assumed to be within a few feet of the microcomputer system. Fig. 2-11 illustrates the more common industrial situation where the transducers are remote from the microcomputer controller. In this situation, the signal conditioning modules are placed at the transducer, and the data is transmitted in analog form, using frequency or current techniques, to the microcomputer's analog input subsystem.

2-8-2 The Microcomputer as a Sequencer

In the analog input subsystems described above, the microcomputer is commonly used as a *sequencer* to control the operation of the analog multiplexer, sample-and-hold, and ADC modules. Its sequencing tasks may be summarized as follows:

1. Select an analog channel by providing an appropriate address to the analog multiplexer.
2. Program the amplifier gain and the low-pass filter cutoff frequency if necessary.
3. Switch the sample-and-hold amplifier to its sample mode

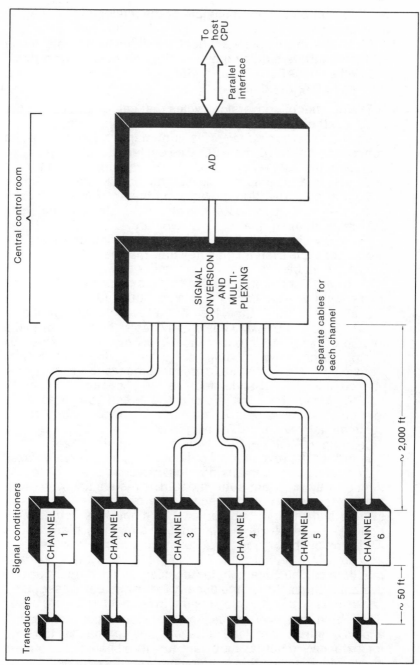

Fig. 2-11. Classical remote data acquisition system.

49

so that an accurate sample of the analog signal may be obtained.

4. Switch the sample-and-hold amplifier to its hold mode and initiate digitizing by strobing the ADC convert line.
5. When the ADC is "ready" with digital data, input, process, and store the data.

The number of conversion cycles that can be completed per second — the system sampling rate, f_s — is also known as the system *acquisition speed.* This is primarily a function of the conversion speed of the ADC. The system acquisition speed may be quite high, ranging from 20 kHz through typical values of 50 kHz to a maximum of several hundred kilohertz. A more important consideration, however, is the amount of effective free time the microcomputer has after managing the analog input subsystem. If the ADC busy/ready flag is *polled* (i.e., periodically checked by inputting the flag through the microprocessor's bus system), this free time may be quite small. The problem may be minimized in a number of ways, but all solutions have in common the need to pass responsibility for the sequencing operations to the analog input subsystem.

A simple solution that does not alter the configuration of Fig. 2-1 is to use the ADC busy/ready flag as an *interrupt* to the microprocessor. Additional time efficiency can be gained by adding a sequencer module to the analog input subsystem whose logic is responsible for sequencing tasks 1 to 4. The sequencer accepts a channel address and a "commence acquisition" command from the microcomputer and generates an interrupt when conversion is complete. Sequencer modules are commercially available, for example, the Datel SCL-1 System Programmer. Their function is illustrated in Fig. 2-12.

A further improvement is obtained by using a *multiplexed with memory* arrangement in which conversions are made continuously by the input subsystem.[3] The results are stored in a read/write memory that is accessible by both the input subsystem and the microcomputer. The memory is usually configured as part of the microcomputer's memory plane and is accessed by the analog input subsystem using direct memory access (DMA) techniques. This approach has the advantage that data can be collected continuously by the data input subsystem with very little time penalty to the microprocessor. This is particularly true if cycle-stealing DMA techniques are used.[6] In addition, the microprocessor can access the data rapidly and as required. The disadvantage of this approach is the need for extensive external hardware (up to 50 integrated circuit chips) which makes this implementation very expensive.

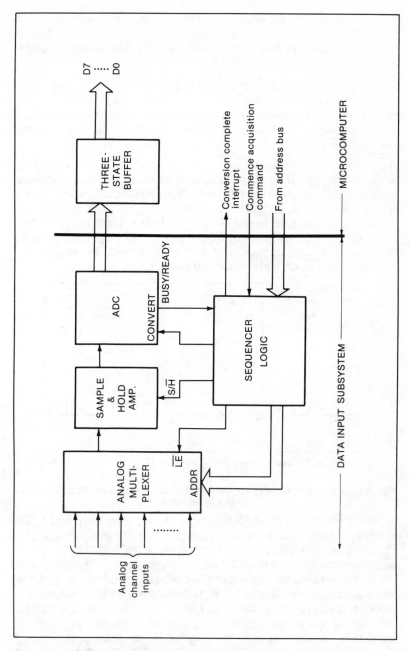

Fig. 2-12. Digital sequencer can free the microcomputer from direct control of the analog input subsystem.

An innovative extension to the basic multiplexed with memory arrangement is seen in Data Translation's Intelligent Analog Peripheral (IAP®). This differs from the basic arrangement presented above in that:

- A microprocessor, the Intel 8085, is used as the logic sequencer in the data input subsystem; and
- The common memory is a "dual-port" memory, accessible independently via an internal IAP bus or via the external system bus.

A sketch of this more advanced configuration is shown in Fig. 2-13. In the event of simultaneous memory access requests from the IAP and from the main system microprocessor, the internal IAP bus takes priority over the system bus. Bus accesses are then interleaved if several bytes from both sources must be read or written simultaneously. Although some delay to the main processor must be expected in these circumstances, such delays will be minimal.

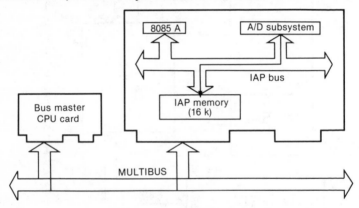

Fig. 2-13. Dual-port memory for very fast data acquisition. (*Courtesy Data Translation, Inc.*)

The use of dedicated microprocessors to sequence the operation of the data input subsystem is increasing. Fig. 2-14A shows a remote data acquisition system (REMDAC®) in which each remote station (Fig. 2-14B) is microprocessor controlled, as is the receiver/transmitter (Fig. 2-14C) which manages the data and communications between the system microcomputer and the remote stations. The receiver/transmitter can be interfaced to the system microcomputer using either its serial or parallel input/output ports. Digital rather than older analog data transmission techniques are used to send data, using a 15-mA current loop, from the remotely located transducers to the microprocessor-controlled receiver/transmitter over a single twisted-cable pair. The advantage of this system lies in the use of microprocessor controllers and digital data transmission techniques. Together, these provide 12-bit data accuracy on each channel, automatic error checking, and reduced microcomputer system overhead. The latter reduction is in the form of the time required of the system microcomputer to acquire a data point. Unfortunately, the REMDAC system uses a nonstandard data transmission scheme which may not be supported by other serial protocols now in use. It should also be noted that external analog signal conditioning of the transducer outputs is still generally required.

2-9 THE MAKE/BUY DECISION

This chapter has concentrated on the principles and issues involved in implementing an analog input subsystem. One of the major decisions to be made if you are designing such a system is whether to purchase a ready-made analog input subsystem or design and build your own. A first step toward resolving this issue is to *define the performance requirements of your input subsystem.* We assume that the transducers have been selected using the criteria specified in Section 3-5. Hence, with the electrical characteristics of each transducer's signal output defined, the following questions must be considered:

- How many input channels are needed?
- What analog signal conditioning is necessary? Factors that must be specified (cf. Chapter 5) include: common or individual signal conditioning lines; single-ended or differential inputs; and gain, DC offset, and low-pass filter requirements for each channel.
- What is the sample rate per channel (from the Sampling Theorem) and therefore the minimum system acquisition speed f_s?
- What is the required minimum system resolution, expressed as an ADC digital word length?
- What is the required system aperture time (from Fig. 2-4)?
- How much system processing of the data is required? This will allow you to decide which input subsystem configuration and microcomputer interfacing approach is appropriate.

Having obtained a reasonable estimate of your input subsystem performance requirements, the make/buy decision can now be made on the basis of:

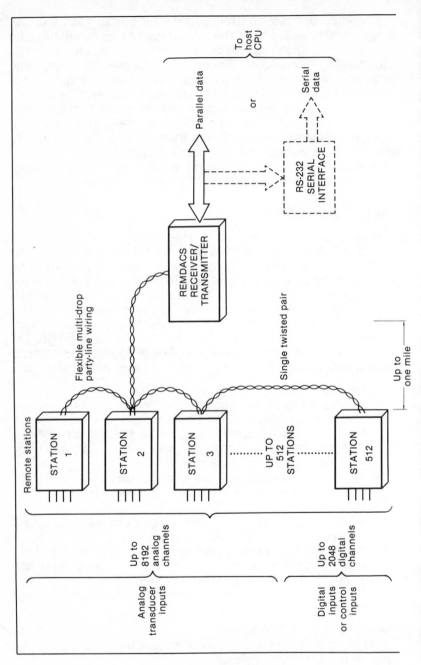

(A) REMDACS® system.

Fig. 2-14. Modern approach to remote

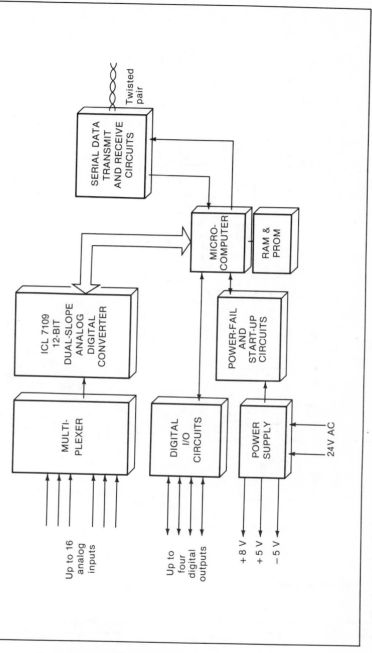

(B) REMDACS® remote data acquisition station.

data acquisition. (*Courtesy Intersil, Inc.*)

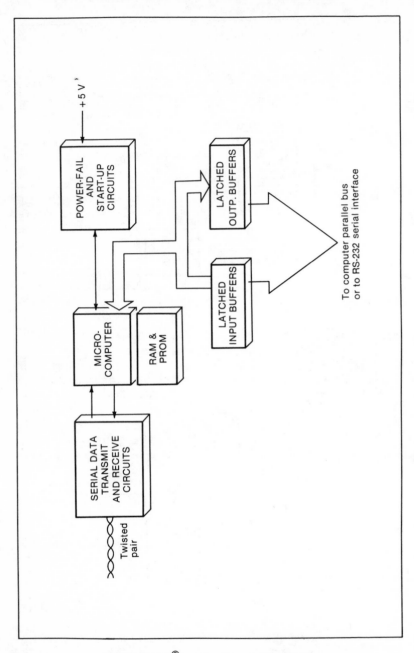

(C) REMDACS® receiver/transmitter station.

Fig. 2-14—cont. Modern approach to remote data acquisition.

- The *time scale* for the project: It is usually much quicker to incorporate a ready-made analog input board into a system than to design and build your own.
- The *cost* of the ready-made product: Allowing for labor and design time, it may still be cheaper to design and produce your own board, even in limited production situations. In a one-off situation, a ready-made input board may win out, but this depends on the next point.
- How closely the ready-made product *meets your requirements:* Often it is necessary to pay for features and performance that are not needed.
- Whether the ready-made product is *physically and electrically compatible* with your microcomputer bus and with the transducers: Some vendors have a rather liberal idea of what constitutes "compatible" and this is aggravated by the current *de facto* microcomputer bus standards in which many pins are undefined. Areas to watch include whether all required power supplies for the analog input board are provided from those available on the microcomputer bus, and whether the analog input boards' data bus lines are three-state buffered and have a reasonable TTL drive capability (see Chapter 9 for more on this point).

In the following chapters, we will examine the analog input subsystem more closely and give specific examples that will facilitate these decisions.

If the decision is made to develop your own analog input subsystem, then the following section summarizes a procedure for selecting appropriate multiplexers, S/H amplifiers, and ADCs.

2-10 A DESIGN APPROACH FOR SELECTING ADCs, SAMPLE/HOLD AMPLIFIERS, AND ANALOG MULTIPLEXERS

In this section, our aim is to develop a systematic step-by-step approach for selecting the analog multiplexer, sample-and-hold amplifier, and analog-to-digital converter components of the data input subsystem shown earlier in Fig. 2-1. For this purpose, let us assume that we have a set of N analog signals which have been through the analog signal conditioning line and have been band-limited to maximum frequencies f_{m1}, $f_{m2} \ldots f_{mi} \ldots f_{mN}$. According to the Nyquist sampling theorem, these signals need to be sampled at frequencies $f_{s1} \ldots f_{si} \ldots f_{sN}$, where $f_{si} \geq 2f_{mi}$. We now wish to multiplex these signals together, digitize them with resolutions $R_1 \ldots R_i \ldots R_N$, and present the coded outputs to the microprocessor subsystem. To select the appropriate ADC, S/H amplifier, and analog multiplexer, the following steps should be taken:

1. *Multiplexer Configuration*

The first step in our procedure is to decide on a multiplexer configuration based on the ideas developed in Section 2-7. From this analysis, we can obtain values for the system sampling frequency or acquisition speed f_s at the multiplexer's output and the time $t_s = \dfrac{1}{f_s}$ available for the S/H and ADC to complete a conversion.

2. *ADC Resolution and Input Characteristics*

The second step is to determine the resolution (R) of the ADC, hence the number of bits(n) required. This decision is based on the input signal that required the greatest resolution and the relationship between R and n, which is given in Table 2-2.

The voltage ranges of the input signals should also be examined. From this, a decision can be made as to whether unipolar or bipolar operation is required for the ADC. In addition, the voltage range of the input signals determines the full-scale deflection of the ADC, and hence an appropriate value for the ADC's reference voltage. Conversely, the choice of an ADC with a particular voltage range may determine the input voltages, and hence the amplifier gains in the signal conditioning line.

3. *System Aperture Time*

The third step is to calculate the system aperture time t_{sa} using Equation 2-6:

$$t_{sa} = \frac{1}{(2^n - 1)\, 2\pi f_m}.$$

In this expression, f_m is the frequency of the input signal with the highest frequency and n is the number of bits selected in step 2.

4. *ADC Selection*

The fourth step is to decide on the broad type of ADC to be employed. As an aid to this choice, Table 2-3 lists various types of ADCs and their characteristic conversion times. Since the resolution R, system sampling time t_s, and system aperture time t_{sa} are known, various choices exist.

Table 2-3. Typical Conversion Times for Integrating and Successive-Approximation ADCs*

Type of Converter	Relative Speed	Conversion Time			
		8 Bits	10 Bits	12 Bits	16 Bits
INTEGRATING	Slow	20 ms	30 ms	40 ms	250 ms
	Medium	1 ms	5 ms	20 ms	—
	Fast	0.3 ms	1 ms	5 ms	—
SUCCESSIVE APPROXIMATION	General-purpose	20 μs	40 μs	50 μs	—
	High performance	10 μs	15 μs	20 μs	400 μs
	Fast	5 μs	10 μs	12 μs	
	High speed	2 μs	4 μs	6 μs	
	Ultra fast	0.8 μs	1 μs	2 μs	

*After Datel-Intersil.

a. If we are dealing with very low frequency or quasi-DC signals so that the ADC's conversion time, t_c, is less than t_{sa}, then no S/H amplifier is required since the ADC will be able to satisfy the system aperture time requirement. The choice of which ADC to use then depends on ensuring that $t_c < t_s$. Under these very low frequency conditions, a slow integrating type of ADC may be preferred because of the noise reduction resulting from the signal-averaging effect of the integrator. Hence, we choose an ADC with the required number of bits and with $t_c < t_s$.

b. At higher frequencies, the value of t_c is usually greater than t_{sa} and an S/H amplifier becomes necessary so that the system aperture time requirement is satisfied by the aperture uncertainty time of the S/H. The choice of a suitable value for the ADC's conversion time, t_c, is then set by the system sampling time, t_s. Hence, we again choose an ADC with $t_c < t_s$ and the correct number of bits.

5. *Sample/Hold Amplifier Selection*

For case (b) in step four, step five is to choose an S/H amplifier that meets the system aperture time (t_{sa}) requirements and that has a sufficiently small droop rate. To satisfy t_{sa}, the appropriate S/H specification to look for is the aperture uncertainty time t_u. We choose an S/H for which $t_u < t_{sa}$.

The droop rate of an S/H amplifier is given by

$$\frac{\Delta V}{\Delta t} = \frac{I_L}{C_H}, \qquad \text{(Eq. 2-13)}$$

where I_L is the leakage current, and C_H is the value of the holding capacitor. Hence, from Equation 2-8, it is necessary to ensure that

59

$$\frac{\Delta V}{\Delta t} < \frac{R(\text{volts})}{2t_c}.$$

Since R and t_c for the ADC are known from step 4, the maximum allowable value of $\Delta V/\Delta t$ can be readily calculated. The data sheets for commercial S/H amplifiers employing an internal holding capacitor usually specify a value for $\Delta V/\Delta t$ itself, while those requiring an external C_H specify a value for I_L. Equation 2-13 shows that a large value for C_H results in a low droop rate. However, a large C_H also results in an increase in the acquisition time t_{acq} during the hold-to-sample transition.

6. *Time Budget*

The final requirement is to check the overall time required for the S/H and ADC to complete a conversion and to compare this with the time available, t_s. That is, from Equation 2-9 we need

$$t_s \geqslant t_{SH} + t_{acq} + t_c (+ t_b),$$

where t_{SH} is the total time associated with the sample-to-hold transition and is therefore the sum of the aperture delay time t_{ad} and the hold settling time t_{set}. The hold settling time is in turn a function of the resolution R, since a high resolution implies a longer waiting period before the hold signal settles to within R(%)/2. Time t_{acq} is the acquisition time for the hold-to-sample transition. It depends on the value of C_H, because, with the limited current drive capability of the main amplifier, a large C_H takes longer to charge. Time t_b only appears in connection with some ADCs and represents the settling time of the output buffer stage of the ADC. If Equation 2-9 is satisfied, then the choice of the S/H and ADC is complete.

In cases where the time budget is not satisfied, it will be necessary to go back and perhaps select a different ADC with a smaller value for t_c. Alternatively, an S/H with improved t_{acq} specifications could be chosen, or the value of C_H could be modified, without causing an unacceptable droop rate.

2-11 REFERENCES

1. H.V. Malmstadt, C.G. Enke, and S.R. Crouch, *Instrumentation for Scientists Series, Module 1: Electronic Analog Measurements and Transducers*, W. A. Benjamin, Inc., 1973.

2. E.L. Zuch, "Principles of Data Acquisition and Conversion," *Digital Design*, 1979, *9:5*, p. 60.

3. R.W. Glines, "Specifying and Testing Sample-Hold Amplifiers," *Teledyne Philbrick Applications Note An-30*, 1977.

4. E.L. Zuch, "Keep Track of a Sample-Hold from Mode to Mode to Locate Error Sources," *Datel/Intersil Data Acquisition and Conversion Handbook*, 1979, p. 164.

5. M. Elphick, *Electronic Design*, 1977, *25:19*.

6. L.A. Leventhal, *Introduction to Microprocessors: Software, Hardware, Programming*, Prentice-Hall International Ed., 1978, p. 493.

Transducers

3-1 INTRODUCTION

The concept of a data domain and its usefulness in under-standing the operation of the analog input subsystem of a microcomputer-based controller were introduced in Chapter 2. That chapter concentrated on the so-called *electrical* data domains. Now we back up one step to consider the transducer, which is the front-end element of the analog input subsystem. Its function is to transform or convert data from the nonelectrical domain into the electrical domain. Devices used in this way are known as *input transducers*. This class of transducers is the subject of this chapter.

Transducers can be classified at many levels. In a microcomputer-based controller, there are input and output transducers. In most cases, the input transducers convert physical data such as force, temperature, and light intensity to the electrical analog data domain. Few input transducers transform physical data directly to the digital data domain. Output transducers are responsible for converting digital data to the analog, time, or nonelectrical data domains. A classic output transducer is the digital-to-analog converter. Other examples include digital-to-position and digital-to-frequency converters.

Two broad classes of input transducers can be identified.[1] The first is illustrated in Fig. 3-1A and represents input transducers whose electrical output voltage or current is self-generated. They are, in effect, voltage or current generators.

An example of this type of device is the thermocouple which senses temperature at its input (a welded pair of dissimilar metals) and generates a small (approximately 1 mV) output voltage due to the Seebeck effect. This class of input transducers can be thought of as a single-stage device since the physical parameter is converted directly to a voltage or a current. In contrast, the second class includes basically two-stage devices (Fig. 3-1B). The first stage involves the transformation of the physical variable to an analog parameter such as resistance, capacitance, inductance, frequency, or charge. The second stage, which requires an external excitation signal, is the primary analog signal conditioning module wherein the analog parameter is converted to a current or a voltage. A strain gauge is an example of such a transducer since it requires an external excitation to transform a small length change into a DC voltage change. This second stage is now commonly provided by manufacturers to facilitate the use of their transducers. There is some price penalty for this primary signal conditioning, but the result is a device having, in most cases, a voltage output in the volt rather than the millivolt range.

A major problem for both readers and writers of articles on transducers is the sheer volume of detail. In Table 3-1, we have summarized *some* of the transducers and the effects they use to transform common physical quantities to the electrical data

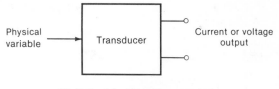

(A) Output I or V self-generated.

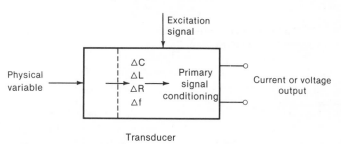

(B) Two-stage device including primary signal conditioning.

Fig. 3-1. Two classes of input transducer.

domain. The list is formidable but by no means comprehensive — in fact, several pages could be devoted to each effect! In this chapter, we will provide an overview of transducers and describe some of the effects they employ to transform information.

As a starting point, let us divide the many types of transducers into three broad categories:

1. *Mechanical,* in which the transducers sense effects that are common in mechanics, such as force, displacement, and velocity.
2. *Fluid,* in which the transducers sense the properties of fluids, such as temperature, pressure, or flow.
3. *Radiation,* which includes devices that sense light, microwaves, and sound.

Within each category, the *physical quantities* selected for discussion are those which are commonly input to microcomputer-based controllers and data loggers (these are noted by an asterisk in Table 3-1). A selection of the *effects* used to sense our chosen physical variables has then been made to ensure complete coverage of the most common, most modern effects and to provide practical information on commercially available devices.

Transducers that use less common effects and/or effects already described in the context of sensing other physical variables are described in Appendix A. Devices used to sense some of the less common physical variables are also described in Appendix A.

3-2 MECHANICAL EFFECT TRANSDUCERS

In this section we describe a range of transducers that are used to sense force, displacement, and proximity. The effects they employ are:

- Variation of resistance with strain
- Piezoelectric effect
- Hall effect
- Reflection or transmission of light
- Movement of tapping point of potentiometer

Devices for measuring velocity and acceleration are presented in Appendix A.

3-2-1 Measurement of Force

Two popular methods of measuring force lend themselves

Table 3-1. Transducers: A Summary

Classification	Physical Parameter	Basic Sensing Technique or Effect Used	Output
MECHANICAL	*Force	*Strain gauge *Piezoelectric crystal	Resistance Charge
	*Displace-ment	*Potentiometer *Hall effect Capacitance change Inductance change Strain gauge Piezoelectric crystal Magneto-resistance Optical encoders	Resistance Voltage Capacitance Inductance Voltage Charge Resistance Digital
	Acceleration	Strain gauge load cell Piezoelectric load cell	Resistance Voltage
	Velocity	Rate of change of displacement Doppler shift	
	*Proximity	*Hall effect *Light reflection/trans- mission	Voltage Current
FLUID	*Pressure	*Strain gauge *Capacitance change *Inductance change *Piezoresistance *Hall effect Pirani gauge	Voltage Capacitance Inductance Resistance Voltage Resistance

	*Temperature	*Thermocouples: Seebeck
		  effect
		*IC Temp. devices:
		    AD590
		    LM135
		Resistance thermometer
		Thermistor
		Radiation
			
			Voltage
			
			Current
			Voltage
			Resistance
			Resistance

	*Level	*Float to displacement device *Conductance *Optical Capacitance Thermal Pressure Sonic echo	
	Flow	Pitot tube Electromagnetic induction Doppler shift	
	Humidity	Distortion to displacement device Conductivity	 Resistance

Table 3-1–cont. Transducers: A Summary

	Anemometry	Rotating cups Thermistor Transistor	Frequency Resistance Voltage
RADIATION	*Light	*Photodiode *Phototransistor Light-dependent resistor Photovoltaic cells	

*Starred transducer types are discussed in the text rather than in an appendix.

to incorporation in electronic systems. Since they form the basis for measuring various other quantities — normally by the addition of mechanical rather than electrical attachments — we will treat them here at the outset and refer back to them from time to time.

The Strain Gauge

The strain gauge uses the fact that when a wire is stretched, its resistance changes. This can be seen from the equation that links the resistance of a conductor to its physical dimensions:

$$R = \frac{\rho l}{A}$$ (Eq. 3-1)

where ρ is the resistivity of the conductor, l is its length, and A is its cross-sectional area. Fig. 3-2 shows schematically the most common type of strain gauge. It consists of a thin metal foil supported on a nonconductive flexible backing about the size of a postage stamp or smaller. The backing facilitates handling and mounting of the gauge on the object to be tested. If the gauge is stretched along its long axis, the length of the conductor increases and its area decreases. The resultant increase in resistance therefore provides a measure of the stretching of the gauge.

The sensitivity of a strain gauge is quoted as a sensitivity factor, k, which relates the fractional change in gauge re-

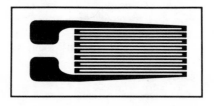

Fig. 3-2. A typical foil strain gauge.

sistance to the fractional change in the length of the gauge according to the equation:

$$\frac{\Delta R}{R} = k \frac{\Delta \ell}{\ell}$$
(Eq. 3-2)

If the gauge is firmly bonded to an object, the fractional change in length (the strain) is the same as that of the object and can be related to the force exerted on the object using the elasticity equation:

$$\frac{\Delta \ell}{\ell} = \frac{EF}{A}$$
(Eq. 3-3)

Here E is Young's Modulus, F is the force exerted on the object in the direction of the length change, and A is the cross-sectional area of the object. Combining these two equations we obtain:

$$F = \frac{1}{k} \frac{A}{E} \frac{\Delta R}{R}$$
(Eq. 3-4)

A typical strain gauge is the Philips PR9810, which has a resistance of 600 ohms and a k value of 2. Its linearity is better than 0.1% for strains up to ± 4000 microstrain (i.e., $\frac{\Delta \ell}{\ell} = 4000 \times 10^{-6}$) and is still better than 1% for strains up to 10,000 microstrain. Mounting the gauge on a surface requires care and close attention to the manufacturer's recommendations to ensure reliability and long life.

Typically, strain gauges operate in the range of ±1000 microstrain or so (to ensure long life). The resistance change which results is therefore small (about 1%) and may be masked by temperature effects. However, temperature-compensated gauges can be purchased which show errors of less than 1 microstrain per degree Celsius when they are attached to the material for which they were designed. Philips adds a letter to the type number of their gauges to indicate the material for which they have been compensated: F for construction steel, S for stainless steel, A for aluminum.

If uncompensated gauges are used, they should be mounted in pairs in opposite arms of a Wheatstone bridge so that temperature-dependent changes in the measuring element are offset by similar changes in the compensating element. Fig. 3-3 shows schematically how a load cell (for use in an automatic weighing machine, for example) may be constructed. Here the compensating element is mounted close to the measuring element so that it suffers the same temperature-induced resistance changes. However, when a load is applied to the load cell, the resistance of the compensating element increases as the circumference of the load cell increases, whereas the resistance of the measuring element decreases as the length of the load cell decreases. The out-of-balance voltage from the bridge circuit of Fig. 3-4 (about 10–50 mV for a properly designed load cell) then gives a measure of the force applied to the load cell.

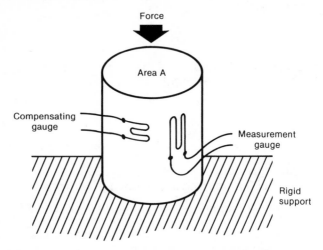

Fig. 3-3. Load cell using two strain gauges for temperature compensation.

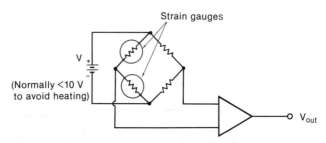

Fig. 3-4. Incorporation of strain gauges into a Wheatstone bridge.

Piezoelectric Crystals

When crystals of certain materials such as quartz or Rochelle salt are deformed, they develop an electric charge on opposite faces of the crystal. The resulting potential difference in these so-called piezoelectric crystals depends on the amount of deformation. Although Fig. 3-5 shows a crystal subjected to a compressional force, crystals are often mounted to be subject to torsional or shearing forces. Although the deformation (a change in length) of the crystal may be quite small (e.g., 10 μm/g (micrometers per gram of weight) in a phonograph pickup), typical outputs range from tens or hundreds of millivolts for small crystals to hundreds of volts for large crystals under high stress. It is useful to think of the crystal as a slightly leaky capacitor that is charged by deforming the crystal. Hence, if a constant deformation is maintained, the voltage developed across the crystal decays with time as the charge leaks away via the internal resistance of the crystal itself. Piezoelectric crystals are therefore used only when the applied force is changing, usually at rates varying from a few hertz up to the megahertz range. A further consequence is that a very high input impedance or charge sensitive amplifier is required for these transducers.

A wide range of load cells based on quartz piezoelectric crystals is made by Kistler, who quotes typical sensitivities of 4 pC/N (picocoulombs per newton) and a linearity of better than 1% of full-scale output. Measurement ranges vary from 0–250 N up to 0–1000 kN. (Note: 1 newton = 0.2248 pound-force). The temperature coefficient is −0.02%/°C. Capacitance varies from about 8 pF (picofarads) for the low range devices to about 700 pF for the high range devices. Using the equation $V = Q/C$, we can calculate the voltage measured across the crystal when the charges quoted above are produced. The input capacitance of the amplifier is in parallel with the capacitance of the crystal for this calculation, but for a rough estimate of sensitivity we may assume that the amplifier capacitance is small compared with the transducer capacitance. Thus, we expect sensitivities approaching 0.5 V/N for the small devices or 5 mV/N for the large devices.

3-2-2 Measurement of Displacement

Resistive Devices

There are many ingenious methods of using a mechanical

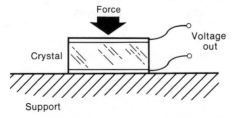

Fig. 3-5. Piezoelectric crystal as a force transducer.

linkage to allow a simple potentiometer or rheostat to be used as a displacement measuring device. Two examples are shown in Fig. 3-6. Although these devices are very simple and robust, their moving contacts require significant force to overcome friction and have limited mechanical life. The resistance element can be designed to have a linear or nonlinear output. The resolution of wire-wound resistance elements is determined essentially by the spacing of the turns. For film-type elements, the resolution is limited by noise considerations (e.g., thermal or Johnson noise, discussed in Chapter 4) to about 5 μm.

A strain gauge may be bonded to a cantilever beam or a reference block to measure small displacements. The system is then arranged so that a movement of the object under observation will bend the beam or will squeeze or stretch the block to which the strain gauge is bonded. Displacements as small as 10 μm are measurable but, depending on the construction of the gauge and the rigidity of the block or beam, considerable force may be necessary to produce the deformation.

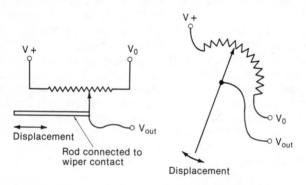

Fig. 3-6. The use of potentiometers as displacement transducers.

Hall Effect Devices

If a slab of p-type semiconductor carrying an electric current is placed in a magnetic field as shown in Fig. 3-7, the positive charges carrying the current feel a force which deflects them to the right. The resulting accumulation of charge along the right-hand side of the slab sets up a measurable voltage, known as the Hall voltage (V_H), which is proportional to both the current flowing (I) and the applied magnetic field, i.e.,

$$V_H = K_H (I \times B), \qquad \text{(Eq. 3-5)}$$

where K_H is the Hall coefficient. The Hall effect is essentially a majority carrier phenomenon which depends only on the bulk properties of the semiconductor material involved. Because Hall effect devices do not have problems due to surface effects, junction leakage currents, or threshold voltages, they can be reproduced easily and are reliable in operation. K_H, however, depends on the concentration of charge carriers and is therefore temperature-dependent.

To use one of these devices as a displacement transducer, a magnet and Hall effect device are mounted so that a changing displacement changes the distance of the magnet from the Hall effect device. This in turn changes the Hall voltage output. The variety of arrangements is large, as can be seen from the bibliography at the end of this chapter. A number of monolithic IC devices are commercially available, and these have some built-in signal conditioning. Some produce an output which varies linearly with a magnetic field (e.g., Texas Instruments' TL173, Sprague UGN-3501M, Siemens SAS 231). This is useful if continuous monitoring of position is required, but only over distances for which a uniform magnetic field gradient is available. Other devices have merely an on/off type of output. These are discussed in the next section.

As an example of the use of monolithic IC sensors, the connections to the SAS 231 are shown in Fig. 3-8. P1 is for zero setting and can be used to introduce an offset of up to ± 150 mT (millitesla). (Note: 1 mT = 10 gauss.) P2 adjusts the sensitivity of the device from less than 20 mV/mT up to about 800 mV/mT. In the absence of P2, the sensitivity is approximately 100 mV/mT. The output (at pin 4) can swing to within 2 V of the sup-

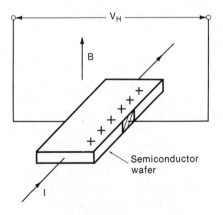

Fig. 3-7. The Hall effect.

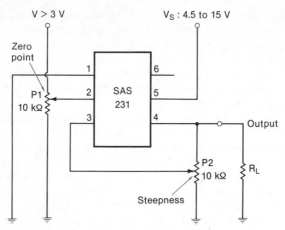

Fig. 3-8. The use of the SAS231 Hall effect transducer. (*Courtesy Siemens Industries Limited*)

ply rail, and it retains its linearity up to this point. Thus, the setting of P2 chooses the sensitivity for the circuit, and the choice of a supply voltage sets the measurement range of this sensor.

3-2-3 Detecting Proximity

Hall Effect Devices

As mentioned in the previous section, some of the Hall effect devices available from electronic component manufacturers have essentially an on/off type of output. The switching occurs when the magnetic field sensed by the device exceeds a threshold value. This can be achieved by a magnet coming within a certain distance of the sensor. The applications of Hall effect sensors as proximity detectors are probably more numerous than their linear displacement applications. As proximity detectors, they are used in brushless motors, pressure sensing, contactless automobile ignition switching, liquid level sensing, and tachometry. To simplify these applications, some Hall effect devices are now available with a magnet built into the package. The proximity of a ferrous material distorts the magnetic field set up at the Hall effect wafer, leading to a change in output.

An example of a sensor without a built-in magnet is the TL170C from Texas Instruments, which is available in a standard plastic transistor package, type TO-92. It has an open collector output and can operate from a 5-V supply for compatibility with TTL integrated circuits. The field required to switch on the sensor seems to vary from sample to sample but is always less than 0.025 T at 25°C, which is quite modest. To switch the device off, the magnetic field must drop by 0.02 T.

Optical Devices

There are basically two ways of using optical devices in a proximity-sensing application. One relies on the reflection of light from an object, and the other relies on an object interrupting a light beam. In both cases, devices are available that contain both the light source (a light-emitting diode, or LED) and the detector (a phototransistor or photodiode) in a single package. Fig. 3-9 shows the packaging for the General Instruments' MCA7 and MCT8, which are examples of the reflective and interruptive types, respectively. Device output currents are usually 100 nA in the dark. They rise with increasing illumination to 100 μA if a single phototransistor (Fig. 3-10A) is used or to a few milliamperes if a photodarlington transistor pair (Fig. 3-10B) is used. The continuously variable output from these devices enables at least the reflective versions to be used as position sensors rather than merely proximity sensors. However, the variability of ambient lighting levels and of the reflectivity of surfaces renders them inaccurate in this role.

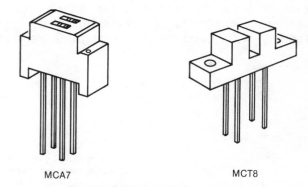

MCA7   MCT8

Fig. 3-9. Optical proximity switches.

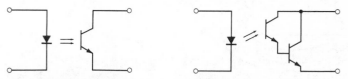

(A) Single phototransistor.   (B) Photodarlington transistor pair.

Fig. 3-10. Electrical configurations for optical proximity switches.

3-3 FLUID TRANSDUCERS

The transducers discussed in this section, and also in Appendix A, are usually used to measure various properties of a fluid such as pressure, temperature, and level. New effects which are introduced as sensing mechanisms include: capacitance change, inductance change, piezoresistance, Seebeck effect, conductance change, and variation of the resistance of a material with temperature. Transducers for measuring flow, humidity, wind velocity, and chemical concentration are discussed in Appendix A.

3-3-1 Measurement of Pressure

A common technique for measuring pressure is to allow the pressure to deform some component of a system, that is, a diaphragm or bellows. Then a displacement transducer converts this physical change to an electrical signal. There are many methods for implementing this technique, some of which are described by O'Higgins.[2] A selection of simple arrangements is shown in Figs. 3-11, 3-12, and 3-13. In Fig. 3-11, the distortion of a closed cylinder due to an internal pressure is monitored by the strain gauge attached to the outside. In Fig. 3-12, the metal diaphragm bows due to the pressure difference across it. This reduces the capacitance between the diaphragm and one of the fixed capacitor plates and increases the capacitance with the other plate. A differential pressure measurement now becomes a differential capacitance

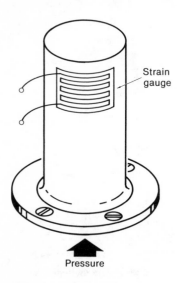

Strain gauge

Fig. 3-11. The use of a strain gauge as a pressure transducer.

Pressure

measurement. A similar technique is shown in Fig. 3-13, which depicts the use of inductive rather than capacitive effects. The diaphragm must be magnetically active so that its bowing will increase the inductance of one coil at the expense of the other.

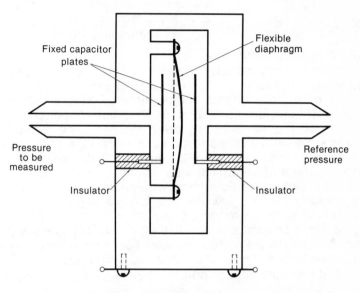

Fig. 3-12. Differential pressure transducer using capacitance changes.
(*From A.J. Diefenderfer,* Principles of Electronic Instrumentation)

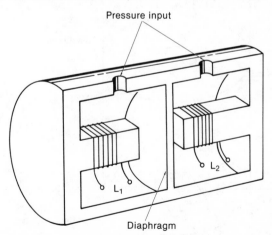

Fig. 3-13. Differential pressure transducer using inductance changes. (*From A.J. Diefenderfer*)

A recent development of this idea occurs in the Hall effect pressure switch illustrated in Fig. 3-14. A magnet is mounted on a diaphragm that distends under pressure, bringing the magnet closer to the Hall effect switch. The device is set to switch at a predetermined pressure. The output voltage V_o is not linearly related to the pressure, but the device can be modified to operate as a linear transducer by employing nonlinear feedback in the signal-conditioning circuit.

Integrated Circuit Pressure Gauges

National Semiconductor markets a series of IC pressure gauges, at the heart of which lies a piezoresistive circuit consisting of a Wheatstone bridge diffused into a wafer of silicon.[3] This wafer is a diaphragm that distorts under the influence of the pressure to be measured. The distortion changes the values of the resistors in the bridge and the out-of-balance voltage becomes a measure of the pressure. An output voltage of about 1 mV/psi is produced. The sensor is available in a monolithic version, without any signal conditioning circuitry, as the LX0503 and LX0603 series. It is also available in a hybrid version, complete with signal conditioning circuitry, as the LX14XX, LX16XX, and LX17XX series. The hybrid packages are more expensive but contain temperature compensation circuitry and buffering amplifiers to provide gain and a low impedance output. They require only a single 9-

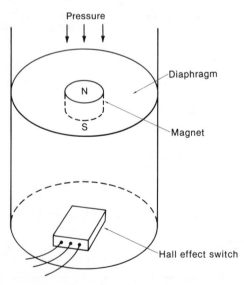

Fig. 3-14. Pressure actuated switch using Hall effect transducer.

to 15-volt DC power supply for their operation. The monolithic devices are much less expensive and may be more attractive to experimenters; one version (LX0505A) is even available in a TO-5 type package. However, they require additional signal conditioning circuitry, one example of which is shown in Fig. 3-15.[4] Other manufacturers — for example, Amtek, Micro Switch, etc. — produce pressure transducers based on the same principle.

3-3-2 Measuring Temperature

Thermocouples

The contact potential difference between two dissimilar metals depends on temperature. If two or more metals are used to make a circuit, and if the junctions are at different temperatures, then the contact potentials do not cancel out and there is a net emf (electromotive force) in the circuit. This is known as the *Seebeck effect* and is the basis of a very common, useful method of temperature measurement. Fig. 3-16 shows the correct way of using the effect. The two junctions between the metals of the thermocouple and the copper leads going to the meter are held at 0°C. The temperature of the A-B metal junction can then be found directly from the appropriate thermocouple tables.[5] Of course, if the input connections to the meter, or to our analog signal conditioning circuitry, are not copper, then there is a risk of another emf being set up at the input. Fortunately, the two connections are normally in close proximity so that their temperatures are the same and the two Seebeck emfs cancel out. This fact is used in the rough-and-ready circuit of Fig. 3-17. This circuit is not capable of the precision of the earlier circuit but is often used because of its simplicity. The temperature found when consulting the thermocouple tables in this case must be interpreted as the approximate difference between the temperature of the A-B metal junction and the temperature of the connections to the measuring system.

The need for the ice/water bath for the reference junctions is a severe disadvantage of the thermocouple when it is required to produce precise results. Because of this, circuits for *cold junction compensation* have been developed which are particularly useful in portable measurement systems. Basically, these circuits sense the ambient temperature of the cold junction and generate an appropriate offset so that the output is proportional to the Seebeck voltage referenced to 0°C. Fig. 3-18 illustrates a typical circuit. Note that Analog Devices markets a modular cold-junction compensator, the 2B56.

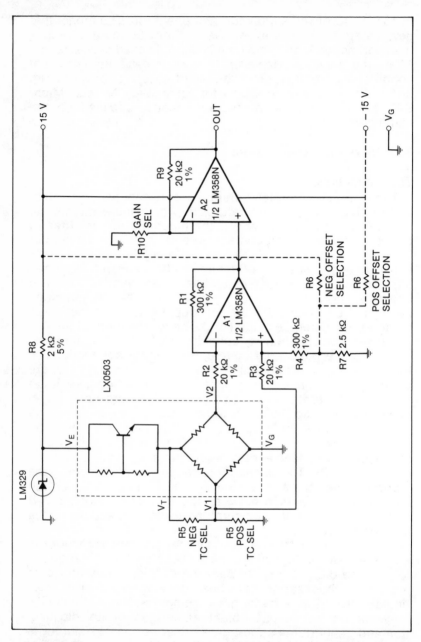

Fig. 3-15. Example of buffering and temperature compensation circuitry for the LX0503 pressure transducer. (*Courtesy National Semiconductor Corporation*)

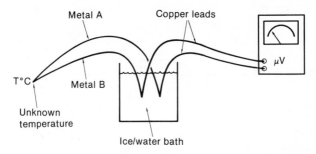

Fig. 3-16. The use of the thermocouple to measure temperature.

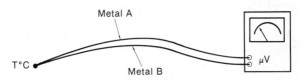

Fig. 3-17. Simplified arrangement of the thermocouple for approximate temperature measurements.

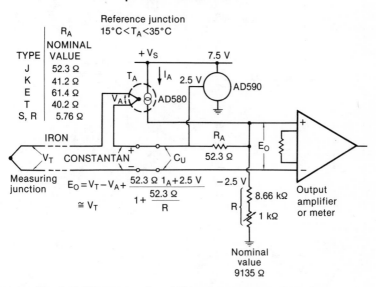

TYPE	R_A NOMINAL VALUE
J	52.3 Ω
K	41.2 Ω
E	61.4 Ω
T	40.2 Ω
S, R	5.76 Ω

Reference junction
$15°C < T_A < 35°C$

$$E_O = V_T - V_A + \frac{52.3 \ \Omega \ I_A + 2.5 \ V}{1 + \frac{52.3 \ \Omega}{R}}$$

$$\cong V_T$$

Nominal value 9135 Ω

Fig. 3-18. Thermocouple cold-junction compensation circuit.

The commonly used thermocouple wire combinations are shown in Table 3-2 and their range and performance are compared in Fig. 3-19.

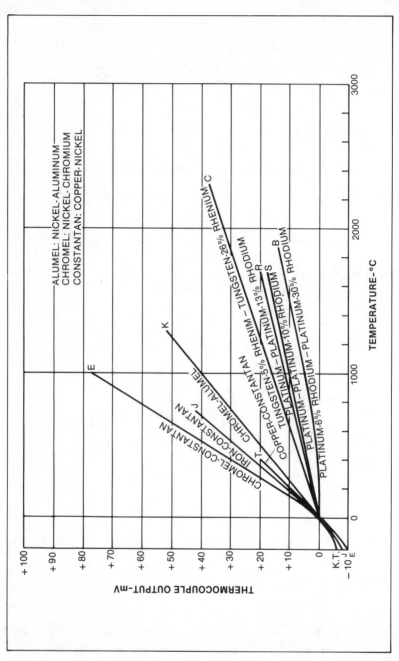

Fig. 3-19. Comparison of thermocouple performance. (*Courtesy Analog Devices*)

temperature variations being measured. It is advisable to minimize self-heating effects by choosing the lowest excitation voltage which will produce the designed output voltage, allowing for the expected line drops. However, because of the low currents involved, even in the worst case (30 V across AD590, 423 μA output current) the power dissipation is only about 13 mW (milliwatts).

LM135 Series

The LM135/LM235/LM335 series from National Semiconductor are variations of a device that produces a voltage proportional to absolute temperature. In its simplest configuration, as shown in Fig. 3-22A, the device behaves as a two-terminal zener diode. The breakdown voltage for the LM335 is 10 mV/K (kelvin) over the range from 0° to 100°C. Larger temperature ranges are available using the LM235 and LM135. The device is outfitted with a third terminal to allow trimming of the output for more accurate calibration as shown in Figure 3-22B. When trimmed at 25°C, some of the devices in this series are capable of accuracy to better than 1°C over their entire operating range. The specifications are quoted at a current of 1 mA, but the device will operate without a noticeable degradation in performance from 400 μA to 5 mA since it has a dynamic impedance of less than 1 Ω. Again, self-heating may introduce noticeable errors, especially if the device is used to monitor the temperature of still air, so the low end of the current range should be used rather than the high end. If the device is always to be used in the same environment, the self-heating effects

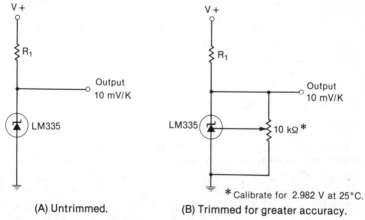

(A) Untrimmed. (B) Trimmed for greater accuracy.

Fig. 3-22. The use of the LM335 temperature sensor. (*Courtesy National Semiconductor Corporation*)

Table 3-4. Wire Length for 1°C Error Due to Ohmic Drop

AWG	Length in Feet at:	
	1 mA	0.5 mA
14	4000	8000
18	1600	3200
22	625	1250

may be calibrated out by suitable adjustment of the trimming potentiometer. However the device may then become inaccurate when moved to a new environment.

A source of error that needs to be considered with these voltage output devices, and which does not apear with the current output devices, is the voltage drop along the leads to the device. The temperature error due to this effect becomes significant when the sensing device is several hundred feet from the supply and measurement circuitry. Table 3-4 indicates the magnitude of the effect.

With a voltage output device such as this, all that is required to obtain an output of 10 mV/°C is to provide an offset voltage of 2.73 V (see Chapter 5). A method suggested by the manufacturers is shown in Fig. 3-23, where the offset voltage is adjusted by means of the 10-kΩ (kilohm) potentiometer and the scale factor is trimmed to 10 mV/°C using the 5-kΩ variable resistor.

Temperature Sensors with Digital Output

At the time of this writing, no sensor is known to be available which produces a digital output without the use of an analog-to-digital converter. However, development work is under way at Rockwell, using a selection of optical effects, such as the temperature-dependence of the gap width of a Fabry-Perot etalon and fiber optics as key parts of the instrument system.[6]

3-3-3 Level Sensing

Float Methods

One of the most common methods for sensing the level of a liquid in a container is to measure the position of a float. The design of such a system involves choosing a displacement transducer and designing the mechanical linkage from this transducer to the float. For example, most automobile fuel-level indicators are of this type, using a rheostat as the displacement transducer. Because of the large number of

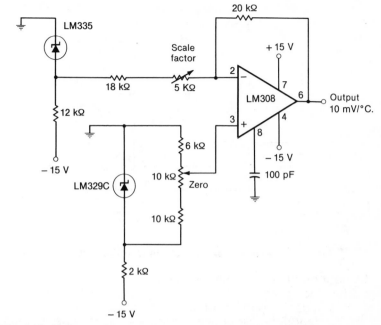

Fig. 3-23. The use of the LM335 to produce a ground-referred Celsius thermometer. (*Courtesy National Semiconductor Corporation*)

possible variations on this theme — mainly mechanical — this method of level sensing will not be discussed further; displacement transducers have already been covered in Section 3-2-2.

Conductance Method

For liquids that show some electrical conductivity, albeit small, an excellent method of level detection is illustrated in Fig. 3-24. The technique relies on this conductivity and on the high-input impedance of such devices as the MOSFET. The CD4049 is a CMOS buffer that produces TTL voltage levels at its outputs. In the absence of any liquid in the tank, all the buffer inputs are held high by the 2.2-MΩ resistors. When the level reaches the wire to a particular input, that input is pulled low by the conduction of current through the liquid, and the buffer output in question goes high. The liquid level is then known to be between the highest sensor with a high output and the lowest sensor with a low output. The circuit works in tap water using ordinary breadboarding wire as the probe. For other liquids, it may prove necessary to change the value of the pull-up resistor.

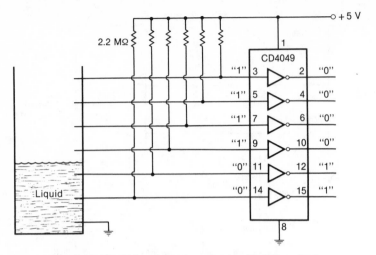

Fig. 3-24. Liquid level sensing circuit with TTL outputs.

If a continuous rather than a quantized measurement of the liquid level is required, then a pair of parallel electrodes running the full depth of the container is needed, as shown in Fig. 3-25. The conductance between the two electrodes is then directly proportional to the depth of the liquid. If the measurements are made with direct current, the positive ions migrating to the cathode and the negative ions migrating to the anode tend to stick to the surface of the electrode and block the access of further ions. This leads to unreliable conductivity measurements. The problem can be avoided by using alternating current.

Optical Transmission

To determine when a liquid is above or below a certain level, optical sensors can be used to detect whether a light beam has been interrupted by the liquid. Two of the many possible configurations are shown in Fig. 3-26. A sensor/source pair

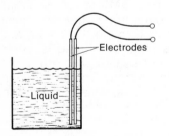

Fig. 3-25. The use of conductance for measurement of liquid level.

86

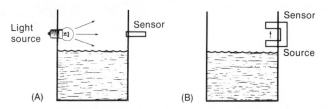

Fig. 3-26. Optical transmission methods for liquid level sensing.

such as the MCT8 discussed in Section 3-2-3 would make a suitable detector for the arrangement in Fig. 3-26B. This device need not be mounted within the tank, as in the diagram, but could be mounted around a sight gauge attached to the tank.

3-4 RADIATION TRANSDUCERS

Transducers in this category are used to sense various wavelengths of the electromagnetic spectrum and of sound. Sensors are commonly required to measure ultraviolet, visible, and near-infrared light; far infrared thermal radiation; microwaves; and gamma radiation. In this section, we will deal only with visible and near infrared light. New devices introduced include the *photodiode* and the *phototransistor.*

3-4-1 Measurement of Light

Photodiode

The semiconductor PN junction, when used as a rectifier, shows a small, temperature-dependent reverse current originating from minority carriers. The latter are created close to the depletion layer by thermal excitation and are swept across the junction by the combined effect of the barrier potential and the reverse bias voltage. This reverse current can be increased by shining light onto the diode to create minority carriers at a higher rate. The reverse current then becomes a measure of the incident light intensity. Since all semiconductor diodes are subject to this effect, manufacturers package them in opaque encapsulation. Scraping the paint off a glass-encapsulated diode allows the photodiode effect to be observed. However, if a predictable response is required of the diode as a photodetector, then it is advisable to obtain a device which is actually marketed as a photodiode. The typical spectral response for a photodiode is shown in Fig. 3-27. Normally the reverse current is directly proportional to the light intensity, with a proportionality constant of about 0.8 $\mu A/(mW/cm^2)$. Alternatively, the photodiode can be used as a *photovoltaic device,* in which the incident light causes a voltage to be developed across the diode. In this case, the open circuit voltage developed is logarithmically related to the light intensity as shown in Fig. 3-28.

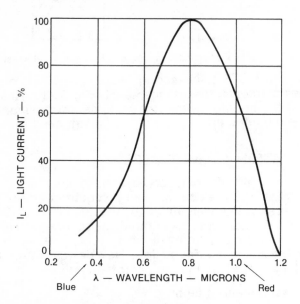

Fig. 3-27. Photodiode spectral response. (*Courtesy Fairchild Semiconductor*)

Phototransistor

Under the normal bias arrangements for a transistor, the collector-base junction is a reverse-biased PN junction. The collector-base junction is therefore capable of acting as a photodiode, with any light falling on the transistor increasing the collector-base reverse leakage current. Once this current enters in the base region, it behaves as normal base current and is amplified by the transistor action. If I_γ is the current which flows from collector to base due to the photodiode effect, then the resulting collector current, I_c, is given by:

$$I_c = (h_{FE} + 1) I_\gamma$$

(Eq. 3-6)

This means that a phototransistor has a much greater sensitivity than a photodiode, although it has a similar spectral response. Typically the phototransistor is operated with the base connection open. The irradiation can then be thought of as providing a base current (I_{CEO}) of about 0.5 $\mu A/(mW/cm^2)$. A typical set of characteristics is shown in Fig. 3-29.

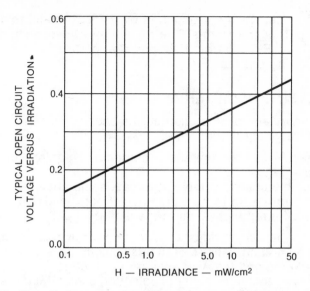

Fig. 3-28. Photodiode output voltage. (*Courtesy Fairchild Semiconductor*)

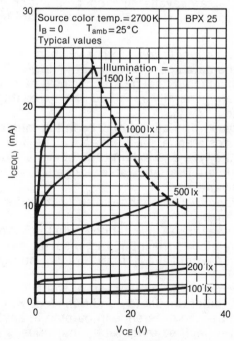

Fig. 3-29. Phototransistor output for a selection of illumination levels with base connection open circuit. (*Courtesy Philips*)

Greater sensitivity is obtained by using a monolithic Darlington pair of transistors. The resulting devices, such as the FPT400 and FPT560 from Fairchild Corporation, are known as photodarlingtons (see Fig. 3-10B).

3-5 SELECTION CRITERIA

The primary aim of this chapter has been to present a selection of transducers that are:

- Used to sense the more commonly required physical parameters.
- Commercially available at a reasonable price.
- Illustrative of the more common effects used to transform data from the physical to the electrical data domain.

This information provides a foundation for understanding the operation and limitations of the devices that are currently being marketed and that will appear in the future.

However, the hard reality of selecting a specific transducer for a given job still remains. The criteria that can be used to make a decision are: availability, cost, output characteristics, and ease of use. The characteristics which are important include:

- *Accuracy or resolution*—Either of these terms may appear in the data specification of the device. They refer to the smallest input change that can be detected at the output and are generally specified as a percentage of the input range.
- *Output type*—The output may be in the form of a current, voltage, resistance, or frequency. The form of output defines the type and extent of later signal conditioning.
- *Input range*—The allowable range of values for the physical variable.
- *Output range*—The change in the output for a full-scale input change.
- *Output linearity*—This defines whether the output is linearly related to the input and, if so, the deviation of the transducer output curve from an ideal straight line (see Fig. 3-30).
- *Repeatability*—The ability of a transducer to repeat readings under duplicate conditions (see Fig. 3-30).
- *Hysteresis*—The difference in outputs at any input value within the specified range when that value is approached from above or below (see Fig. 3-30).

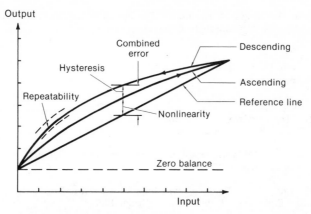

Fig. 3-30. Illustrative transducer performance parameters.

- *Temperature stability* — The change in the output per unit change in temperature.
- *Response time* — The time required for the output to rise to 63% of its full-scale output.
- *Output impedance* — The effective resistance between the output terminals of the transducer.

Before beginning the search for an acceptable transducer for a given application, it is important to specify the required input range, linearity, accuracy, and response time. Once these specifications have been satisfied from the range of available transducers, the remaining transducer characteristics can then be traded off against cost to obtain the best cost/performance benefit you can afford. A large-output voltage range combined with a low-output impedance is generally sought as the ideal since this minimizes the required analog signal conditioning. However, this combination may be very expensive in relation to your available budget, and you may have to select a less costly device requiring a little or a lot of additional analog signal conditioning. In all cases, though, the cost/performance ratio should be minimized, keeping in mind the minimum performance specifications that can be tolerated and the amount of later analog signal conditioning that will be required.

3-6 BIBLIOGRAPHY

General

Ohr, S., "Focus on Transducers: Semiconductors Make Inroads, But Electromechanicals Hold Their Own." *Electronic Design,* July 5, 1979, p. 89.

Baumbick, R.J., and J. Alexander, "Fiber Optics Sense Process Variables." *Control Engineering,* March 1980, p. 75.

Force

Hall, J., "What's Going On in Weighing?" *Instruments and Control Systems,* August 1978, p. 29.

Displacement

Garratt, J.D., "Survey of Displacement Transducers Below 50 mm." *Journal of Physics E: Scientific Instruments,* 1979, *12,* p. 563.

Hudson, C., "A Guide to Optical Shaft Encoders." *Instruments and Control Systems,* May 1978, p. 33.

Cullum, W.M., "Angle Sensing Transducers for Shaft to Digital Conversion." *Australian Electronics Engineering,* October 1980, p. 27.

Bridges, M., "Conductive Plastic Potentiometer." *Australian Electronics Engineering,* September 1980, p. 69.

Proximity

Dance, B., "Hall Effect Devices and Their Applications." *Electronics Industry,* May 1979, p. 21.

Polczynski, M., "Hall-effect Sensor Provides Low-cost, Reliable Isolation." *Electronic Design,* January 8, 1981, p. 271.

Dance, B., "Hall Effect and Other Semiconductor 'Magnetic' Devices." *Australian Electronics Engineering,* July 1978, p. 8.

Dance, B., "Optocoupling and Optical Interrupter Devices; 2." *Australian Electronics Engineering,* January 1980, p. 24.

Pressure

Salmon, J., "Semiconductor Pressure Transducers." *Control and Instrumentation,* January 1979, p. 30.

Shepherd, I., "Reviewing Pressure Transducer Technologies to Aid Selection." *Control and Instrumentation,* January 1979, p. 35.

Moore, R., "Pressure Transmitters: One Manufacturer's Approach to Reliability." *Control Engineering,* May 1980, p. 93.

Bicking, R., "P-to-V Transducer Available in Control Market After Automotive Baptism." *Control Engineering,* November 1978, p. 51.

Morris, H.M., "D/P Cell Outputs Either Current or Frequency." *Control Engineering,* February 1979, p. 53.

Temperature

MacDonald, N.H., "Thermocouple Type Selection to Suit the Application." *Control and Instrumentation,* September 1978, p. 31.

Dance, M., "MPUs Allow High Precision Thermometry." *Electronics Industry,* May 1979, p. 12.

Kadis, A., "A-D Convertor-on-a-chip Is the Basis of Digital Thermometer." *Electronic Design,* January 22, 1981, p. 133.

Analog Devices, "Two-terminal IC Temperature Transducer—AD590." *Analog Devices Product Description and Application Note.*

Level

Hall, J., "Guide to Level Monitoring." *Instruments and Control Systems,* October 1978, p. 25.

Morris, H.N., "Sensing Interface Levels Poses Many Challenges." *Control Engineering,* August 1978, p. 41.

Homas, K., "Reflections on Liquid Level Measurement: An Intelligent Approach." *Control and Instrumentation,* September 1979.

3-7 REFERENCES

1. D.H. Sheingold, *Transducer Interfacing Handbook: A Guide to Analog Signal Conditioning,* Analog Devices Inc., Norwood, MA 02062, 1980.

2. P.J. O'Higgins, *Basic Instrumentation,* McGraw-Hill, 1966.

3. National Semiconductor, *The Pressure Transducer Handbook,* National Semiconductor Corp., Santa Clara, CA 95051, 1977.

4. National Semiconductor, "LX0503, LX0603 Series Monolithic Pressure Transducers" National Semiconductor Corp., Application note 1979.

5. Omega Engineering Inc., "Temperature Measurement Handbook," Omega Engineering, Stamford, CT, pp. A-8–A-40.

6. K.A. James, W.H. Quick, and V.H. Strahan, "Fiber Optics: The Way to True Digital Sensors?" *Control Engineering,* February 1979, p. 30.

Signals and Noise

4-1 INTRODUCTION

The transducers described in Chapter 3 are devices for converting a measurement of some physical quantity from the physical into the electrical data domain, as the first stage of its path to the microcomputer. The electrical signal at the output of the transducer is therefore a carrier of encoded information about the physical or chemical property being measured. Unfortunately, the signal also contains an unwanted component, known as *noise*, which is unrelated to the property of interest.

Noise in its broadest sense can be regarded as any part of the total signal which is not required. Thus, what may be noise in one application could become required information in another. Pressure fluctuations in air are a typical example. Frequencies less than 10^{-2} Hz are important in meteorology, while frequencies between 16 Hz and 20 kHz cover the audio range. Hence, audio signals may (literally!) be regarded as noise by the meteorologist.

The control of noise in a microcomputer system becomes of interest to the designer when the noise obscures a signal of interest. The purpose of this chapter is to discuss some of the sources of noise and to suggest some techniques by which this noise can be reduced. If we are to successfully separate the information from the noise, and hence selectively eliminate the noise, we must also know something about the *characteristics of the information.* Therefore, we begin by discussing the characteristics of signals.

4-2 CHARACTERISTICS OF SIGNALS

Fig. 4-1A shows the sort of signal that might originate from a transducer. It is a time-varying voltage (or current, resistance, etc.) where the information we require is contained in the instantaneous value of the voltage. This is known as the *time domain representation.* In principle, using either Fourier analysis or Fourier transforms, we may break down any such signal into a number of sine waves of various frequencies, amplitudes, and phases. This gives us a representation of the signal in the *frequency domain* which may have the form shown in Fig. 4-1B.

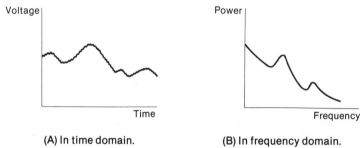

(A) In time domain.   (B) In frequency domain.

Fig. 4-1. Typical signal.

The ability to picture signals in either the time or the frequency domain is a very useful concept when dealing with the analog input subsystem, because the frequency spectrum of a signal provides the major means of distinguishing information content from noise. It also provides information on the bandwidth required for the analog subsystem, i.e., what range of frequencies must be allowed through to avoid distorting the signal and thereby changing the instantaneous voltage from what it should be.

To completely analyze the frequency domain of the signal is tedious and unnecessary when trying to estimate the bandwidth of the signal. One can get an idea of the range of frequencies required to represent a given signal without significant distortion by comparing the signal in question with a few well known waveforms. These waveforms are shown in Fig. 4-2, with their corresponding frequency domain representations. If the waveform is rounded and repetitive, then the frequencies of the components can be identified visually. If the waveform is repetitive but angular, it can be thought of as being composed of square waves or triangular waves. The square wave produces the more stringent requirements of the two and, as can be seen from Fig. 4-2, has frequency components extending up to infinity. Often, a reasonable representation can be achieved by preserving components up to $9f_o$, where f_o is the fundamental frequency. If the waveform is not repetitive, it can be considered as a collection of humps, either rounded or angular. Based on the widths of these humps, the range of frequencies required to produce an adequate representation can also be estimated from Fig. 4-2.

As an example of the application of these ideas, consider the signal shown in Fig. 4-3. It is close in form to a square wave of period T_2 superimposed on a sine wave of period T_1. The fre-

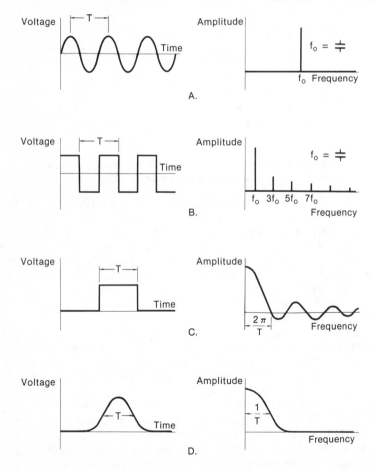

Fig. 4-2. Examples of transformations from time to frequency domain of simple waveforms.

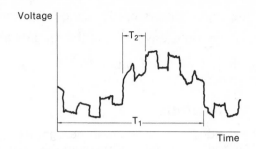

Voltage

Time

Fig. 4-3. Approximate signal frequency analysis through square-wave identification.

quency domain representation has components of $f = \dfrac{1}{T_1}, \dfrac{1}{T_2}$, $\dfrac{3}{T_2}, \dfrac{5}{T_2}, \dfrac{7}{T_2}, \dfrac{9}{T_2}$, etc. The information we want may be contained entirely in the squarish component of the time domain version of the signal, in which case the frequency domain component at $f = \dfrac{1}{T_1}$ can be regarded as noise. This leaves a frequency domain representation of the information content similar to that shown in Fig. 4-2B. The analog input system can now be designed to allow the appropriate frequency bands to pass through and to discriminate against the rest.

Fig. 4-4 represents a second example, which is basically a slowly varying voltage with occasional peaks. Here we must estimate the width, in the time domain, of the narrowest peak that must pass through the system undistorted. Referring to Fig. 4-2D, we see that most of the power in the frequency domain representation appears below $f = \dfrac{1}{T}$.

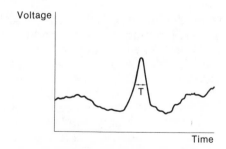

Voltage

Time

Fig. 4-4. Approximate signal frequency analysis through peak width identification.

If the analog input subsystem is designed to handle frequencies up to $f = \dfrac{1}{T}$ only, any peaks in the original signal that are narrower than T seconds will suffer distortion by being broadened and reduced in amplitude.

4-3 SOURCES OF NOISE

Noise can be divided into three main categories: stochastic noise (i.e., random, internal, or unavoidable noise); deterministic noise (i.e., environmental, external, or avoidable noise); and quantization noise. These are discussed below.

4-3-1 Stochastic (Random) Noise

The main sources of stochastic noise are: thermal or Johnson noise, shot noise, and flicker or 1/f noise.

Thermal noise is due to the random thermal motion of the charge carriers in a component such as a resistor. This motion gives rise to small voltages fluctuating across the resistor. The resulting mean-square noise voltage is given by

$$V_n^2 = 4kTR \, \Delta f, \qquad \text{(Eq. 4-1)}$$

where k is Boltzman's constant (1.38×10^{-23} J/K), T is the absolute temperature, R is the resistance of the component, and Δf is the bandwidth of the system. This voltage is described as a "white noise" since it is evenly spread through the frequency spectrum. Reducing the system bandwidth will reduce its effect, but we can never completely eliminate this noise because of the finite bandwidth of the signal.

To give an idea of the size of this effect, for a 1-MΩ resistor at room temperature and a measurement bandwidth of 1 MHz, the RMS noise voltage is 130 μV. A 10-kΩ resistor measured over the audio-frequency bandwidth (about 20 kHz) would produce 1.8 μV of noise.

Shot noise is produced whenever current carriers cross a barrier, such as a PN junction in a semiconductor device. The name appeared in the days when vacuum tubes were the main electronic device. The arrival of a pulse of electrons at the anode was likened to the shot from a scattergun arriving at its target—there was a spread in the arrival times of the individual particles. Even when we are dealing with supposedly constant currents rather than single pulses, the effect is still present and leads to a random fluctuation in the instantaneous magnitude of the current. The RMS value of this current fluctuation is given by

$$i_n = \{2qI\Delta f\}^{1/2}, \qquad \text{(Eq. 4-2)}$$

where q is the charge on the electron, I is the average current and Δf is again the bandwidth of the system. Bipolar transistors, which rely on conduction across semiconductor PN junctions for their operation, generate this kind of noise, whereas field effect transistors, whose gate/channel junctions carry only a small leakage current, do not introduce significant shot noise into a system.

Using typical figures of I = 1 mA and Δf = 1 MHz, i_n from Eq. 4-2 is roughly 0.02 μA. As with thermal or Johnson noise, shot noise is also spead uniformly through the frequency spectrum and thus can be described as white noise.

Flicker noise is sometimes known as "1/f noise" because its power spectrum, rather than being flat, is inversely proportional to frequency. It therefore consists mainly of low frequency energy (flicker) and is the dominant noise below about 1 kHz in bipolar transistors. It is significantly greater in solid state devices than in vacuum tube devices and is thought to result from random variations in diffusion processes. However, the phenomenon is not well understood and is sometimes linked with long-term drift. Since this type of noise increases toward DC, we must avoid DC for sensitive measurements. The usefulness of chopping amplifiers, which convert a DC signal to an AC signal before amplifying it, becomes apparent.

4-3-2 Deterministic (Environmental) Noise

The main sources of deterministic or environmental noise are: power line hum at 60 Hz and higher order harmonics of 60 Hz; wide-band or radio-frequency interference (RFI) caused by narrow, high-energy switching spikes; and local radio and TV transmitters.

In general, deterministic noise, or *interference* as it is sometimes known, originates from any electrical source that radiates electromagnetic signals. This interference is picked up by any conductor in the microcomputer system that can act as an antenna. The most common interference comes from the power distribution network and therefore occurs predominantly at 60 Hz. However, harmonics at 120 Hz, 180 Hz, and 240 Hz can be significant and should not be ignored. Other sources of interference may produce a wider noise power spectrum and are therefore more difficult to eliminate. Such sources include lightning, ignition systems, arcing relays, and switchgear or brushes on electric motors — anything that produces an electrical discharge. The sensitivity of a wire or component to electromagnetic interference is roughly proportional to its length and cross-section, and its resistance to ground. The effect of this noise type depends heavily on the amount of voltage amplification that follows the component responsible for the pickup.

Not all environmental noise comes directly from radiated electromagnetic waves. Some may be conducted into the microcomputer system from the mains and needs to be filtered out by the power supply. This interference comes from nearby equipment drawing current from the mains in large quantities or in bursts. It is a particularly important source of noise in industrial environments.

The position of environmental noise in the noise spectrum is shown in Fig. 4-5. The flat portion is due to the effects of thermal noise and shot noise, and the rise in noise power at low frequencies is due to flicker noise. Most of the environmental noise is likely to come in the region where flicker noise is giving way to the thermal and shot noise as the dominant noise source. This leaves a relatively "quiet" region in the range 10^3 Hz–10^5 Hz before medium-band radio begins to have an effect.

4-3-3 Quantization Noise

When the signal from the transducer is finally digitized after analog signal conditioning, an approximation occurs in the conversion from the continuously variable analog domain to the discrete steps of the digital domain. This conversion introduces an error — noise — into the measurement which may be as large as the *quantization level* (the ADC resolution). If the noise already present in the signal is less than the quantiza-

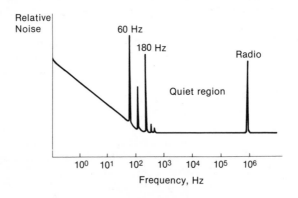

Fig. 4-5. The noise spectrum.

tion level, then the quantization noise will predominate and the precision and accuracy of the measurement will be limited by the resolution of the ADC. If, however, the RMS value of the noise present is at least as large as the quantization level, then the effect of the ADC is to add white noise to the signal. The amount of white noise is given by $\Delta V/\sqrt{12}$, where ΔV is the quantization level.

4-4 QUANTIFYING NOISE

When considering the effect of noise, its absolute magnitude is not as important as is its size compared with the information content of the signal. This becomes clear if we look back to the earlier example of thermal noise. The 1.8 μV of noise from the 10-kΩ resistor is insignificant when superimposed on a 1-volt signal at the output of an amplifier. However, at the amplifier's input, where the information content may be as little as 1 to 10 μV, there is almost as much noise as information. After amplifying the signal by a factor of 10^6 for input to the ADC, we may well have an output signal comprising about 5 V of information mixed with about 2 V of noise.

The amount of signal compared with the amount of noise is measured by the *signal-to-noise* ratio (S/N) which is usually defined by the expression

$$S/N = 20 \log V_s/V_n, \qquad \text{(Eq. 4-3)}$$

where V_s is the rms signal voltage and V_n is the RMS noise voltage.

If we have a functional block, such as an amplifier in the analog input subsystem, then the effect of this block on the signal-to-noise ratio is measured by the *noise figure* of the block, which is given by

$$NF = (S/N)_{in} - (S/N)_{out}, \qquad \text{(Eq. 4-4)}$$

where the signal-to-noise ratio is measured in dB (decibels) as defined in Eq. 4-3. Thus, if the amplifier introduces additional noise into the system, $(S/N)_{out}$ for the output is less than $(S/N)_{in}$ for the input and the resulting noise figure is greater than 0 dB.

For any analog signal input to the microcomputer, we have seen that there are normally several sources of noise content. These sources are usually independent and therefore have no fixed phase relationship to one another, i.e., they are *uncorrelated.* To sum the contributions from the independent sources, we must add the mean squares of the voltages, giving, for instance,

$$V_{n(total)}^2 = V_t^2 + V_s^2 + V_f^2 \qquad \text{(Eq. 4-5)}$$

where the total noise content is assumed to originate from the thermal, shot, and flicker effects.

4-5 DEALING WITH NOISE

In principle, deterministic or environmental noise is avoidable, whereas stochastic noise is inherent in the components of the analog input subsystem and therefore unavoidable. The first step, then, in maximizing the S/N ratio of the signal is to minimize the deterministic noise to the extent possible. This is accomplished by careful attention to the electrical and mechanical design of the analog input subsystem, including grounding, shielding and cabling, decoupling, and power supply filtering. The second step is to minimize stochastic noise by choosing good quality (low drift, low noise figure) amplifiers and transducers, particularly when dealing with low-level signals.

Having taken these precautions to minimize the *entry* of noise into the analog input subsystem, the third step in maximizing the S/N ratio is to enhance the signal by reducing the amount of noise accompanying the signal. *Signal enhancement* relies on the fact that a signal has definite bandwidth, phase, or magnitude characteristics that allow it to be distinguished from the noise.

The basic signal enhancement techniques include:

1. *Control of the bandwidth* of the subsystem. The use of this technique to avoid aliasing and for noise reduction was discussed in Chapter 2. It is particularly successful for noise reduction when the frequency spectra of the signal and the noise do not overlap. Even in the general case, by restricting the bandwidth of the system to the minimum needed to let the required signal pass through, the amount of noise included with the signal can be kept to a minimum.

2. *Averaging or integrating* where successive samples of the signal are added together. This technique demands that the signal maintain the same phase relationship (i.e., is synchronized) with the sampling pulse and therefore relies on the phase characteristics of the signal. It is particularly useful when the frequency spectra of the signal and the noise significantly overlap so that controlling the bandwidth by filtering would result in an unacceptable corruption of the signal.

3. *Magnitude discrimination* is commonly used in the digital domain where noise immunity is achieved by defining voltage ranges that correspond to logical ones and zeros. Some magnitude discrimination circuitry is often used with YES/NO transducers, such as proximity detectors, so that small disturbances at their output will not be mistaken for "YES" signals.

In the following subsections, we will concentrate on the techniques used to prevent environmental noise from entering the analog input subsystem. The selection of a good quality amplifier to minimize stochastic noise and the control of bandwidth by filtering are discussed in Chapter 5 (Analog Signal Conditioning).

4-5-1 Cabling, Screening, and Grounding

Environmental noise in a circuit can be greatly reduced by proper shielding and grounding. Shielding is achieved by surrounding the circuit or signal cable by a conducting material, which is connected to a ground or to the system common (common bus), to prevent the entry of electromagnetic radiation. This is why many electronic systems have metal cabinets or chassis. However, the possibility of one part of the circuit picking up unwanted signals from another part of the same circuit should not be ignored. Wires feeding high-impedance inputs followed by substantial amplification are most susceptible. They may need to be carefully located away from power lines or other carriers of large AC signals and be provided with extra shielding. It is normal to use shielded cable to conduct the signal from one part of an analog input subsystem to another, but incorrect grounding of the shield can lead to increased, rather than decreased, noise pickup.

In any system, a common bus line exists from which all voltages are measured. We refer to this as the *system common.* If the system common is connected to the earth, say, via a water pipe, then a *system ground* is established. The analog subsystem (Fig. 4-6) is made up of a number of functional blocks, each with its own common rail, which are in turn connected to the system common. Ideally all commons should have zero impedance between them and to ground, but in practice this is not the case. Wires, PCB tracks, and metal chassis and shields all have finite resistances, and some capacitive or inductive coupling always exists between nominally common points and the system ground. It is therefore most important to determine where the return currents from the various functional blocks are flowing. This is because, when the return currents are combined with the finite resistances of their common rails, they generate different potentials along the system common. If two or more adjacent commons are connected, then a *ground loop* is formed, and the different potentials cause a circulating current to flow. In addition, the topology of the ground loop can cause it to act as an antenna so that the RF interference that it picks up can contribute to the ground loop current.

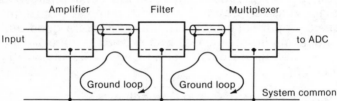

Fig. 4-6. The origins of ground loops.

A useful circuit model can be developed as shown in Fig. 4-7. Here the distributed resistances associated with the ground leads are represented by equivalent lumped values. In this diagram:

Z_i is the input impedance of the amplifier,
R_S is the source resistance,
R_{CG} is the resistance of the shield surrounding the cable that links the source to the amplifier,
R_{CS} is the resistance of the central lead of the cable,
R_{SG} is the resistance between the source and the source common,
R_{PG} is the resistance between the ground input of the amplifier and the amplifier common,

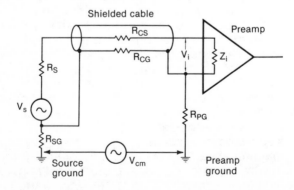

Fig. 4-7. Circuit model for effect of ground loop noise.

104

V_s is the source voltage, and
V_{cm} is the common-mode noise voltage source between
the amplifier common and the source common.

The voltage V_{cm} results from the current flowing in the ground loop, RF pickup, and any other noise voltage sources. With respect to the S/N ratio of the system, the important factor is how much of V_{cm} actually appears at the input terminal of the amplifier. Hence, if we determine the noise input voltage V_i in terms of V_{cm}, the result can suggest several approaches to minimizing the effect of V_{cm} by attempting to make $V_i = 0$.

If V_s is assumed to be zero and $Z_i \gg R_{CS} + R_S$, then analysis of the circuit shows that the input signal V_i reaching the amplifier due to V_{cm} is given by:

$$V_i = V_{cm} \frac{R_{CG}}{R_{SG} + R_{CG} + R_{PG}} \qquad \text{(Eq. 4-6)}$$

Consideration of this result suggests several methods for removing the effects of V_{cm}, i.e., for making V_i in Eq. 4-6 equal to zero:

1. $V_{cm} = 0$. This may be achieved by *single point grounding* in which the source and pre-amplifier are physically connected to the same common point. However, even with shielding, some RF pickup can still occur.
2. $R_{CG} = 0$. This can be attempted by bolting both the source and the amplifier commons to the same large metal plate.
3. $R_{SG} = \infty$. This amounts to "floating the source" by disconnecting it from ground if practicable. This means, however, that the return current to the source flows through the shield of the cable and is therefore susceptible to interference.
4. $R_{PG} = \infty$. This implies "floating the amplifier," which is possible if it is operated from a battery or isolated power supply. If the amplifier is mains-operated, then removing the power-line ground is not recommended! Deliberate insertion of a resistor R_{PG} (about 100 Ω) which is very much greater than R_{CG}, effectively floats the amplifier input terminals.

An alternative approach to those outlined in connection with Fig. 4-7 is to make proper use of the differential inputs of the amplifier, and to rely on its high common-mode rejection ratio, to eliminate the common-mode interference signal V_{cm}. The general layout is illustrated in Fig. 4-8. It is important to notice that the shield should not be connected to the local common at both ends, since this configuration would add another ground loop to the system. Furthermore, it is better for the shield to be connected to the common at the source end rather than at the amplifier end. This is because stray capacitances will complete the ground loop and allow currents to flow, induced by interference. It can be shown that, in the former case, these currents flow through the shield and do not affect the difference voltage sensed at the amplifier input; whereas, in the latter case, they flow in the signal leads and do affect the voltage sensed by the amplifier.[1] Note that if two separate screened cables are used instead of the single twin-cored cable shown, the connecting cables should be of the same length and geometry to equalize cable resistances and capacitances.

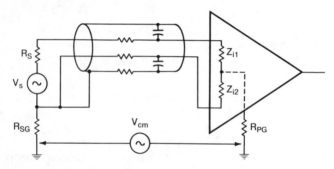

Fig. 4-8. Use of differential amplifier to discriminate against common-mode noise.

4-5-2 Decoupling Analog Circuits

Not all of the environmental noise enters a circuit as picked-up radiation. Some of it may enter via the power supply leads as illustrated in Fig. 4-9, which shows the input noise voltage that is equivalent to various noise voltages on the power supply rails. A well-designed power supply provides much protection against interference from other users of the mains supply. But even a good power supply cannot keep certain parts of a microcomputer system from affecting other parts through the power rails if the power supply leads to the individual parts are routed incorrectly.

Most of the trouble occurs because amplifiers are loosely represented as three-terminal devices (two terminals for a differential input, one for the output) and the return path for the load current is forgotten. This return path is normally via the *system common,* with respect to which the output voltage is

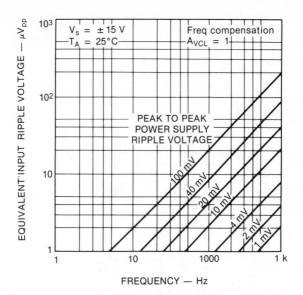

Fig. 4-9. Equivalent input ripple voltage, due to power supply ripple, as a function of frequency.

specified or via its substitute, one or both of the supply rails. Such forgotten current paths can cause unexpected feedback within a circuit or can cause coupling between two circuits connected to the same common. This mechanism can contribute to the V_{cm} shown in Fig. 4-7 or to the ground loop currents shown in Fig. 4-6.

Fig. 4-10 shows how these return currents can cause coupling between the functional blocks in the analog subsystem. R_1, R_2, and R_3 represent the resistance of the connecting wire; a few inches of #20 wire would typically have a resistance between 1 and 10 mΩ. The return currents are such that normally those from the later stages are much greater than those from the early stages ($I_1 < I_2 < I_3$), with I_3 probably around 10 mA. This means that the "earth" voltage at point B will be around 100 μV different from that at point A. This may not be much of a problem at point B, since we are dealing with high-level signals at this end of the analog input subsystem. But the fact that I_3 also has an effect on the "earth" of the preamp and the filter, where the signals are smaller, can lead to significant coupling and consequently corruption of the signal. The elimination of this coupling, then, requires two things. Not only should we use a single ground as indicated in Section 4-5-1, but also each functional block should have a separate lead to connect it to ground, as shown in Fig. 4-11, so that no

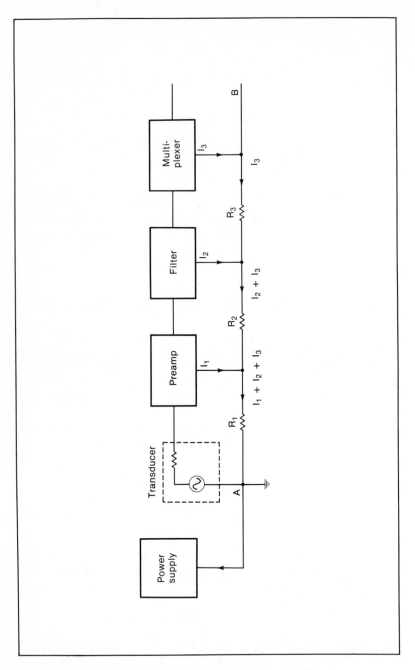

Fig. 4-10. Coupling caused by the use of a common path for return currents.

108

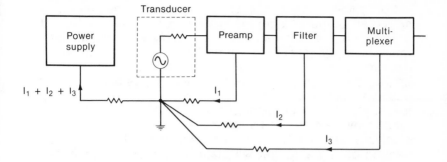

Fig. 4-11. Decoupling by the use of separate paths for return currents.

two signals share the same return path. A further consequence of this reasoning is that the ground point should be
close to the transducer and that the preamp ground lead
should be kept as short as possible. Since the preamp is where
the signal is smallest, this is where the greatest care must be
taken to reduce the amount of coupling between one functional block and the next.

Fig. 4-12 shows how a capacitor can be used to reduce the
length of the current loop for high frequencies and *decouple*
one stage from another. Allowing signal currents to flow along
shared power supply rails can cause variations in the supply
voltage at other functional blocks in the analog input subsystem leading to unwanted coupling between the blocks.
Merely connecting the capacitor from the negative rail to the
current common can leave quite a long loop, which may show
significant inductive effects at high frequencies.

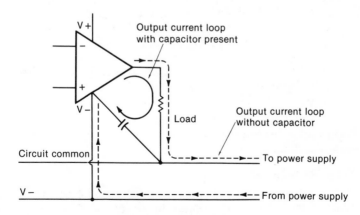

Fig. 4-12. Use of a capacitor to shorten current path.

For some amplifiers (depending on the design of the amplifier output stage), it may be best to connect the capacitor to the V⁺ terminal rather than the V⁻ terminal.[2] Even if the system is expected to handle only low frequencies, decoupling of this form is often necessary to keep the amplifier from oscillating at high frequencies because of the positive feedback via the inductance of the power supply leads. However, the capacitance in parallel with this inductance may then produce a resonant circuit. The insertion of a small resistance between the power supply rail and the V⁻ connection on the amplifier will damp out such a resonance. A fully decoupled amplifier may be configured as in Fig. 4-13.

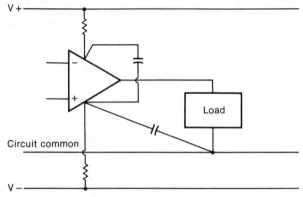

Fig. 4-13. Decoupled amplifier.

In short, to minimize coupling problems:

- Identify the complete current path for all signals, especially the commonly forgotten return path.
- Keep these current paths separate from power supply rails by careful routing and/or the insertion of by-pass capacitors.
- Avoid having two signals share the same path. The common rail is the most likely place to find signals sharing a path, and problems here can be solved largely by single-point earthing.

Decoupling of the digital ICs within the microprocessor subsystem is discussed in Section 10-5-2.

4-5-3 Impedance Matching

A traditional starting point for minimizing noise in a system has been to consider the noise figure for the amplifier. This is because, for a given signal from a transducer, we wish to in-

110

troduce the least possible degradation to the signal-to-noise ratio. However, the noise figure of an amplifier is a function of the source resistance (the resistance of the transducer, in this case) as well as a function of frequency, so we cannot consider just the amplifier in isolation. An example of the behavior of the noise figure for an instrumentation amplifier is shown in Fig. 4-14, which is reproduced from the data sheets on the μA725. Fig. 4-14B, which is derived from Fig. 4-14A, shows that the noise figure goes through a minimum for a source resistance just below 100 kΩ when the measurements are taken at 1 kHz. So, for optimum amplifier performance, a transducer would need to be chosen with an output resistance of 100 kΩ — which is not necessarily easy or even practical. For critical applications, a transformer can be placed between the transducer and the amplifier to match the output impedance of the transducer with the optimum value (100 kΩ) required by the amplifier. Before discussing this possibility, it is useful to consider whether the impedance matching is worthwhile.

First, we need to discover why the noise figure for the amplifier depends on the resistance of the transducer. Fig. 4-15 represents the front end of the analog input subsystem, as far as nonenvironmental sources of noise are concerned. The transducer is represented by a source of noise, V_{ni}^2, in series with its internal resistance. The amplifier is represented by a perfect (noiseless) amplifier with two noise sources on its input. The amplifier's noise voltage e_n can be thought of as largely thermal noise and its noise current i_n as largely shot noise. However, both voltages will contain flicker noise, so their values will vary with frequency. Since the perfect

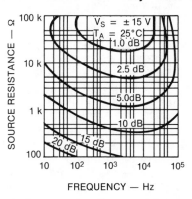

(A) Narrow band spot noise contours.

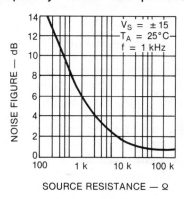

(B) Noise figure for a function of source resistance.

Fig. 4-14. Noise figure for μA725 instrumentation amplifier.

amplifier, with its infinite input impedance, does not allow current into its input, all of the noise current flows through the transducer. This develops a noise voltage across it which is directly proportional to the transducer's internal resistance. The amount of noise added to the signal by the amplifier therefore increases with transducer resistance. The amplifier noise figure increases for *low* values of transducer resistance, however, because the noise output of the *transducer* (assumed to be entirely thermal) *decreases* as the transducer resistance decreases (Eq. 4-1). Because the noise figure depends on the ratio of noise added by the amplifier to the noise already present in the signal, the noise figure is increased just as effectively by reducing the transducer noise as by increasing the noise added by the amplifier. This does not necessarily lead to a degradation in the signal-to-noise ratio seen at the output of the amplifier.

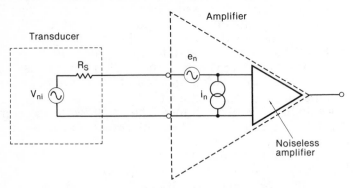

Fig. 4-15. Circuit model for amplifier noise sources.

So, although the noise figure provides a useful means of comparing two amplifiers, we must not place too much weight on its variation with source resistance when considering matching a transducer to an amplifier. In exacting situations, the gains to be made by impedance matching may be worthwhile, but at this stage we need to consider the magnitude of the amplifier noise before a decision can be made. Graphs like Fig. 4-16 help to provide a very direct answer to this question. In the worst case shown, using about the maximum useful bandwidth for this amplifier, the total noise referred to input is less than 10 μV, and the question becomes: Is this significant compared with the information content of the signal from the transducer? The answer, in many cases, is a resounding no. Having made this assessment, one can then turn to solving bandwidth problems and minimizing environmental noise.

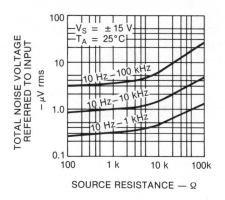

Fig. 4-16. Broadband noise for µA725 instrumentation amplifier.

As an example, consider the thermocouple, which has one of the smallest outputs of the commonly used transducers. With a thermocouple output of about 40 µV/°C, noise of about 1 µV on measurements of 1 kHz bandwidth will restrict the temperature resolution to 0.025°C, which is more than adequate for most purposes. Clearly, attention to the frequency and bandwidth of the measurement is far more important in this case than attention to impedance matching.

Even if the noise magnitude obtained from Fig. 4-16 is not small compared with the information content of the signal from the transducer, it is worth considering whether the amplifier noise will still be swamped by transducer noise. This is quite possible, because all that has been included in Fig. 4-16 is the thermal noise from the transducer. A substantial amount of shot or flicker noise may be generated, and if this is the case, there is probably again little to be gained from impedance matching.

If the amplifier noise does have a significant effect, then what can be done about it? Finding a transducer that has an internal resistance matched to the characteristics of our amplifier, while retaining the best signal-to-noise ratio, is likely to be impossible. Finding an amplifier that will match our transducer is also improbable. The solution, then, is to insert a transformer between the transducer and the amplifier. For a low-resistance transducer, this steps up the output voltage of the transducer, increasing the thermal noise voltage while preserving the signal-to-noise ratio so that the transducer noise dominates the amplifier noise. Thus the degradation of the signal-to-noise ratio by the amplifier is minimized by ensuring that the noise added by the amplifier is as small as possible compared with the noise already present.

113

4-6 REFERENCES

1. V.J. Lovoula, "Preventing Noise in Grounded Thermocouple Measurements," *Instruments and Control Systems,* January 1980, p. 31.

2. P. Brokaw, "An IC Amplifier Users' Guide to Decoupling, Grounding, and Making Things Go Right for a Change," *Application Note G17/329-4700,* Analog Devices Inc., Norwood, MA 02062.

Analog Signal Conditioning

5-1 INTRODUCTION

In Chapter 2, the analog input subsystem (Fig. 2-1) of a micro-computer-based data acquisition or control system was introduced as the hardware module responsible for data input. A key element of this subsystem was the analog signal conditioning line, whose functions were discussed in Section 2-3. In Fig. 5-1, the analog signal conditioning line has been expanded to illustrate the functions that may be necessary to transform a transducer's electrical output into a high-level voltage, suitable for further operations such as data transmission, analog signal processing, and/or analog-to-digital conversion. The need for primary signal conditioning was discussed in Section 2-1. The aim of this chapter is to present the circuits and components that implement the primary signal condition-ing, isolation, filtering, offsetting, and gain/scaling functions.

The physical location and the extent of the analog signal conditioning vary widely according to the application. In most cases, the line shown in Fig. 5-1 is located with the transducer. Hence, if the transducer is located away from the microcom-puter, the output from the line must be transmitted to the microcomputer in either analog or digital form. A received analog signal is then multiplexed with other analog inputs and digitized for input to the microprocessor. For digital data

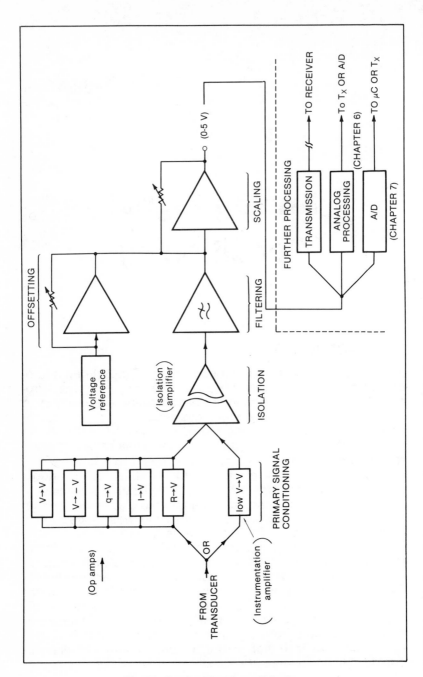

Fig. 5-1. Analog signal conditioning.

transmission, analog-to-digital conversion is done in the field. An additional option is analog processing of the signal, which may be done in the field but is more commonly implemented at the microcomputer.

An important prerequisite to successfully designing and implementing an analog signal conditioning line is to appreciate the characteristics and limitations of the various types of amplifiers available. We therefore begin this chapter by discussing the properties of real amplifiers as a guide toward selecting the correct amplifier for your application.

5-2 OPERATIONAL AMPLIFIERS

Amplifiers are required to implement many of the functional blocks of Fig. 5-1. The most common and versatile amplifier, the *operational amplifier* (OA, or *op amp*), is discussed in this section in terms of its ideal and real electrical characteristics. In Section 5-3-1, we use the OA to implement the primary signal conditioning operations illustrated in Fig. 5-1. However, for small noisy signals in the presence of high common mode voltages, an OA may not be adequate and an *instrumentation amplifier* (IA), such as that described in Section 5-3-2, may be necessary. On the other hand, in some applications it is essential that there be no direct ohmic contact between the analog signal conditioning subsystem and the microcomputer. In such cases, an *isolation amplifier* (ISO A) must be employed. This special type of amplifier is described in Section 5-4.

5-2-1 Ideal Operational Amplifiers

An OA has two input terminals, known as the inverting (−) and noninverting (+) inputs, and a single-ended output. The load is normally connected between the output and the circuit common (Fig. 5-2). Since the OA is a direct-coupled differential amplifier, the output voltage, V_o, is directly proportional to the difference between the input signals. That is,

$$V_o = A_{VOL} (V_2 - V_1), \tag{Eq. 5-1}$$

where A_{VOL} is the open-loop difference gain. Since A_{VOL} is very large, an OA is almost always used in a *closed-loop configuration,* employing one of a variety of feedback networks which then define the operational behavior of the amplifier, as illustrated in Section 5-3. The feedback holds the two inputs at virtually the same potential, so that if the (+) input is connected to ground, then the (−) input is also held at ground, even though there is no direct ohmic contact. Under these con-

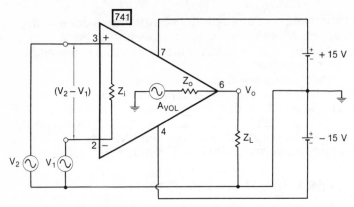

Fig. 5-2. Operational amplifier.

ditions the (−) input is known as a *virtual ground* or summing junction.

In a real OA, a small output voltage, V_o, exists due to the common-mode input voltage, V_{cm}, which is the average of the two input voltages. That is,

$$V_o = A_{cm} \left(\frac{V_1 + V_2}{2} \right), \qquad \text{(Eq. 5-2)}$$

where A_{CM} is the common-mode gain. The common-mode rejection ratio (CMRR) is defined as

$$\text{CMRR} = A_{VOL}/A_{cm} \qquad \text{(Eq. 5-3)}$$

and is therefore a measure of the effectiveness of a real OA in rejecting common-mode signals.

When analyzing OA circuits, it is useful to begin by defining the properties of an ideal OA. These are summarized in Table 5-1. Real OAs differ from the ideal in a number of respects, so for comparison, the properties of a typical real OA (the 741) are summarized in Table 5-2. From this comparison, it is clear that the typical OA is a good approximation to the ideal.

Table 5-1. Ideal Operational Amplifier Properties

- Infinite open-loop gain, A_{VOL}
- Infinite common-mode rejection ratio (CMRR)
- Infinite bandwidth
- Infinite input impedance, Z_i
- Zero output impedance, Z_o
- Zero offset voltage, V_{OS}
- Zero drift
- $V_2 - V_1 = 0$

Table 5-2. Real Operational Amplifier Specifications

Name	Description	Symbol	Typical Value	Units
ABSOLUTE MAXIMUM VALUES				
Supply voltage	Maximum voltages that can be applied to the + and − supply terminals.	V_{CC}, V_{CC}	±18	V
Differential input voltage	Maximum voltage difference that can be applied between the non-inverting (+) and inverting (−) inputs.		±30	V
Input voltage	Maximum voltage that can be applied to either input. Gives the maximum common-mode voltage.		±15	V
Power dissipation	Maximum value is obtained when input tries to drive output to one supply rail while output is connected to other rail.	P_D	500	mW
MAJOR DC PARAMETERS				
Input bias current	Mean value of the base current to the input transistors; $I_B = (I_{B1} + I_{B2})$.	I_B	100	nA
Input offset current	Difference between the base currents of the input transistors; $I_{OS} = I_{B1} - I_{B2}$.	I_{OS}	20	nA
Input offset current drift	Variation of I_{OS} with temperature.	$\Delta I_{OS}/\Delta T$	1	nA/°C
Input offset voltage	Input voltage required to null the output with zero source voltage.	V_{OS}	1	mV
Input offset voltage drift	Variation of V_{OS} with temperature.	$\Delta V_{OS}/\Delta T$	10	μV/°C
Input resistance	Ratio of change in input voltage with change in input current, measured at one input.	Z_i	1	MΩ
Voltage gain	Change in output voltage with differential input voltage, under open-loop conditions.	A_{VOL}	10^5 100	V/V dB
Common-mode rejection ratio	Ratio of open-loop gain, A_{VOL}, to common-mode gain, A_C.	CMRR	100	dB
Power supply rejection ratio	Ratio of change in input offset voltage, V_{OS}, with change in supply voltage.	PSRR	−90	dB
Short-circuit output current	Maximum available output current.	I_{SC}	5	mA
Output impedance	Ratio of output voltage change to output current change.	Z_o	75	Ω

Table 5-2–cont. Real Operational Amplifier Specifications

Name	Description	Symbol	Typical Value	Units
	MAJOR AC PARAMETERS			
Gain-bandwidth product	Measures variation of A_{VOL} with frequency; information is usually in graph form, as in Fig. 5-5.	GBW	10^6	Hz
Risetime	Small signal output response time to a square pulse input; t_r is measured between 10% and 90% points on output pulse, at unity gain.	t_r	0.3	μS
Bandwidth	Frequency range from DC to frequency f_M where output is -3 dB for unity gain amplifier; note BW $= 0.35/t_r$ (μs).	BW	10^6	Hz
Slew rate	Large signal maximum rate of change of output voltage with time.	SL	1	V/μS
Overshoot	Maximum overshoot of output voltage due to a square pulse input, as expressed as a percent of the final output; is a measure of the stability of the amplifier.		5	%

5-2-2 Parameters of Real Operational Amplifiers

The differential front end of an OA consists of a matched pair of *bipolar junction transistors* (BJTs) or *field effect transistors* (FETs), as shown in Fig. 5-3. The input terminals are connected to the bases of the BJTs which must therefore draw their bias currents, I_{B1} and I_{B2}, from the external input circuits. Hence, two conditions need to be satisfied:

- Each input must have some form of DC current path to ground.
- The resistance of each of these paths should be the same so that equal bias currents develop equal common mode input voltages.

As an example, the inverting amplifier of Fig. 5-4 has a DC path to ground for each of its inputs, and R_3 has been chosen such that

$$R_3 = R_i/R_f = R_iR_f/(R_i + R_f). \qquad \text{(Eq. 5-4)}$$

In this case, it has been assumed that $R_s \ll R_i$.

Because the input transistors of real OAs are not identical, their base currents, I_{B1} and I_{B2}, and their base/emitter voltages, V_{BE1} and V_{BE2}, are unequal. The resulting input offset current, I_{OS}, and input offset voltage, V_{OS}, lead to a net nonzero output

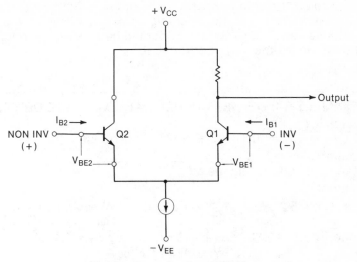

Fig. 5-3. Operational amplifier input.

voltage even when both inputs are grounded. We must therefore introduce an external input offset voltage that will null the output for zero source voltage. This can be done either by using the offset null circuit provided by the manufacturers, as in Fig. 5-4, or by applying a small offset voltage of the appropriate polarity at either OA input.[1]

Although the presence of I_B, I_{OS}, and V_{OS} in real OAs leads to an output error voltage, a more serious problem is that these parameters are temperature-dependent, so that this output er-

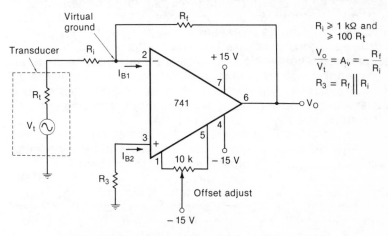

Fig. 5-4. Inverting amplifier with I_B and V_{OS} control.

ror voltage drifts with temperature. Example 5-1 shows the effect of a 10°C temperature change for two different input resistances and indicates that R_i should be as small as possible to minimize the output drift due to I_{os}.

EXAMPLE 5-1: OFFSET CURRENT AND VOLTAGE DRIFT

Given:

741 OA; $\Delta T = 10°C$; $R_i = 500$ kΩ or 10 kΩ.

Require:

Total input voltage change ΔV_i.

Solution:

From Table 5-2   : $\dfrac{\Delta I_{os}}{\Delta T} = 1$ nA/°C $\dfrac{\Delta V_{os}}{\Delta T} = 10$ μV/°C

Hence for $\Delta T = 10°C$: $\Delta I_{os} = 10$ nA $\Delta V_{os} = 0.1$ mV

$$\Delta V_i = \Delta I_{os} R_i + \Delta V_{os}$$

If $R_i = 500$ kΩ   : $\Delta V_i = (10 \times 10^{-9})$ $(500 \times 10^3) + 0.1$ mV

$\Delta V_i = 5.1$ mV

If $R_i = 10$ kΩ   : $\Delta V_i = (10 \times 10^{-9})$ $(10^4) + 0.1$ mV

$\Delta V_i = 0.2$ mV

Operational amplifiers are available with simple BJT inputs, with cascaded BJTs in a Darlington configuration (Sections 3-4-1 and 11-4-3), or with FET inputs. In general, BJT inputs have large bias currents (~200 nA), small offset voltages (~1 mV), and modest (~2 MΩ) input impedances, Z_i; and FET inputs have very small bias currents (~20 pA), large offset voltages (~10 mV), and high input impedances (~100 MΩ). Darlington, or super-beta, inputs represent a compromise between these extremes. The choice of a BJT, Darlington, or FET input OA depends on whether bias currents or offset voltages are more significant in a particular application. It is important to minimize bias current when an OA is required as a buffer, as a current-to-voltage converter, or in situations involving charged capacitors, such as in sample-and-hold amplifiers and operational integrators. This is because the DC bias currents tend to discharge the capacitors even though the AC input impedance to the OA may be very high. A small offset voltage, V_{os}, is important in direct coupled circuits involving low-level DC signals, because V_{os} is easily amplified along with the signal. This can result in a large, temperature-dependent DC error voltage. A small V_{os} is also important for precision comparators if transitions at incorrect levels are to be avoided. In summary, an OA with a BJT input is preferred in DC applications where low source impedances exist and small offset voltages are important, while a FET input is preferred when very high source impedances exist and low bias currents are important.

5-2-3 AC Parameters of Real Operational Amplifiers

When choosing an OA, the important AC considerations are the *frequency dependence of the open loop voltage gain* (A_{VOL}) and the *slew rate*. Fig. 5-5 shows that A_{VOL} decreases with increasing frequency in such a way that the gain-bandwidth product remains constant. Although for circuit analysis it is usually assumed that A_{VOL} is infinite, in practice it is necessary only to ensure that A_{VOL} is large compared with the closed loop gain (A_{CL}) over the range of frequencies of interest. In particular, if A_{CL} is the ideal closed loop gain (i.e., for $A_{VOL} = \infty$) and A'_{CL} is the acutal closed loop gain, then the percentage difference between A_{CL} and A'_{CL} at the maximum frequency of interest is as follows:

(a) For 30% difference, $A_{VOL} \geq 2.5A_{CL}$
(b) For 10% difference, $A_{VOL} \geq 10A_{CL}$ (Eq. 5-5)
(c) For 1% difference, $A_{VOL} \geq 100A_{CL}$

Example 5-2 illustrates the technique for choosing A_{VOL}. Note that the maximum frequency of interest in case (a) is the 3-dB frequency, f_c.

EXAMPLE 5-2: CHOICE OF A_{VOL}

Given:
Inverting amplifier, gain $A_{CL} = -10$ for $0 < f < 1$ kHz

From Equation 5-5:
For 10% error, $A_{VOL} \geq 10 \times 10 = 100$ at 1 kHz.
For 1% error, $A_{VOL} \geq 100 \times 10 = 1000$ at 1 kHz.

For a 741 OA, Fig. 5-5 shows that $A_{VOL} = 1000$ at 1 kHz. Hence a 741 can meet the 1% specification.

If the required frequency range is increased to $0 < f < 10$ kHz, then from Fig. 5-6, A_{VOL} at 10 kHz is 10^4 and a 741 would not meet the 1% specification.

Slew rate (SR) is the maximum rate of change of the OA output voltage with time and may be expressed as:

$$SR = \left(\frac{\Delta V_o}{\Delta t}\right)_{MAX} = \frac{I_{MAX}}{C_c} \text{ volts/}\mu s \qquad \text{(Eq. 5-6)}$$

where C_c is the OA *compensation capacitor* and I_{MAX} is the maximum current available from the OA to charge C_c. The slew rate is a large signal effect which is caused by current limiting within the OA and occurs when the maximum charging rate of the compensation capacitor is reached. The compensation capacitor is required to stabilize the OA by preventing high-frequency self-oscillation. The capacitor introduces a single-pole, low-pass filter into the transfer function of the OA so that its gain becomes very small at frequencies where oscillation might otherwise occur. In an application, the slew rate can be estimated as follows:

- For a rectangular pulse of magnitude V, the switching time Δt becomes:

$$\Delta t = V/SR \qquad \text{(Eq. 5-7)}$$

- For a sinusoidal output signal of amplitude V_p and frequency f, the required slew rate is given by:

$$SR \geqslant 2\pi f V_p \qquad \text{(Eq. 5-8)}$$

The value of C_c is governed by two conflicting requirements. Equation 5-6 shows that a small C_c results in a high slew rate. However, a small C_c implies a high cut-off frequency for the low-pass filter and therefore a possibly unstable amplifier. The normal procedure is to make C_c as small as possible while still maintaining stability, and OA manufacturers usually give recommended values of C_c for different values of A_{CL}. However, a number of common monolithic OAs, such as the 741, are internally compensated. This results in an OA that is stable under all conditions but at the expense of a limited slew rate.

5-3 PRIMARY SIGNAL CONDITIONING

The primary conditioning block of the analog subsystem is required to undertake one of a number of possible operations, depending on the type of transducer employed. These operations include:

- Inverting and noninverting voltage amplification.
- Current-to-voltage conversion.
- Charge-to-voltage conversion.
- Resistance-to-voltage conversion.
- True differential voltage amplification.
- Resistance-to-voltage conversion using a resistance bridge.

These operations are usually carried out using OAs, but in difficult situations an instrumentation amplifier or even an isolation amplifier may become necessary. Although frequency-to-voltage conversion is shown in Fig. 5-1, its discussion should be considered within the broader context of data transmission and reception techniques.

5-3-1 Operational Amplifier Implementation

Practical circuits for each of the operations listed above are provided in Figs. 5-4 and 5-6 through 5-11. The industry standard 741 OA is used, except in Fig. 5-8 where an FET input CA3140 from RCA is needed for the charge-to-voltage converter. With each circuit, we have listed in order the equations that describe the circuit and allow the required component values to be selected. These formulae should be adequate,

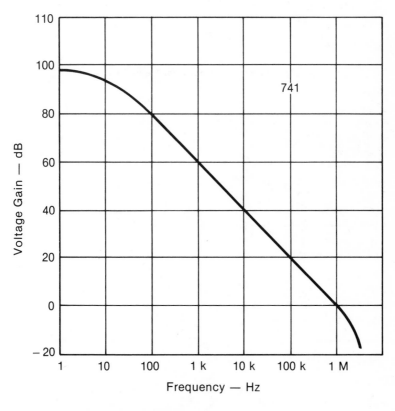

Fig. 5-5. Open-loop frequency response for 741 OA.

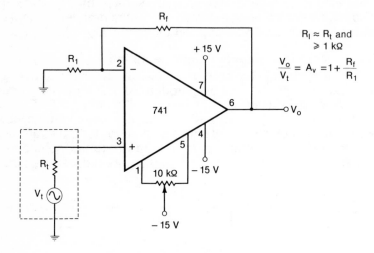

Fig. 5-6. Noninverting voltage amplifier.

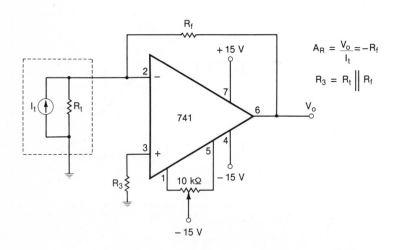

Fig. 5-7. Current-to-voltage converter.

provided that the procedures given in Section 5-2-2 for selecting an OA are followed.

Component values should normally be chosen to provide a medium level ($\sim$ 1 volt) signal output. To minimize transducer loading and consequent input signal attenuation, the input impedance, Z_i, of the OA circuit should be at least one hundred times the output impedance, R_t, of the transducer if the transducer is a voltage source. It should be less than one hundredth of R_t if the transducer is a current source. In other words,

$$Z_i \geqslant 100\ R_t \text{ (voltage source)}$$
$$Z_i \leqslant 0.01\ R_t \text{ (current source)}$$

(Eq. 5-9)

The amplifier configurations and design formulae in the circuits of Figs. 5-4 and 5-6 through 5-11 ensure that these conditions are satisfied. Note also that the gain of the voltage amplifiers (Figs. 5-4, 5-6, and 5-10) should generally be limited to a maximum of about 100 per OA. With typical gain-

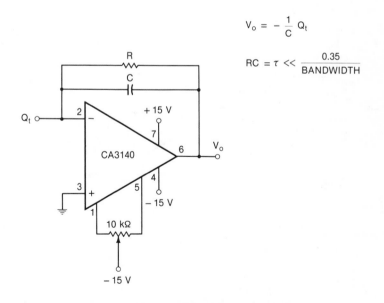

$$V_o = -\frac{1}{C} Q_t$$

$$RC = \tau \ll \frac{0.35}{\text{BANDWIDTH}}$$

Fig. 5-8. Charge-to-voltage converter.

127

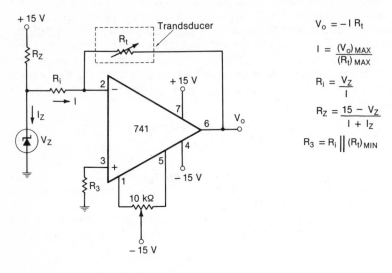

Fig. 5-9. Resistance-to-voltage converter.

$$V_o = -I R_t$$

$$I = \frac{(V_o)_{MAX}}{(R_t)_{MAX}}$$

$$R_i = \frac{V_Z}{I}$$

$$R_Z = \frac{15 - V_Z}{I + I_Z}$$

$$R_3 = R_i \parallel (R_t)_{MIN}$$

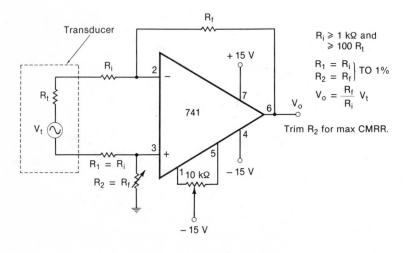

Fig. 5-10. Differential amplifier.

$$R_i \geq 1 \text{ k}\Omega \text{ and } \geq 100 R_t$$

$$\left. \begin{array}{l} R_1 = R_i \\ R_2 = R_f \end{array} \right\} \text{ TO 1\%}$$

$$V_o = \frac{R_f}{R_i} V_t$$

Trim R_2 for max CMRR.

128

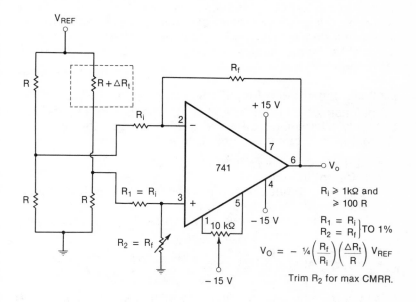

Fig. 5-11. Resistance bridge amplifier.

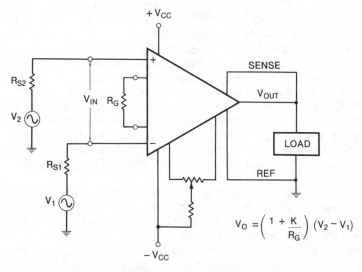

Fig. 5-12. Basic instrumentation amplifier.

bandwidth products of about 10^6, the bandwidth of the OA is approximately 10 kHz, which approaches the maximum that an 8-bit microcomputer system can satisfactorily handle. However, although increased gain can be obtained at the expense of reduced bandwidth, it is generally better to use additional OAs if necessary, since large gain magnifies the effect of I_{os} and V_{os}.

5-3-2 Instrumentation Amplifiers

The instrumentation amplifier (IA) shown in Fig. 5-12 is basically a precision differential voltage amplifier. Its main characteristics can be summarized as follows:

- Suitable only for voltage amplification.
- Differential input.
- Very high input impedance and very low output impedance.
- Stable voltage gain, usually controlled by a single gain-setting resistor, R_G.
- Very high CMRR.
- Low offset and drift.
- High linearity.

It is important to note that an IA is *not* an operational amplifier and that optimizing an IA as a voltage amplifier means losing versatility.

Instrumentation amplifiers are used in hostile environments where it is difficult to acquire useable signals. Typical problems include: wide temperature variations, electrical noise, interference, significant common-mode voltages, ground loops, and voltage drops due to finite lead resistances. If these problems are combined with the low signal levels associated with some types of transducers, such as thermocouples, then an instrumentation amplifier can be an excellent solution. However, if the common-mode voltages exceed the amplifier's supply voltage, or if very high isolation impedances are required between the signal source and the rest of the data acquisition system, then an isolation amplifier may be necessary.

Fig. 5-12 shows that, in addition to the signal inputs and the gain resistor terminals, an IA normally has some form of offset null facility and a pair of feedback terminals labeled *sense* (V_s) and *reference* (V_R). When an IA is used in its basic configuration, V_s and V_R are connected as in Fig. 5-12. However, V_s can be used to sense remotely and hence to stabilize the voltage signal at the load itself. Or it can be used to allow a current booster inside the feedback loop, which increases the output power without loss of precision. V_R can be used to introduce a bias voltage into the output so that V_{OUT} is not necessarily referenced to ground.

Instrumentation amplifiers can be implemented in a number of ways using OAs, or they can be purchased in modular or monolithic form from various manufacturers, including Burr-Brown, Datel-Intersil, and Analog Devices.[2] Since commercial IAs tend to be fairly expensive (around \$30), an inexpensive alternative is to construct an IA using three OAs as in Fig. 5-13. This circuit is basically the same as that employed in many commercial IAs, but it needs careful matching of the resistance values if reasonable performance is to be achieved.

5-4 ISOLATION AMPLIFIERS

An isolation amplifier (ISO A) or isolator is essentially an instrumentation amplifier or operational amplifier which has its

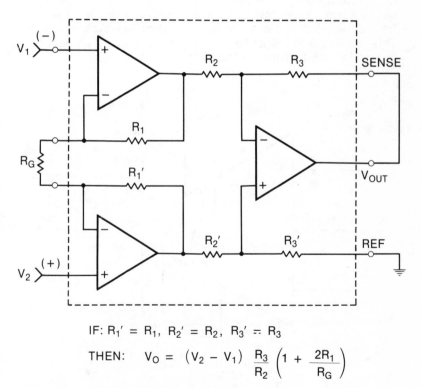

IF: $R_1' = R_1$, $R_2' = R_2$, $R_3' = R_3$

THEN: $V_O = (V_2 - V_1) \dfrac{R_3}{R_2} \left(1 + \dfrac{2R_1}{R_G}\right)$

Fig. 5-13. An instrumentation amplifier constructed from OAs.

131

input stage ohmically isolated both from its output stage and from the power supply input. The circuit symbol and terminals for a typical ISO A are shown in Fig. 5-14. The main features of an ISO A are:

- Ability to handle very high common-mode voltages (CMV) of up to several thousand volts.
- Very high rejection of noise, interference, and any other unwanted common-mode signals.
- Very high impedance leakage paths from the input to the power common.

Environments in which isolation amplifiers are useful include power stations, industrial process control systems, automatic test equipment, and patient monitoring in hospitals. Typical applications within these environments include the recovery of small signals superimposed on large common-mode voltages, or the avoidance of troublesome ground loops and their associated noise. The fully floating input allows a simple two-wire connection so that the transducer is completely independent of the system ground. This technique amounts to "floating the amplifier," as described in Section 4-5-1 of the Noise chapter.

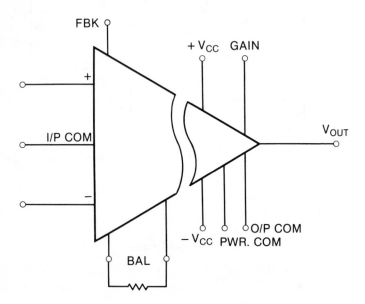

Fig. 5-14. Isolation amplifier type AD277.

In the context of this book, a most important application is the protection of the microcomputer and its input and output subsystems from transients or fault conditions. This is particularly serious in industrial plants, where the leads carrying a signal from a remote monitoring point to a central microcomputer can pick up several hundred volts of common-mode interference. This will almost certainly damage the analog input line and probably the microprocessor, unless an isolator is inserted between the remote transducer and the input subsystem.

In medical procedures involving patient monitoring, it is essential to protect the patient from leakage currents and amplifier fault conditions. It is equally important to protect the amplifier from the large voltage pulses (5 kV) associated with defibrillation. The special properties of an isolation amplifier provide an effective solution to both of these problems.

In an isolation amplifier, the method of coupling across the *isolation barrier* between the input stage and the rest of the amplifier can be magnetic, optical, or any other way which avoids direct ohmic contact. A precision isolation amplifier, such as the one shown in block form in Fig. 5-15, normally uses transformer coupling in which the input signal modulates a 50–100-kHz carrier wave. The external DC power supply runs an oscillator whose output is transformer-coupled across the isolation barrier to a rectifier and filter, which produces the necessary DC voltages to operate the input stage. This stage can be either an instrumentation amplifier or else an uncommitted operational amplifier. In some commercial models, the fully floating DC voltages are available to power the input transducer if required. The signal from the input amplifier modulates the carrier and is transferred back across the barrier by a second transformer to a phase-sensitive detector and low-pass filter at the output. Because of the technique employed to transfer the signal across the barrier, the bandwidth of an isolation amplifier covers frequencies only in the range of DC to about 2 kHz.

Isolation amplifiers are available from several manufacturers and, although expensive, they sometimes represent the only viable solution in difficult situations.

5-5 FILTERING

The need to filter the analog signal was discussed in Chapters 2 and 4, and two major reasons were presented for controlling the signal bandwidth. The reasons were to minimize the noise content of the signal (Sections 2-3 and 4-5) and to prevent

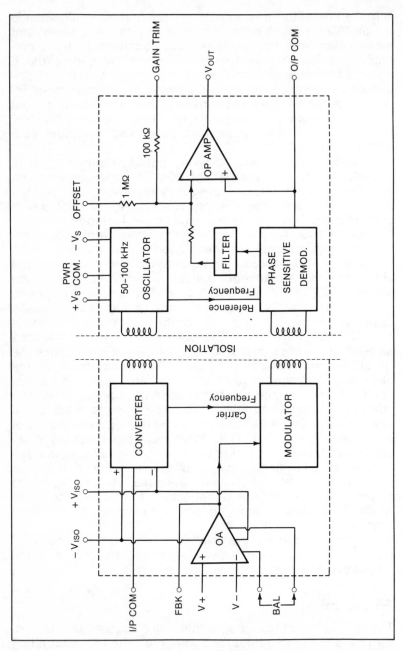

Fig. 5-15. Composite block diagram for Analog Devices' Model 227 and Burr Brown's Model 3450 isolation amplifiers.

134

aliasing when sampling the analog signal (Section 2-6-3). For whichever reasons we restrict the bandwidth, the ideal filter would pass the signals in the allowed frequency band without attenuation and would totally block any signals outside this band. Of course, real filters cannot achieve this behavior, though with enough spent on time and components they can approach it. Rather than attempt an exhaustive treatment of filters in this section, our aim is to present practical circuits that are effective as anti-aliasing and noise suppression filters. Additional theoretical and practical information is readily available elsewhere.[3]

5-5-1 First-Order Filters

First-order filters are the simplest available, requiring only a resistor and a capacitor for their construction. The *low-pass filter* shown in Fig. 5-16A is followed by an optional buffer. This buffer may be used to prevent subsequent modules of the analog input subsystem from loading the filter and altering its characteristic behavior from that indicated in Fig. 5-16B. The heavy line in Fig. 5-16B shows a convenient and simplified representation of the transfer function of a first-order filter. The gain (V_o/V_i) of the filter block is considered to be flat from zero to f_c, the cut-off or "corner" frequency (the gain A comes only from the buffer), and then to decrease at 20 dB/decade as the frequency is further increased. This "roll-off" of 20 dB/decade is typical of first-order filters and represents their major limitation compared with the abrupt cut-off of an "ideal" filter. The true response of the first-order filter (the light line in Fig. 5-16B is a smooth curve that approaches the straight lines

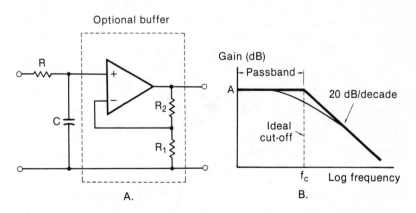

Fig. 5-16. A first-order low-pass filter (A) and its transfer function (B).

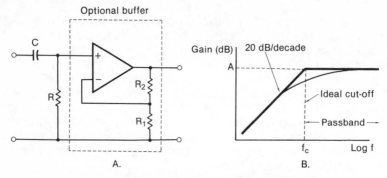

Fig. 5-17. A first-order high-pass filter (A) and its transfer function (B).

asymptotically at both the high and low frequency extremes and is 3 dB below the simplified response at the corner frequency.

The similarities between the first-order *high-pass filter* and its low-pass counterpart can be seen clearly by comparing Fig. 5-17 with Fig. 5-16. Note that interchanging the resistor R and capacitor C produces a 20 dB/decade roll-off at low frequencies in Fig. 5-17 while leaving an approximately unattenuated passband above f_c. It is a general principle of high/low-pass filters that interchanging the Rs and Cs converts any high-pass filter to a low-pass filter and vice versa. The corner frequency in each case is given by:

$$f_c = \frac{1}{2\pi RC}.$$ (Eq. 5-10)

5-5-2 Second-Order Filters

One way to steepen the roll-off beyond the 20 dB/decade of a first-order filter is to cascade two first-order filters that have the same f_c. However, this leads to a gain reduction of 6 dB instead of 3 dB at the corner frequency, with possibly unacceptable signal attenuation penetrating into the passband. There are various designs for second-order filters that achieve a 40 dB/decade roll-off outside the passband with only a 3-dB gain reduction at the corner frequency. Of these designs, we mention the *Sallen and Key filter* (also known as the VCVS) here because filters of this design can easily be cascaded to produce higher order filters while suffering only 3-dB gain reduction at the corner frequency.

Fig. 5-18 shows the circuit of a second-order Sallen and Key *low-pass* filter. The *high-pass* version is obtained by interchanging R_1 with C_1 and R_2 with C_2. Typically, in both cases we put $R_1 = R_2$ and $C_1 = C_2$. The corner frequency is then given by:

$$f_c = \frac{1}{2\pi R_1 C_1}. \qquad \text{(Eq. 5-11)}$$

The value of R_1 should be greater than 1 kΩ to prevent loading the output of the previous amplifier and less than 1 MΩ to minimize the output error voltage due to I_{os}. The value of C_1 should be greater than 100 pF to minimize the effect of stray capacitance and less than 1 μF as this is the practical upper limit for ceramic or polyester capacitors. The use of electrolytic or tantalum capacitors must be avoided because they are polarized.

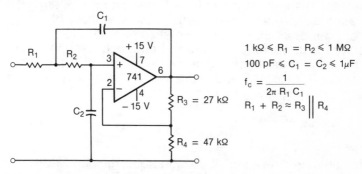

Fig. 5-18. Sallen and Key second-order, low-pass filter.

To obtain a transfer function that is maximally flat in the passband (known as the *Butterworth* response), the gain of the op amp must be set according to the equation:

$$\text{Gain} = \frac{R_3 + R_4}{R_4} = 1.6 \qquad \text{(Eq. 5-12)}$$

This produces a filter with a gain of 1.6 in the passband (4 dB), a roll-off of 40 dB/decade outside the passband, and a gain reduction of 3 dB at the corner frequency. It should be noted that precise resistor values are essential if the correct Butterworth response is to be obtained. This may require the use of trimming resistors to set R_3/R_4 to its exact value. The values of R_3 and R_4 should also be comparable to R_1 and R_2 to minimize the output error voltage from input bias currents (cf. Equation 5-4).

5-5-3 Higher Order Filters

By cascading first- and second-order filters, filters of any order can be obtained which have a roll-off of 20 dB/decade per order beyond f_c. However, to obtain the Butterworth (maximally flat) response so that a gain reduction of only 3 dB oc-

Table 5-3. Gain Required of Sallen and Key Filter When Used as One Stage of a Higher Order Filter

	1st stage	2nd stage	3rd stage
2nd order	1.6	—	—
3rd order	first order	2.0	—
4th order	1.15	2.24	—
5th order	first order	1.38	2.38
6th order	1.07	1.6	2.48

curs at the corner, the gain of each stage must be carefully selected. The gain selected for a Sallen and Key filter will differ according to whether it is used as one stage of a higher order filter or as an independent second-order filter. The gain required in a specific situation is obtained from the Butterworth polynomial of the appropriate order.[4] These gains are compiled in Table 5-3, and suggested resistor values to obtain these gains are given by Berlin.[5]

5-5-4 Choice of Filter

Type

In common data acquisition situations, the bandwidth of the signal of interest will extend from near DC to some maximum frequency f_{MAX}. A low-pass filter is therefore needed to reject noise above f_{MAX}. The corner frequency is usually selected above but near to f_{MAX} except when the Nyquist frequency, f_N, is *below* f_{MAX} (Fig. 5-19). If the sampling rate cannot be increased to move f_N *above* f_{MAX}, then the corner frequency *must* be placed at f_N to prevent aliasing. We will return to this troublesome situation presently.

At low frequency, below the signal frequencies of interest (we hope), environmental noise or 1/f noise may be larger than the signal of interest. Here, a sharp cutoff (high order), high-

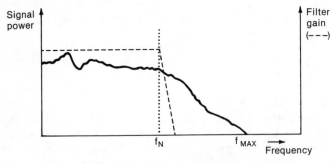

Fig. 5-19. Required filter response when $f_N < f_{MAX}$.

pass filter is necessary to keep the signal from being swamped by this noise. Hence, a low-pass filter in series with a high-pass filter is commonly used with broad band signals, particularly when low-frequency noise is significant.

Particularly troublesome narrow band interference can be rejected using a "notch" filter. On the other hand, a signal which covers a relatively restricted frequency range can be selectively passed using a single bandpass filter.[6]

Order

A sharp roll-off (meaning high order) is necessary when the signal size, including noise, is still significant at frequencies near a selected corner frequency. In the situation described above, for example, where $f_{MAX} > f_N$ and the corner frequency f_c is placed at the Nyquist frequency, a signal whose frequency is in the octave above f_c will be attenuated by less than 6 dB by a first-order filter before being presented to the ADC. After digitization, the resulting alias of this relatively large, unwanted signal will cause significant distortion of the ADC output.

Clearly, high-order filters provide better rejection of unwanted signals than do low-order filters, but at greater expense. To save on time, cost of components, and board space, it is thus best to select the lowest order filter that will produce acceptable rejection. However, since Sallen and Key filters require only one resistor and one capacitor more than a first-order active filter, it is usually cost effective to choose an even order *above* the minimum order required and to implement this using cascaded Sallen and Key filters.

5-6 SCALING AND OFFSETTING

The signal appearing at the input of the gain/scaling block in Fig. 5-1 is typically of medium peak-to-peak amplitude ($\sim$1 V), is band-limited, and may or may not have a DC voltage component as a result of the transduction and primary signal conditioning. The need for scaling and offsetting was discussed in Chapter 2 (Section 2-3), where it was observed that their purpose is to transform a selected input voltage range, v_1 to v_2, to the voltage range of the ADC (typically 0–5 V). *Offsetting* is used to shift the DC level of the signal so that its minimum value is zero volts. The final amplification of the signal, to provide the maximum voltage range that can safely be applied to the ADC, is described as *scaling*.

Before discussing a circuit that will implement these operations, let us facilitate circuit calibration by considering the *order* in which these operations are performed. The order providing the easiest calibration procedure, and the one that we recommend, is first to *offset* and then to *scale* the input signal. This approach is illustrated in Fig. 5-20A and may be expressed as:

$$OUTPUT = (INPUT - OFFSET)\ GAIN \qquad (Eq.\ 5\text{-}13)$$

The advantage of this technique is that circuit calibration becomes a simple two-step process. The alternative approach is illustrated in Fig. 5-20B and may be expressed as:

$$OUTPUT = [GAIN\ (INPUT)] - [OFFSET] \qquad (Eq.\ 5\text{-}14)$$
$$= [GAIN\ (v_2 - v_1)] - [GAIN \cdot v_1]$$

The disadvantage of this approach is that the circuit calibration process is iterative and therefore time-consuming. This is because the scaling that is done first involves the repeated application of v_1 and v_2 and the repeated observation of V_1 and V_2. Note also that V_2 may exceed the absolute maximum permissible ADC input voltage (typically $V_{REF} + 0.3$ V) so that the ADC input protection circuitry discussed in Chapter 7 becomes essential.

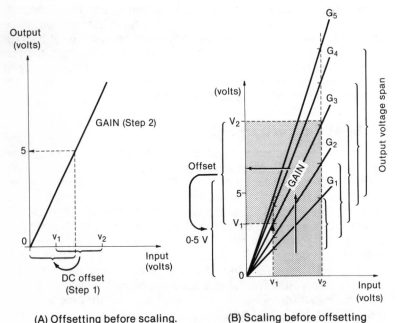

(A) Offsetting before scaling. (B) Scaling before offsetting

Fig. 5-20. Circuit calibration.

A circuit that implements the approach described in Equation 5-13 is shown in Fig. 5-21. From Equation 5-13, the voltage output, V_{OUT}, is given by:

$$V_{OUT} = [V_{IN} + (-R_2/R_1 \cdot V_{REF})] \cdot (-R_4/R_3) \qquad \text{(Eq. 5-15)}$$

The variable offset voltage, V_{OFFSET}, used to null v_1 is obtained from OA1 which is configured as an inverting amplifier with a gain of $-R_2/R_1$. For offsetting, an input voltage V_{IN} of v_1 volts is applied (usually from an external voltage reference source), and the gain of the offset amplifier is adjusted using R_2 until V_{OUT} is zero. Hence,

$$v_1 = (R_2/R_1) \cdot V_{REF} \qquad \text{(Eq. 5-16)}$$

The input reference voltage, V_{REF}, is usually unipolar and $\sim$1–5 volts so that offset voltages in the range of -10 to 10 volts can be easily generated. Circuits for V_{REF} are provided in Chapter 12. The offsetting operation is implemented at the input of the scaling amplifier, OA2, which is configured as an inverting, summing amplifier.

For scaling, input voltage v_2 is applied and the gain of the scaling amplifier adjusted, using R_4, until V_{OUT} is equal to V_{MAX} of the ADC[V_{MAX}(ADC)]. Substituting for v_1 from Equation 5-16 and with V_{IN} equal to v_2, Equation 5-15 becomes:

$$V_{OUT} = V_{MAX} (ADC) = [v_2 - v_1] \cdot (-R_4/R_3) \qquad \text{(Eq. 5-17)}$$

An advantage of the inverting configuration is that gains of less than unity can be set through R_4 to attenuate input signals whose span exceeds V_{MAX} (ADC).

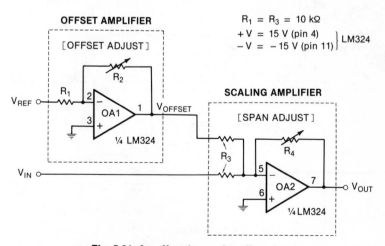

Fig. 5-21. An offsetting and scaling circuit.

Because the offsetting and scaling operations are done with high-level voltages (typically 0.5 to 5 V) and with low amplifier voltage gains (0.5 to 3), the input offset voltages and currents of the amplifiers have negligible effect and can be ignored in this circuit. Resistors R_1 and R_3 define the input impedance of OA1 and OA2 respectively ($Z_i = R_3/2$ for OA2) and have been set at 10 kΩ to ensure that neither amplifier will load its signal source.

5-7 COMMERCIAL DATA ACQUISITION MODULES

Continual improvements in analog, digital, and hybrid device

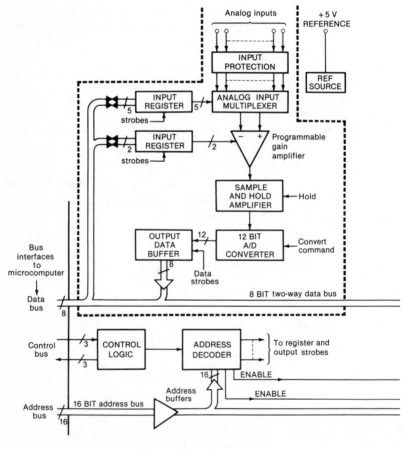

(A) Analog Devices' RTI1200.

Fig. 5-22. Analog

technology have led to the introduction of powerful and flexible analog input subsystems to the commercial marketplace. Four of these commercial systems, which are typical of those currently available, are illustrated in Figs. 5-22 and 5-23. All four have the following features in common:

- The analog input line contains an analog multiplexer, a programmable gain instrumentation amplifier (PGIA), a sample-and-hold amplifier, and an analog-to-digital converter.
- The analog input line is sequenced by on-board timing and control logic rather than the (external or on-board) microprocessor.

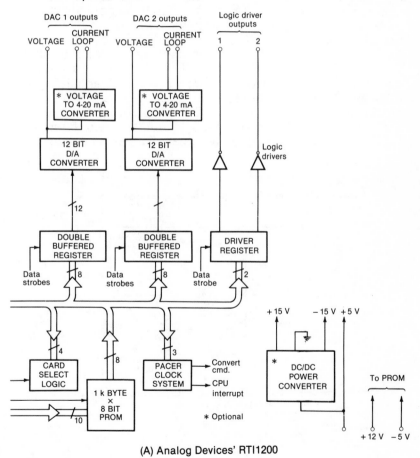

(A) Analog Devices' RTI1200

input boards.

- The only signal conditioning provided is the PGIA.

As a result of this last point, virtually all of the analog signal conditioning functions described in this chapter and illustrated in Fig. 5-1 must be implemented *externally* to the commercial analog input section. The only exception is the scaling of the signal.

5-7-1 Scaling/Gain

The primary purpose of the PGIA is to scale the analog input signal under software control by digitally switching the gain resistor of the instrumentation amplifier. In addition, the amplifier provides the constant, high-input impedance and high common-mode rejection ratio that characterize an instrumentation amplifier. The *range* and *number* of gain values that can be selected by software vary widely. The PGIAs in both Analog Devices' RTI-1200 (Fig. 5-22A) and Intel's iSBC 88/40 (Fig. 5-23B) have four gain settings that are selected by a 2-bit code. For the RTI-1200, gains of 1, 2, 4, and 8 are available, while the iSBC 88/40 provides gains of 1, 5, 50, and 250. The PGIA in National's BLC-8715 (Figure 5-23A), on the other hand, provides seven gain values of 1, 2, 5, 10, 20, 50, and 100 which are selected by a 3-bit code. In most modules, the control byte that specifies the gain for a particular channel is latched by a

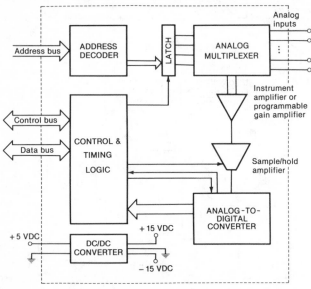

(B) Burr Brown's MP8418.

Fig. 5-22 — cont. Analog input boards.

memory-mapped register. The format diagram for the BLC-8715 gain control byte is shown in Fig. 5-24. To select a gain of 50 for differential input channel 8, for example, the following sample 8080 program segment would be needed:

```
PGIAGN EQU   1018H          ; address of the PGIA
         .
         .
         .
         LXI   H, PGIAGN    ; set up the PGIA address
         MVI   M, 10000110B ; output the gain control byte.
         .
         .
         .
```

Although the PGIA gain is easily specified, the limited values available mean that the user must invariably provide some external signal amplification to establish a preferred full-scale input value for final scaling by the PGIA.

An additional, rarely mentioned performance limitation may be imposed on the data input subsystem by the PGIA due to its relatively long settling time. This is the time required for the PGIA output to settle to within a specified percentage of the predicted output voltage, after the application of a step function input. This time varies from about 1 μs to 1 ms, depending on the quality of the device and the percentage specified. But the more serious problem is that *the settling time increases significantly at large (>10) gain values.* This can be seen clearly in Fig. 5-25, which shows the effect on the 3607 PGIA from Burr-Brown, particularly the effect on the 0.01% curve which is relevant for 12-bit accuracy. The importance of this effect is illustrated by the sample time (channel-select to data-in-memory time) specifications of the iSBC 88/40 data input section, where the ADC conversion time, t_c, is 50 μs. Although the sample time is only 55 μs at gains of 1 and 5, this time extends to 250 μs at a gain of 50 and to 2.5 ms at a gain of 250! Hence, if high PGIA gain values are used to provide the bulk of the signal amplification, then a significant time penalty is imposed by the PGIA and the effective system data acquisition speed must suffer. If acquisition speed is important, then most of the required signal amplification must be provided externally so that low PGIA gain values (and hence fast settling times) can be used for final scaling. We suspect that the gain values of many data input modules are deliberately kept low to minimize this problem.

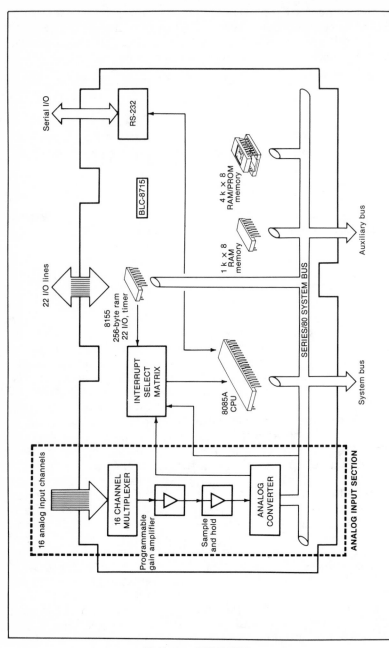

(A) National BLC-8715.
Fig. 5-23. Microcomputer boards containing

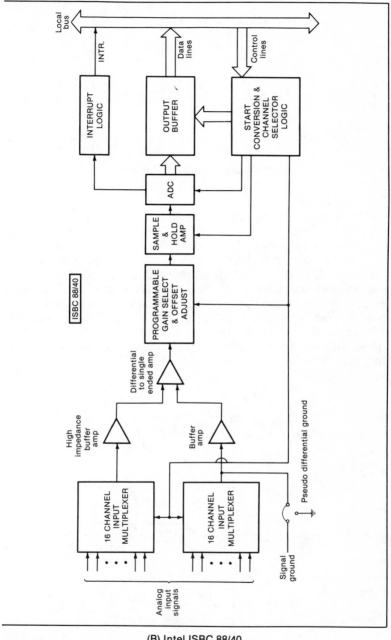

(B) Intel ISBC 88/40.

an analog input section.

147

7	6	5	4	3	2	1	0	
Channel No.				"1" = Single "0" = Differential	Gain			
					0	0	1	X1
					0	1	0	X2
					0	1	1	X5
					1	0	0	X10
					1	0	1	X20
					1	1	0	X50
					1	1	1	X100

Fig. 5-24. PGIA gain control byte for the BLC-8715.

5-7-2 Offsetting

Since the analog input sections of most commercial modules do not provide an offset signal conditioning facility, other techniques must be devised. The most obvious method is to use an external offset circuit of the type described in Section 5-6, but an alternative technique, using the analog multiplexer in differential mode, is illustrated in Fig. 5-26. Here, the signal and the offset reference voltage are applied to the differential input lines for the selected channel, and the PGIA amplifies the *difference* between them. Note that by first offsetting and then scaling, we retain the order recommended in Section 5-6 as best for calibration.

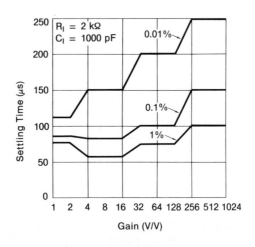

Fig. 5-25. Settling time vs. gain for the Burr Brown 3607 PGIA.

148

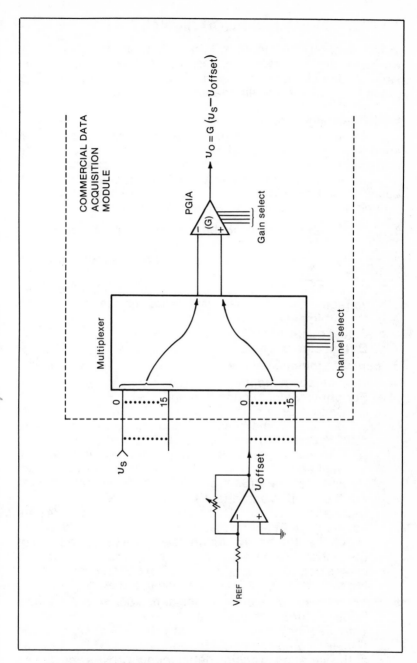

Fig. 5-26. Signal offsetting in commercial data acquisition modules.

5-8 DESIGNING AN ANALOG SIGNAL LINE

In this section, our aim is to bring together, in the form of a workable design procedure, the factors that must be considered to implement an analog signal conditioning line. This procedure will then be illustrated with a design example.

5-8-1 Procedure

Since the character and performance of the analog signal conditioning line depend primarily on the specifications of the transducer, it is usual to begin at the primary signal conditioning end of the line and work forward. In the procedure detailed below, it is assumed that the conditioning line is to be configured as shown in Fig. 5-1. Here are the steps:

1. *Select a transducer* using the procedure outlined in Section 3-5.
2. Specify the *output characteristics of the transducer.* These include:
   a. Type of output signal, e.g., low-level voltage, high-level voltage, charge, current, resistance, frequency.
   b. Output impedance, R_t.
   c. Signal bandwidth.
   d. Output signal range.
3. *Estimate the noise input* (Section 4-3: Sources of Noise).
4. Select *suitable amplifiers.*
   a. For primary signal conditioning.
      (1) Choose an amplifier type, i.e., ISO A, IA, FET OA, or BJT OA on the basis of the required DC parameters (Section 5-2-2), including Z_i, I_B, V_{OS}, and CMRR.
      (2) Choose a specific amplifier of the required type on the basis of the required AC parameters — bandwidth and slew rate (Section 5-2-3) — and thermal stability.
   b. For the filtering and offset/scaling modules.
      General-purpose BJT OAs such as the LM324 and 741 are generally satisfactory, although it is wise always to check that the bandwidth and slew rate (Section 5-2-3) of the chosen OA are adequate. In practice, this usually means completing design steps 5(b) and (c) before finalizing the selection of OAs for these modules.
5. Specify the *requirements of each signal conditioning block.*
   a. Primary signal conditioning.
      This section refers specifically to the design of the primary signal conditioning module using OAs. Because of the variation in design detail found with IAs and ISO As

from different manufacturers, we have not attempted to provide design details on these two amplifier types. If either is chosen in step 4(a), the reader should consult the appropriate manufacturer's data sheet for design details. Hence, for an OA:

(1) Determine the required amplifier configuration as a result of step 2(a) and refer to the appropriate circuit diagram (Figs. 5-4 and 5-6 to 5-11).

(2) Set the maximum output voltage, $V_{o(MAX)}$, of the primary conditioning block at 1 volt (peak-to-peak) and the voltage gain of the amplifier (A_v), if appropriate, at less than 100 per OA (Section 5-3-1).

(3) Calculate the required circuit component values using the equations in the order in which they are provided in the appropriate diagram.

b. Filtering.

(1) Specify the type, order, and corner frequency, f_c (Section 5-5-4).

(2) Select a value for the filter resistor R_1 (1 k$\Omega < R_1 < 1$ MΩ) and calculate C_1 using:

$$C_1 = \frac{1}{2\pi R_1 f_c} \qquad \text{(From Eq. 5-11)}$$

(3) Determine the gain, A_{CL}(filter), of the filter block and values for the gain resistors (Equation 5-12 and Section 5-5-3).

c. Offsetting and scaling.

(1) Specify the maximum signal subrange of interest and hence calculate the minimum input voltage range ($\Delta v = v_2 - v_1$) to the offset/scaling block.

(2) Specify the maximum base signal value of interest and hence calculate the maximum base input voltage (v_1) to the offset/scaling block.

(3) Choose V_{REF} for the offsetting block and specify V_{MAX} (ADC).

(4) For the scaling/offsetting circuit of Fig. 5-21:
Calculate $R_{4(MAX)}$ for the scaling amplifier using

$$R_{4(MAX)} = \frac{V_{MAX}(ADC) \cdot R_3}{\Delta v} \qquad \text{(From Eq. 5-17)}$$

Calculate $R_{2(MAX)}$ for the offset amplifier using

$$R_{2(MAX)} = \frac{v_1 R_1}{V_{REF}}. \qquad \text{(From Eq. 5-16)}$$

5-8-2 Example

This example describes the design of an analog signal conditioning line for a thermocouple, using the procedure in Section 5-8-1.

1. *Transducer: thermocouple.*

2. *Transducer output characteristics.*
   a. Output signal: low-level voltage.
   b. $R_t \approx 0$ ohms.
   c. Signal bandwidth: DC to $\sim10^{-2}$ Hz.
   d. Signal range: 0 to 40 mV (20°C to 950°C)

3. *Noise input.*
   Common-mode RFI on the thermocouple leads is likely to be significant ($\sim$mV).

4. *Amplifiers.*
   a. For primary signal conditioning.
      (1) Since there is no mention of large common-mode signals, an ISO A is not required. An amplifier with high CMRR is necessary, but since the output impedance of the thermocouple is very low, an IA is not necessary. Hence, choose a BJT OA for moderate z_i, low V_{OS}, and medium CMRR.
      (2) Choose an LM308 for its low drift of 5 μV/°C.
   b. For filtering and offset/scaling modules, choose an LM324, BJT OA.

5. *Requirements.* Primary signal conditioning.
   a. (1) Choose a differential amplifier configuration (Fig. 5-10).
      (2) Gain $= \dfrac{1 \text{ volt}}{V_{t(MAX)}} = 1/40 \times 10^{-3} = 25.$
         This is less than the upper limit of 100, so only one OA is necessary.
      (3) From Fig. 5-10 and choosing $R_i = 18$ kΩ,

      $$R_f = \frac{V_o R_i}{V_{t(MAX)}} = \frac{1 \times 18}{40 \times 10^{-3}} = 450 \text{ k}\Omega. \text{ Hence, choose } R_f = 470 \text{ k}\Omega.$$

   b. Filtering.
      (1) Choose a second-order, low-pass Sallen and Key filter (Fig. 5-18) as adequate for this application. Since the signal frequency range is 0–10^{-2} Hz, choose $f_c = 1$ Hz as adequate if there is no significant noise in the vicinity of f_{MAX}.

(2) Choose $R_1 = 270$ kΩ. Hence,

$$C_1 = \frac{1}{2\pi R_1 f_c} = \frac{1}{2\pi \cdot 270 \times 10^3 \cdot 1} = 0.59 \ \mu F$$

Hence, choose $C_1 = 0.57 \ \mu F$.

(3) From Equation 5-12, gain of second-order Sallen and Key filter is 1.6. Choose $R_3 = 270$ kΩ, $R_4 = 470$ kΩ for the required gain and to be comparable with R_1 and R_2 so as to minimize bias current error.

c. Offsetting and scaling.

(1) Minimum signal subrange of interest: 10 mV (ΔV)
Hence $\Delta v = \Delta V \cdot$ [primary signal conditioning gain]·[A_{CL} (filter)]

$$= (10 \text{ mV}) \cdot (25) \cdot (1.6) = (10 \text{ mV}) \cdot (41.6)$$
$$= 0.42 \text{ volt}$$

(2) Maximum base signal value of interest: 30 mV (V_1)
Hence $v_1 = V_1 \cdot (41.6) = 30 \text{ mV} \times 41.6$
$$= 1.25 \text{ volts}$$

(3) Choose $V_{REF} = -5$ V (note the required polarity); V_{MAX} (ADC) = 5 V.

(4) With R_1 and R_3 chosen at 10 kΩ,

$$R_{4(MAX)} = \frac{V_{(MAX)}(ADC) \cdot R_3}{\Delta v} = \frac{5 \times 10}{0.42} = 119 \text{ kΩ}$$

Select $R_{4(MAX)} = 150$ kΩ.

$$R_{2(MAX)} = \frac{v_1 R_1}{V_{REF}} = \frac{1.25 \times 10}{5} = 2.5 \text{ kΩ}$$

Select $R_{2(MAX)} = 3$ kΩ.

5. *Final tuning.*
The circuit design for the thermocouple analog signal conditioning line is shown in Fig. 5-27. Because of the importance of eliminating the effects of V_{OS}, an offset null potentiometer (P1) has been included (the LM308 has no internal offset compensation circuit). Note also that C1 is the compensation capacitor recommended for the LM308.

5-9 BIBLIOGRAPHY

Operational Amplifiers
Fairchild, *Linear Op Amp Data Book.* 1979.

Instrumentation Amplifiers and Isolation Amplifiers
Analog Devices, *Data Acquisition Products Catalog.* 1978.

Analog Devices, *Isolation and Instrumentation Amplifier Designer's Guide.*

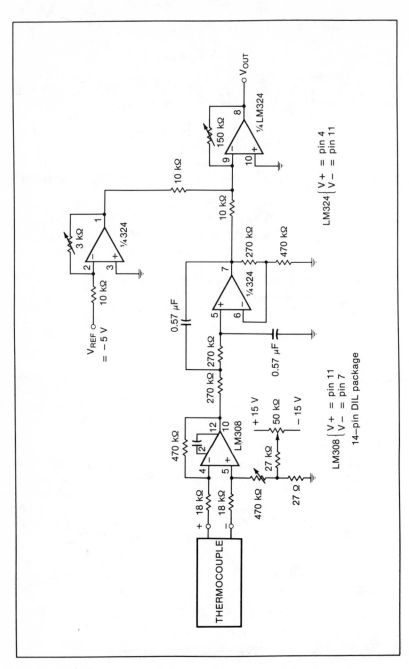

Fig. 5-27. Analog signal conditioning line for a thermocouple.

G. R. Riskin, "A User's Guide to IC Instrumentation Amplifiers." *Analog Devices, Application Note.*

Burr Brown, *1979 General Catalog and 1979-80 Supplement.*

Datel-Intersil, *Data Acquisition Component Handbook.*

5-10 REFERENCES

1. H.M. Berlin, *Design of Op-Amp Circuits, with Experiments,* Howard W. Sams & Co., 1977.

2. Burr-Brown, P. O. Box 11400, Tucson, AZ 85734; Datel-Intersil, 10710 N. Tantau Ave., Cupertino, CA 95014; Analog Devices, P. O. Box 280, Norwood, MA 02062.

3. For a theoretical treatment, see J.G. Graeme, G.E. Toby, and L.P. Huelsman, *Operational Amplifiers: Design and Applications,* McGraw-Hill Kogakusha Ltd., 1971; for the practical approach, see H. M. Berlin, *Design of Active Filters, with Experiments,* Howard W. Sams & Co., 1977.

4. J. Millman, and C.C. Halkias, *Integrated Electronics,* McGraw-Hill Kogakusha Ltd., 1972, p. 550.

5. Berlin, *Design of Active Filters,* 1977.

6. Berlin, *Design of Active Filters,* 1977.

Analog Signal Processing

6-1 INTRODUCTION

Signal processing can be defined as the set of mathematical operations that may be applied to a signal to modify its characteristics. The term also refers to the way in which several signals can be combined to produce a desired result. Although the signal conditioning operations of amplification, filtering, scaling, and offsetting discussed in Chapter 5 are themselves processing operations, we regard them as essential to any analog input subsystem. In this chapter, we describe a number of additional operations that can be used to make a signal more useful or results more meaningful. A further distinction is made between signal conditioning and signal processing: The *signal conditioning* operations are all *linear;* that is, the output of a functional block is directly proportional to the magnitude of the input signal or, for two or more input signals, the output is a simple linear superposition of the individual signals. However, many *signal processing* operations are *nonlinear,* so direct proportion and simple addition do not apply.

In this chapter our aims are to:

- Illustrate the function or purpose of signal processing.
- List some of the more common mathematical operations available to implement a particular process.
- Describe in some detail the analog implementation of these operations.

- Discuss some of the factors that determine where the signal processing should take place within the microprocessor subsystem, that is, whether the processing should be done by the analog or digital hardware or by the software.
- Demonstrate the usefulness of signal processing by way of some typical applications.

6-1-1 Signal Processing

Some of the functions or purposes of signal processing can be briefly listed as:

- Linearizing the output from a transducer.
- Compression and/or expansion of the dynamic range of a signal.
- Determining the peak, average, or RMS value of a signal.
- Computing some property of a signal or combination of signals.
- Waveform shaping.
- Decision making, including the use of windows and hysteresis.
- Transforming data from the time domain to the frequency domain.
- Correlation.

Some of these processes can be readily understood by referring to Figs. 6-1 through 6-4. Fig. 6-1 shows a transducer whose output signal varies nonlinearly with the physical variable. By passing this signal through a linearizing block, whose transfer function is the inverse of the transducer's response, an output is developed which is a linear function of the physical variable.

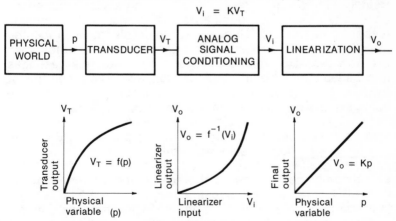

Fig. 6-1. Linearization of the signal from a transducer.

157

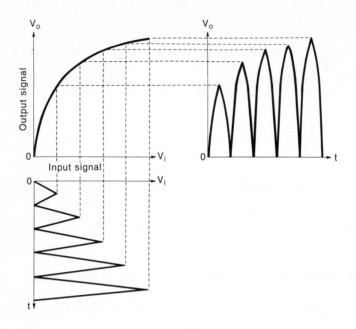

Fig. 6-2. Compression of the dynamic range of a signal.

Figure 6-2 shows how a nonlinear transfer function can be employed to compress the dynamic range of a signal, where the dynamic range is the ratio of *maximum* to *minimum* amplitude of a signal. This signal processing technique is useful, for example, with speech or music which have an extremely wide dynamic range. It is therefore usually expressed on a logarithmic (i.e., decibel) scale to match the dynamic response of the ear. Hence, if a voice signal is presented directly to, say, an 8-bit ADC, the louder passages may overflow the ADC while the softer but still audible passages may be less than the first quantization level. The resolution of the ADC could be increased to 10, 12, or 16 bits. In addition to being expensive, however, this option would require two bytes per point for input to an 8-bit microprocessor and would provide excessive resolution on the louder passages. By using analog signal compression to limit the large signals and amplify the small signals, the full dynamic range of the voice signal can be compressed within the limited range of, say, an 8-bit ADC. If the original dynamic range of the signal is to be subsequently recovered, then an expansion process employing the inverse of the compression function must be introduced.

Some applications require only certain characteristics of a

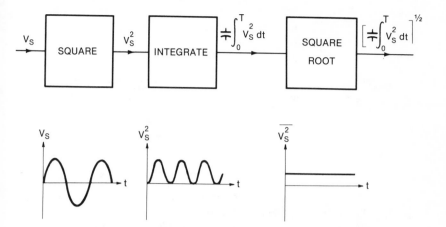

Fig. 6-3. Block diagram showing the operations and waveforms required to obtain a true RMS value of a signal.

signal rather than its complete representation. Typical characteristics include its peak, average, and RMS value. Signal processing is used to obtain these quantities and involves such operations as precision rectification, averaging or integration, and squares and square roots. By way of example, Fig. 6-3 shows the steps needed to obtain the RMS value of a signal.

In many situations, the signal from the transducer is not of prime importance in itself. More important is a derived quantity obtained by carrying out a set of mathematical calculations on the signal or signals. A typical example, illustrated in Fig. 6-4, is the measurement of AC electrical power dissipation. Here, separate signals representing the current and the voltage are multiplied to give the instantaneous power, and the result is averaged to give the mean power dissipation. By taking logarithms, the power can then be expressed on a decibel scale. Such calculations constitute one of the major functions of signal processing.

Decision-making processes usually involve the use of comparators, which we regard as being equivalent to a simple 1-bit ADC. Consequently, we defer consideration of these processes until Chapter 7.

6-1-2 Mathematical Operations
The mathematical operations that may be employed to carry out a signal processing function can be conveniently classified as either continuous or discontinuous, depending

159

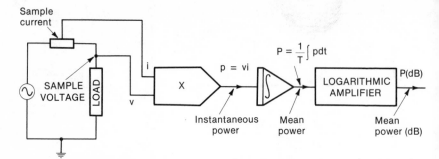

Fig. 6-4. Measurement of a AC power dissipation in a load.

upon whether the operation is smooth or contains sudden jumps. Continuous operations include:

- Addition and subtraction.
- Integration and differentiation.
- Multiplication and division.
- Square and square root.
- Logarithms and anti-logarithms (exponentials).

Building upon these basic operations, we can derive more complex operations such as:

- Raising to an arbitrary power.
- True RMS.
- Vector sums.
- Trigonometric functions.

Basic discontinuous operations involve the use of ideal diodes and comparators, from which may be derived such operations as modulus, or absolute value, and hysteresis. Piecewise linear functions use a finite set of straight lines as an approximation to a continuous function.

One approach to the subject of signal processing is to take each mathematical operation and list some of the useful signal processing functions for which the operation is central. Consider, for example, the multiplying operation. Some of the signal processing applications that use this operation include wattmeters, phase-sensitive detectors, linearization, ratio determinations, RMS calculations, voltage-controlled amplifiers and filters, generation of polynomials, and vector sums. In the sections that follow, we have adopted this descriptive approach, organizing the material by mathematical operation of interest together with its analog implementation. Each section also illustrates the use of the math operation in simple signal processing applications.

6-1-3 Signal Processing Options

When designing a complete microcomputer-based data acquisition or control system, decisions must often be made about whether to carry out the required signal processing in hardware (analog or digital) or in software. Chapter 2 (Section 2-4) introduced some of the factors that need to be considered in making these decisions. These included flexibility, reliability, precision, speed, real-time processing, ease of implementation, complexity, cost, and overall system resource management. Of course, other less tangible factors such as the background, experience, and personal preferences of the designer also have a significant effect upon the decisions.

Flexibility is clearly one of the main virtues of the software approach. System modifications can generally be implemented quickly by modifying the software — a straightforward process if good documentation exists. However, with the ready availability of voltage-controlled or programmable amplifiers, filters, and oscillators, considerable flexibility can now also be built into an analog system.

When considering *precision,* the drift, noise, offsets, and possible need for recalibration of an analog system need to be balanced against the finite resolution imposed by the quantization process in the ADC and against the possible truncation errors introduced in software calculations.

Two further considerations are the required *bandwidth* (and therefore the response time) of the system and whether results of calculations are required in *real time* to perform further control or decision-making operations. If, for example, a system is performing a logging, monitoring, or "babysitting" function where data is accumulated over a long period and can be processed at leisure, then a relatively slow software-based approach is appropriate. In addition, if the microcomputer forms part of a control system involving mechanical or electromechanical elements, then the response time of these devices is usually so long that the speed of the computing system is not a problem. However, if processed information is required at a faster rate than the time available for the microcomputer to execute the necessary set of instructions, then a hardware implementation may be the only option. For an 8-bit processor, a realistic upper limit to the sampling rate is about 10 kHz if significant real-time processing is needed. If the software approach is too slow, then the further decision must be made whether to carry out the required signal processing using hard-wired digital logic or analog components.

The *ease of implementation* of a particular operation is an important factor when deciding which domain to use for signal processing. Such operations as multiplication and integration require only a single device in the analog domain but are much more complex to implement in software or in digital hardware. However, linearizing the response of a transducer may be much easier in software, for example, using table look-up techniques.

The question of *cost* is clearly related to the ease of implementation, because a complex approach is also usually an expensive one. For example, suppose we wish to multiply two fast signals. There are digital processing boards that carry out this operation, but they cost about $1000 compared to a precision analog multiplier, which costs about $10.

Some processing functions are so *complex* that their implementation in the analog domain would require an excessive number of components, with the resulting problems of reduced reliability and degraded signal/noise ratio. A typical example is determining the Fourier transform of a signal. In such cases, the only viable option may be to carry out the calculations in software and to accept the likely speed limitations.

A final general point is the *management of resources* for the entire system. It may be possible, after considering all the factors discussed above, to implement a particular signal processing operation in software. But considering the other tasks that the microcomputer needs to perform, perhaps at the same time, it may be necessary to implement the operation outside the microcomputer in the analog domain.

Since this book is concerned with the analog electronics associated with a microcomputer system, the rest of this chapter is devoted to analog signal processing and its practical realization. It is our belief that the rapid advances in microcomputer technology have led to some neglect of the analog domain. Part of our intent, therefore, is to redress the balance and to show that an optimum system results when the most appropriate technology is used to implement a particular process. An important final point is that this is a fun area in which there is almost unlimited scope for ingenuity and imagination on the part of the designer. Since the field is so vast, we can do no more than to introduce some of the analog building blocks and to provide a few ideas as starting points for the reader's own creativity.

6-2 ADDITION AND SUBTRACTION

The simplest mathematical operations are addition and sub-

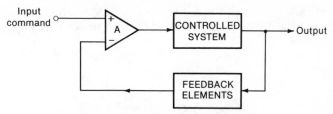

Fig. 6-5. Closed-loop control system.

traction. These are also all-pervasive operations in signal processing, being used whenever two or more signals, whether constant (as in offsetting) or time dependent, need to be linearly combined. For example, in a control system the action required of the controller often depends on the *difference* between the input signal (the desired state of the system) and the output signal (the actual state of the system). The required subtraction operation can be done conveniently in the analog domain as shown in Fig. 6-5. There a transducer samples the output and feeds back a signal for subtraction from the input command to produce an "error" signal for the controller. Sometimes more than two signals need to be combined in this fashion to achieve the required control system behavior.

The basic configurations for the addition and subtraction operations have been introduced in Chapter 5 (Section 5-6), where the scaling amplifier of Fig. 5-21 adds an offset voltage to the signal being conditioned. The addition operation relies on the "virtual ground" property of the inverting amplifier input, which is shown in Fig. 5-4. Using this idea in Fig. 6-6, we can write:

$$I_1 = \frac{V_1 - O}{R_1} = V_1/R_1$$

$$I_2 = \frac{V_2 - O}{R_2} = V_2/R_2$$

$$I_3 = \frac{V_3 - O}{R_3} = V_3/R_3$$

$$I_f = \frac{O - V_o}{R_2} = -V_o/R_f$$

Fig. 6-6. Summing amplifier.

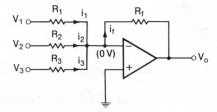

163

Remembering that the input to an OA has a high impedance and that effectively no current flows into it, we can say that

$$I_f = I_1 + I_2 + I_3.$$

This gives

$$-\frac{V_o}{R_f} = \frac{V_1}{R_1} + \frac{V_2}{R_2} + \frac{V_3}{R_3}, \text{ or}$$

$$V_o = -R_f \left(\frac{V_1}{R_1} + \frac{V_2}{R_2} + \frac{V_3}{R_3} \right). \qquad \text{(Eq. 6-1)}$$

Thus, the output voltage is proportional to the weighted sum of the input voltages. Each input voltage sees only its associated input resistor connecting it to a "ground," so that the inputs do not interact with each other. Any number of inputs may therefore be added in this fashion.

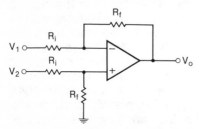

Fig. 6-7. Subtractor.

The difference amplifier of Fig. 5-10 may form the basis for a subtractor as shown in Fig. 6-7. The V_T of Fig. 5-10 becomes the difference $(V_1 - V_2)$ in Fig. 6-7 so that:

$$V_o = \frac{R_f}{R_i}(V_1 - V_2). \qquad \text{(Eq. 6-2)}$$

However, since this circuit does not contain a virtual earth to isolate the inputs from one another, it is often best to subtract by inverting one of the input voltages and then use a summing amplifier.

An example of the use of subtraction appears in Fig. 3-23, where the output of the LM335 temperature sensor is 10 mV/°K. To obtain a temperature measurement voltage of 10 MV/°C, we need only subtract 273 × 10 mV or 2.73 V by appropriate adjustment of the 10-kΩ zero potentiometer, since °C = °K − 273.

6-3 INTEGRATION AND DIFFERENTIATION

The operations of integration and differentiation are often required in signal processing. As indicated in Chapter 3, a transducer may generate a signal that is proportional to the derivative, or to the integral, of the variable of interest. Integration and differentiation are also important in control systems where the control action is often determined in part by the integral of the controlled variable or its derivative. A third use for integration is in signal averaging, since the average value of a voltage, $\overline{V}$, over a time period T is given by:

$$\overline{V} = \frac{1}{T} \int_{0}^{T} V(t)dt \qquad \text{(Eq. 6-3)}$$

Although the integration or differentiation of the signal can be done in software with comparatively little overhead, the circuits introduced in this section do not add much hardware to the analog input subsystem and can free the microprocessor for more important tasks. This is necessary, for example, at high data acquisition rates when the microprocessor may be fully committed to reading data and taking appropriate control action. Such a situation is likely to occur, for example, when an accelerometer is used to obtain position information. (This is, in fact, a quite common way of obtaining position information, especially for navigation systems in aerospace applications.) A high sampling rate is necessary to avoid missing short duration changes in acceleration. If these bursts of acceleration are not adequately sampled, then substantial errors in position can result, because position requires two integrations of acceleration. A similar problem arises when flowrate is used to calculate the volume of a fluid delivered to a vessel.

6-3-1 The Integrator
The basic circuit of an integrator is shown in Fig. 6-8. Since the noninverting input of the amplifier is a virtual ground (see Section 5-2-1), the input voltage, V_i, appears across R, causing

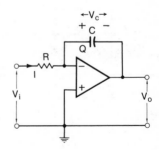

Fig. 6-8. Basic integrator.

a current $I = V_i/R$ to flow toward the amplifier input. This current cannot flow into the inverting input of the OA because of its high input impedance, and so it builds up a charge, Q, on the capacitor. The tendency of this charge to change the voltage at the inverting input will cause the output voltage to change in the opposite direction, providing the necessary voltage across the capacitor to hold the charge Q and to maintain the inverting input as a virtual ground. Thus,

$$V_o = -V_c = -Q/C.$$

Since $Q = \int_0^T I\, dt$ and $I = V_i/R$,

then $V_o = -\dfrac{1}{C}\int_0^T I\, dt = -\dfrac{1}{RC}\int_0^T V_i\, dt.$ (Eq. 6-4)

Of course, this explanation ignores the problems caused by the input bias currents and the input offset voltage of the amplifier. Fig. 6-9 shows how these problems can be overcome when the requirement is for the *continuous integration, averaging, or smoothing of AC signals.* The 10-MΩ resistor in parallel with the capacitor reduces the DC gain of the amplifier so that the input offset current and voltage will not be integrated. As a result, they push the amplifier into saturation. However, this improvement is obtained at the expense of limiting the low-frequency performance of the circuit — it will not work accurately below 10 Hz. The effects of the input bias current and input offset voltage have been further reduced by including the resistor in the noninverting input connection and by using the external offset balancing circuit, respectively. The trimming resistor should be adjusted to produce minimum drift of the output when $V_i = 0$ volts.

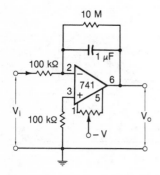

Fig. 6-9. Integrator with reduced DC gain and hence reduced drift.

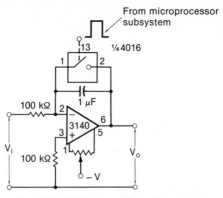

Fig. 6-10. Integrator with reset control.

When *operation down to DC is necessary,* a resetting facility is required so that the capacitor can be discharged at the start of an integration period. Fig. 6-10 shows how this can be done using an analog switch controlled by a TTL pulse from the microprocessor subsystem. The time t = 0 in Equation 6-4 can now be defined as the time at which the switch opens and allows the capacitor to commence accumulating charge.

6-3-2 The Differentiator

The basic circuit of a differentiator can be obtained from the integrator circuit of Fig. 6-8 by interchanging the capacitor and the resistor. A similar argument to that used for the integrator yields for the differentiator:

$$V_o = -RC \frac{dv_i}{dt} \qquad \text{(Eq. 6-5)}$$

The fact that the DC gain of this circuit is zero minimizes the problems resulting from amplifier input offsets. However, the very high gain of the circuit at high frequencies now makes environmental noise more of a problem. Hence, because of their high-frequency components, any voltage spikes reaching the input will be easily transmitted by the input capacitor to produce a large effect at the output. The usual solution, shown in Fig. 6-11, is to insert a resistor before the input capacitor to limit the high frequency gain of the amplifier. This circuit works well at 1 kHz, but the presence of the 270-Ω resistor seriously affects the accuracy of the differentiation for frequencies higher than this. Reducing the size of the capacitor by a factor of ten will extend the frequency range upward by a factor of ten but, as can be seen from Equation 6-5, this will also reduce the output signal size by the same factor. However, analog differentiators are not popular and should be

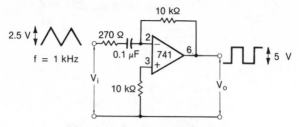

Fig. 6-11. Practical differentiator.

avoided if possible because of their great susceptibility to noise and the limitation on the bandwidth of input signals that can be effectively differentiated. Similar problems still exist in attempting to carry out the differentiation in software, due to the large sampling rate required to detect fast edges. Hence, differentiation should be avoided as a signal processing technique insofar as possible.

6-3-3 The Ratemeter

The ratemeter is a form of differentiator whose output voltage, instead of being proportional to the rate of change of input voltage, is proportional to the rate of arrival of input pulses. Measuring the rate of arrival of pulses is a common way of making a tachometer, for example (cf. Section 3-2-3). However, using the microprocessor to do the counting (Section 7-3) and then to calculate the pulse rate may consume a disproportionate amount of its time at high pulse rates. The circuit of Fig. 6-12 is then an attractive alternative. A positive pulse arriving at the input will charge C_1 to its peak value via D_1. Between this pulse and the next one, C_1 will discharge rapidly into C_2 via D_2. C_2 is continuously discharging slowly through R, so the height to which its output voltage rises depends on the rate of pulses arriving. Output voltage V_o also depends on the pulse height but not on the *pulse shape.*

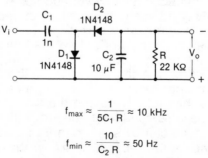

$$f_{max} \approx \frac{1}{5C_1 R} \approx 10 \text{ kHz}$$

$$f_{min} \approx \frac{10}{C_2 R} \approx 50 \text{ Hz}$$

Fig. 6-12. Diode pump ratemeter.

Because of this, the circuit is more useful than the integrator of Fig. 6-8, which could otherwise be used as a ratemeter. The circuit output's dependence on pulse height can be overcome simply by passing the input pulses through a clipping circuit such as that shown in Fig. 7-5.

6-4 PRECISION RECTIFICATION

In signal processing, we often need to half- or full-wave rectify a signal or to determine its peak or absolute value. These applications require one or more diodes which, ideally, should have the characteristics shown in Fig. 6-13A. Unfortunately, the characteristics of real diodes look more like those shown in Fig. 6-13B. There it can be seen that real diodes require a minimum forward voltage, V_F, of about 0.6 volt for silicon devices or 0.2 volt for germanium, before they will conduct. Hence, when rectifying low-level ($\sim$1 volt) signals, this error can be significant. The problem can be overcome by putting the diode in the feedback loop of an operational amplifier as in Fig. 6-14 to produce a *precision diode.* In this case, the turn-on voltage V_s is given by:

$$V_s = V_F/A \qquad \text{(Eq. 6-6)}$$

where A is the open loop gain of the OA. Therefore, if $V_F = 0.6$ volt and $A = 10^5$, then the turn-on voltage becomes 6 μV!

A simple application of the precision diode is the peak-reading detector, shown in Fig. 6-14, which is used to measure the peak value of a transient signal. The capacitor charges up to the maximum value of the signal and holds that value until it is reset, perhaps using an analog switch under micro-processor control as with the integrator (Fig. 6-10). The output buffer stage should have very low input bias currents to minimize any unwanted discharge of the capacitor.

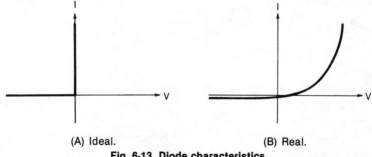

(A) Ideal.   (B) Real.

Fig. 6-13. Diode characteristics.

169

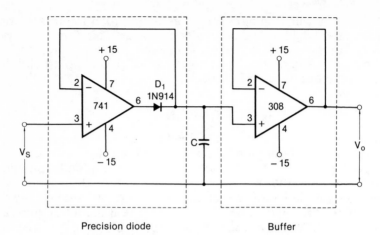

Fig. 6-14. Precision peak detector with output buffer.

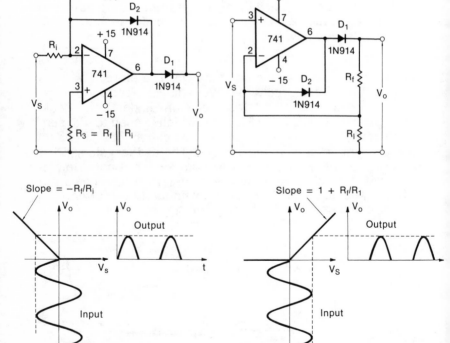

Fig. 6-15. Precision half-wave rectifiers and their transfer characteristics.

Fig. 6-15 shows two versions of a precision half-wave rectifier in which basic inverting or noninverting amplifiers have been modified by the addition of diodes D_1 and D_2. Diode D_1 is the basic rectifying diode, and D_2 clamps the output of the OA to zero when D_1 is OFF. For the noninverting rectifier, if V_s is positive then the OA output is positive, D_1 is ON, and D_2 is OFF. However, if V_s is negative then the OA output is also negative, D_1 is OFF, and D_2 is ON and maintains a feedback path to the inverting input. It is important to note that the rectified output is taken from the cathode of D_1 and not directly from the output of the OA. Also, as the transfer characteristics in Fig. 6-15 show, the gain of the rectifier is the same as that for the corresponding simple amplifier.

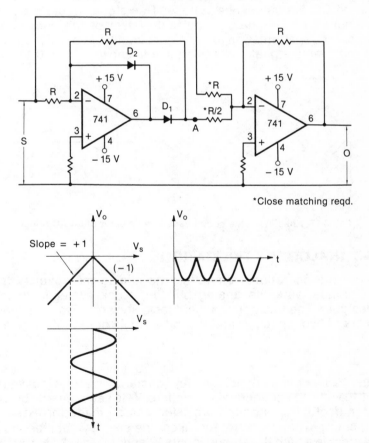

*Close matching reqd.

Fig. 6-16. Precision full-wave rectifier, modulus, or absolute circuit, and its transfer characteristics.

171

Finally, Fig. 6-16 shows one version of a precision full-wave rectifier or absolute value circuit in which a half-wave rectifier is followed by a summing amplifier. In this circuit, if V_s is positive then the half-wave rectifier is OFF, the signal at point A is zero, and $-V_s$ appears at the output of the summing amplifier. However, if V_s is negative then $+V_s$ appears at point A and the output becomes

$$V_o = -(2V_s - V_s) = -V_s \qquad \text{(Eq. 6-7)}$$

A typical application for the full-wave rectifier is the measurement of the out-of-balance signal from an AC bridge. The bridge output (Fig. 6-17) would be detected by a differential or instrumentation amplifier, full-wave–rectified to give its magnitude and then averaged by an integrator to give the required DC out-of-balance voltage. This signal would then be presented to the analog input subsystem of the microcomputer for transformation to the digital domain. A block diagram of the overall signal processing line is shown in Fig. 6-17.

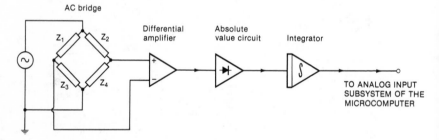

Fig. 6-17. Absolute value circuit used in a detector of an AC bridge.

6-5 ANALOG MULTIPLICATION

After the operational amplifier, the analog multiplier is the next most versatile analog building block available to the designer. The basic functional block, shown in Fig. 6-18, consists of two inputs, V_x and V_y, and a single output, V_o, where:

$$V_o = \frac{V_x V_y}{V_R} \qquad \text{(Eq. 6-8)}$$

and V_R is a dimensional scaling constant with a typical value of 10 volts. In commercial multipliers, V_R is set internally by the manufacturers, although provision can be made for external trimming. The necessity for V_R can be seen by considering a system in which the analog inputs V_x and V_y can take any value within the range of -10 to $+10$ volts. If both V_x and V_y have a

Fig. 6-18. Basic multiplier.

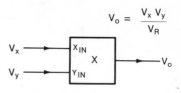

$$V_o = \frac{V_x V_y}{V_R}$$

value of 10 volts, then simple multiplication gives an output of 100 volts! However, if $V_R = 10$ volts then the output is scaled to a maximum value of 10 volts.

Another basic consideration is the *polarity* of the input signals V_x and V_y, which are shown schematically in Fig. 6-19. In a true *four-quadrant* multiplier, input signals of either polarity are accepted and the output preserves the correct polarity. Some multipliers operate only in one or two quadrants, however. For a one-quadrant multiplier, both V_x and V_y must be positive. For two-quadrant multipliers, one signal input can have either polarity.

In addition to the basic multiplier block, many monolithic and modular analog multipliers have an uncommitted operational amplifier, attached as shown in Fig. 6-20, together with a pair of matched resistors and an additional input, V_z. As an example, Fig. 6-21 shows the Analog Devices AD533 monolithic device wired as a multiplier. The X_o, Y_o, and Z_o offset potentiometers are used to zero the output when V_x, V_y or V_x and V_y are zero. The set gain potentiometer is used to trim the value of the scale factor, V_R, to its design value of 10 volts.

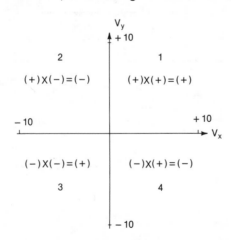

Fig. 6-19. Input variables showing multiplication quadrants.

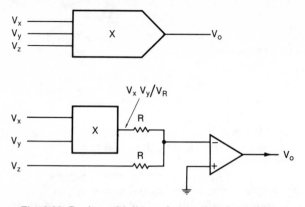

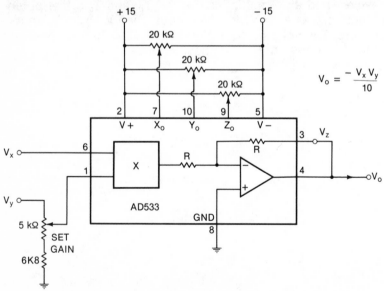

Fig. 6-20. Basic multiplier and operational amplifier.

The purpose of the operational amplifier is illustrated in Fig. 6-22, where it can be seen that, by placing the basic multiplier block within the feedback loop, an analog divider is obtained. Care must be exercised when using the circuit of Fig. 6-22B to ensure that the denominator, V_x, always remains either positive or negative and finite to prevent the possibility of division by zero. If the denominator is allowed to pass from a positive value, through zero, to a negative value, then division by zero will necessarily result. Analog dividers are therefore in-

Fig. 6-21. Typical monolithic device (AD533) connected as a multiplier.

herently one- or two-quadrant devices. Similarly, if the two inputs of the multiplier are connected as in Fig. 6-22C, then the output is the square of the input. This same block placed in the feedback loop (Fig. 6-22D) implements the square root operation. Note that in this case the input, V_z, must be negative to

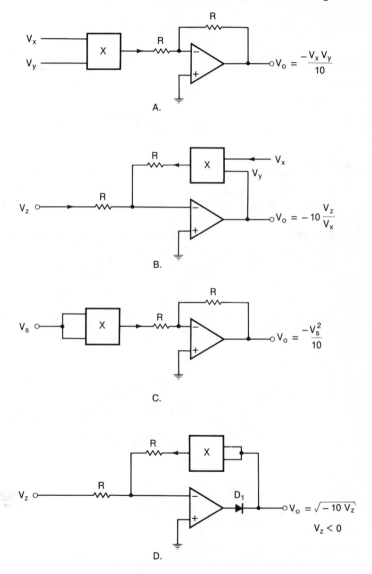

Fig. 6-22. Basic operations of an analog multiplier.

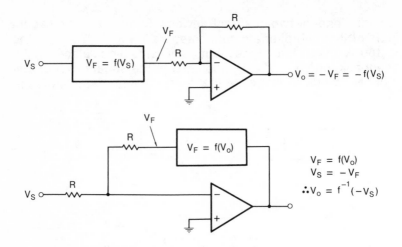

Fig. 6-23. General principle for obtaining the inverse of a function.

prevent the invalid operation of attempting to take the square root of a negative number. The diode is intended to physically prevent this possibility.

The examples given in Fig. 6-22 are specific cases of a more general principle that is illustrated in Fig. 6-23. This figure shows that if there is an operational block that implements the function

$$V_o = -f(V_s),$$

then placing this block in the feedback loop of an OA generates the inverse function

$$V_o = f^{-1}(-V_s). \qquad \text{(Eq. 6-9)}$$

Analog multipliers can be used in a wide range of applications. Perhaps the simplest is shown in Fig. 6-24 where the multiplier is used as a simple amplifier with a voltage-controlled gain. Multipliers are also extremely useful in function-generating circuits if a voltage-controlled oscillator

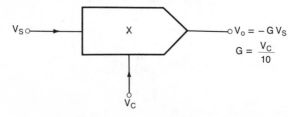

Fig. 6-24. Simple amplifier with voltage-controlled gain.

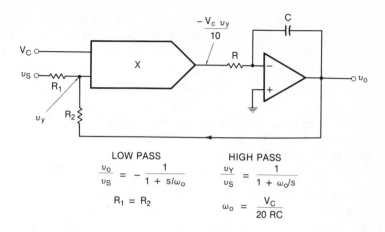

$$\frac{v_o}{v_S} = -\frac{1}{1 + s/\omega_o}$$

$$R_1 = R_2$$

$$\frac{v_Y}{v_S} = \frac{1}{1 + \omega_o/s}$$

$$\omega_o = \frac{V_C}{20\,RC}$$

Fig. 6-25. Single-pole, voltage-controlled high- or low-pass filter.

or filter is required. Fig. 6-25 shows a simple, single-pole filter in which the corner frequency, W_o, is given by:

$$W_o = \frac{V_c}{20\,RC} \qquad \text{(Eq. 6-10)}$$

This result shows that W_o is directly proportional to the value of the control voltage, V_c. In practical circuits, a ten to one tuning range is easily achievable. An interesting feature of this circuit is that it can operate as either a low-pass or a high-pass filter depending on the point at which the output signal is obtained. Note also that the circuits of Figs. 6-24 and 6-25 could be very useful for implementing a microcomputer-controlled analog signal conditioning line. The control voltages, V_c, would be generated by the microprocessor through a DAC to specify the required gain and corner frequency.

Many ingenious multiplier circuits are possible that implement a particular function. For example, a Wheatstone bridge consisting of nominally equal resistances, R, has an out-of-balance voltage due to a resistance change, ΔR, that is given by:

$$V_s = \left(\frac{X}{1 + X} \right) V \qquad \text{(Eq. 6-11)}$$

where $X = \Delta R/2R$ and V is the supply voltage. That is:

$$X = \frac{V_s/V}{1 - (V_s/V)} \qquad \text{(Eq. 6-12)}$$

Usually X has to be kept much less than unity to ensure

177

reasonable linearity between X and V_s. However, Fig. 6-26 shows how the function of Equation 6-12 can be fully implemented using a multiplier and two operational amplifiers. The final output is given by

$$V_o = \frac{10 \ (V_s/10)}{1 - (V_s/10)} \qquad \text{(Eq. 6-13)}$$

which is of exactly the form required by Equation 6-12. Thus, V_o remains a linear representation of the resistance change, ΔR, even when ΔR is large.

As a final example, Fig. 6-27 shows how combinations of multipliers and summing amplifiers can be connected to generate a polynomial with arbitrary coefficients. In general, if the sequence consists of n multipliers and summing amplifiers, then a polynomial of order x^n can be generated. By adjusting the values of the coefficient potentiometers, A_0, A_1 . . ., the circuit can be used to model any arbitrary function to which a polynomial can be fitted. The circuit is therefore very useful for such tasks as linearizing or generating trigonometric functions by polynomial approximation.

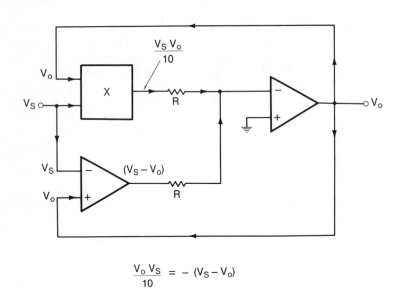

$$\frac{V_o V_s}{10} = - (V_s - V_o)$$

$$\therefore V_o = \frac{10 \ (V_s/10)}{1 - (V_s/10)}$$

Fig. 6-26. Linearization of the out-of-balance output voltage from a Wheatstone bridge.

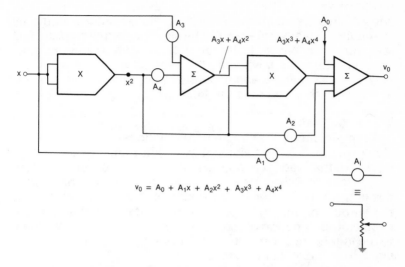

$$v_0 = A_0 + A_1x + A_2x^2 + A_3x^3 + A_4x^4$$

Fig. 6-27. Generating an arbitrary polynomial using multipliers and summing amplifiers.

6-6 LOGARITHMIC CIRCUITS

There are three main application areas for which a circuit with a logarithmic response may be required, namely:

1. *Linearization of transducer output.* The resistance of a thermistor, for example, varies exponentially with temperature. If this resistance variation is converted to a voltage variation and the signal applied to a logarithmic amplifier, the resulting output is then directly proportional to temperature.
2. *Computation.* The logarithm of the ratio of two voltages is necessary, for example, to obtain a measurement of optical absorbance for chemical analysis, quality control, and pollution monitoring.
3. *Compression/expansion.* This signal processing function was described in Section 6-1-1 and is illustrated in Fig. 6-2. A logarithmic amplifier can be used to provide the nonlinear transfer characteristic required to compress the dynamic range of a signal.

The choice whether to implement the logging or antilogging operation in the analog domain or in the digital domain is determined by the factors outlined in Section 6-1-3. If it is decided to perform the logging or antilogging operation in the analog domain, two implementation options are available: namely, to use one of the circuits shown below or to purchase one of the special-purpose logarithmic amplifiers currently available from several manufacturers. The former approach is relatively inexpensive in terms of component costs and may be more interesting, whereas the second approach will probably be more reliable and accurate; and it may be less expensive overall if labor costs are important.

6-6-1 Logarithms

A simple circuit that implements the logarithm operation is shown in Fig. 6-28. The element with logarithmic behavior is included in the feedback loop. Using the virtual ground concept as in Section 6-3-1, it can be seen that the current flowing through the transistor in the feedback loop is $I_f = V_i/R_i$. Now the output voltage, V_o, is equal to the voltage drop across the base-emitter junction of the transistor, and this is proportional to the logarithm of the current I_{BE} flowing through the junction, since $I_{BE} = I_o \exp(V_{BE}/kT)$. Hence,

$$V_o = -V_{BE} \propto \log I_{BE} \propto \log I_f \qquad \text{(Eq. 6-14)}$$
$$\propto -\log V_i$$

This circuit will produce a reasonably accurate logarithm function over an input voltage range of 1 mV to 10 V if the input offset voltage is carefully nulled. The resulting output voltage varies typically from 0.3 to 0.6 volt. Unfortunately, because of the dependence of I_{BE}, and therefore V_o (Equation 6-14), on absolute temperature, T, the circuit shown in Fig. 6-28 is almost useless. A practical log circuit which overcomes this problem is shown in Fig. 6-29. Here transistor T_2 is operated at essentially constant current, so that temperature alone causes

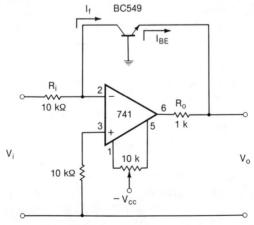

Fig. 6-28. Simple logarithmic amplifier.

changes in the base-emitter voltage. Since T_1 and T_2 are a matched pair in a single package, the temperature-dependent voltage change in T_2 will exactly offset the temperature-dependent change in the logging element T_1. The circuit performs well in the range $1\,mV \leqslant V_i \leqslant 100\,V$, giving $0.5\,V \leqslant -V_o \leqslant 5.5\,V$ such that each factor-of-ten increase in input voltage causes the output voltage to change by 1 V.

6-6-2 Antilogarithms

To obtain antilogarithmic behavior, a circuit similar to the logging circuit of Fig. 6-28 can be used, but with the input resistor interchanged with the transistor (see Fig. 6-30). The current flowing through transistor T_2 into the feedback loop is then proportional to e^{V_i}, or the antilogarithm of input voltage, leading to:

$$- V_o \propto antilog(V_i) \qquad \text{(Eq. 6-15)}$$

Again, the simple circuit suffers badly from the temperature-dependent behavior of the transistor base-emitter junction, so it is advisable to use a matched pair of transistors for temperature compensation, as shown in Fig. 6-30. OA1 is used as a subtractor (see Section 6-2) to subtract a temperature-dependent voltage generated across T_1 from the input voltage. Since the circuit is a signal expander, the input voltage must be attenuated by R_1 and R_2 to ensure that it can be handled by the antilogging element and that the output will stay within the capability of OA2.

The logarithmic and antilogarithmic amplifiers just described can be used as building blocks to perform more complex mathematical operations.[2] For instance, to obtain the logarithm of the ratio of two voltages — which is needed for the absorbance measurement mentioned earlier — the arrangement shown schematically in Fig. 6-31 can be used.

6-6-3 Companding Converters[3]

We have already seen that a logarithmic amplifier provides an effective means of compressing the dynamic range of a signal. An alternative way of achieving this signal compression is to use an analog-to-digital converter which has an approximately logarithmic transfer function, as shown in Fig. 6-32A. To recover the full dynamic range of the signal on output from the microprocessor, a DAC having an antilog transfer function of the type shown in Fig. 6-32B must be used.

One of the most common classes of ADC is the digital servo ADC (Fig. 6-33), in which a DAC is used in the feedback loop of

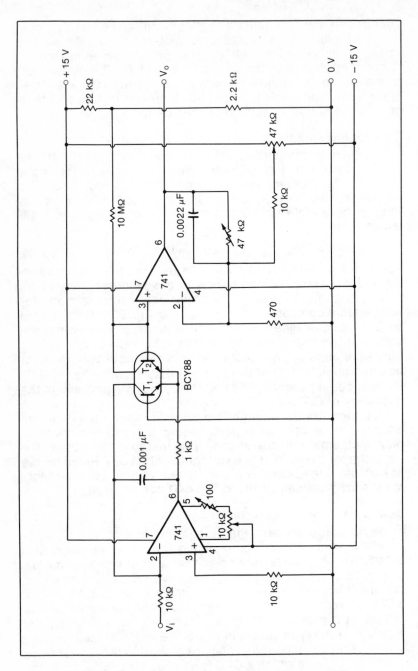

Fig. 6-29. Temperature-compensated logarithmic amplifier.

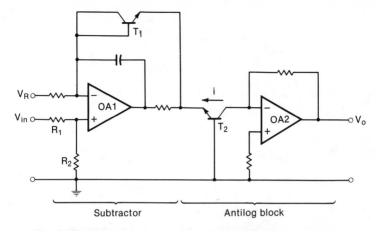

Fig. 6-30. Temperature-compensated antilogarithmic amplifier.

a digital system which may or may not be the microprocessor. The system guesses the binary equivalent of the analog signal V_i using, in most cases, either a ramp or successive approximations technique.[4] This digital guess is applied to the DAC whose output is compared with V_i. In describing multipliers in the previous section, it was seen that if an analog block such as a multiplier, having transfer function $f(V_s)$, is placed in the feedback loop of an op amp (OA), the inverse transfer function is implemented at the output of the OA. The same principle may be applied to the DAC in Fig. 6-33, so that if the transfer function of the DAC is antilogarithmic, the ADC will have a logarithmic transfer function.

DACs used in this way are described as *companding* (for compressing/expanding). Their antilog transfer function expands the dynamic range of a signal during digital-to-analog conversion, while their use in the feedback loop of a digital servo ADC results in a log transfer function for the ADC, and this compresses the dynamic range of the signal. The DAC-76 from Precision Monolithics Inc. (Santa Clara, CA) is an exam-

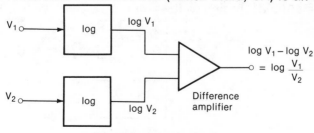

Fig. 6-31. Log ratio circuit.

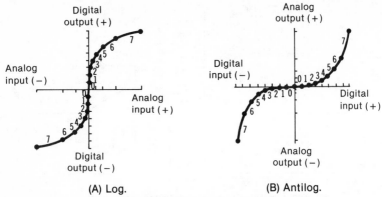

(A) Log.   (B) Antilog.

Fig. 6-32. Transfer functions.

ple of a companding DAC. It is an 8-bit device that uses three bits to divide its full scale range into eight unequal segments (0 to 7 in Fig. 6-32B) and four bits to divide each segment linearly into sixteen equal steps. The eighth bit is a sign bit. With this arrangement, the resolution of the DAC-76 drops from 0.025% of full scale (12-bit resolution) in segment 0 to 3.2% (5-bit resolution) in segment 7.

6-7 PIECEWISE LINEAR APPROXIMATIONS

The foregoing sections have outlined methods of processing a signal to produce an output voltage that is a precise, well-defined function of the input. For some purposes, however, we can approximate a required complex transfer function by using a linear relationship over a restricted range. Or, by using a succession of straight line segments, we can approximate the function over an extended range. This technique is known as *piecewise linear approximation.*

6-7-1 Resistive Network

The resistance of a thermistor decreases exponentially with temperature according to the relation

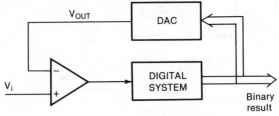

Fig. 6-33. Digital servo ADC.

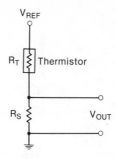

Fig. 6-34. Thermistor output
linearizing.

$$R \propto Ae^{-BT} \qquad \text{(Eq. 6-16)}$$

where T is the temperature of the thermistor and A and B can be found from the manufacturer's specifications. A technique producing an output voltage that varies approximately linearly with the temperature of a thermistor is illustrated in Fig. 6-34. The output voltage of the circuit is given by:

$$f(T) = \frac{V_{OUT}}{V_{REF}} = \frac{R_S}{R_S + R_T} = \frac{1}{1 + R_T/R_S} \qquad \text{(Eq. 6-17)}$$

A value for R_s must be chosen so that the transfer function f(T) is approximately linear over a specified temperature range. This can be done graphically by drawing lines of the form shown in Fig. 6-35, where the degree of linearity can be judged visually and the optimum value of R_s can be selected for the temperature range required. Alternatively, the selection can be made analytically by differentiating Equation 6-17 with respect to T and by finding the value of R_s for which df/dT is approximately constant over the temperature range required. Both methods are described more fully elsewhere.[5,6] Thermistors already linearized in this fashion can be obtained in a single package, together with their linearizing resistor(s), from manufacturers such as Omega Engineering, Inc. Such devices

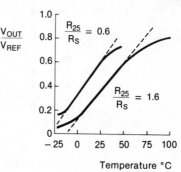

Fig. 6-35. Typical linearized
thermistor output.

185

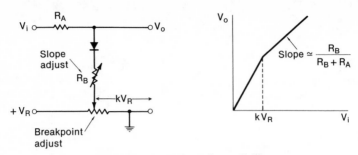

Fig. 6-36. Nonlinear voltage divider.

can often be connected either as voltage dividers (as in our example) giving $V_{OUT} \propto T$, or as temperature-sensitive resistors giving $R \propto T$, according to the needs of the application.

6-7-2 Diode Shaping

A diode-shaping network can be used to produce a nonlinear voltage divider to build up an arbitrary function from straight line segments as illustrated in Fig. 6-36. When the input voltage, V_i, is less than the voltage, kV_R, set by the breakpoint adjusting potentiometer, then the diode is reverse-biased and the output voltage, V_o, is equal to V_i. When V_i exceeds kV_R, the diode conducts and V_i is attenuated by the voltage divider consisting of R_A and R_B so that:

$$V_o \approx V_i \frac{R_B}{R_A + R_B} \qquad \text{(Eq. 6-18)}$$

A number of these circuits can be cascaded to produce an arbitrary transfer function as shown in Fig. 6-37. The resistor values must be chosen to provide the required breakpoints and slopes so that the resulting transfer function V_o/V_i, which consists of a set of straight line segments, is an adequate approximation to the required function. Unfortunately, this sim-

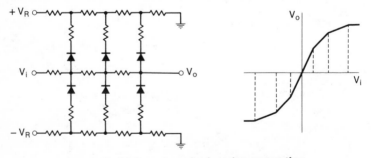

Fig. 6-37. Arbitrary transfer function generation.

ple passive circuit suffers from the problem that the positions of the breakpoints are affected by the voltage drops across the diodes. This effect is also temperature-dependent. Fig. 6-38 shows a practical circuit that eliminates the diode effect and linearizes the output of a chromel-constantan thermocouple to within about ±0.5°C over the range of 0–650°C.[7] Such a circuit can be used to produce an increase in slope at the breakpoint merely by reversing the sense of the diodes.

6-7-3 Variable Reference ADC

Linearization of a transducer output can be done at the digitization stage by changing the reference voltage to the ADC according to the size of the analog input signal. Keithley Instruments (Cleveland, OH) have developed a digital thermometer based on this idea[8], so that the advantages of using a thermocouple as the sensor can be obtained without the need for linearization circuitry of the type shown in Fig. 6-38. The Keithley thermometer uses a dual slope ADC (the Intersil 7106) with ten reference voltages available to it. During the rampdown phase of the measurement, a multiplexer selects one reference voltage after another, thus changing the scaling factor according to the size of the input voltage. The first few breakpoints (the points at which the ADC switches from one reference to the next) occur at 0, 43, 128, 170, and 340°C. Hence, the nonlinear output of the thermocouple is represented as a series of straight line segments, much as in Section 6-7-2. Unfortunately, BCD or binary outputs do not appear to be available for input to the microprocessor.

6-8 FOR THE FUTURE

Because of the emphasis in this book on analog electronics in microcomputer systems, this chapter has concentrated on the implementation of signal processing in the analog domain. Digital signal processing is, of course, a strong competitor. It deserves careful consideration on the basis of the factors listed in Section 6-1-3 before a decision is made. Both approaches should remain roughly competitive in the near future given that advances in technology will improve the stability and reliability of analog integrated circuits and, by speeding up microprocessors, will improve the real-time performance of digital processing.

But what of the more distant future of analog signal processing? Perhaps the field of microcomputers can provide a clue. The I8080 microprocessor represented a breakthrough in digital electronics and led the way to the implementation of a

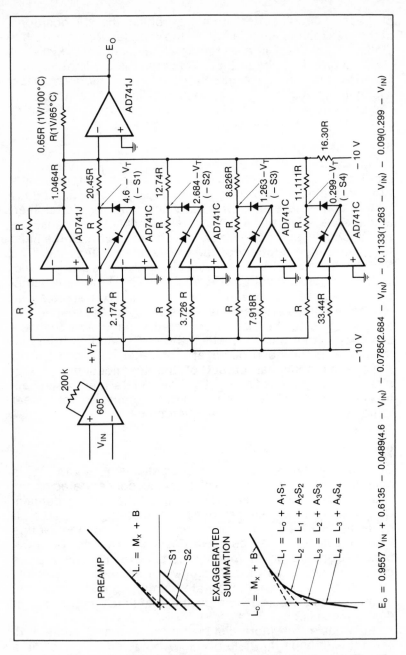

Fig. 6-38. Thermocouple linearization using piecewise linear approximation.
(Courtesy D. H. Sheingold, Analog Devices)

digital computer on a single silicon chip. In the same way, we believe the next breakthrough in the area of analog signal processing must surely be a first step toward the implementation of an analog computer on a single silicon chip. The problems of programmability, stability, space for resistors and capacitors, and power consumption are, of course, enormous and will almost certainly require a new technology. If the economics and demand are right, the new technology will come.

A small taste of this concept can be seen in the I2920 analog signal processor from Intel.[9] This device, which was announced at the 1979 International Solid State Circuits Conference, is a digitally implemented analog signal processor. As such, it goes only part way toward our concept of, and belief in, a true monolithic analog computer. Although the

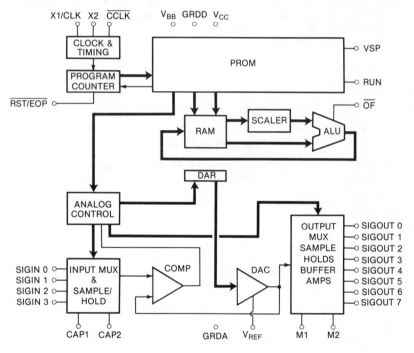

- 192 × 24-bit program store (EPROM)
- 9-bit ADC
- 25-bit arithmetic processor
- 40 × 25-bit RAM
- DC to 10 kHz frequency range
- ± 5 V power supplies
- 28-pin package
- N-MOS fabrication
- 192 instruction capacity

Fig. 6-39. Intel's 2920 analog signal processor.

I2920 looks and acts like an analog component, it uses sampled data techniques to implement the required transfer function in the digital domain. A block diagram of the 2920 is shown in Fig. 6-39 along with a summary of its most important features.

The importance of the I2920 and the difficulties that lie ahead in developing a monolithic analog computer are aptly summarized by McGowan in his 1979 article in *Control Engineering* describing the I2920:

> No one, we were told (at the 1979 International Solid State Circuits Conference) had the sophistication necessary to implement both digital and analog circuitry on a monolithic LSI chip. Or at least, no one cared to share it. Even so, the 2920 must be seen as a development only; a *trend setter* to be sure but not a breakthrough. The nature of an analog signal makes it an untidy partner to digital circuitry and the marriage of the two remains a troublesome prospect in large scale integration.[10]

6-9 REFERENCES

1. G.B. Clayton, *Operational Amplifiers.* Newnes-Butterworths, London, 1971.

2. R.A. Pease, "Compute Accurate Reciprocals with Super-matched Dual Transistors." *Electronic Design, 6,* March 15, 1979, p. 96.

3. M.K. Parsin, "Companding Converters Squeeze Twelve Bits into Seven." *Control Engineering,* February 1980, p. 71.

4. J. Titus, C. Titus, and D. Larson, *Microcomputer-Analog Converter Software & Hardware Interfacing.* Howard W. Sams & Co.,Inc., 1978.

5. C.S. Molee and P. Vitale, "Thermistors Make Good Thermometers." *Electronic Design, 8,* April 12, 1978, p. 90.

6. D.H. Sheingold, "Transducer Interfacing Handbook." *Analog Devices,* 1980, p. 96.

7. D.H. Sheingold, p. 103.

8. J. McLeod, "ADC Compensates for Thermocouple Nonlinearity." *Electronic Design,* March 31, 1981, p. 38.

9. H. Gee, M. Tanenhaus, and R. Fritts, "Signal Processor 'Digitizes' Analog Design Problems." *Electronic Design,* March 31, 1981, pp. 161-168.

10. M.J. McGowan, "Processing Analog Signals Digitally on a Single Programmable Chip." *Control Engineering,* 1979, 26:10, p. 68.

Analog-to-Digital Conversion

7-1 INTRODUCTION

Analog-to-digital conversion means transforming an analog representation of information into some form of digital representation. The physical device that implements this transformation is the analog-to-digital converter or ADC. In general terms, the ADC can be described as a data domain converter (see Section 2-2) since, like the transducer, its function is to transform the representation of data from one domain to another. The ADC can therefore be thought of as the bridge between the analog input subsystem (Chapters 2–6) and the microprocessor subsystem (Module 2), as represented in Fig. 7-1.

The field of data acquisition can be classified into two broad areas: *digitizing* of continuous analog data, and *event logging.* Digitizing with sampling techniques and a multibit ADC has already been described at the systems level in Chapter 2. That chapter also presented a design procedure for selecting the required ADC, sample-and-hold amplifier, and analog multiplexer for a particular application. Numerous books and articles are also available which describe, in detail, the various techniques of analog-to-digital conversion and the complementary process of digital-to-analog conversion.[1] It is not our intention to duplicate that material in this chapter but

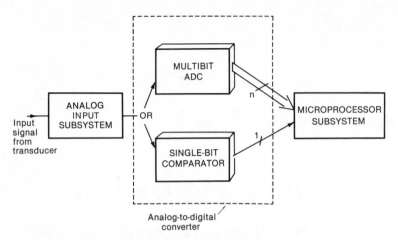

Fig. 7-1. The ADC is a bridge between the analog and digital data domains.

rather to emphasize some rarely mentioned *peripheral analog electronics* which are required for successful, reliable, and precise analog-to-digital conversion. We also emphasize the system calibration procedures that must be considered before meaningful data can be transferred to, and used by, the microprocessor.

Event logging, the second major data acquisition subclass, requires that an event be identified and subsequently counted. Event identification is usually performed using a single-threshold to two-threshold (window) comparator circuit which, in a sense, can be regarded as a single-bit ADC (see Fig. 7-1). Analog signal conditioning through the analog input subsystem is generally required in advance of the comparator, and the counting in a microcomputer-based system is handled by the microprocessor subsystem. Section 7-3 is devoted to a discussion of single-bit comparator circuits, together with the software and hardware issues that must be addressed in designing a reliable microcomputer-based event logger.

7-2 MULTIBIT DIGITIZING AND THE ADC

In this section, we describe a number of the peripheral analog circuits required for the correct operation of an analog-to-digital converter (ADC). We also describe the procedure used to calibrate the ADC. The additional components are illustrated in block form in Fig. 7-2. They include:

- A clock with a well-defined frequency for the internal operation of the ADC.

- A stable reference voltage so that the ADC can compare the incoming analog signal with a known and stable reference.
- An overload protection circuit to limit the range of the input signal applied to the ADC.
- An input buffer to minimize the effect of the differing output impedances of the various voltage sources that may be connected to the input of the ADC.

Calibration of the system involves:

- Setting the zero and full scale inputs to the subsystem by the necessary offsets and gains of the analog signal conditioning line.
- Setting the zero and full scale values for the ADC.
- Considering the interaction between the input subsystem and the microcomputer's software.

By way of example, Fig. 7-2 shows a feedback type of ADC in which a DAC and some conversion logic have been placed in the feedback loop of a precision comparator. The exact form of converter is determined by the type of conversion logic employed, typical examples being the servo and tracking ADCs and the very popular successive-approximation ADC.

Depending on the complexity and the attendant cost of the monolithic, hybrid, or modular ADC purchased, virtually all of the peripherals shown in Fig. 7-2 are either available on board or must be supplied by the user. The simplest and therefore the cheapest ADCs may only contain the DAC and the conversion logic. For such devices the user must supply not only the peripherals but also the precision comparator. Typical examples within this class include Analog Devices' AD7570 and Datel's MC8B.[2] A large class of devices, such as National Semiconductor's ADC 0800 and 0808, provide an on-board comparator, with the user supplying the rest of the peripherals.[3] At the top of the range, ADC systems are available which include all of the blocks shown in Fig. 7-2, with the exception of an external power supply and possibly a protection circuit. A typical example in this class is Analog Devices' AD572. In the following subsections, we discuss each of the peripheral blocks in turn, outlining their particular characteristics and their implementation when they are not provided on board by the manufacturer.

7-2-1 Clocks

The clock input to an ADC usually requires a square wave having rise and fall times compatible with the type of logic

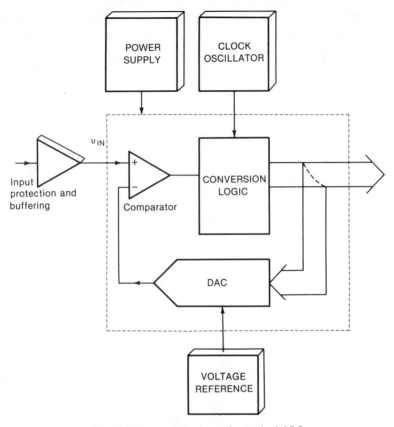

Fig. 7-2. The architecture of a typical ADC.

family used to implement the digital conversion logic. The specification sheets for ADCs that require an external clock give the range of clock frequencies that can be employed. ADCs employing an internal clock may either operate at a fixed frequency (e.g., 500 kHz for AD572) or be adjusted over a limited range using external resistors and capacitors (e.g., AD7570).

External clocks can be generated using one of the circuits given in Section 10-4, one chosen to satisfy the frequency, rise-time, and mark-to-space ratio requirements of the ADC. A further possibility in microcomputer applications is to use a divided-down version of the microprocessor's clock to provide the clock input to the ADC (cf. Fig. 7-9).

If an internal ADC clock or a separate external clock is employed, then it will operate asynchronously with respect to the microprocessor's clock. This fact needs to be taken into

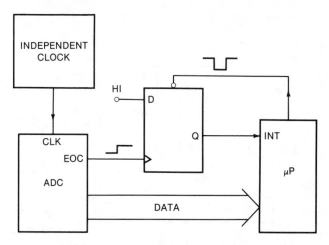

Fig. 7-3. Data transfer between ADC and microprocessor using a simple vectored interrupt structure.

account when interfacing the ADC to the microcomputer. Using the microprocessor's clock may, in some cases, lead to simplification since the analog input subsystem, including the ADC, is then slaved to the system clock.

Transfer of the output data from the ADC into the microprocessor can be accomplished either via interrupts or by polling. The interrupt arrangement is sketched in Fig. 7-3, where the *end-of-conversion* (EOC) signal from the ADC provides the interrupt flag. Since the EOC line usually stays high until a new conversion is initiated, the D-type, positive edge-triggered flip-flop has been inserted to prevent multiple servicing of the interrupt, which would occur if EOC were connected directly to the interrupt input. If polled operation is employed, as in Fig. 7-4, then a D-type flip-flop driven by the microprocessor's clock should be employed to resynchronize the ADC with the rest of the system, particularly if separate clocks are employed for the ADC and the processor.

7-2-2 Voltage Reference

As outlined in Section 12-6, the stability of the voltage reference must be better than half the resolution of the ADC if meaningful results are to be obtained. Table 12-1, which compares the number of ADC bits to the resolution, may therefore be used to determine the required stability of the voltage reference. With ADC modules or monolithic devices featuring an internal reference, the necessary stability is guaranteed by the manufacturer, provided that the specified temperature

195

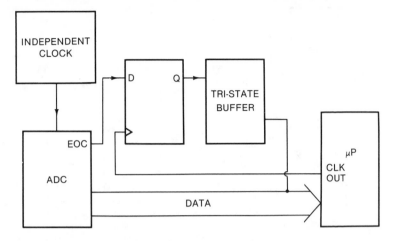

Fig. 7-4. The ADC's end-of-conversion flag should be resynchronized with the microprocessor clock for polled data transfer operation.

range is not exceeded. If an external source is required, Section 12-6 can be consulted to determine the most suitable source to meet the needs of the particular ADC.

7-2-3 Input Protection

Specification sheets for the ADC usually list an absolute maximum analog voltage that can be tolerated between the analog input and the analog common without damaging the device. If unexpectedly large voltages are likely which would exceed the maximum allowable value, then some form of protection circuit should be connected across the input. In principle, the easiest procedure is to connect a zener diode between the analog input and the common, as illustrated in Fig. 7-5A. The zener diode would have a breakdown voltage which is greater than the maximum analog input voltage of interest but less than the absolute maximum allowable voltage. An alternative approach is to connect a pair of diodes, as in Figure 7-5B, between the input line and the supply voltages so that the input voltage is constrained to lie between $V_{cc} + V_D$ and $-(V_{ss} + V_D)$, where V_D is the forward voltage drop across the diode. This arrangement gives good protection, particularly if germanium diodes, with their low value of $V_D \sim 0.2$ volt, are employed.

In some critical applications, however, the rounded knee of the zener's breakdown characteristic (Fig. 11-13B) or the finite turn-on voltage, V_D, of the diodes (Fig. 6-13B) may lead to inadequate protection. This will be the case, for instance, when

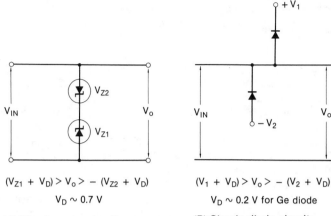

$(V_{Z1} + V_D) > V_o > - (V_{Z2} + V_D)$

$V_D \sim 0.7$ V

(A) Simple zener circuit.

$(V_1 + V_D) > V_o > - (V_2 + V_D)$

$V_D \sim 0.2$ V for Ge diode

(B) Simple diode circuit.

Fig. 7-5. Input circuit protection.

the maximum voltage of interest is very close to the maximum allowable voltage. Under these conditions, some form of precision voltage limiter may be needed, such as the one shown in Fig. 7-6. In this circuit, the diodes are placed within the feedback loop of the operational amplifier. As a result, their natural

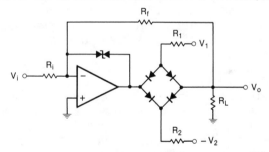

(A) Circuit diagram.

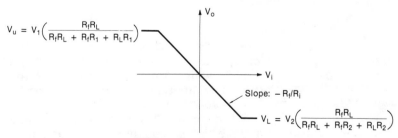

$$V_u = V_1 \left(\frac{R_f R_L}{R_f R_L + R_f R_1 + R_L R_1} \right)$$

Slope: $- R_f/R_i$

$$V_L = V_2 \left(\frac{R_f R_L}{R_f R_L + R_f R_2 + R_L R_2} \right)$$

(B) Transfer characteristics

Fig. 7-6. Precision limiter.

turn-on voltage V_D is reduced to V_D/A, where A is the (very large) open loop gain of the operational amplifier.

7-2-4 Input Buffering

The direct analog input to many ADCs has a comparatively low input impedance in the range from 2 to 10 kΩ. As a consequence, some form of input buffer circuit is required if loading of the signal source is to be avoided. It is customary to use an external operational amplifier wired as a voltage follower, although for some commercial devices such as Analog Devices' AD572 an optional buffer amplifier is available as part of the module. If some additional gain is required in the analog input line, it is possible to provide both gain and buffering by using an operational amplifier in its noninverting amplifier configuration, which has an inherently high input impedance.

7-2-5 Miscellaneous Considerations

Power Supply Decoupling

Although ADCs have built-in immunity to fluctuations and noise on their power supply rails, for optimum performance it is good practice to bypass the supply rails by means of capacitors placed as close as physically practical to the power supply inputs to the ADC. Good quality 1-μF to 5-μF tantalum capacitors should be used, which are bypassed in turn by 0.01-μF disc ceramic capacitors to improve the high-frequency decoupling.

Grounding and Layout

Analog and digital signal grounds should be kept separate where possible. This prevents noisy digital signals from flowing in the analog ground circuit and inducing spurious analog signal noise. In addition, the analog signal input line should be shielded in critical applications and kept physically separate from the input clock line.

7-2-6 System Calibration

Fig. 7-7 shows the path that data follows on its way from the transducer to the microprocessor. In particular, it highlights those blocks or subsystems which are directly relevant to the system calibration process. Ultimately, system calibration involves defining the *data baseline* and the *scale factor* at the microprocessor. The data baseline is that value of the data variable (DV_1, for example) which will be represented as binary zero ($00 \ldots 00_2$). The scale factor is the change in the value of the data variable (ΔDV) which is required to cause a binary

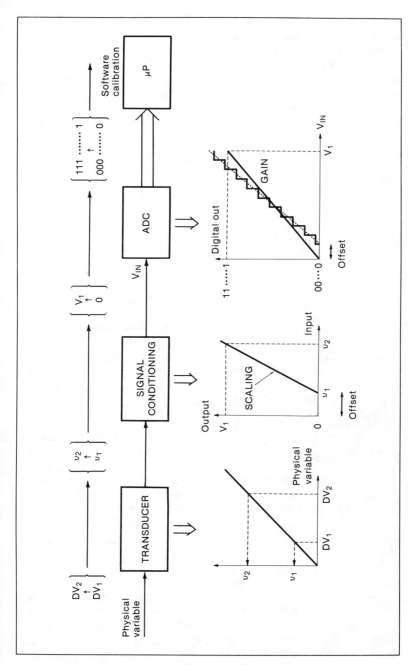

Fig. 7-7. System calibration summary.

199

change equal to the resolution of the ADC (i.e., ΔDV per binary step). For instance, say that the output of the analog signal conditioning line described for a temperature transducer in Section 5-8-2 is digitized using a 10-bit ADC. In this case the calibration process ensures that the required temperature range of 20° to 950°C results in corresponding binary changes of zero to full-scale. The microprocessor must also be made aware, via software, that the temperature baseline is 20°C and that the scale factor is as follows:

$$\text{Scale factor} = \frac{DV_2 - DV_1}{2^n - 1} \qquad \text{(Eq. 7-1)}$$

$$= \frac{950 - 20}{2^{10} - 1} = \frac{930}{1023}$$

$$= 0.91°C \text{ per binary step.}$$

Hence, system calibration is a three-stage process in which:

1. The *ADC must be calibrated* so that a zero to full-scale voltage change at the input to the ADC results in a corresponding binary zero to binary full-scale change at its output.
2. The *analog input subsystem must be calibrated* through offsetting and scaling so that the data variable range of interest $(DV_2 - DV_1)$ will result in the zero to full-scale input voltage range required by the ADC.
3. The *software must be calibrated* by defining the data baseline and the scale factor.

ADC Calibration

The transfer function of an ideal analog-to-digital converter is shown in Fig. 7-8A. Numerous departures from this ideal are possible.[4] The two which can be externally compensated are shown in Figs. 7-8B and C, namely, *offset error* and *gain error.* The offset error is a measure of the extent to which the real transfer function for an ADC is displaced from the ideal. It is essentially the ADC zero error. The gain error is a measure of the extent to which the *slope* of the ADC transfer function differs from that of the ideal.

Calibrating the ADC therefore involves nulling out the offset and gain errors using the variable resistance circuit configurations recommended by the manufacturer (cf. Fig. 7-9) as follows. An input voltage of half the ADC resolution (volts) should be applied to the ADC, and its offset or zero potentiometer should be adjusted until the least significant bit begins to flicker. An input voltage of full scale minus half the ADC resolution should then be applied and the gain poten-

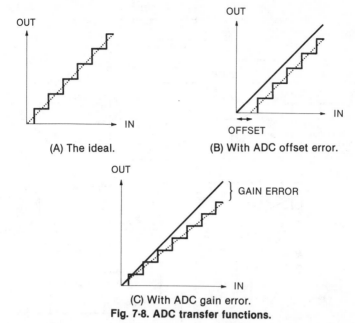

(A) The ideal.

(B) With ADC offset error.

(C) With ADC gain error.

Fig. 7-8. ADC transfer functions.

tiometer adjusted until the binary output begins to flicker between 11 . . . 10 and 11 . . . 11 (110 and 111 in Fig. 7-8A). The ADC is now calibrated for a resolution as defined by Equation 2-1.[5]

This procedure is simple in concept, but there are practical difficulties, namely, the need for either:

1. An adjustable voltage reference source whose short-term stability is better than R(volts)/10, and a precision digital voltmeter; or
2. A precision voltage reference source.

The voltage reference source selected for the ADC (cf. Section 7-2-2) can be used, after buffering and scaling, with a precision DVM as illustrated in Fig. 7-10. On the other hand, precision voltage reference sources are available—the DVC-8500 digital voltage calibrator from Datel-Intersil, for example. Both options are expensive.

Input Subsystem Calibration

This was discussed in Section 5-6 under the heading "Scaling and Offsetting." The ideal procedure is to apply the data baseline value of the data variable (DV_1) to the transducer (see Fig. 7-7) and adjust the offset potentiometer for zero volts from the analog signal conditioning block. One should then apply

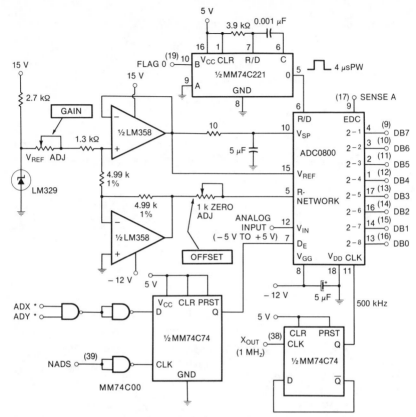

Fig. 7-9. ADC interface circuit showing gain (V_{REF} adjust) and offset (zero adjust) circuits. (*Courtesy National Semiconductor Corp.*)

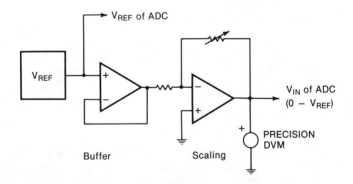

Fig. 7-10. A voltage source circuit for ADC calibration.

the maximum value of the data variable to the transducer and adjust the scale potentiometer to provide the specified full-scale input voltage for the ADC. In practice, however, it is usually very difficult to adjust and then hold the data variable at the prescribed minimum and maximum values. Hence, a stable voltage reference is customarily used to simulate the output voltage from the transducer, perhaps after primary signal conditioning (cf. Fig. 5-1), under these conditions. The required voltages can usually be identified by referring to the calibration data supplied by the transducer manufacturer.

Software Calibration

To complete the system calibration process, values for the data baseline and for the scale factor must be built into the system software. There are basically three methods for doing this. The first method requires the most software, most likely including a floating point package. By this method, the user enters, via a keypad, the data baseline value (DV_1) and the maximum data value (DV_2). The software then calculates the scale factor using Equation 7-1. The second method is simpler, in that the user is asked to enter the data baseline and scale factor values. The third approach is simply to write the required values into the code during software development. The first two approaches are normally found in intelligent or semi-intelligent data loggers and digital control systems, while the latter approach characterizes the dedicated, microcomputer-based digital control systems.

It is beyond the scope of this book to discuss in detail the software structures that can be used to manage system calibration. However, one or two important points can be made by way of overview. First, if the scale factors allowed in the system are kept to multiples of two — i.e., $\times$ ¼, $\times$ ½, $\times$ 1, $\times$ 2, $\times$ 4, etc. — then the software can be kept relatively simple, since multiplication and division can be done by left or right shifts of the appropriate byte or word, respectively. In addition, if the largest data variable range is assigned a scale factor of one (e.g., 1°C per binary step), then it is easy to rescale the analog signal conditioning line for scale factors of, say, $\times$ ½ (½°C per binary step) and $\times$ ¼ under software control. This is done using a programmable gain amplifier whose gain would be set to $\times$ 2 and $\times$ 4, respectively. This automatic scale expansion, with its consequent improvement in system resolution (cf. 1°C per binary step to ½°C, etc.), is a straightforward software exercise once the primary signal conditioning is organized. It is also possible to control the automatic adjustment of the offset voltage, which is required for a nominated data baseline value, by means of software. This is achieved using a digital-to-analog converter in place of the offset amplifier in the analog signal conditioning line.

7-3 SINGLE-BIT DIGITIZING: EVENT LOGGING

In many situations, it is not necessary to know the precise magnitude of a signal but only whether or not a signal is present. In other words, we may want only to detect or count events without specifying their exact nature. A typical example of event detection is an automatic door-opening system, where a light beam is broken by a person approaching the door. The event detected is the breaking of the beam, and this event initiates the opening of the door. The system knows nothing about the event except that the beam has been broken. Whether it was broken by an adult or a child, or even by an inanimate object, is unimportant. What does matter is that something is approaching the door and so the door needs opening.

If a microcomputer system is designed as an event logger, then the problem for the analog input subsystem is to distinguish between an event and the absence of an event. In the example just used, a transducer responds to a reduction in light level. The door-opening system should not respond to reductions caused, for example, by the presence of dust or cigarette smoke in the beam. But the door should react if the transducer output drops all the way to the level set by the ambient lighting in the absence of a beam. The occurrence of an event, then, is generally defined by the transducer output dropping below or rising above a *specific level* or *threshold.* Further examples of event logging arise in the use of other proximity-detecting transducers (Section 3-2-3), such as the Hall effect transducer or the infrared sensor; and in nuclear radiation measurement, where the object is to detect the presence or absence of a pulse from a particle detector.

In some cases, a pulse that is within a small voltage *range* will represent the occurrence of an event. In these cases, we need a circuit to detect whether the signal is above a certain threshold but also below a higher level, in other words, to detect whether the signal lies within a particular *window* or *allowable range.* Section 7-3-1 deals with single-threshold circuits, and Section 7-3-2 is devoted to window circuits for event detection. In these sections, we will assume that the transducer output has been conditioned and possibly processed, by one or more of the techniques outlined in Chapters 5 and 6, to produce a positive voltage.

7-3-1 Single-Threshold Circuits

The purpose of a single-threshold event detection circuit is to determine whether the voltage obtained from the transducer after signal conditioning is greater or less than a preset reference voltage. If so, the circuit must produce an output voltage compatible with the logic levels of the micro-processor subsystem (cf. Section 8-3-2). This function is usual-ly performed using a monolithic comparator such as the popular LM311. Here, however, we describe circuits using the LM339, which is not only easier to use but also has many im-proved specifications, including lower input offset voltage and currents, lower input bias currents, and lower supply current drain. In addition, its open collector output allows it to be con-nected directly to most logic families (cf. Section 9-2-1: CMOS ICs and voltage buffering) even if they are operating at a higher supply voltage than the comparator.

Fig. 7-11 shows the basic comparator configuration. It pro-vides an asserted high output whenever the input voltage, V_i, exceeds the threshold voltage, V_{REF}. The supply voltage, V^+, should be at least 1.5 V greater than the threshold voltage and is normally the same as V_{LOGIC}, where V_{LOGIC} is the supply voltage (normally +5 V) from which the digital circuits of the microprocessor subsystem are fed.

A disadvantage of this simple circuit is that, if the input voltage crosses the threshold voltage slowly, the comparator is prone to enter oscillation due to input noise or stray capacitive feedback. The most reliable solution to this prob-lem is to apply *hysteresis* (cf. Section 10-2) to the comparator as shown in Fig. 7-12. The positive feedback supplies the

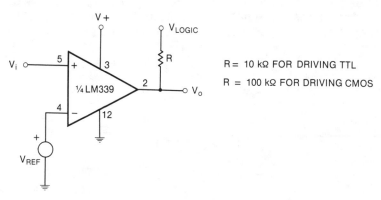

Fig. 7-11. Single-threshold event detection circuit.

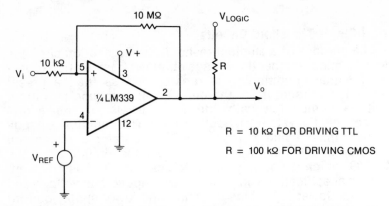

Fig. 7-12. Single-threshold event detection circuit with hysteresis.

hysteresis and has the effect of raising the threshold for the low-to-high transition by about $V_{LOGIC}/10^3$ above V_{REF}. It also lowers the threshold for a high-to-low transition by about $V_{LOGIC}/10^3$ below V_{REF}.

7-3-2 Window Circuits

Because of the open collector output stage of the LM339 comparator, the outputs of two comparators can be wired together, as illustrated in Fig. 7-13. This produces a simple window circuit whose output is asserted high only when the input voltage lies between a lower reference voltage ($V_{REF\ LOW}$) and an upper reference voltage ($V_{REF\ HIGH}$). If $V_i < V_{REF\ LOW}$, then the output transistor of the upper comparator is off while that of the lower comparator is on and sinks current to bring V_o to within about 250 mV of the earth rail. If $V_{REF\ LOW} < V_i < V_{REF\ HIGH}$, then the output transistor of each comparator is off and V_o is pulled up to about V_{LOGIC} by R. When $V_i > V_{REF\ HIGH}$, then the output transistor of the upper comparator turns on and sinks current to bring V_o to within about 250 mV of the earth rail.

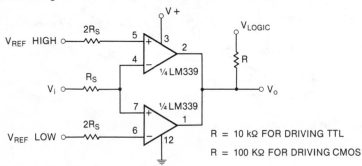

Fig. 7-13. Window comparator for event detention.

The resistors on the comparator inputs reduce the input off-set voltages, which are generated by the input due to bias currents flowing through unequal source resistances. Depending on the accuracy required of the window limits, these resistors may not be necessary. R_s represents the output impedance of the signal source, and the resistors labeled $2R_s$ include the output resistance of the reference voltage sources.

7-3-3 Microprocessor Subsystem Interaction

The single- or double-threshold circuits described in the previous sections produce an output which is asserted (usually high) when the single- or double-threshold conditions, respectively, are satisfied. From the point of view of the microprocessor subsystem, this output should be treated as a *flag input,* because it specifies the occurrence of an event. This opens up a range of microprocessor design issues relating to the handling of flag inputs, which are discussed in detail in a number of textbooks on microcomputer interfacing. The two important interfacing issues that must be addressed here are:

1. Whether to *poll* the flag or whether to use the flag as an *interrupt.*
2. Whether to use a D-type, positive edge-triggered flip-flop between the comparator and the microprocessor bus system to act as a flag register. The functions of this register are to stretch a short-duration flag so that it is not missed by the microprocessor, or to shorten a long-duration flag to avoid multiple servicing. The latter function is achieved by clearing the flag register under software control once the flag input has been serviced (see Fig. 7-14).

For event logging, the tendency is to use vectored or polled interrupts instead of polling. This is because the polling approach almost always requires that the microprocessor be dedicated to polling the flag to ensure that an event is not lost. Again, for the reasons given above, a flag register is almost always used.

There are, however, a number of other hardware/software issues specifically related to event logging. The most important of these is the need to buffer or *prescale* the pulse stream coming from the comparator circuit. The need for a prescaler depends on the event rate, the regularity of event occurrence, the technique for detecting the flag, and the presence of other likely overheads on the microprocessor besides summing the counts from various channels. In most cases, the other processor overheads mean that, even with interrupt detection of the event flag or flag register, a prescaling circuit is generally used. Fig. 7-14 illustrates a very simple but nonetheless effective prescaling circuit that was used in a four-channel event logger by one of the authors (PFG).[6] For this circuit, a microprocessor interrupt is generated after every twelve events (Q_C and Q_D both asserted). The output from IC1, which sets the flag register and generates an interrupt, also clears the counter so that accumulation of counts can continue while the microprocessor services the interrupt. The responsibilities of the software can be summarized as follows:

- *At system initialization,* the prescaling counter must be cleared.
- *After an event interrupt,* the prescaler count (twelve in the circuit of Fig. 7-14) must be added to the accumulated channel count which is usually stored in memory. The flag register must then be cleared before interrupts are re-enabled.
- *At the end of the accumulation period,* which is usually flagged by a timer interrupt, the residual count must be retrieved by reading the counter outputs and be added to the accumulated channel count. The prescaler must then be cleared and disabled until the start of the next accumulation period.

System count rates in excess of 100 kHz can be handled using interrupts and prescaling in this way, as long as the events occur regularly. At the other extreme, very slow event rates can also require a circuit of the type shown in Fig. 7-14 if the events occur nonuniformly. Such is the case, for example, in logging naturally occurring gamma rays; the gammas tend to occur in "bursts" which are characteristic of radioactivity.[7] Although the event rate lies between 1 and 100 Hz, depending on the gamma energy window which is preset at the comparator inputs (Fig. 7-13), the time between gammas may be less than a microsecond, so a buffer is essential to ensure that no events are lost.

When the count rates are high or if the interrupt frequency needs to be kept down, perhaps due to the number of channels involved or due to the processing overheads required of the microprocessor, then a more substantial prescaler is needed. Intel's 8253 programmable interval timer (Fig. 7-15) and/or its equivalents represent ideal LSI devices for this purpose. With three 16-bit presettable down counters, the 8253 can replace

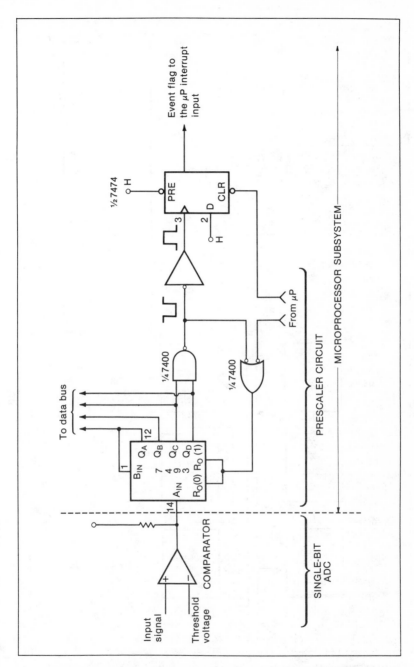

Fig. 7-14. Prescaler circuit and flag register for an event logger.

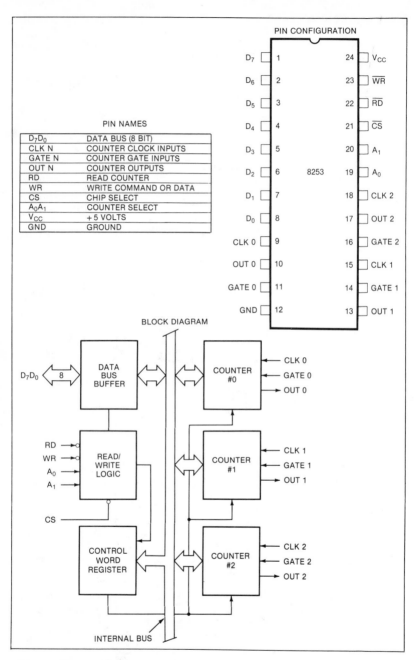

Fig. 7-15. The 8253 programmable interval timer. (*Courtesy Intel Corp.*)

the function of the simple prescaling circuit of Fig. 7-14 and at the same time provide three channels (three prescaler counters) in one IC package! The flag register flip-flop also becomes unnecessary, because the terminal count output of the 8253 is cleared when the counter is reset by loading the appropriate mode control byte.

7-4 REFERENCES

1. J.A. Titus, C.A. Titus and D.G. Larsen, *Microcomputer-Analog Converter Software & Hardware Interfacing.* Howard W. Sams & Co., Inc., 1978; G.B. Clayton, *Data Converters.* The Macmillan Press Ltd., London, 1982; E.L. Zuch, Ed., *Data Acquisition and Conversion Handbook: A Technical Guide to A/D-D/A Converters and Their Applications.* Datel-Intersil, Mansfield, MA 1979.

2. Analog Devices, *Data Acquisition Components and Subsystems Catalog.* Norwood, MA, 1980, p. 10-69; Datel-Intersil, *Data Acquisition Component Handbook,* 1980, p. 26C.

3. National Semiconductor Corp., *Data Acquisition Handbook.* Santa Clara, CA, 1978, pp. 2-8 and 2-19.

4. Zuch, 1979, pp. 40–48.

5. Manufacturers often recommend a gain adjusted with an input voltage of $V_{FULLSCALE} (1 - \frac{3}{2} \cdot 2^{-n})$, which results in a resolution of 100×2^{-n}, (%) and a quantization error of $+$ LSB at the most significant bit.

6. P.F. Goldsbrough, "An 8080-Based Data Logger for a Seabed Natural Gamma Spectrometer." *Proceedings of Conference on Microprocessors and Allied Technology at Canberra, 1977.* Canberra Branch of the Australian Computer Society, ACT, pp. 113–119.

7. Goldsbrough, 1977.

MODULE 2

THE MICRO-PROCESSOR SUBSYSTEM

Electrical Properties
of Microcomputer ICs

8-1 INTRODUCTION

Microprocessor subsystems, such as those illustrated in Figs. 1-4, 1-5, and 1-7, consist of an assembly of complex digital integrated circuits which are manufactured by a variety of fabrication processes. However, there are essentially only two broad integrated circuit categories (logic families) in use in microprocessor subsystems: *MOS* and *bipolar.* The MOS (*metal oxide semiconductor*) logic family, of which PMOS, NMOS, CMOS, and HMOS are common in microcomputer systems, uses MOS field-effect transistors (MOSFETs) as its principal circuit element. The bipolar logic family uses the bipolar transistor — either pnp or npn — as its principal circuit element. Its most common subfamilies are TTL (transistor-transistor-logic) and LS (low-power Schottky) TTL.

This chapter:

- Introduces the broad electrical properties that characterize the MOS and bipolar logic families so that their roles in the microprocessor subsystem, and the reasons for using them, can be appreciated.
- Explains the DC and AC specification terminology essential to the successful design of a microprocessor bus system. This is done by briefly considering the operation and interaction of the basic gates from each logic family.

8-2 MOS AND BIPOLAR IC FAMILIES

8-2-1 Characterizing Properties

Each fabrication process endows its corresponding logic family with a distinct set of electrical characteristics which, while varying somewhat within the family, are broadly consistent for that family. The electrical properties which characterize an IC family include:

- Packing density.
- Speed of operation.
- Power consumption.
- Current drive capability and input current loading of a family IC.

Table 8-1 gives the figures for these properties for members of the MOS and bipolar IC families.

Packing density is a measure of the number of transistors that can be fabricated on a silicon wafer of up to 1.5 cm^2. It is usually quoted in terms of the number of basic gates that can be fabricated per mm^2. In this form, it provides only a rough measure for comparison since the number of transistors per gate is not constant from one IC family to the next. Generally, MOS gates require approximately half the transistors of an equivalent bipolar gate (see Section 8-2-3). Thus from Table 8-1 it is evident that the packing density of MOS is at least an order of magnitude better than that of bipolar.

Table 8-1. Characteristics of Major Fabrication Technologies*

	BIPOLAR		MOS		
	Standard TTL	Low Power (LS) Schottky TTL	NMOS (Silicon Gate)	CMOS	HMOS
Gate propagation delay t$_{AV}$(ns)	10	9.5	25	~30	2
Gate power dissipation P$_D$ (mW)	12	2	1	50 nW at DC to 1 W at 1 MHz	0.4–1
Packing density (gates/mm^2)	20	25–35	100–18?	40–90	250
Fan-out (standard load**)	10	5	~1	~1	~1
Fan-in (standard load**)	1	1/2	1/4	~1/40	1/4
Power supply voltage (volts)	5.0 ± 5%	5.0 ± 5%	5.0 ± 5%	3 to 18	2 to 5

*After Krutz, 1980, and Williams, 1970.
**Standard load is 40 μA for a high; 1.6 mA for a low.

The *speed of operation* is a measure, in megahertz (MHz), of how fast a family member flip-flop can change state without error. This factor is determined by the *propagation delay times* of the gates which are used to form the flip-flop. The two times usually quoted, t_{pHL} and t_{pLH}, are illustrated in Fig. 8-1 for an inverter. The time t_{pHL} is that which is required for the output to go from a *h*igh to a *l*ow when commanded to do so by an input pulse. The time t_{pLH} is that which is required for an output to go from a *l*ow to a *h*igh. Since these two times are not normally the same, the propagation delay time quoted by a manufacturer is usually the average, t_{AV}, of t_{pHL} and t_{pLH}:

$$t_{AV} = (t_{pHL} + t_{pLH})/2 \qquad \text{(Eq. 8-1)}$$

Hence,

$$\text{speed (MHz)} \approx 1/t_{AV} \, (\mu s) \qquad \text{(Eq. 8-2)}$$

Note that while bipolar ICs are faster than MOS on average, HMOS stands out as a high performer even compared with bipolar ICs.

Power consumption is an important IC family characteristic from the point of view of the total current demand placed on the power supply by the microprocessor subsystem. It is sometimes specified by the manufacturer in terms of the average power dissipation, P_D, for the IC, or even for a gate within the IC. However, it is more often given in terms of the

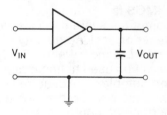

Fig. 8-1. Gate-switching characteristics.

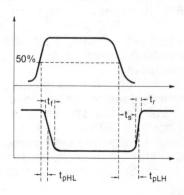

217

average current drain, I_{cc}. The P_D may then be calculated as:

$$P_D = V_{cc}I_{cc} \qquad \text{(Eq. 8-3)}$$

Notice in Table 8-1 that the power demand of MOS ICs is significantly less than that of bipolar ICs.

The *current drive* and *input current loading* of a family member IC determine the number of IC packages — memory ICs, for example — that can be connected to the data, address, and control buses of the microprocessor. The *current drive* or *fan-out* capability of an IC is specified as the maximum current drive the IC can provide while maintaining a specified high or low output voltage; it clearly characterizes the *outputs* of a logic family. *Inputs* are similarly characterized by the current load which each input represents to a driving device — the data bus, for example. The amount of current needed by an input is sometimes known as the *fan-in* of the input. Both factors are commonly quoted in terms of a "unit load." Table 8-1 shows that bipolar has a better current drive capability than MOS. However, it also has a worse fan-in than MOS so that its inputs require more current. Both factors will be discussed in more detail in Section 8-3-1 and their importance should become clearer in Chapter 9, where we explore the issues involved in making the bus system work.

8-2-2 The Role of MOS and Bipolar ICs

MOS is the dominant fabrication technology used in microcomputer systems. This dominance is due primarily to the superior packing density of NMOS and HMOS compared with that of standard and LS TTL (Table 8-1). So, MOS technology has been used to implement those subsystem functions which are complex and require large-scale integration (LSI), such as the microprocessor, memories (both ROM and RAM), and peripheral controllers (Fig. 1-3). Most of these devices are manufactured using the NMOS technology, although some 16-bit microprocessors, such as Intel's 8086, use the high performance HMOS, in which the dimensions of the MOSFETs have been reduced to achieve improved packing density and switching speed, together with reduced power consumption (see Table 8-1).

In addition to the high packing density of MOS, a complementary feature that is essential in making this technology suitable for LSI devices is its low power dissipation per gate. Although NMOS shows an order of magnitude improvement in power dissipation over standard TTL, NMOS integrated circuits still run much hotter than medium-scale integration TTL devices. So, the time-honored "finger test" for determining IC

Table 8-2. Comparison of Power Consumption of Various Microprocessors

Device	Manufacturing Technology	I_{CC} (mA)	Power (W)
8085	NMOS	170	0.85
6800	NMOS	240	1.2
8086	HMOS	275	1.375
NCS800	CMOS	10	0.050
RCA COSMAC	CMOS	3	0.015 @ 4 MHz and 5 V
		20	0.100 @ 4 MHz and 10 V

failure due to overheating does little more than provide a scorched finger for NMOS LSI devices! Table 8-2 shows the very large power consumption of NMOS LSI microprocessors and the very impressive improvement which is possible with CMOS. A long-standing problem of CMOS, however, has been the considerable increase in power consumption which occurs at high switching frequencies such as are found in microcomputer systems (cf. Tables 8-1 and 8-2). For this reason, CMOS microprocessors have not been popular. National Semiconductor Inc., however, produces a CMOS microprocessor (the NSC800, Fig. 8-2) capable of running at approximately the same speeds (1.6 μs instruction cycle time) as the 8085A, 6800, and Z-80, 8-bit NMOS processors but requiring only 50 mW at 5 V V_{cc}. It also operates with a supply voltage of from 3–12 V!

Two significant disadvantages of the MOS technology are its low current drive capability of one standard TTL load (Table 8-1) and lower switching speed compared with bipolar devices. Gate propagation delays have been improved dramatically with the introduction of HMOS, but NMOS is about 2.5 times slower (Table 8-1) than TTL. So, current NMOS processors cannot be expected to have the same real-time processing capability as discrete bipolar logic or bipolar processors such as Intel's 3000 series. Their limited current drive capability means that bus buffering is almost essential, even in relatively small microcomputer systems. We will discuss this further in Chapter 9.

Because of the lower packing density and relatively high power dissipation per gate of bipolar technologies compared with MOS technologies, the bipolar family is used to provide the small- and medium-scale IC functions which are needed in microcomputer systems. These include the basic logic functions (inversion, NAND, NOR, AND and OR), decoders for address decoding, latches for data output, and three-state buffers for

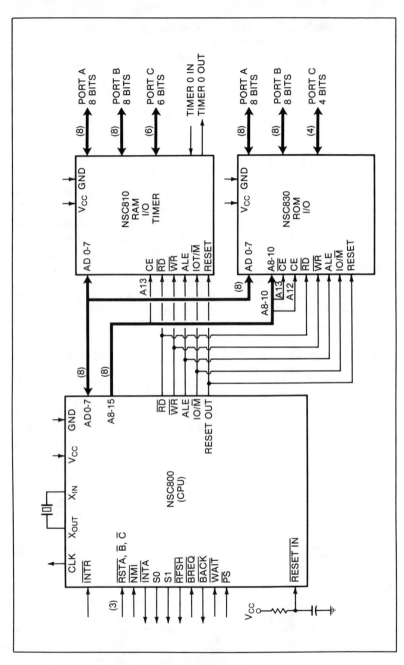

Fig. 8-2. The NSC800 CMOS Microprocessor.

data input. The high current drive capability of bipolar logic means also that TTL ICs are used to provide the current drive required for the address, data, and control buses but lacking with the MOS microprocessors. This bus buffering function is a common application of bipolar logic in the microprocessor subsystem, although MOS ICs with specially designed output stages for improved current drive are also used (e.g., the Intel 8212 buffer/latch).

8-2-3 Operation of the Basic MOS and Bipolar Gates

In this section, we will discuss in broad outline the operation of the basic gate circuit (the inverter) for each logic family. This will help in understanding the interaction of gates and from that, the nature of the DC and AC specifications which are provided to cope with these interactions.

The Bipolar Gate

It is helpful to begin by considering a single bipolar transistor used as a switch, as in Fig. 8-3A. Here, an npn transistor is used in a common-emitter configuration. By driving the base of the transistor with a large base current (I_B), when V_{IN} is ~ 5 V, the transistor saturates, a large collector current flows (the transistor switch is closed), and the output voltage, $V_{CE\ (SAT)}$ (Fig. 8-3B), is ~ 0.3 V. With no base current drive when V_{IN} is ~ 0 V, the transistor is cut off, no collector current flows (the transistor switch is open) and the output voltage is approximately V_{CC}. Therefore, the circuit acts as a voltage inverter when driven in this way.

While this circuit is very simple, it unfortunately suffers from a relatively slow switching speed because of the two major effects illustrated in Fig. 8-1:

- The time required after V_{IN} (and therefore I_B) drops before the base region of the transistor is cleared of the excess charge that builds up when the transistor is saturated. This is the charge storage time t_s.
- The time required to charge and discharge the external load capacitance C_L. This effect controls the times t_r and t_f.

In Fig. 8-4, the circuit of a basic TTL gate, which overcomes these problems, is shown. The operation of this circuit has been described many times and is summarized in Table 8-3.[2] A high at output Y is obtained by turning on Q_3 (Q_4 is off) to connect the output to V_{cc} through R_4, Q_3, and D_1, while a low is obtained by turning on Q_4 (Q_3 is off) to connect Y to digital com-

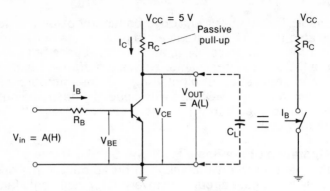

(A) Bipolar transistor used as a switch.

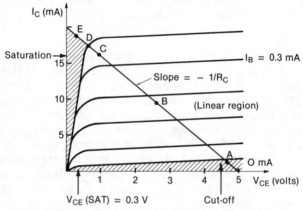

(B) Output characteristics for transistor in (A).

Fig. 8-3. Bipolar gate.

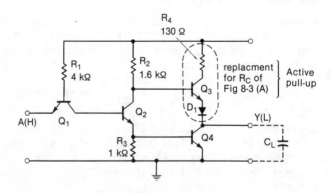

Fig. 8-4. Basic TTL inverter gate.

Table 8-3. Operation Summary for TTL Circuit

A	Q_1	Q_2	Q_3	Q_4	Y
LOW	ON	OFF	ON	OFF	HIGH
HIGH	OFF	ON	OFF	ON	LOW

mon. Q_2 is needed to drive the so-called "totem-pole" (or push-pull) output stage and D_1 is needed to ensure that Q_3 and Q_4 cannot be turned on together for an extended period — a useless condition at best! The charge storage time, t_s, of Q_2 has been reduced — consequently improving the overall switching speed of the gate — by the action of Q_1 at the moment (t_2 in Fig. 8-1) when input A is grounded. Q_1 clears the base region of Q_2 of its excess saturation charge, effecting a reduction in t_s. Time t_r is improved by the use of Q_3 to provide higher current drive for charging C_L, while t_f is reduced since Q_1 and Q_2 of a load gate provide an effectively lower input resistance for the TTL gate during this time.

Additional improvements in the switching speed of TTL gates involve a further reduction in t_s by preventing the transistors from being driven deeply into saturation. This is done by connecting Schottky diodes between the base and collector of the transistors of the TTL gate, as illustrated in Fig. 8-5. Schottky diodes[3] have a forward voltage drop (V_f) of only 0.2 V and their effect is summarized in Table 8-4. As the transistor saturates, V_{BC} becomes positive and forward biases the Schottky diode. The diode then shunts part of the base current away from the base of the transistor as it begins to saturate and so prevents the buildup of charge carriers in the base. TTL gates manufactured in this way are known as Schottky (S) TTL. The

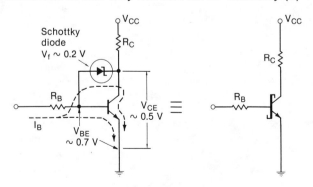

Fig. 8-5. Schottky-clamped bipolar transistor.

Table 8-4. Effect of Schottky Diode on a Saturated Transistor

Position on Transistor's Output Characteristics	V_{BE} (V)	V_{CE} (V)	$V_{BC} = V_{BE} - V_{CE}$ (V)
A* (cut-off)	0	~ 5	−5
B (linear)	0.65	$\sim \dfrac{V_{CC}}{2} = 2.5$	~ -1.85
C (onset of saturation)	0.7	0.7	0
D (Schottky condition)	0.75	0.55	+0.2
E (deep saturation)	0.8	0.2	+0.6

*See Fig. 8-3B.

so-called *Low*-power Schottky (LS) TTL gates have considerably increased resistor values which reduce their power consumption to approximately 2 mW per gate while maintaining a t_{AV} (9.5 ns) which is comparable with standard TTL. For this reason, and a lower input current loading, LS TTL has effectively replaced standard TTL in most modern digital systems, including microcomputers.

The MOSFET Gate

Bipolar transistors are current-controlled devices (see Fig. 8-3B). Although they are easy to fabricate, so explaining the early popularity of bipolar logic, their detailed operation is relatively complex. Field effect transistors (FET), on the other hand, are voltage-controlled devices whose operation is relatively simple. They are also easily fabricated. The n-channel MOSFET (Fig. 8-6A) consists of n-type semiconductor inserts, known as the drain and the source, in a p-type semiconductor material. The region between the drain and source is known as the *channel.* To control the flow of current I_D, the resistance of the channel can be altered by applying a control voltage, V_{GG}, between the gate and drain. The gate consists of an oxide layer which isolates the channel from the metal contact — hence the name, MOS, for metal oxide semiconductor.

To produce the MOSFET equivalent of the bipolar switch circuit shown in Fig. 8-3A, an external supply, V_{DD}, and a load resistor, R_D, are connected in series with the channel via the drain and source, as illustrated in Figs. 8-6A and B. If V_{IN} is ~ 0 V (a low), a p-type channel exists and the reverse-biased pn junctions prevent current flow in the channel. (Note that this is the origin of the broken lines in the MOSFET symbol.) The MOSFET switch is therefore open and V_{OUT} will be $\sim V_{DD}$ (a high). Conversely, if V_{IN} is $\sim V_{DD}$, an n-type channel is established, current I_D flows and V_{OUT} is ~ 0 V.

In practice, the load resistance R_D is replaced by a MOSFET

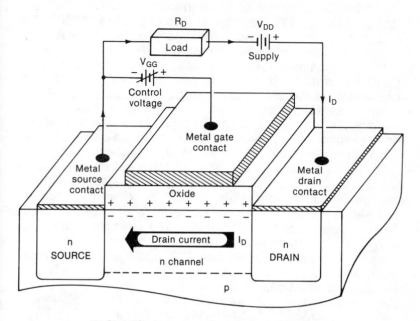

(A) Simplified cross section of planer MOSFET.

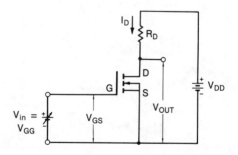

(B) A MOSFET used as a switch.

Fig. 8-6. MOSFET gate.

which has been turned on by connecting its gate to V_{DD} as illustrated in Fig. 8-7. The channel area of this load MOSFET is adjusted to provide a load resistance of ~ 100 kΩ. Given that the off resistance of Q_2 is ~ 10^{10} Ω, then V_{OUT} is ~ 5 V when Q_2 is off. The type of MOSFET discussed above is used almost exclusively in MOS ICs and is described as an n-channel *enhancement* device, because a channel is established only when a control voltage is applied to the gate. However, the n-channel enhancement MOSFET tends to turn on without any applied voltage. To prevent this, doped *silicon gates* are often used (as in Intel's 8080A and 8085A microprocessors).[4]

While the power consumption of NMOS at 1 mW per gate is lower than that of LS TTL (2 mW per gate), it is still significant and becomes very important in LSI ICs which have tens of thousands of NMOS transistors. The 8085, for example, has an average power consumption of 850 mW! The power consumption of NMOS transistors is due to the drain current drawn from the V_{DD} power supply when Q_2 (Fig. 8-7) is on and the output is low. This problem has been eliminated and power consumption dramatically reduced in the Complementary-MOS (CMOS) circuit of the type illustrated in Fig. 8-8. Here, a p-channel MOSFET has been used to replace Q_1 in Fig. 8-7 so that the inverter now consists of a complementary pair of MOSFETS which require opposite voltages (high or low) to switch them on and off. Table 8-5 summarizes the operation of this inverter circuit. Notice that in either output state either Q_1 or Q_2 is always turned off. As a result, power consumption is very low (about 1 μW). It is frequency-dependent, however,

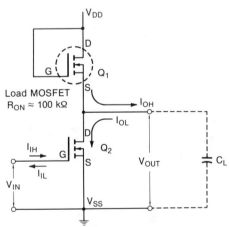

Fig. 8-7. An n-channel (NMOS) inverter gate.

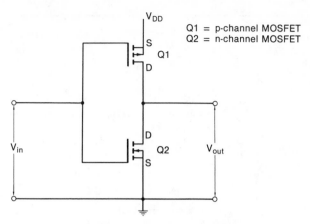

Fig. 8-8. A CMOS inverter gate.

since current from the power supply flows only during the short ($\sim$ 50 ns) period when the gate is switching and both Q_1 and Q_2 are momentarily on.

8-3 DC AND AC ELECTRICAL SPECIFICATIONS

The DC and AC characteristics of integrated circuits are provided by manufacturers as a minimally complete description of the electronic behavior of their ICs. The *DC characteristics* are concerned with the current and voltage specifications for the IC under steady-state or stable input and output conditions; these are presented in tabular form in Fig. 8-9. The *AC characteristics* are concerned with the behavior of the inputs and outputs of the IC with time and include both rise and fall times and the setup and hold times which are necessary for satisfactory IC operation. These times are provided by manufacturers both in tabular form and as graphic displays of the tabulated data, known as "timing diagrams." A typical AC specification sheet is shown in Fig. 8-10.

Table 8-5. Operation of CMOS Inverter in Fig. 8-8

V_{IN}	Q_1	Q_2	V_{OUT}
Logic 1 = V_{DD}	OFF	ON	Logic 0 $\approx$ 0 V
Logic 0 = 0 V	ON	OFF	Logic 1 = V_{DD}

227

DC CHARACTERISTICS

($T_A = 0°C$ to $70°C$; $V_{CC} = 5$ V $\pm 5\%$; $V_{SS} = 0$ V; unless otherwise specified)

Symbol	Parameter	Min.	Max.	Units	Test Conditions
V_{IL}	Input Low Voltage	−0.5	+0.8	V	
V_{IH}	Input High Voltage	2.0	V_{CC} + 0.5	V	
V_{OL}	Output Low Voltage		0.45	V	I_{OL} = 2 mA
V_{OH}	Output High Voltage	2.4		V	I_{OH} = −400 μA
I_{CC}	Power Supply Current		170	mA	
I_{IL} = I_{IN}	Input Leakage		±10	μA	$V_{in} = V_{CC}$
I_{LO}	Output Leakage		±10	μA	0.45 V ≤ V_{out} ≤ V_{CC}
V_{ILR}	Input Low Level, RESET	−0.5	+0.8	V	
V_{IHR}	Input High Level, RESET	2.4	V_{CC} + 0.5	V	
V_{HY}	Hysteresis, RESET	0.25		V	

(A) MOS − 8085 Microprocessor.

Fig. 8-9. DC specifications

electrical characteristics over recommended operating free-air temperature range (unless otherwise noted)

PARAMETER		TEST CONDITIONS†		SN54LS'			SN74LS'			UNIT
				MIN	TYP‡	MAX	MIN	TYP‡	MAX	
V_{IH}	High-level input voltage			2			2			V
V_{IL}	Low-level input voltage					0.7			0.8	V
V_{IK}	Input clamp voltage	$V_{CC} = $ MIN, $I_I = -18$ mA				-1.5			-1.5	V
V_{OH}	High-level output voltage	$V_{CC} = $ MIN, $V_{IH} = 2$ V, $V_{IL} = V_{IL}$ max, $I_{OH} = $ MAX		2.4	3.4		2.4	3.1		V
V_{OL}	Low-level output voltage	$V_{CC} = $ MIN, $V_{IH} = 2$ V, $V_{IL} = V_{IL}$ max	$I_{OL} = 12$ mA		0.25	0.4		0.25	0.4	V
			$I_{OL} = 24$ mA		0.35	0.5		0.35	0.5	
I_{OZH}	Off-state output current, high-level voltage applied	$V_{CC} = $ MAX, $V_{IH} = 2$ V, $V_O = 2.7$ V				20			20	µA
I_{OZL}	Off-state output current, low-level voltage applied	$V_{CC} = $ MAX, $V_{IH} = 2$ V, $V_O = 0.4$ V				-20			-20	µA
I_I	Input current at maximum input voltage	$V_{CC} = $ MAX, $V_I = 7$ V				0.1			0.1	mA
I_{IH}	High-level input current	$V_{CC} = $ MAX, $V_I = 2.7$ V				20			20	µA
I_{IL}	Low-level input current	$V_{CC} = $ MAX, $V_I = 0.4$ V				-0.4			-0.4	mA
I_{OS}	Short-circuit output current§	$V_{CC} = $ MAX		-30		-130	-30		-130	mA
I_{CC}	Supply current	$V_{CC} = $ MAX, Output control at 4.5 V	'LS373		24	40		24	40	mA
			'LS374		27	45		27	45	mA

† For conditions shown as MIN or MAX, use the appropriate value specified under recommended operating conditions.

‡ All typical values are at $V_{CC} = 5$ V, $T_A = 25°C$.

§ Not more than one output should be shorted at a time and duration of the short circuit should not exceed one second.

(B) Bipolar — 74LS373 Octal Latch.

for integrated circuits.

229

AC Characteristics

Symbol	Parameter	Limits (ns)										Test Conditions
		2716		2716-1		2716-2		2716-5		2716-6		
		Min.	Max.	Min.	Max.	Min.	Max.	Min.	Max.	Min.	Max.	
t_{ACC}	Address to Output Delay		450		350		390		450		450	$\overline{CE} = \overline{OE} = V_{IL}$
t_{CE}	$\overline{CE}$ to Output Delay		450		350		390		490		650	$\overline{OE} = V_{IL}$
t_{OE}	Output Enable to Output Delay		120		120		120		160		200	$\overline{CE} = V_{IL}$
t_{DF}	Output Enable High to Output Float	0	100	0	100	0	100	0	100	0	100	$\overline{CE} = V_{IL}$
t_{OH}	Output Hold from Addresses, $\overline{CE}$ or $\overline{OE}$ Whichever Occurred First	0		0		0		0		0		$\overline{CE} = \overline{OE} = V_{IL}$

Capacitance [4] $T_A = 25°$ C, f = 1MHz

Symbol	Parameter	Typ.	Max.	Unit	Conditions
C_{IN}	Input Capacitance	4	6	pF	$V_{IN} = 0V$
C_{OUT}	Output Capacitance	8	12	pF	$V_{OUT} = 0V$

AC Test Conditions:

Output Load: 1 TTL gate and $C_L = 100$ pF *
Input Rise and Fall Times: ≤20ns
Input Pulse Levels: 0.8 V to 2.2 V
Timing Measurements Reference Level:
    Inputs   1 V and 2 V
    Outputs 0.8 V and 2 V

AC Waveforms (1)

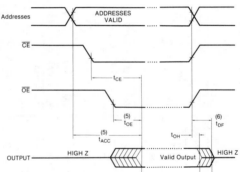

NOTE: 1. V_{CC} must be applied simultaneously or before V_{PP} and removed simultaneously or after V_{PP}.

2. V_{PP} may be connected directly to V_{CC} except during programming. The supply current would then be the sum of I_{CC} and I_{PP1}.

3. Typical values are for $T_A = 25°C$ and nominal supply voltages.

4. This parameter is only sampled and is not 100% tested.

5. $\overline{OE}$ may be delayed up to $t_{ACC} - t_{OE}$ after the falling edge of $\overline{CE}$ without impact on t_{ACC}.

6. t_{DF} is specified from $\overline{OE}$ or $\overline{CE}$, whichever occurs first.

Fig. 8-10. AC specifications for the I2716 MOS-type EPROM.

In Section 8-2-1, two electrical specifications of ICs were introduced as aids in describing MOS and bipolar ICs: P_D, a DC specification, and t_{AV}, an AC specification. However, to assess the electrical compatibility of ICs in the bus-oriented microprocessor subsystem, the complete range of DC and AC specifications must be used. These are illustrated in Figs. 8-9A and 8-10. So, the microcomputer systems designer must be able to read and appreciate the meaning of these specifications.

8-3-1 Interaction of Basic Gates

In Section 8-2-3, we presented the circuits for and explained the operation of the basic TTL (Fig. 8-4), NMOS (Fig. 8-7), and CMOS (Fig. 8-8) gates. Each output stage of these circuits consists of two series transistors connected between the power supply and digital common, and each input connects directly to the input (base or gate) of a transistor. Hence, in Fig. 8-11, which illustrates the interaction of a driver and its load, only a generalized output stage for the driver and input stage for the load have been used. Each transistor is represented as a box.

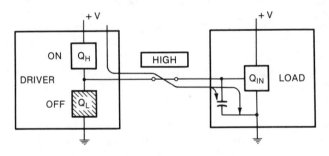

(A) Driver output as a high.

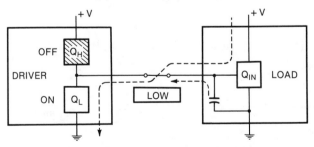

(B) Driver output as a low.

Fig. 8-11. Interaction of basic gates.

The output of the driver can be asserted high or low by connecting the output line to either the power supply (+V) or to digital common. For a *high*, (Fig. 8-11A), Q_H turns on and connects the output to +V while Q_L simultaneously turns off to isolate the output from digital common. Current flows from +V through Q_H of the driver and Q_{IN} of the load to digital common, and the driver output is said to *source* current.

To assert the output *low* (Fig. 8-11B), Q_H turns off and Q_L turns on so that the output line is isolated from +V and connected to digital common. An interesting consequence of this is that the load must now provide current which flows from +V through Q_{IN} of the load, into Q_L of the driver, and then to digital common. The current direction is therefore reversed and the driver output must now *sink* current.

We now examine the DC specifications which are defined to quantify this gate interaction.

8-3-2 DC Specifications

The DC characteristics provided by manufacturers can be divided into two groups—voltage and current—as shown in Table 8-6. Within each group, the voltages and currents are specified for an input (I) and output (O) when either is asserted high (H) or low (L). The strict definitions of these characteristics are detailed and rather circular; they have been provided in Appendix C for completeness. Our task here is to interpret the DC characteristics so as to provide a feel for their intent. This interpretation is shown schematically in Fig. 8-12.

Outputs

When Q_H in Fig. 8-12 switches on (Q_L off) so that the driver output is asserted high, the voltage to which the output rises is known as the output high voltage (V_{OH}). The magnitude of this high voltage depends on the current (I_{OH}) being sourced by Q_H (see Fig. 8-13A) and may be expressed as:

$$V_{OH} = V - I_{OH}R_{OH}, \qquad \text{(Eq. 8-4)}$$

where R_{OH} is the output resistance of the gate for a high.

Table 8-6. Convenient Grouping of DC Specifications

Condition	Voltage (V)	Current (I)
Input high (IH)	V_{IH}	I_{IH}
Input low (IL)	V_{IL}	I_{IL}
Output high (OH)	V_{OH}	I_{OH}
Output low (OL)	V_{OL}	I_{OL}

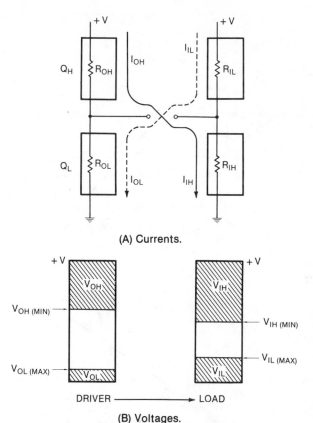

(A) Currents.

(B) Voltages.

Fig. 8-12. DC specifications for ICs.

Hence, if I_{OH} increases to supply a greater load (for example, through the addition of extra RAM ICs to a memory plane), then V_{OH} will drop. To ensure the integrity of the high-level output voltage, manufacturers guarantee a minimum worst-case output voltage, $V_{OH}(MIN)$, for a specified maximum output current, $I_{OH}(MAX)$. These figures are usually used in design/analysis work.

Similar considerations apply when the output of the driver is asserted low. The magnitude of the output low voltage (V_{OL}) may be expressed as:

$$V_{OL} = V_L + I_{OL}R_{OL} \qquad \text{(Eq. 8-5)}$$

where V_L is the output low voltage when I_{OL} is zero, and R_{OL} is the output resistance of the gate for a low. In this case, the output voltage rises as the sink current, I_{OL}, increases (Fig.

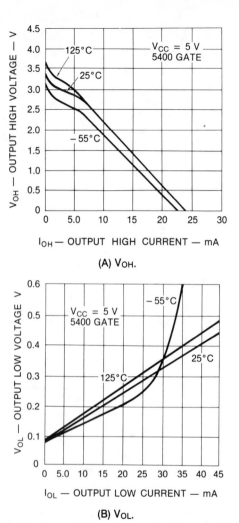

(A) V_OH.

(B) V_OL.

Fig. 8-13. Variations in the output voltages of a TTL gate with load current.

8-13B). A V_{OL}(MAX) is therefore specified under conditions of some I_{OL}(MAX).

The output current and voltage specifications for the I8085 and 74373 have been highlighted in Fig. 8-9 to illustrate typical values for this group of DC specifications for "TTL compatible" ICs. Note that I_{OH} (MAX) and I_{OL} (MAX) define the current drive capability of the output.

Inputs

Since each gate input acts as a current load for the driver

gate, manufacturers provide separate DC current specifications for when the input is driven high (I_{IH}) and low (I_{IL}) by the driver gate. From Fig. 8-12A, it can be seen that these two currents depend on the input resistance of the load as well as on the voltages applied by the driver to the load input. Hence, I_{IH} and I_{IL} may be expressed as:

$$I_{IH} = \frac{V_{OH}}{R_{IH}} \text{ and } I_{IL} = \frac{V - V_{OL}}{R_{IL}} \qquad \text{(Eq. 8-6)}$$

It should be noted that while $I_{OH} = I_{IH}$ and $I_{OL} = I_{IL}$ in Fig. 8-12, in practice the input and output high and low currents will not normally be equal. This is because the output currents represent the drive capability of the driver, while the input currents represent the current loading presented by a *single* gate input.

V_{IH} and V_{IL} are the input voltages which the gate input will recognize as a high and low, respectively. Worst-case values, V_{IH} (MIN) and V_{IL} (MAX) (see Fig. 8-12B), are defined which are worse than the corresponding output voltages for the driver. In this way, a completely loaded-down driver will generate output voltages which will be recognized by the load gate. The input voltages and currents for the 8085 and 74373 are shown in Fig. 8-9.

Current Sourcing and Sinking: Guidelines To Avoid Confusion

The *direction* of current flow is indicated, by convention, in the DC specifications (Fig. 8-9) by the *sign* of the current — a *negative* sign indicating that current is flowing *out* of a terminal. Under these circumstances, a device is said to *source* current. Likewise, current flowing *into* a terminal is shown, by convention, as *positive*. In this case, the device is said to *sink* current. There is an inherent source of confusion, we believe, in the use of these descriptions: since the terms "sourcing" and "sinking" are applicable to both the inputs and outputs of an IC. Note, for example, in Fig. 8-11A that a gate *output* sources current when at a high but, for a low, it is the *input* of the load gate (Fig. 8-11B) which sources the current.

To analyze the design of bus systems, however, it is more important to identify the *driving device,* on the one hand, and its *load,* in the form of the inputs being driven, on the other hand. Thereafter, it is the *magnitude* of the drive current capability at both a high and a low which is important, rather than the *direction* of this current flow. Thus, when discussing bus design/analysis in Chapter 9, we will:

- Clearly identify the device which is driving the bus and its load.

- Use current magnitudes and avoid reference to the direction of current flow.
- Define direction of current flow (when necessary) by referring to the *asserted state* of the *driver output.* The gate in-

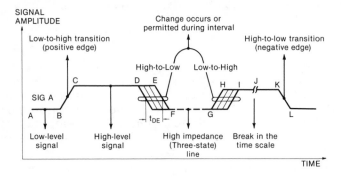

(A) Single-line timing symbols.

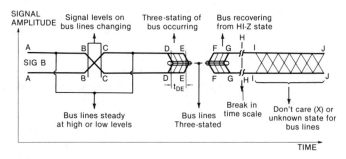

(B) Bus timing symbols.

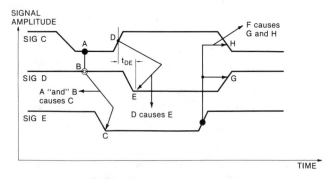

(C) Signal interaction symbols.

Fig. 8-14. Summary of graphic symbols used on timing diagrams.

puts that represent the load for a driver will be assumed to accept current from or provide current to the driver, as required by the voltage level on the line.

8-3-3 AC Specifications

Timing Diagrams

The timing diagrams, or AC waveforms, are probably the most important part of the AC characteristics data sheet, since they illustrate the specifications (see Fig. 8-10). At the time of writing, there was not a drafting standard for timing diagrams, although an informal consensus has developed and firmed.[5] Fig. 8-14 represents our attempt to consolidate and summarize this consensus.

We divide the symbols into three groups:

- Single-line timing symbols (Fig. 8-14A).
- Bus timing symbols (Fig. 8-14B).
- Signal interaction symbols (Fig. 8-14C).

In the illustrations, each displayed waveform is a plot of signal amplitude versus time, the passage of time being represented from left to right. In Fig. 8-14A, for example, the low-to-high transition BC of the signal line (known as a "positive edge" because of its slope when drawn) precedes the high-to-low transition, KL (a "negative edge"), in time. The time axis does not normally maintain a constant scale since the clear pictorial presentation of timing information is usually of paramount importance. Therefore, the rise and fall times for single lines (BC, DE and HI, KL in Fig. 8-14A) and the changing time of bus lines (BC, DE, and FG in Fig. 8-14B) are usually exaggerated in scale to clearly display the change of condition or level on the line or bus. Likewise, any extended period during which a signal line or bus is stable is compressed for manageable display by using the "break-in-time" symbol (J and H in Figs. 8-14A and B, respectively).

Elapsed times are defined on the diagrams (for example, by t_{DE} in Figs. 8-14B and C), while maximum, minimum, and/or typical values, as appropriate, are tabulated in the "AC specifications." If accurate timing specifications are required (for example, in very fast memory systems where a few nanoseconds error can be critical), then the *signal rise and fall times* and the *timing measurement reference levels* become extremely important. This data is normally hidden in small print and minute diagrams somewhere in or around the AC specifications (see "AC Test Conditions" in Fig. 8-10).

The illustration of the interaction of signals, (as in Fig. 8-14C) is on the increase but is by no means universal. This information is extremely important, however, since it establishes for the reader a cause/effect relationship among the many signal lines displayed. Note also that the signal name is normally placed at the left end of its timing diagram.

Capacitive Loading

One of the important points we made in Section 8-2-3 was that the output rise and fall times of TTL and CMOS gates, and therefore their propagation delay times, are dependent on the *load capacitance* that the gate must drive (see Fig. 8-15). Because of this, the timing specifications for device outputs are quoted and guaranteed by manufacturers for capacitive loads up to a nominated worst-case value (C_L). Beyond this, a degradation (lengthening) of the timing specifications can be expected.

The capacitance which a gate output must drive therefore represents its *AC load* (DC current loading is discussed in Section 8-3-2) and clearly a worst-case value can be identified for a particular set of timing specifications. Typically, the propagation delay times for TTL are guaranteed for maximum AC loads of either 15 pF or 50 pF, while for MOS and CMOS the times are often quoted for loads of 50 pF, 100 pF, or 150 pF. Note, for example, that the "test condition" for the 2716 timing specifications (in Fig. 8-10) is a C_L of 100 pF.

The maximum number of inputs which an output can drive before degradation of the timing specifications occurs — that

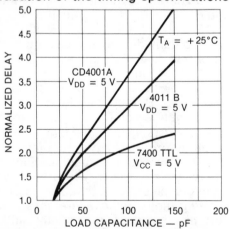

Fig. 8-15. Normalized propagation delay versus load capacitance for TTL and CMOS.

is, the AC fan-out (N_{AC}) of the gate — can now be calculated if you know the input capacitance (C_{IN}) of each driven gate and the effective stray capacitance occurring along the signal path (C_W). Since these capacitances are in parallel and must therefore be added, then:

$$C_L \geqslant \left[\sum_{i=1}^{N_{AC}} (C_{IN})_i + C_W \right] \qquad \text{(Eq. 8-7)}$$

Motorola, for example, quotes a C_L of 130 pF for the M6800 and C_{IN} values of 100 pF for each PIA or ACIA and 15 pF for each MPU, RAM, or ROM input.[6] With an assumed 25–30 pF for C_W then from Equation 8-7, the AC fan-out of the MPU is about 7 to 10 family components. Input capacitance values for TTL, MOS, and CMOS are typically in the range of 1–5 pF, with TTL traditionally having a lower value than MOS and CMOS. Modern MOS and CMOS ICs, however, have input capacitances which are now comparable to the load capacitance-limited TTL packages.

8-4 REFERENCES

1. R.L. Krutz, *Microprocessors and Logic Design.* Wiley, 1980, p. 156.

2. G.E. Williams, *Digital Technology: Principles and Practices.* SRA Inc., 1977, pp. 34, 35, 56; R. Tocci, *Digital Systems: Principles and Applications.* Prentice-Hall International, Inc., London, 1980.

3. J. Millman and C.C. Halkias, *Integrated Electronics: Analog and Digital Circuits and Systems.* McGraw-Hill Kogakusha Ltd., 1972, pp. 228–230.

4. C.A. Holt, *Electronic Circuits: Digital and Analog.* Wiley, 1978, p. 93.

5. P.R. Rony, "Interfacing Fundamentals: Timing Diagram Conventions." *Computer Design,* 1980, *19:1,* p. 152; W.I. Fletcher, *An Engineering Approach to Digital Design.* Prentice-Hall, 1980, p. 451; C.A. Holt, *Electronic Circuits: Digital and Analog.* Wiley, 1978, p. 296.

6. Motorola, Inc., "M6800 Microprocessor Applications Manual." *Microcomputer Applications Engineering,* 1975, pp. 4–19, 20.

Making the Bus System Work

9-1 INTRODUCTION

In this chapter we begin the discussion of the electronic engineering of the microprocessor subsystem. Our approach is to concentrate on the bus structure of this subsystem since it is through the address, data, and control buses that all of the blocks of the subsystem must be successfully interconnected, as illustrated in Fig. 1-3. We will assume that the logical design of the microprocessor subsystem is fully understood, has been successfully completed, and these decisions made:

- Amount and type of memory.
- Number and type of peripheral controllers.
- Required memory and input/output decoding.

We also assume that the appropriate components have been selected to fulfill these logical requirements. The next task in the design process is to ensure, through additional design if necessary, the *electrical compatibility* of all the components interconnected via the system bus. To do this satisfactorily, we need to examine both the DC and the AC conditions on the bus.

9-2 DC CONDITIONS: VOLTAGE AND CURRENT DRIVE

To consider the electrical compatibility of the components, we begin by examining the DC or steady-state characteristics of these components. Fig. 8-9 presented examples of the DC specifications for an NMOS component (the 8085 microprocessor) and a bipolar component (the 74LS373 octal latch), illustrating the current and voltage specifications that typically characterize the components of a microprocessor subsystem:

- V_{IH}, V_{IL}, V_{OH}, V_{OL}.
- I_{IH}, I_{IL}, I_{OH}, I_{OL}.

These parameters were defined in Section 8-3-2 and illustrated in Fig. 8-12. To assist in the DC analysis and to avoid the confusion which we feel is inherent in the use of either the sign of a current or the terms "sourcing" and "sinking," we use current *magnitudes* exclusively. We show direction of current flow *on the bus,* when necessary, by identifying the bus driver, its load, and the voltage level on the bus line.

9-2-1 DC Voltage Requirements

The requirements that ensure the DC voltage compatibility of a bus driver and its load are illustrated in Fig. 9-1 and can be expressed in the following way. For whichever device is driving the bus:

1. Its minimum guaranteed output voltage for a high (V_{OH} [MIN]) must exceed the minimum guaranteed input voltage which will be recognized as a high (V_{IH}[MIN]) by each load device, i.e.,

$$V_{OH}(MIN) > V_{IH}(MIN) \qquad \text{(Eq. 9-1)}$$

2. Its maximum guaranteed output voltage for a low (V_{OL} [MAX]) must be less than the maximum guaranteed input

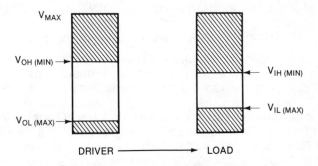

Fig. 9-1. Requirements for DC voltage compatability of a bus driver and its load.

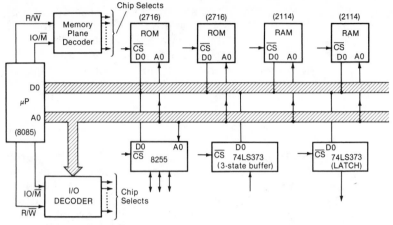

Fig. 9-2. A small microprocessor subsystem.

voltage which will be recognized as a low (V_{IL}[MAX]) by each load device, i.e.,

$$V_{OL}(MAX) < V_{IL}(MAX) \qquad \text{(Eq. 9-2)}$$

To see how these requirements are applied, consider Fig. 9-2, which shows a microprocessor subsystem in block diagram form. For simplicity, only the data and address bus lines, D0 and A0, are shown. To check the electrical compatibility of all the elements in a subsystem such as this, the designer must:

- Tabulate the DC characteristics of each element, as in Table 9-1.
- Identify, for the data, address, and control buses, each possible bus driver and its load.
- Ensure that the requirements of Equations 9-1 and 9-2 are satisfied by checking the worst-case DC output voltages of the driver for both a high (V_{OH}[MIN]) and low (V_{OL}[MAX]) against the corresponding worst-case input voltages (V_{IH}[MIN] and V_{IL}[MAX] respectively) of its load.

For a microprocessor subsystem such as that of Fig. 9-2, the address bus lines of the microprocessor represent the simplest case to examine since these lines act as bus driver on all occasions. The shaded portion of the DC voltage specifications on Table 9-1 shows that the 8085's V_{OH}(MIN) of 2.4 volts does, in fact, exceed the V_{IH}(MIN) of the 2716 EPROM, 2114 RAM, 8255 PPI, and 8251 USART which, together, represent the load for the 8085's address bus lines. Thus Equation 9-1 is satisfied. A notable exception, however, is the 2708 EPROM whose V_{IH}(MIN) of 3 volts is 0.6 volt higher than the

242

Table 9-1. DC Characteristics for the Fig. 9-2 Subsystem ICs*

	μP	ROMS		RAM	I/O			Buffers		
	8085	2708	2716	2114	8255A	8251A	74LS373	74LS244*	74LS245**	CMOS
$V_{OH}(MIN)$	2.4 V	3.7 V @ 100 μA / 2.4 V @ 1 mA	2.4 V	2.4 V	2.4 V	2.4 V	2.4 V	2.4 V	2.4 V @ 3 mA / 2.0 V @ 15 mA	~ V_DD
$V_{OL}(MAX)$	0.45 V	0.45 V	0.45 V	0.4 V	0.45 V	0.45 V	0.4 V @ 12 mA / 0.5 V @ 24 mA	0.4 @ 12 mA / 0.5 @ 24 mA	0.4 V @ 12 mA / 0.5 V @ 24 mA	~ 0.05 V
$V_{IH}(MIN)$	2.0 V	3.0 V	2.2 V	2.0 V	2.0 V	2.0 V	2.0 V	2.0 V	2.0 V	0.7 V_DD
$V_{IL}(MAX)$	0.8 V	0.65 V	0.8 V	0.8 V	0.8 V	0.8 V	0.8 V	0.8 V	0.8 V	0.3 V_DD
$I_{OH}(MAX)$	400 μA	100 μA/1mA	400 μA	1 mA	400 μA	400 μA	6.5 mA	15 mA	15 mA	1.7 mA
$I_{OL}(MAX)$	2 mA	1.6 mA	2.1 mA	2.1 mA	2.5 mA	2.2 mA	12 mA/24 mA	24 mA	24 mA	1.7 mA
I_{IH}	10 μA	10 μA	10 μA	10 μA	10 μA	10 μA	20 μA	20 μA	20 μA	1 μA
I_{IL}	10 μA	10 μA	10 μA	10 μA	10 μA	10 μA	0.4 mA	0.2 mA	0.2 mA	1 μA
I_{OZH}	10 μA	10 μA	10 μA	10 μA	10 μA	10 μA	20 μA	20 μA	20 μA	
I_{OZL}	10 μA	10 μA	10 μA	10 μA	10 μA	10 μA	20 μA	20 μA	20 μA	

*IC Specifications:
2708 : 1K × 8-bit EPROM
2716 : 2K × 8-bit EPROM
2114 : 1K × 4-bit RAM
8255 : PPI, parallel I/O port
**Schmitt trigger inputs.

8251 : USART serial port
74LS373 : Octal latch with 3-state O/P's
74LS244 : Octal buffer/line driver/line receiver
74LS245 : Octal transceivers with 3-state O/P's

guaranteed worst-case high voltage for the 8085 of 2.4 volt. (The use of pull-up resistors to overcome this problem is discussed later.) Table 9-1 also shows that the 8085's V_{OL}(MAX) of 0.45 volt is less than the V_{IL}(MAX) of its address bus load devices, so that Equation 9-2 is also satisfied.

The data bus must be checked in the same way. The DC voltage characteristics of the components listed in Table 9-1 apply equally to their address, data, and control lines, so only the additional components driven by the 8085's data bus lines, but not by its address bus lines (the 74LS373 for example), need additional checking. Table 9-1 shows that the output voltage levels of the 8085 are indeed adequate to drive the data input lines of the 74LS373 to a high or low.

Remember, too, that the data bus is *bidirectional* and that each of the EPROMs, RAMs, and input devices will drive the data bus, for data input to the microprocessor. Therefore, the *output voltage specifications* of these devices must also be checked against the input voltage specifications of the 8085 which, in this case, becomes the load. The nonshaded portions of Table 9-1 show that, as data bus drivers, each of the RAMs, ROMs, and I/O devices is voltage compatible with the 8085 as load.

Pull-Up Resistors

The DC voltage compatibility of virtually all of the components discussed so far is typical of microcomputer systems in general. This is due to the "TTL compatibility" of most MOS integrated circuits, whereby the DC voltage specifications of such devices are guaranteed to be compatible with standard TTL devices. What can be done, however, when DC voltage levels are incompatible as, for example, with the 8085 and 2708?

The problem is overcome by connecting a "pull-up" resistor between the output of the driving device and the +5-V microcomputer power supply rail (V_{CC}), as illustrated in Fig. 9-3. The effect of these resistors is to "pull-up" a high voltage to a value which is approximately equal to V_{CC} and which is, in any case, greater than the V_{IH}(MIN) of the problem-causing load device. The position of the resistors on the bus is unimportant and is usually selected on the basis of convenience during printed circuit board layout. Resistor values of 2–10 kΩ are typically used, the larger resistor values reducing the current loading (see Section 9-2-2) on the driver but also reducing its V_{OH} at a high.

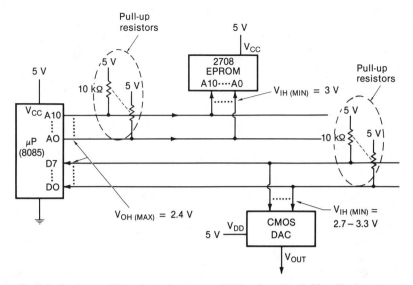

Fig. 9-3. Overcome DC voltage incompatabilities in a 5-volt (V_{CC}, V_{DD}) system using pull-up resistors.

CMOS ICs and Voltage Buffering

A similar incompatibility of DC voltage levels arises when a CMOS IC, such as a CMOS digital-to-analog or analog-to-digital converter, is connected to the bus lines of the microprocessor subsystem. Since CMOS ICs can operate with a power supply voltage, V_{DD}, of 3–18 V, a simple pull-up resistor may not always solve a high-level voltage incompatibility. Rather, special voltage level buffering, as illustrated in Fig. 9-4, may need to be employed. Two distinct situations can be identified: $V_{DD} = 5$ V, and $V_{DD} > 5$ V.

1. First, the situation where $V_{DD} = 5$ V. In Table 9-2, we have summarized the application of Equations 9-1 and 9-2 to the situations where CMOS acts either as a bus driver or as a bus load for a TTL-compatible IC such as an 8085 microprocessor. This table shows that CMOS and TTL are voltage-compatible *except* when CMOS is acting as the load and the bus line is high (see the shaded box in Table 9-2). In this case, illustrated in Fig. 9-3, V_{OH}(MIN) of a TTL-compatible driver (the 8085) does not exceed the V_{IH}(MIN) of the CMOS load so that the TTL driver's high voltage will not be recognized by the CMOS IC. The problem is simply solved, as for the 2708 discussed earlier, by using pull-up resistors to increase the V_{OH} of the TTL-driven bus line.

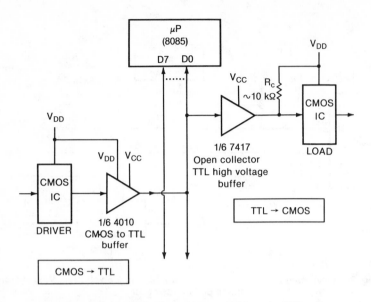

Fig. 9-4. Voltage level buffering is needed to solve DC voltage incompatabilities when V$_{DD}$ exceeds 5 volts.

2. When V$_{DD}$ exceeds the nominal 5 V V$_{CC}$ value for TTL ICs, problems occur whether the CMOS IC is acting as bus driver or bus load. Consider first that *the CMOS IC is acting as the load* for a TTL-driven bus, as in Fig. 9-4. The high-level voltage incompatibility described for the case when V$_{DD}$ = 5 V is now accentuated since the V$_{IH}$(MIN) of the CMOS IC may exceed 5 V. So, using pull-up resistors to pull the TTL-driven bus lines up to ~5 V for a high will not solve the problem. An open-collector TTL gate, whose structure is illustrated in Fig. 9-5, must be used to provide the required voltage level translation of the microprocessor's V$_{OH}$(MIN) of 2.4 V (Table 9-2) to a value which exceeds the V$_{IH}$(MIN) of 0.7 V$_{DD}$ for CMOS. In an open-collector TTL buffer, the active pull-up transistor of standard TTL (see Fig. 8-4) has been omitted so that an external resistor (R$_C$) must be provided. The effect of this pull-up like resistor is

Table 9-2. DC Analysis of a CMOS/TTL Interface

	Bus Voltage Level Condition			
Bus Driver	V$_{OH}$(MIN) > V$_{IH}$(MIN) (Eq. 9-1)		V$_{OL}$(MAX) < V$_{IL}$(MAX) (Eq. 9-2)		Bus Load
CMOS	~ V$_{DD}$	2.0 V	~ 0.05 V	0.8 V	TTL
TTL	2.4 V	0.7 V$_{DD}$	0.45 V	~ 0.3 V$_{DD}$	CMOS

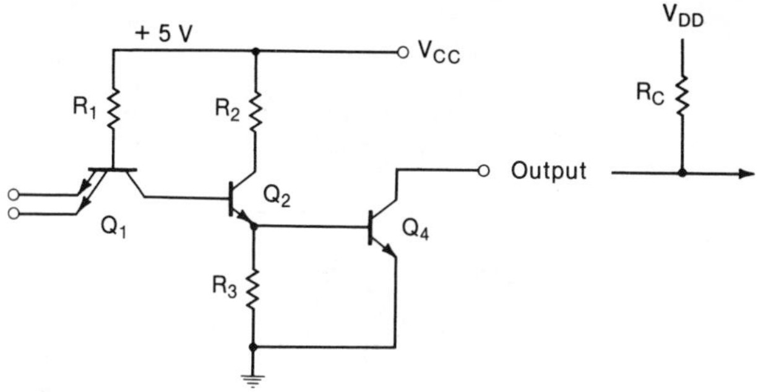

$$R_{c(MIN)} > \frac{V_{CC} - V_{OL}}{I_C} = \frac{V_{CC} - V_{OL}}{I_{OL} - I_{IL}} \quad ; \quad R_{c(MAX)} < \frac{V_{CC} - V_{OH}}{I_{CEX} + I_{IH}}$$

(I_{CEX} = open collector OFF
leakage current)

Fig. 9-5. An open collector TTL gate can be used as a TTL-to-CMOS buffer.

to allow V_{OH} to rise to V_{DD}. Using the equations in Fig. 9-5, the value of R_C must exceed a minimum $R_C(MIN)$, to ensure an adequate low voltage level and optimize the propagation delay time of the buffer at the expense of increased power consumption, and be less than a maximum, $R_C(MAX)$, to ensure an adequate high voltage level and minimize power consumption, but increase the propagation delay time:

$$R_C(MIN) < R_C < R_C(MAX) \qquad \text{(Eq. 9-3)}$$

If *the CMOS IC is acting as bus driver* (Fig. 9-4), the $V_{OH}(MIN)$ of the CMOS IC driver is $\sim V_{DD}$, and this may destroy the input stage of the microprocessor. Hence, for a CMOS IC to safely drive the microprocessor when V_{DD} exceeds V_{CC}, a CMOS-to-TTL buffer must be used to translate the CMOS ICs $V_{OH}(MIN)$ of V_{DD} to a value less than V_{CC} but exceeding the $V_{IH}(MIN)$ of the TTL-compatible microprocessor of 2 V (see Table 9-2). A 4010 hex, noninverting buffer from Fairchild Inc., whose circuit diagram is shown in Fig. 9-6, will accomplish this task.

9-2-2 DC Current Requirements

Equations 9-1 and 9-2 define the criteria for ensuring the DC voltage compatibility of a bus driver and its load. An analogous set of equations defines the criteria for ensuring the DC *current* compatibility of a bus driver and its load:

$$I_{OH}(MAX) \geqslant \sum_{i=1}^{N} [I_{IH}(MAX)]_i \qquad \text{(Eq. 9-4)}$$

$$I_{OL}(MAX) \geqslant \sum_{i=1}^{N} [I_{IL}(MAX)]_i \qquad \text{(Eq. 9-5)}$$

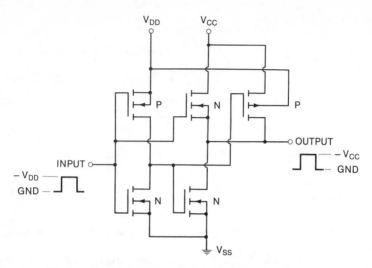

Fig. 9-6. Circuit schematic for the 4010 hex, noninverting CMOS-to-TTL buffer.

where N = number of active devices. That is, the maximum guaranteed output drive current capability of the driver, when asserting the bus high (I_{OH}[MAX]) or low (I_{OL}[MAX]), must exceed the current demand of the load under either of these conditions. If either of the DC current requirements is not satisfied, the output voltage of the driver for a high may drop below V_{OH}(MIN), while the output voltage for a low may exceed V_{OL}(MAX). The resulting high-level and low-level voltages may not then be recognized by the load devices as high and lows respectively.

Fig. 9-7 illustrates the application of Equation 9-4 to the address bus lines of a small microprocessor subsystem. The microprocessor is the bus driver in this example and it has an I_{OH}(MAX) of 400 μA (see Table 9-1). From Table 9-1, I_{IH}(MAX) is 10 μA for MOS devices such as the RAM and ROM and 20 μA for LS TTL devices such as decoders and latches. So a maximum of forty MOS devices or twenty LS TTL devices could be driven by the microprocessor to a high. These figures, however, represent the two extremes since the load on the address bus usually consists of a mixture of MOS and LS TTL devices. Therefore, *between* twenty and forty IC inputs could be driven by each address bus line. If this number is inadequate, then the DC current drive capability of the address bus must be improved by using a current buffer, or *line driver,* such as the 74LS244 (see Table 9-1) whose I_{OH}(MAX) is 15 mA. With this IC, the worst-case drive capability of the address bus lines can be increased by a factor of at least 30. For the 8085, where the low-order eight bits of the address bus are multiplexed onto the data bus, an octal latch, such as the 74LS373, must be used to latch the low address byte, A7-A0. This latch also acts as a line driver and increases the current drive capability of the A7-A0 lines by a factor of at least 10 (see Table 9-1).

The data bus presents a slightly more complex situation because of its bidirectional nature. Assuming for the moment that three-state devices neither drive nor load the data bus, then Equations 9-4 and 9-5 must again be satisfied. Remember that all microcomputer input devices (ROMs, RAMs, PPI, etc,) also must be considered as bus drivers. The two main cases are shown in Fig. 9-8. Fig. 9-8A illustrates the case for the data bus analogous to that described above for the address bus where the microprocessor is bus driver. Since the current drive capability of the microprocessors' address and data bus lines is the same, this case requires no additional consideration. It is worth noting, however, that the current loading on the microprocessors' data bus lines is considerably less than that on its address bus lines due to the large number of load devices which have their data input lines three-stated.

Fig. 9-8B illustrates the situation in which an input device is acting as data bus driver. It can be seen from Table 9-1 that the output drive capability of typical ROMs, RAMs, and input devices is as good as, if not better than, that of the 8085 microprocessor. Hence, the conclusions drawn above con-

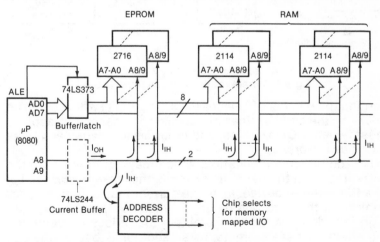

Fig. 9-7. Illustration of the drive current capability/load current demand on the *address bus* when it is asserted high.

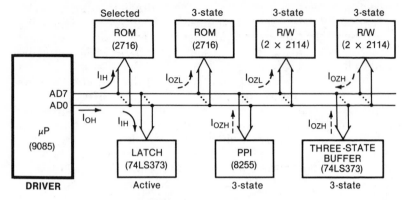

(A) 8085 acts as a bus driver.

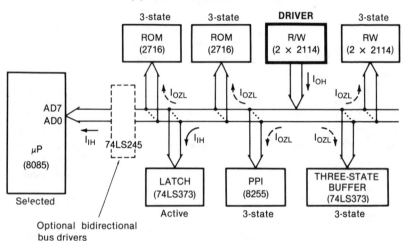

(B) An input device acts as a bus driver.

Fig. 9-8. Current requirements on the data bus.

cerning the number of devices (MOS or LS TTL) which could be driven by the address lines of the microprocessor also apply to most typical ROMs, RAMs, and input devices when acting as data bus drivers.

An additional complication, which may act to increase the current load on the data bus driver, is the *leakage current,* I_{OZ}, of a three-stated device. I_{OZ} is the current that is sourced to or sunk from the data bus by an IC whose outputs are in their high impedance state. The problem that arises in predicting the effect of these currents, as an additional load on the bus driver, is that the *direction* of flow of leakage current (to or from the three-stated device) depends on the voltage levels that *would* appear if the outputs were *not* three-stated. On average, approximately half of the three-stated outputs will drive the bus while the other half will load the bus resulting in a net zero additional current loading on the bus driver IC. (See Fig. 9-8A.) However, in the worst case (Fig. 9-8B), *every* three-stated device acts as a current load on the bus and Equations 9-4 and 9-5 must be rewritten as:

$$I_{OH}(MAX) \geqslant \sum_{i=1}^{N} [I_{IH}(MAX)]_i + N' \cdot I_{OZL} \qquad \text{(Eq. 9-6)}$$

$$I_{OL}(MAX) \geqslant \sum_{i=1}^{N} [I_{IL}(MAX)]_i + N' \cdot I_{OZH} \qquad \text{(Eq. 9-7)}$$

where N' is number of three-stated input devices. To provide for the unpredictable nature of this leakage current effect, *bidirectional bus drivers* are usually used, as shown in Fig. 9-8B. These bus drivers also allow for the increase in the number of devices on the data bus and provide isolation for the microprocessor from the rest of the microcomputer system. A package such as the 74LS245 (Table 9-1) increases the drive capability of the microprocessor's data bus by about a factor of 10.

To avoid having to current buffer each input device connected to the data bus, subsystem elements are normally grouped in clusters of up to twenty on a single printed circuit card or module, which is then connected to further modules via a backplane or flat cable. The data, address, and control buses of each module are then buffered where they enter or exit a module as illustrated in Fig. 9-9.

9-3 AC CONDITIONS AND BUS TIMING

Ensuring the DC voltage and current compatibility of all the components that are interconnected through the microcomputer's bus system under *static,* or DC, conditions was shown in the previous section to be a straightforward, if nontrivial, task. Ensuring that the same components will respond satisfactorily to each other under *dynamic,* or AC, conditions, when the microprocessor is running at full speed, is a much more difficult and less straightforward task. It requires detailed study of the relationship, with time, of the various address, data, and control signals—a topic described generally as *bus timing.* The data required for this study is provided by manufacturers in tabular form as "AC characteristics" or "AC

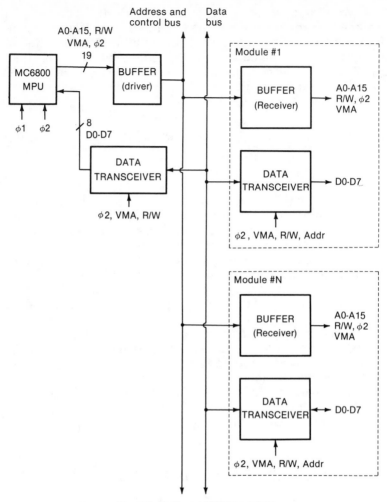

Fig. 9-9. Buffered M6800 system.

specifications" and graphically as "timing diagrams" or "AC waveforms."

Bus timing considerations are important in the electronic engineering of a microcomputer system to ensure that data can be transferred reliably between a microprocessor and its memory and I/O peripheral controllers without loss or corruption. A peripheral controller that is too slow, for example, will not be able to provide or accept data within the timing constraints of the microprocessor. An improperly timed enabling of an input device (a memory, for example) can result in the microprocessor and the input device simultaneously attempting to drive the data bus (*bus contention*) with consequent data corruption and possible IC damage.

The design-analysis-redesign cycle which is necessary to ensure the AC compatibility of the microcomputer's components is a tedious, iterative process which can leave even experienced digital system designers confused and frustrated (Fig. 9-10). The reasons for this become clear very quickly when a timing cycle is attempted. The most common problems include:

- Each IC is treated by the manufacturer as an independent device and is given a separate set of timing specifications. Figs. 9-11A and B show the timing specifications Intel provides for its 8085 microprocessor. To successfully interface the 2114, 1K × 4-bit RAM whose timing specifications are shown in Figs. 9-12A and B involves comparing the timing data presented in Figs. 9-11 and 9-12 while taking into account the AC characteristics of the interface ICs! The task, therefore, is very difficult because of its magnitude and because there are very few timing specifications which are obviously common.

- The timing diagrams which are provided are complete and thorough and give no indication of the likely importance of any of the timing parameters (Fig. 9-11A).

Fig. 9-10. Bus timing can be very confusing!

- A drawing standard for timing diagrams is only slowly emerging, so that even diagrams from the same manufacturer look different according to *when* they were drawn (cf. Figs. 8-10, 9-11A, and 9-12A); and different manufacturers select different styles (cf. Figs. 9-11A and 9-13).

Because of these difficulties, most designers of standard, uncomplicated microcomputer systems use memories and peripheral ICs provided by the microprocessor manufacturer. The assumption (and hope!) is that a particular "family" of microcomputer ICs, such as Intel's MCS85 family or Motorola's 6800 family (Fig. 9-14), will be AC compatible. Problems generally occur when components from different manufacturers are mixed, when timing constraints are extremely tight, or, less commonly, when high speed ($\sim$ 10 MHz) systems are to be designed for which "standard" components are too slow.[1]

Our aim in this Section (9-3) is to provide a generalized approach to bus timing analysis which can be used to check that the ICs of the microprocessor subsystem will work together satisfactorily when the microprocessor is running at full speed.

9-3-1 Microprocessor Read and Write Timing Requirements

The first step in any systematic AC design/analysis procedure is to carefully study the read and write timing requirements of the microprocessor's bus signals, since the microprocessor is usually chosen first and is the bus controller in most microcomputer system applications. Such a study will:

1. *Simplify the timing diagrams* if necessary, since, at first sight, the read and write timing diagrams for a microprocessor can appear to be very complex. With complex timing diagrams, redrawing the diagrams in simplified form, showing only the major timing specifications, can be very useful as a learning and clarification exercise.

2. *Identify the sequence* in which the processor's bus signals are asserted. This provides a feel for the operational requirements of the microprocessor during its read and write cycles. The sequence can be determined by studying the microprocessor's operating description, which is usually found in the user's manual. A useful aid illustrating the sequence information in complex timing diagrams is the *signal-flow diagram* which shows, in flow

chart form, the sequence in which the signals are asserted, together with the critical times.

3. *Identify the critical times* associated with the microprocessor's read and write cycles. These times are usually easily identified as a result of the sequence study. For a read cycle, the critical time(s) is the *system access time* (t_{sac}), which is the maximum time that the system has to drive the data bus with stable data after the address and/or read control lines have stabilized. For a write cycle, the critical times include the *data set-up* and *data-hold times,* which are usually defined with respect to the trailing edge of the write control signal, and the *write control signal width*.

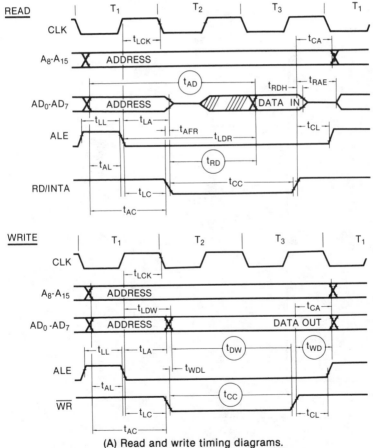

(A) Read and write timing diagrams.

Fig. 9-11. Timing data for the Intel 8085 microprocessor.

AC CHARACTERISTICS

$T_A = 0°C$ to $70°C$; $V_{CC} = 5V \pm 5\%$; $V_{SS} = 0V$

Symbol	Parameter	8085A [2]		8085A-2 [2] (Preliminary)		Units
		Min.	Max.	Min.	Max.	
t_{CYC}	CLK Cycle Period	320	2000	200	2000	ns
t_1	CLK Low Time (Standard CLK Loading)	80		40		ns
t_2	CLK High Time (Standard CLK Loading)	120		70		ns
t_r, t_f	CLK Rise and Fall Time		30		30	ns
t_{XKR}	X_1 Rising to CLK Rising	30	120	30	100	ns
t_{XKF}	X_1 Rising to CLK Falling	30	150	30	110	ns
t_{AC}	A_{8-15} Valid to Leading Edge of Control[1]	270		115		ns
t_{ACL}	A_{0-7} Valid to Leading Edge of Control	240		115		ns
t_{AD}	A_{0-15} Valid to Valid Data In		575		350	ns
t_{AFR}	Address Float After Leading Edge of READ (INTA)		0		0	ns
t_{AL}	A_{8-15} Valid Before Trailing Edge of ALE[1]	115		50		ns
t_{ALL}	A_{0-7} Valid Before Trailing Edge of ALE	90		50		ns
t_{ARY}	READY Valid from Address Valid		220		100	ns
t_{CA}	Address (A_{8-15}) Valid After Control	120		60		ns
t_{CC}	Width of Control Low (RD, WR, INTA) Edge of ALE	400		230		ns
t_{CL}	Trailing Edge of Control to Leading Edge of ALE	50		25		ns
t_{DW}	Data Valid to Trailing Edge of WRITE	420		230		ns
t_{HABE}	HLDA to Bus Enable		210		150	ns
t_{HABF}	Bus Float After HLDA		210		150	ns

(B) Tabulated data.

Fig. 9-11 — cont. Timing data for

Symbol	Parameter	8085A Min	8085A Max	8085A-2 Min	8085A-2 Max	Units
t_{HACK}	HLDA Valid to Trailing Edge of CLK		110		40	ns
t_{HDH}	HOLD Hold Time	0		0		ns
t_{HDS}	HOLD Setup Time to Trailing Edge of CLK	170		120		ns
t_{INH}	INTR Hold Time	0		0		ns
t_{INS}	INTR, RST, and TRAP Setup Time to Falling Edge of CLK	160		150		ns
t_{LA}	Address Hold Time After ALE	100		50		ns
t_{LC}	Trailing Edge of ALE to Leading Edge of Control	130		60		ns
t_{LCK}	ALE Low During CLK High	100		50		ns
t_{LDR}	ALE to Valid Data During Read		460		270	ns
t_{LDW}	ALE to Valid Data During Write		200		120	ns
t_{LL}	ALE Width	140		80		ns
t_{LRY}	ALE to READY Stable		110		30	ns
t_{RAE}	Trailing Edge of READ to Re-Enabling of Address	150		90		ns
t_{RD}	READ (or $\overline{INTA}$) to Valid Data		300		150	ns
t_{RV}	Control Trailing Edge to Leading Edge of Next Control	400		220		ns
t_{RDH}	Data Hold Time After READ $\overline{INTA}$[7]	0		0		ns
t_{RYH}	READY Hold Time	0		0		ns
t_{RYS}	READY Setup Time to Leading Edge of CLK	110		100		ns
t_{WD}	Data Valid After Trailing Edge of $\overline{WRITE}$	100		60		ns
t_{WDL}	LEADING Edge of $\overline{WRITE}$ to Data Valid	40		20		ns

Notes:

1. A_8–A_{15} address Specs apply to IO/$\overline{M}$, S_0, and S_1 except A_8–A_{15} are undefined during T_4–T_6 of OF cycle whereas IO/$\overline{M}$, S_0 and S_1 are stable.

2. Test conditions: t_{CYC} = 320 ns (8085A)/200 ns (8085A-2): C_L = 150 pF*

3. For all output timing where C_L = 150 pF use the following correction factors:
25 pF ≤ C_L < 150 pF; −0.10 ns/pF;
150pF < C_L ≤ 300pF: +0.30 ns/pF

4. Output timings are measured with purely capacitive load.

5. All timings are measured at output voltage V_L = 0.8 V. V_H = 2.0 V. and 1.5 V with 20 ns rise and fall time on inputs.

6. To calculate timing specifications at other values of t_{CYC} use Table 7.

7. Data hold time is guaranteed under all loading conditions.

(B) Tabulated data.

the Intel 8085 microprocessor.

As an example of this approach, consider the 8085A read and write timing diagrams shown in Fig. 9-11A. These were prepared using Intel's description of the operation of the 8085 in the MCS-85 User's Manual,[2] the simplified timing diagrams shown in Fig. 9-15, and the signal-flow diagram shown in Fig. 9-16. Note the use of the logic OR symbol in the signal flow diagram to cope with the t_{AD} or t_{RD} specifications for the system access-time. During clock time T_1, the processor establishes the high and low address bytes by asserting A15=A8 with the required high order address byte and AD7-AD0 (the pin-outs on which data and low address are multiplexed) with the required low order address byte. A strobe signal, ALE, is asserted for the first half of T_1 to provide an enable for the external latch that is required to catch and hold

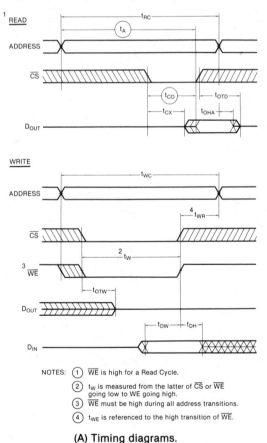

NOTES:
1. $\overline{WE}$ is high for a Read Cycle.
2. t_W is measured from the latter of $\overline{CS}$ or $\overline{WE}$ going low to WE going high.
3. $\overline{WE}$ must be high during all address transitions.
4. t_{WE} is referenced to the high transition of $\overline{WE}$.

(A) Timing diagrams.

Fig. 9-12. Timing specifications for

A7-A0. In time T_2, the appropriate read or write control signal is asserted and either the data bus (AD7-AD0) floated in preparation for a read operation or asserted with data for a write-to-peripheral operation. Time T_3 is where the peripheral read or write occurs and it is in this clock-cycle period that the most important times can be identified. For the 8085A read operation, the "stable-address-to-data-in time", t_{AD}, and "the stable-control-to-data-in time", t_{RD}, define the *system access-times.* For a write operation, the data set-up (t_{DW}) and data-hold (t_{WD}) times are defined with respect to the trailing edge of $\overline{WR}$.

Although the bus architecture of a microprocessor dictates the sequence and role of various control signals, the important

READ CYCLE[1]

SYMBOL	PARAMETER	2114-2		2114-3, 2114L3		2114, 2114L		UNIT
		Min.	Max.	Min.	Max.	Min.	Max.	
t_{RC}	Read Cycle Time	200		300		450		ns
t_A	Access Time		200		300		450	ns
t_{CO}	Chip Selection to Output Valid		70		100		100	ns
t_{CX}	Chip Selection to Output Active	0		0		0		ns
t_{OTD}	Output 3-state from Deselection	0	40	0	80	0	100	ns
t_{OHA}	Output Hold from Address Change	10		10		10		ns

WRITE CYCLE[2]

SYMBOL	PARAMETER	2114-2		2114-3, 2114L3		2114, 2114L		UNIT
		Min.	Max.	Min.	Max.	Min.	Max.	
t_{WC}	Write Cycle Time	200		300		450		ns
t_W	Write Time	100		150		200		ns
t_{WR}	Write Release Time	20		0		0		ns
t_{OTW}	Output 3-state from Write	0	40	0	80	0	100	ns
t_{DW}	Data to Write Time Overlap	100		150		200		ns
t_{DH}	Data Hold from Write Time	0		0		0		ns

NOTES: 1. A Read occurs during the overlap of a low $\overline{CS}$ and a high $\overline{WE}$.

2. A Write occurs during the overlap of a low $\overline{CS}$ and a low $\overline{WE}$.

AC CONDITIONS OF TEST

Input Pulse Levels.............................0.8 V to 2.4 V
Input Rise and Fall Times ....10 ns
Input and Output Timing Levels ....1.5 V
Output Load..................1 TTL Gate and C_L = 50 pF*

AC CHARACTERISTICS T_A = 0°C to 70°C, V_{CC} = 5V ± 5%, unless otherwise noted.

(B) Tabulated data.

the Intel 2114, 1K X 4-bit RAM.

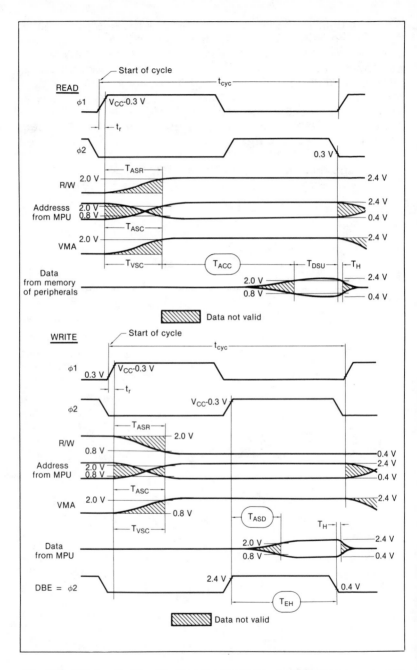

Fig. 9-13. Read and write diagrams for the Motorola M6800 microprocessor.

read and write times generally are common to most microprocessors: the system access-time for a read operation; and the data set-up, data-hold, and control-enable times for a write operation. For the M6800 (Fig. 9-13), whose timing diagrams appear less cluttered, these times are: T_{ACC} (READ); and $T_{ASD} - T_{ED}$, T_H, and T_{ED} (WRITE).

9-3-2 Peripheral Timing Requirements

Having identified the role, sequence, and critical times for the various microprocessors' control signals, we turn now to the timing requirements of the peripheral IC(s). If a system design is in its early stages, the timing diagrams for the peripheral will provide the additional data necessary to design an appropriate interface block (see Section 9-3-3). If the interface block between the microprocessor and a peripheral has already been designed, then a timing analysis (described in Section 9-3-4) may be carried out.

In either case, the timing specifications for the peripheral must be *compared* with those of the microprocessor. This can be done by placing photocopies of the respective timing diagrams side by side. Better still, the photocopies can be cut apart and reorganized so the read and write timing diagrams for the peripheral are placed below those of the microprocessor, as illustrated in Fig. 9-17 for an 8085/2114 read operation. This facilitates the comparison, given that the critical microprocessor times have been identified. Unfortunately, the time scales for the microprocessor and peripheral timing diagrams are not normally the same, so comparisons are difficult. At the other extreme, drawing microprocessor and peripheral timing diagrams to a common scale is difficult and not normally worth the effort. A middle path which we recommend is a neat re-sketching of the peripherals' timing diagrams. Try, by eyeballing, to match the scale of the peripherals' timing diagrams to that of the microprocessor. This process is greatly eased if there is at least one signal line which is common to both timing diagrams. In microprocessor systems, the address bus will normally suffice in this role; in Figs. 9-18 and 9-19, where a re-sketching has been tried, the address bus was used as the reference for rescaling the 2114's read and write timing diagrams.

With the timing diagrams for the microprocessor and peripheral juxtaposed, the comparison process, for either the design of interface logic or a timing analysis, is facilitated.

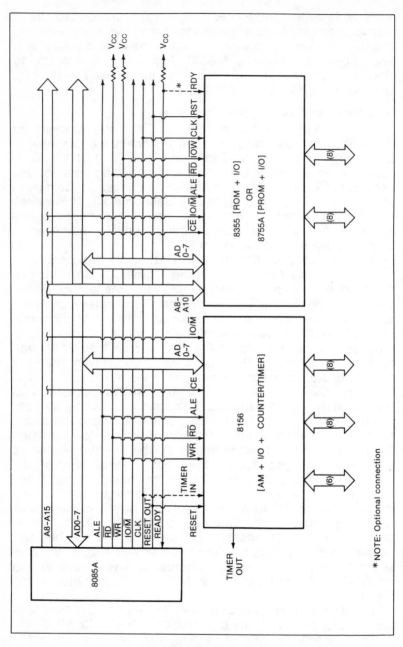

(A) Intel MCS85 family.

Fig. 9-14. Microprocessor

9-3-3 Interface Logic

A comparison of the microprocessor/peripheral timing diagrams can facilitate and provide the necessary understanding for the logical design process. As we will see, the comparison is sometimes critical to the success of a design.[1]

Consider, as an example, Intel's 2114 1K × 4-bit read/write memory, whose timing specifications are juxtaposed to those of the 8085 in Figs. 9-18 and 9-19. For a *read cycle* (Fig. 9-18), the microprocessor, in conjunction with the necessary interface logic, must provide the 2114 with a 10-bit address (A9-A0) and assert its chip-select ($\overline{CS}$) input. The function of $\overline{CS}$ is to

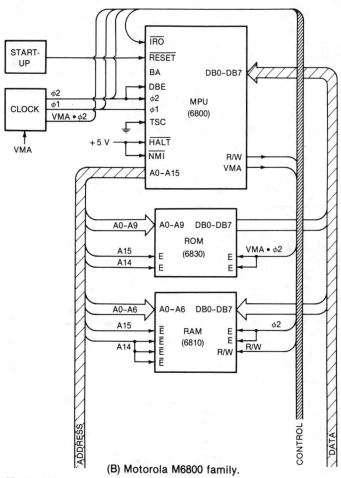

(B) Motorola M6800 family.

"families" of ICs.

enable the internal logic of the 2114 as well as its (three-stated) output buffers. A *write cycle* (Fig. 9-19) also requires that the $\overline{WE}$ input be asserted for a minimum time, t_W, during which the address must remain stable. Data set-up (t_{DW}) and data hold (t_{DH}) times are specified for the 2114 with respect to the trailing edge of the write pulse that must be applied to the $\overline{WE}$ input.

A satisfactory interface block, shown in Fig. 9-20, was generated in the following way. Either one level of *bus buffering* in a medium-sized, single PC board system, or two levels of buffering in a multi-board system, will be needed to provide the necessary current drive for each bus line. Because of the multiplexing of data (D7–D0) and low-order address (A7–A0) onto the same bus lines (AD7–AD0 in Fig. 9-18), the low address byte, A7–A0, must be latched by ALE during clock time T_1. Since ALE is asserted *before* AD7–AD0 stabilizes with the low address byte (Fig. 9-15) and is dropped time t_{LA} before AD7–AD0 is floated, an IC which latches on a negative edge must be used.

The $\overline{CS}$ *input control signal* to the 2114 presents an interesting problem which only becomes obvious from a comparative study of the 8085 and 2114 timing diagrams (Fig. 9-18).

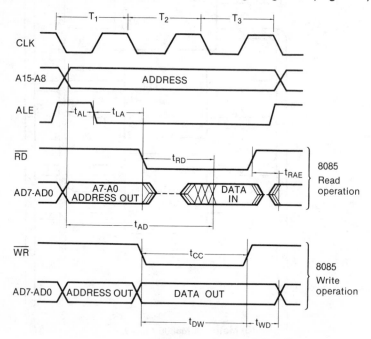

Fig. 9-15. Simplified 8085 read and write timing diagrams.

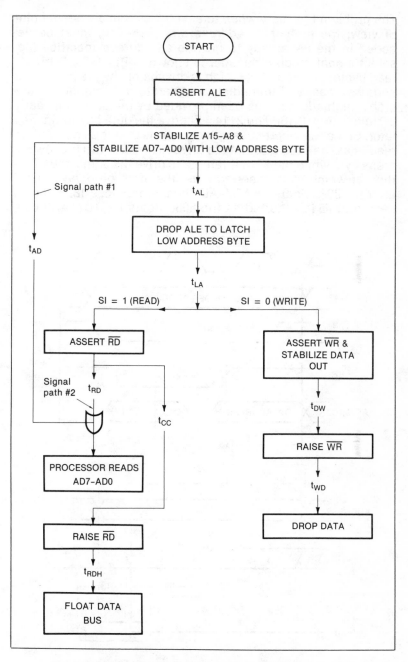

Fig. 9-16. Signal flow diagram for 8085 read and write cycles.

The problem is simply *when* to assert $\overline{\text{CS}}$. From a system point of view, the high-order address bits (A15–A10) must be decoded in the usual way to provide an address-specific chip-select signal. Such a decoder is shown in Fig. 9-20. During a read cycle, this decoder, which is driven only by the high-order address lines, will immediately generate a $\overline{\text{CS}}$ signal when a stable high address has been provided by the 8085, e.g., early in time T_1 (Fig. 9-18). The 2114 will drive the data bus at time t_{CX} later. Since the worst-case value for t_{CX} is 0 ns, bus contention results as the 8085 attempts to drive AD7–AD0 with the low address byte while the 2114 attempts to drive the same lines. The time at which $\overline{\text{CS}}$ is asserted must therefore be *delayed* until after the 8085 floats its AD7–AD0 bus. From Fig. 9-18, it can be seen that $\overline{\text{RD}}$ is asserted as the 8085 floats its AD7–AD0 bus,

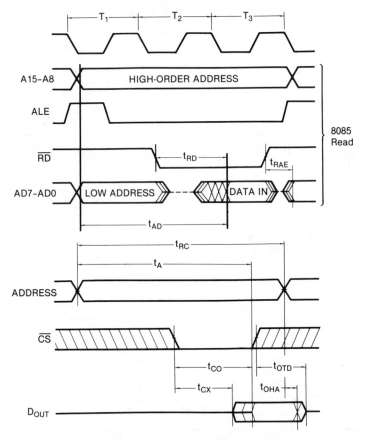

Fig. 9-17. Unscaled comparison of the 8085 and 2114 read timing diagrams.

266

and so $\overline{RD}$ must be gated with the decoder output to adequately delay the CS assertion time.

However, the 2114 must also be enabled during an appropriate write (Fig. 9-19) operation and so $\overline{RD}$ *or* $\overline{WR}$ must be used to enable the decoder. Finally, WE must be driven by the 8085's $\overline{WR}$ control signal, which is asserted during the time that data is stable on the AD7–AD0 bus.

9-3-4 Timing Analysis

After completing a logical design of the interface block between the microprocessor and its peripheral, with the aid of their timing diagrams, a *timing analysis* of the design should be done to determine whether the interface will work when the processor is running at full speed. To this end, the signal paths

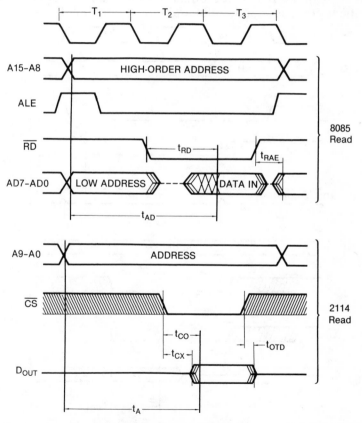

Fig. 9-18. Comparison of the 8085 read timing diagram with a rescaled 2114 read timing diagram.

267

to and from the peripheral must be identified and the critical processor and peripheral timing specifications checked. For a *read operation,* the important signal path (or paths) is defined by the system access time requirement of the microprocessor and is one of the following:

1. The stable-address-to-data-in path.
2. The stable data path.

Path 1 involves a round trip from processor to peripheral (by the address) and from the peripheral back to the microprocessor (by data). For the *write operation,* a one-way signal path from processor to peripheral can be identified as a result of the data set-up and data-hold requirements of the peripheral. The resulting signal path is path 2. After studying each of these paths, the usual next step is to compare the critical processor and peripheral timing specifications.

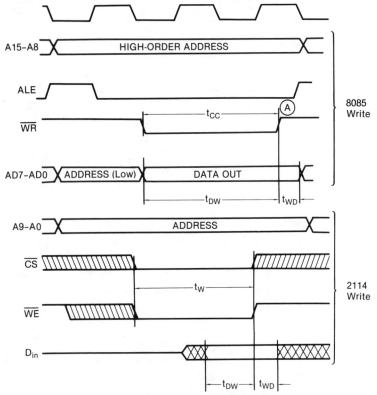

Fig. 9-19. Comparison of the 8085 write timing diagram with a rescaled 2114 write timing diagram.

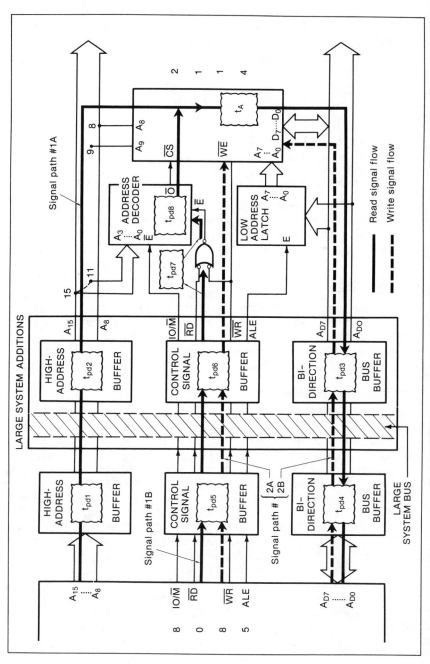

Fig. 9-20. Signal path analysis for the 8085/2114 read and write cycles.

As an example, the signal paths for the 8085/2114 interface are shown in Fig. 9-20. The system access time of the 8085 is specified in terms of the stable-address-to-data-in time (t_{AD}) and the stable-control-to-data-in time (t_{RD}). Therefore two read signal paths must be checked; they are identified as path 1A and path 1B, respectively, in Fig. 9-20. For each of these paths, the following timing inequalities can be seen in Fig. 9-18 (path 1) and Fig. 9-19 (path 2):

- Path 1A: $t_{AD}(8085) > T_A(2114)$ (Eq. 9-8)
- Path 1B: $t_{RD}(8085) > t_{CO}(2114)$; $t_{RAE}(8085) > t_{OTD}(2114)$ (Eq. 9-9)
- Path 2A: $t_{CC}(8085) > t_W(2114)$ (Eq. 9-10)
- Path 2B: $t_{DW}(8085) > t_{DW}(2114)$; $t_{WD}(8085) > t_{DH}(2114)$ (Eq. 9-11)

By checking these inequalities against the AC specification tables in Figs. 9-11B and 9-12B for the 8080 and 2114, respectively, it is possible to identify the signal path(s) that may cause a timing failure. This then becomes the *critical signal path*,[4] for which design modifications will be necessary.

Before considering options that may provide a solution to a timing failure problem, we need to examine several factors which may contribute to a timing failure: logic delay, capacitive loading, logic element threshold variations, and transit time. Each factor has the general effect of delaying the arrival time of the microprocessor's address, data, and control signals at the peripheral. The delays are normally cumulative.

Signal Propagation Delays

The critical assumption in the timing analysis presented above is that no delay accrues as the address, data, and control bus signals pass through the buffers, gates, decoders, etc., on their way to the 2114. In reality, significant delays do occur. These are specified by the manufacturer as "propagation delay times" (see Section 8-2-1) and range from ∿ 5–50 ns for TTL (higher for CMOS) depending on the complexity of the IC. In contemporary microcomputer systems, where the system access time (t_{sac}) of the microprocessor ranges down to ∿ 200–300 ns, IC propagation delay represents the most significant factor to be considered, after the timing specifications of the processor and peripheral, in timing analysis calculations.

This factor is particularly important in analyzing the round-trip signal paths (1A and 1B in Fig. 9-20) associated with a read operation where the delays are cumulative. In general terms, the timing inequality for the read operation and signal paths 1A and 1B can be expressed as[5]:

$$t_{sac} > t_{DA} + \sum_{i=1}^{N} (t_{pd})_i \qquad \text{(Eq. 9-12)}$$

where,

t_{DA} is the device access time, and

$\sum_{i=1}^{N} (t_{pd})_i$ is the sum of the propagation delays for the N devices along the path (1A or 1B) of interest.

So from Fig. 9-21, Equations 9-8 and 9-9 become:

- Path 1A: $t_{AD}(8085) > t_A(2114) + \sum_{i=1}^{4} (t_{pd})_i$ (Eq. 9-13)

- Path 1B: $t_{RD}(8085) > t_{CO}(2114) + \sum_{i=1}^{6} (t_{pd})_i$

  $t_{RAE}(8085) > t_{OTD}(2114) + \sum_{i=1}^{6} (t_{pd})_i$ $\Big\}$ (Eq. 9-14)

For the write operation and signal path 2, the effect of signal propagation delays is minimal as the signals ($\overline{WR}$ and data) travel from the microprocessor toward the peripheral at essentially the same time. The effect is to shift the data set-up and data-hold reference point (point A in Fig. 9-19) by the *difference* in propagation delay times down paths 2A and 2B. This effect is known as *signal skew.* Equation 9-11 therefore becomes:

Path 2: $t_{DW}(8085) + \Delta T > t_{DW}(2114)$

  $t_{WD}(8085) - \Delta T > t_{DH}(2114)$ $\Big\}$ (Eq. 9-15)

where

$$\Delta T = [\Sigma(t_{pd's} \text{ path 2A}) - \Sigma(t_{pd's} \text{ path 2B})].$$

Note that a positive value for ΔT indicates that $\overline{WR}$ is delayed with respect to D7–D0 so that reference edge A in Fig. 9-19 is transposed to the right.

The significance and importance of signal propagation delays as a factor in timing analysis can be readily assessed by noting that $\Sigma(t_{pd})_i$ for paths 1A and 1B is typically in the range of 40–80 ns for TTL ICs, and ΔT for paths 2A and 2B is $\sim$ 10–20 ns. These times can be as much as five times larger for CMOS components! Signal propagation delay is therefore a very significant factor for the read signal paths (path 1) where device and system access times can differ by $\sim$ 100 ns (Eq. 9-11). It is, however, very much a second order effect for the write signal path (path 2 in Fig. 9-20) unless the device and system data set-up and data-hold times are within a few ns of each other.

Capacitive Loading

The importance of capacitive loading in timing analysis calculations stems from the fact that the times quoted in the AC characteristics for an IC are the worst-case times that can be expected when an IC output drives into the nominated load capacitance, C_L (in 8-10, 9-11B, and 9-12B). The *actual times* will vary according to the actual capacitive load (C_{actual}) which the signal output under consideration must drive. A correction time or "error" ($\pm \Delta T$) must be applied to the nominated time to account for a deviation (ΔC_L) of the actual load capacitance from the nominated value. The correction time can be determined from graphical data of the type shown for the 8080 in Fig. 9-21. Or it can be determined algebraically from a nominated correction factor, k, where:

$$\Delta T = k \Delta C \qquad \text{(Eq. 9-16)}$$

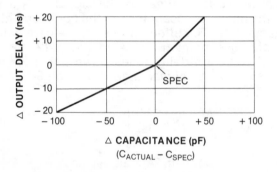

$\triangle$ CAPACITANCE (pF)

($C_{ACTUAL} - C_{SPEC}$)

Fig. 9-21. Variation in 8080 timing specifications with changes in load capacitance from $C_L = C_{SPEC}$.

An example of these correction factors is provided in Fig. 9-11B for the 8085[6] where:

k = − 0.1 ns/pF	25 pF ≤ C_L ≤ 150 pF
k = + 0.3 ns/pF	150 pF ≤ C_L ≤ 300 pF

The value of k for Schottky TTL (from Fig. 9-22) is ∼ 0.05 ns/pF, while for CMOS, k is typically ∼ 0.4–0.8 ns/pF. For gates, decoders, buffers, etc., the actual propagation delays can be read directly from graphs such as that shown in Fig. 9-23.

Clearly then, capacitive loading is another variable which must be considered in timing analysis calculations. For NMOS microprocessors, memories, and peripherals, and for TTL gates, decoders, buffers, and so on, the effect of variations in C_L on the timing specifications is minimal and can usually be

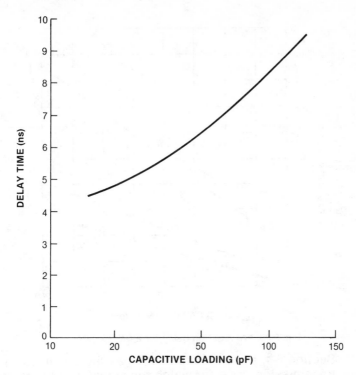

Fig. 9-22. Propagation delay for a Schottky TTL gate.

ignored, except perhaps where the times are particularly tight (i.e., within 10–20 ns). However, for CMOS elements, capacitive load variations may be a first-order effect because of the larger k values for CMOS compared with TTL.

Logic Element Threshold Variations

In Section 8-3-3 we mentioned that it is necessary to consider the signal rise and fall times in situations where timing is tight. The reason is that small timing shifts can develop due to variations in the measurement reference levels of the ICs used in the interface design. These reference levels can vary widely between IC families (1.5 V for TTL, 0.5 V_{DD} for CMOS) and even within a family (1.5 V for TTL, 1.3 V for LS TTL). The effect of such variations can be seen clearly in Fig. 9-24. Because the times involved are ∼nanoseconds, however, this is usually only a second-order effect and can be ignored in most cases.

Transit Time

Signal transit time is the time required for the signal (address, data, or control) to travel down the PC trace. As we will

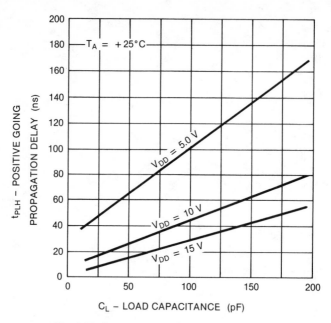

Fig. 9-23. Propagation delay for a CMOS gate.

see in Section 9-4, in some circumstances the bus lines can act as transmission lines, for which the signal travel time per unit length[7] is given by:

$$t_p \approx \sqrt{L(C + C_L)} \qquad \text{(Eq. 9-17)}$$

where,

L is the inductance/unit length,
C is the capacitance/unit ($\sim$ 1.5 pF/in for GIO epoxy),
C_L is the load capacitance.

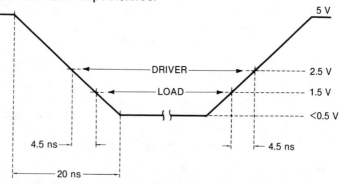

Fig. 9-24. Timing delays can occur when the switching thresholds of the bus driver and load differ.

274

The effect is minor at ~ 2 ns/ft except where the microprocessor/peripheral timing specifications are within a few nanoseconds as with high speed memories, for example.

9-3-5 Timing Incompatibility: The Options

The timing analysis described in the previous section will occasionally uncover a timing incompatibility between the microprocessor and the peripheral/memory. This will occur because of one or more of the following:

- The microprocessor is too "fast" for the interface. This problem is most likely with memory ICs since their access time performance continues to struggle to keep up with the system access times allowed by state-of-the-art microprocessors.
- The peripheral is too "slow" for the microprocessor. This is identical to the previous problem in relative terms, but it is included to cover the situation in which the bus architecture of the peripheral may lead to a serious signal, and therefore timing, incompatibility. This is almost inevitable when microprocessors and peripherals from different manufacturers are mixed. Interfacing Motorola's asynchronous serial communications chip — the M6850 ACIA — to an Intel 8085 is a case in point which one of the authors (PFG) has had the delight to experience.
- Interface delays occur, including propagation delays, capacitive loading, and transit time.

Timing incompatibilities can be rectified by:

1. Reducing the effects of propagation delays, capacitive loading, and transit time.
2. Changing peripherals/memories for faster and/or bus-compatible devices.
3. Slowing down the microprocessor system clock.
4. Using "memory ready" timing techniques.

Option 1 is extreme and is used only in circumstances where the microprocessor/peripheral or memory timing is very tight and where it is necessary to keep the microprocessor running at maximum clock speed. Likewise, option 2 is rather extreme since there may simply be no other peripheral on the market which offers the same system performance capability as the offending IC. This leaves options 3 and 4 as those most commonly employed to rectify a timing incompatibility.

Table 9-3. 8085 Microprocessor Timing Specifications Depend on the Clock Period, T*

		8085A			8085A-2	
READ	t_{AL}	$(1/2)\ T - 45$	MIN	t_{AL}	$(1/2)\ T - 50$	MIN
	t_{LA}	$(1/2)\ T - 60$	MIN	t_{LA}	$(1/2)\ T - 50$	MIN
	t_{LL}	$(1/2)\ T - 20$	MIN	t_{LL}	$(1/2)\ T - 20$	MIN
	t_{LCK}	$(1/2)\ T - 60$	MIN	t_{LCK}	$(1/2)\ T - 50$	MIN
	t_{LC}	$(1/2)\ T - 30$	MIN	t_{LC}	$(1/2)\ T - 40$	MIN
	t_{AD}	$(5/2 + N)\ T - 225$	MAX	t_{AD}	$(5/2 + N)\ T - 150$	MAX
	t_{RD}	$(3/2 + N)\ T - 180$	MAX	t_{RD}	$(3/2 + N)\ T - 150$	MAX
	t_{RAE}	$(1/2)\ T - 10$	MIN	t_{RAE}	$(1/2)\ T - 10$	MIN
	t_{CA}	$(1/2)\ T - 40$	MIN	t_{CA}	$(1/2)\ T - 40$	MIN
WRITE	t_{DW}	$(3/2 + N)\ T - 60$	MIN	t_{DW}	$(3/2 + N)\ T - 70$	MIN
	t_{WD}	$(1/2)\ T - 60$	MIN	t_{WD}	$(1/2)\ T - 40$	MIN
	t_{CC}	$(3/2 + N)\ T - 80$	MIN	t_{CC}	$(3/2 + N)\ T - 70$	MIN
	t_{CL}	$(1/2)\ T - 110$	MIN	t_{CL}	$(1/2)\ T - 75$	MIN
	t_{ARY}	$(3/2)\ T - 260$	MAX	t_{ARY}	$(3/2)\ T - 200$	MAX
	t_{HACK}	$(1/2)\ T - 50$	MIN	t_{HACK}	$(1/2)\ T - 60$	MIN
	t_{HABF}	$(1/2)\ T + 50$	MAX	t_{HABF}	$(1/2)\ T + 50$	MAX
	t_{HABE}	$(1/2)\ T + 50$	MAX	t_{HABE}	$(1/2)\ T + 50$	MAX
	t_{AC}	$(2/2)\ T - 50$	MIN	t_{AC}	$(2/2)\ T - 85$	MIN
	t_{1}	$(1/2)\ T - 80$	MIN	t_{1}	$(1/2)\ T - 60$	MIN
	t_{2}	$(1/2)\ T - 40$	MIN	t_{2}	$(1/2)\ T - 30$	MIN
	t_{RV}	$(3/2)\ T - 80$	MIN	t_{RV}	$(3/2)\ T - 80$	MIN
	t_{LDR}	$(4/2)\ T - 180$	MAX	t_{LDR}	$(4/2)\ T - 130$	MAX

*N is equal to the total WAIT states.

Slowing the Microprocessor System Clock

Although the majority of microprocessors will not run at very low clock frequencies approaching DC, they will operate over a considerable clock frequency range. For the 8085A, for example, this frequency range is from 3.125 MHz down to 500 kHz (320–2000 ns in Fig. 9-11B). Since the bus timing specifications for microprocessors are referenced to the clock, the timing specifications are almost always a function of the clock frequency. This can be seen clearly in Table 9-3 for the 8085, where the critical read and write times (starred) are directly proportional to the clock period (T).

Slowing the microprocessor clock is thus a very simple way of rectifying a timing problem caused by a "fast" microprocessor or a "slow" peripheral. The ways in which the clock frequency can be altered are discussed in Section 10-4. The consequence of slowing down the clock, however, is that the execution time for all instructions is increased because these times are also a function of the clock period. Consequently, the system data throughput may be significantly and critically reduced. This being the case, an alternative solution may need to be found and *memory-ready timing* may provide the answer.[8]

Memory-ready Timing

This technique represents a compromise between slowing down the clock on the one hand and attempting to minimize propagation delays on the other. The approach is to lengthen only those parts of the microprocessor's read and write cycles which involve the critical read and write times. This is done by generating a "memory-ready" signal which is dropped when a read and write request is made by the microprocessor of the peripheral/memory and is reasserted only after a fixed time interval. Fig. 9-25 illustrates how this is usually done. The memory-ready signal is then used to drive appropriate circuitry to lengthen the critical read and write times.

For the 8080 and 8085 microprocessors, read and write cycle stretching is done by dropping their *READY* input lines, which has the effect of forcing the processor into a *wait state,* as in Fig. 9-26A. Fig. 9-26B shows Intel's suggestion for a pulse generator that will insert one wait state. The M6800 microprocessor, on the other hand, illustrates an alternative strategy, wherein the active or asserted high half-cycle of $\phi2$ (where the read and write operations occur; see Fig. 9-13) can be stretched from a minimum of 500 ns to a maximum of 5 μs using a special memory-ready input to the MC6875 clock IC. Fig. 9-27 shows a block diagram of the 6875 (Fig. 9-27A) and the effect on Φ2 of dropping the memory-ready input (Fig. 9-27B).

The advantage of the memory-ready timing technique is that the microprocessor can continue to run at maximum clock frequency except during the time-critical periods during the read and write cycles. The technique contains the worst of both worlds, however, since there is still some reduction in system throughput *and* additional clock hardware is required.

9-4 TRANSMISSION LINE EFFECTS

In Section 9-3-4 we saw that, contrary to what we would hope for, a signal requires a finite time to travel down a bus line. Being aware of this signal delay and making allowance for it when necessary is important in bus timing. The delay is caused by distributed inductance and capacitance on the bus

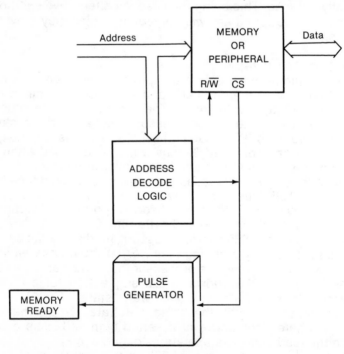

Fig. 9-25. Circuit for generating a "memory-ready" timing pulse for the microprocessor.

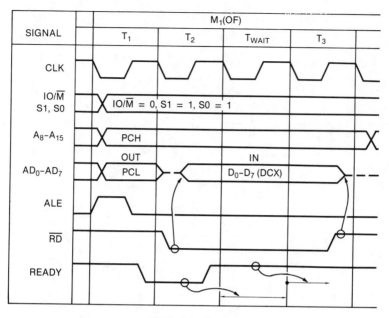

(A) Timing diagram.

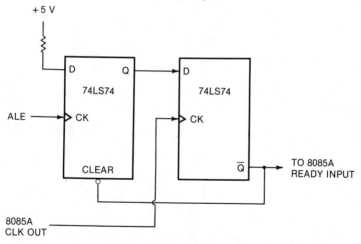

(B) Circuit for inserting the single "wait state" illustrated in (A).

Fig. 9-26. 8085 "wait state" timing.

line which, as a result, is described as a *transmission line* and is modeled as illustrated in Fig. 9-28.[9]

In addition to the signal delay down the bus line, the second and usually more serious effect is the generation of unwanted

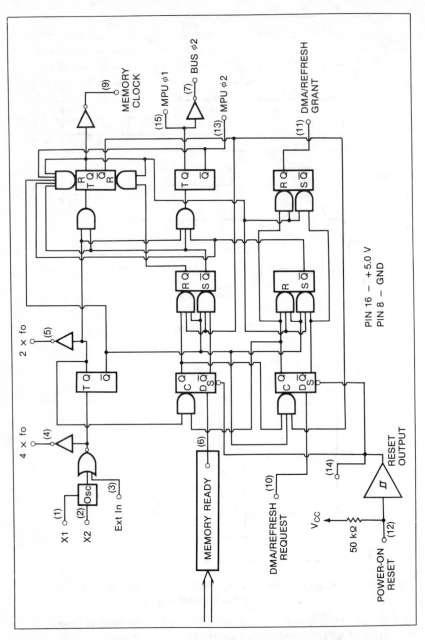

(A) Motorola 6875 clock IC has "memory-ready" input for stretching O_2 of the clock.

Fig. 9-27. Motorola 6875

reflections from both the load and source ends of the line leading to the "ringing effect." This effect is often observed on the leading and trailing edges of the signals and is illustrated in Fig. 9-28. This and the less common rounding of signal edges can delay the effective triggering time of the microprocessor subsystem logic and may lead to false triggering. In this section, we will look at how these reflections arise, determine when problems are likely to occur, and describe common solutions.

9-4-1 Occurrence and Basic Principles

To understand how reflections occur, we need to follow the life of the pulse or signal step as it propagates down the bus line. Transmission line theory shows that, at each instant, the pulse "sees" a characteristic line impedance Z_o which is given by:

$$Z_o = \sqrt{\frac{L}{C}} \qquad \text{(Eq. 9-18)}$$

where L is the inductance per unit length and C is the capacitance per unit length and Z_o has the following properties:

- Z_o is independent of the length of the line and is a pure resistance.
- Z_o has the same value at all points along the line.
- The value of Z_o depends only on the cross-sectional geometry of the line and the nature of the dielectric medium between the conductors.
- Typical values for Z_o are:
  50, 75, or 93 Ω for coaxial cable,
  100–120 Ω for a twisted pair,
  100 Ω for a PCB track with a ground plane on the other side of the board,
  120 Ω for a backplane bus line adjacent to a ground rail.

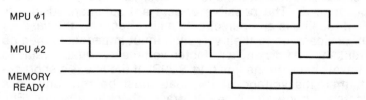

(B) Effect of "memory-ready" on clock signals.
"memory-ready" timing.

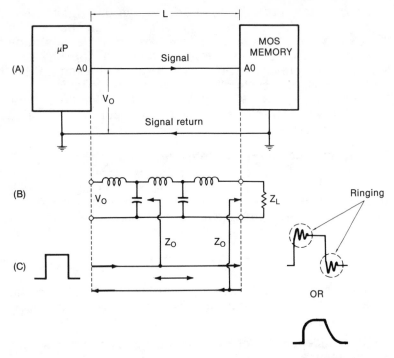

Fig. 9-28. Microprocessor bus lines (A) may behave as transmission lines (B) which, if improperly terminated, can lead to multiple signal reflections and ringing (C).

The signal travels at ~ 0.6 times the velocity of light (C) and for a line of length (L) the transit time (t_D) is:

$$t_D = \frac{L}{0.6C} \qquad \text{(Eq. 9-19)}$$

As the step, V_o, propagates along the line, it charges up the distributed capacitance along the line. What happens when the signal step reaches the load[6] depends entirely on its input impedance Z_L. The possible effects are summarized in Fig. 9-29. If the line is an open circuit, as is effectively the case for MOS devices due to their very high input impedance, then no current should flow and a reflected voltage V_r, equal in value to V_o, travels back up the line (Fig. 9-29B). If the line is a short circuit, then the voltage at the load must be zero and so a reflected voltage step $V_r = -V_o$ travels back up the line (Fig. 9-29E). For load impedances between these extremes (Figs. 9-29C and D), the reflected voltage V_r is given by:

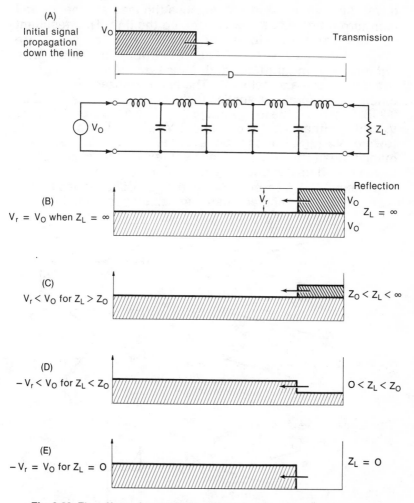

(A)
Initial signal
propagation
down the line

V_o

Transmission

V_o

Z_L

(B)
$V_r = V_o$ when $Z_L = \infty$

Reflection

V_r

V_o

$Z_L = \infty$

V_o

(C)
$V_r < V_o$ for $Z_L > Z_o$

$Z_o < Z_L < \infty$

(D)
$-V_r < V_o$ for $Z_L < Z_o$

$O < Z_L < Z_o$

(E)
$-V_r = V_o$ for $Z_L = O$

$Z_L = O$

Fig. 9-29. The effect of terminating a line in various load resistances.

$$V_r = \left[\frac{Z_L - Z_o}{Z_L + Z_o} \right] V_o = \rho_v V_o \qquad \text{(Eq. 9-20)}$$

where ρ_v is the voltage reflection coefficient.

The longer term effect is illustrated in Fig. 9-30 for the conditions where $V_r = +\frac{1}{2}V_o$ (Fig. 9-30A) and where $V_r = -V_o$ (Fig. 9-30B). Consider first the condition where $\rho_v = +\frac{1}{2}$ (Fig. 9-30A). As illustrated in Fig. 9-29C, at time t_D, the voltage at the load end is $V_o + V_r = \frac{3}{2}V_o$. The reflected step, $\frac{1}{2}V_o$, travels back up the line and is reflected from the (assumed) short circuit at the

283

driver. An inverted step $-V_o$ reaches the load at time $3t_D$ and is in turn reflected as $-\frac{1}{4}V_o$ back up the line. The resultant voltage at the load at time $3t_D$ is therefore $\frac{3}{2}V_o - \frac{1}{2}V_o - \frac{1}{4}V_o = \frac{3}{4}V_o$. The reflections continue with diminishing magnitude and cause the load voltage to oscillate above and below V_o. The line stabilizes after $\sim 10t_D$. Similar considerations applied to the case where $\rho_V = -\frac{1}{2}$ (Fig. 9-29B) show that the load voltage this time rises slowly toward V_o. Thus, either oscillations about V_o ($Z_L > Z_o$) or a slow rise toward V_o ($Z_L < Z_o$) can be expected if $Z_L \neq Z_o$; and the magnitude of the effect depends entirely on the mismatch between the characteristic impedance Z_o of the line and the load impedance Z_L. However, if $Z_L = Z_o$ (i.e., the load impedance is *matched* to the characteristic impedance of the line), no

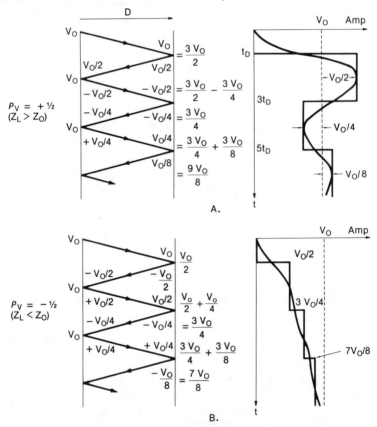

Fig. 9-30. Reflections on an improperly terminated bus line leading to (A) ringing or (B) rounding.

reflections occur, and voltage V_o is established at the load after time t_D.

9-4-2 When Do Problems Occur?

Whether a line is ideal, or whether it acts as a transmission line, depends on the round trip delay time t_d of a pulse out-and-back along the line compared with the rise-time t_r or fall-time t_f of the pulse. If we have a signal whose rise time, t_r, exceeds the round trip delay time ($t_r > t_d$), then the reflection effects illustrated in Fig. 9-30 will be obscured by the inherent rise time of the signal. If, however, t_d is greater than t_r (or t_f), the interconnection will behave as a transmission line and the condition governing the need for considering transmission line effects can be written as:

$$\left.\begin{array}{l} 2t_D > t_r \text{ (or } t_f) \\ \text{i.e., } \dfrac{2L}{0.6C} > t_r \text{ (or } t_f) \end{array}\right\} \qquad \text{(Eq. 9-21)}$$

Substituting for C yields:

$$L \geqslant 9t_r \text{ (or } t_f) \qquad \text{(Eq. 9-22)}$$

where,

L is in centimeters and t_r is in nanoseconds.

The time requirement of Equation 9-21 can also be expressed as a requirement on the length of the transmission line. So, for standard TTL, $t_r = 10$ ns and $t_f = 5$ ns so that, from Equation 9-22, if L exceeds ~ 45 cm then transmission-line effects must be considered. For NMOS and CMOS, whose rise times are longer than those of TTL by at least a factor of 2, the length of the bus lines required before transmission line effects need be considered is ~ 100 cm.

As a result of these length figures, we conclude that transmission line effects are not a problem on the bus of the microprocessor subsystem where track lengths are unlikely to exceed 45 cm. Problems are likely, however, when long lengths of cable, such as flat ribbon, coaxial, and twisted pairs, are being driven. Problems are also likely to occur with the IEEE488 bus system (Hewlett Packard's GPIB®), which can interconnect up to fifteen "smart" instruments over a total distance of 20 m.[10]

9-4-3 Solution: Bus Termination

Although the properties of a transmission line strictly apply only to a line of infinite length, a pulse traveling along a line of finite length can be "fooled" into thinking that the line is infinite, if the line is terminated by a load resistance R_L with the same value as Z_o. If the condition $R_L = Z_o$ is satisfied, then the line is said to be *matched* or "terminated in its characteristic impedance." Under these conditions, the pulse traveling along the line is completely absorbed by the load and no reflection occurs. This is, in fact, the intermediate case between the $Z_L > Z_o$ and $Z_L < Z_o$ cases which are illustrated in Figs. 9-29C and D. This solution to transmission line effects is known as *resistive termination.* An alternative approach the electronics industry is turning to is *diode termination.* We will examine both solutions.

Resistive Termination

Two types of resistive termination are used in the microprocessor subsystem: series and parallel.[11] These are illustrated in Figs. 9-31 and 9-32, respectively. Series termination can be used when the driver is driving a high input impedance load such as MOS ICs. In this case, series resistance R_s is added so that the total resistance, including the output resistance of the driver R_o, is equal to Z_o. The signal which initially propagates down the line is now $V_o/2$ from the usual voltage divider action. The signal is reflected without inversion from the open circuit (see Fig. 9-29B), leaving the output at $\frac{1}{2}V_o + \frac{1}{2}V_o = V_o$. When the reflection reaches the driver end, it sees resistance, $R_s + R_o = Z_o$, to ground through the signal generator and is totally absorbed. No further reflections occur. For TTL, R_o is $\sim 80 \, \Omega$ and experimentally a series resistance of 33 eQ has been found to be satisfactory.[12] The resistor consumes very little power and the dc voltage drop across R_s due to the DC load currents is negligible even for TTL (1 mA across $33 \, \Omega = 33$ mV worst case).

Parallel termination is preferred, particularly when driving a low input impedance load such as TTL, and it has the practical advantage of high rise and fall times. For cables, the load, $R_L = Z_o$, is usually placed directly across the line as in Fig. 9-32A. For TTL and MOS drivers, however, this resistance $\sim 130 \, \Omega$ acts to load down the output which may not then rise

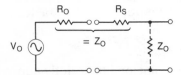

Fig. 9-31. Series termination of a bus line.

above the V_{IH}(min) of the load gate. An $R_L = Z_o$ connected to V_{cc} as in Fig. 9-32B can also provide the correct termination via the power supply to digital common. This approach, however, loads the driver for a low and may destroy the bottom driver transistor because of the ~ 50 mA sink current (5 V, 100 Ω) it

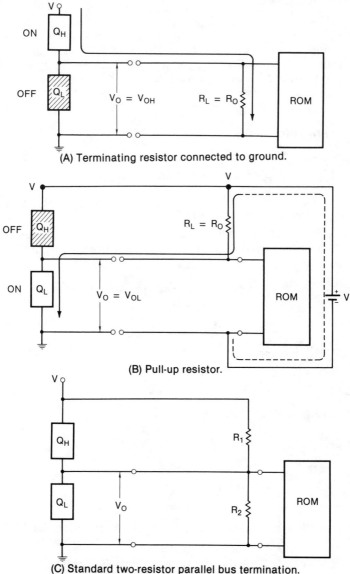

(A) Terminating resistor connected to ground.

(B) Pull-up resistor.

(C) Standard two-resistor parallel bus termination.

Fig. 9-32. Single-resistor parallel bus termination.

would be required to handle. As a result, the two-resistor configuration of Fig. 9-32C is normally used to minimize the current loading on the driver while providing an effective load resistance equal to Z_o.

The resistors are chosen so that:

$$Z_o = \frac{R_1 R_2}{R_1 + R_2} \qquad \text{(Eq. 9-23)}$$

Also the open circuit output voltage V_{oc}, appearing from the voltage dividing action of R_1 and R_2, is made to be greater than the guaranteed input high voltage V_{IH}. That is,

$$V_{oc} = V_{cc}\left[\frac{R_2}{R_1 + R_2}\right] \geq V_{IH} \qquad \text{(Eq. 9-24)}$$

If a parameter K defined by

$$K = V_{oc}/V_{cc} \qquad \text{(Eq. 9-25)}$$

is introduced, then from Equations 9-23 and 9-24,

$$R_1 = Z_o/K \qquad \text{(Eq. 9-26)}$$
$$\text{and } R_2 = Z_o/(1 - K) \qquad \text{(Eq. 9-27)}$$

Therefore, given a value of Z_o for the line, and by selecting a value for K to satisfy Equation 9-24, the values of R_1 and R_2 can be determined, as in Example 9-1.

EXAMPLE 9-1: DETERMINING VALUES FOR R_1 and R_2

Given:
  $Z_o = 120\ \Omega$
  $V_{IH} = 2\ V$
  $V_{cc} = 5\ V$

Assume K = 0.7, so that $V_{oc} = 3.5$ V

Therefore from Equation 9-26:

$$R_1 = \frac{120}{0.7} = 190\ \Omega$$

and from Equation 9-27:

$$R_2 = \frac{120}{0.3} = 400\ \Omega$$

Using preferred values, make $R_1 = 180\ \Omega$ and $R_2 = 390\ \Omega$.

Open collector drivers, such as the Fairchild 96101 quad two-input positive NAND buffer, can be employed to drive a bus

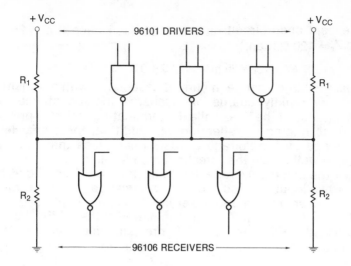

Typical values: $R_1 = 180\ \Omega$
$R_2 = 390\ \Omega$

Fig. 9-33. Open-collector gates used as bus drivers on terminated bus lines.

line (Fig. 9-33). An estimate of their required current sinking capability can be obtained by noting that when the line is *low*, a current I, given by:

$$I = (V_{cc} - V_{OL})/R_1 \qquad \text{(Eq. 9-28)}$$

flows through the driver's output transistor to ground. If, as is shown in Fig. 9-33, both ends of the line are terminated then the total sink current I_s becomes:

$$I_s = 2I = 2\left(\frac{V_{cc} - V_{OL}}{R_1}\right) \qquad \text{(Eq. 9-29)}$$

Thus, for the data given in Example 9-1, and assuming $V_{OL} \sim 0.5\ V$,

$$I_s = 2\left(\frac{5 - 0.5}{180}\right) = 50\ mA \qquad \text{(Eq. 9-30)}$$

Therefore, the 96101 with a guaranteed current sinking capability of 80 mA is an appropriate driver.

The pull-up mechanism following a low-to-high transition on the line involves the rapid interruption of the quiescent low current which, acting across the characteristic impedance Z_o, generates a voltage change:

$$\Delta V = \Delta I Z_o$$

This voltage change, together with V_{OL}, just matches the final

289

quiescent open circuit high voltage V_{oc}. Hence if $\Delta I = 25$ mA and $Z_o = 120\ \Omega$ then,

$$\Delta V + V_{OL} = 25\ \text{mA} \times 120\ \Omega + 0.5 = 3.5\ \text{V} = V_{oc}.$$

Thus, the large change in current associated with a transition can very rapidly charge or discharge the inductance and capacitance of the line, while the terminating resistors prevent spurious ringing or reflections. In addition, the signal level developed by the voltage dividers guarantees that the high state is well above the threshold high level.

For the line receivers, a device such as the Fairchild 96106 quad two-input NOR receiver is recommended because of its higher noise margin and lower input loading than a standard TTL gate. The recommended termination of the IEEE488 bus is illustrated in Fig. 9-34. The higher resistor values are provided so that with up to fifteen parallel terminators,

$$R_L \approx \frac{1}{15}\ (3\ \text{K}/\!/6.2\ \text{K}) \approx 130\ \Omega.$$

A consequence of having a matched line concerns the output characteristics of the pulse generator driving the line,

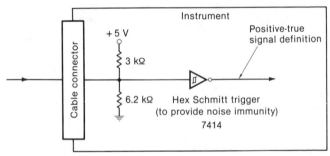

(A) For an output device.

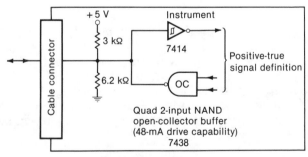

(B) For a bidirectional bus.

Fig. 9-34. Recommended IEEE

which may, for example, be the output from a TTL gate. If the output delivers a pulse of magnitude V_E into an open circuit and has an output impedence R_o, then the voltage V_o of the pulse appearing on a terminated line is given by:

$$V_o = V_E \left(\frac{Z_o}{Z_o + R_o} \right) \qquad \text{(Eq. 9-31)}$$

For example, if the line is a coaxial cable with $Z_o = 50\ \Omega$, and the driver is the output from a standard TTL gate with $V_E = 5\ V$ and $R_o = 80\ \Omega$, then from Equation 9-31, $V_o \approx 1.9\ V$, which is less than the guaranteed input high voltage of 2 V. Consequently, in such a situation, a special line driver with a low output impedance and a high current drive capability is required.

An alternative approach is to increase the value of Z_o. However, for the geometry and dimensions encountered in a typical system it is difficult to increase Z_o above about 150–200 Ω. In any case, a large value for Z_o increases the crosstalk be-

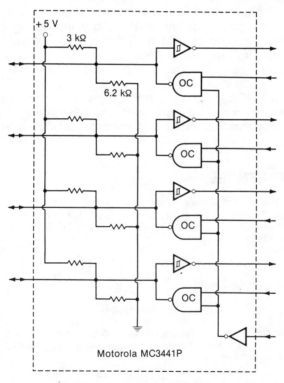

(C) Commercial transceiver.

488 bus termination.

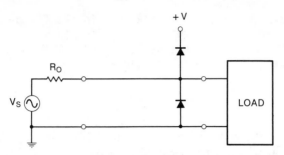

Fig. 9-35. Diode termination.

tween adjacent lines and tends to pick up more noise. Consequently a compromise value for Z_o of about 100 Ω is often adopted, since it can be driven fairly readily with acceptable crosstalk and is easily realized in practice.

Diode Termination

The technique used in this approach is to connect Schottky diodes from the signal line to V_{cc} and from the signal line to ground as illustrated in Fig. 9-35.[13] The effect of the diodes is to "kill" the voltage excursions above + 5 V and below 0 V, which accompany ringing on an unterminated line, without dissipating any more power than on an open line. Fairchild's 10-K series ECL (emitter-coupled logic) includes the F10014 active terminator, a 16-pin dual-in-line package that contains fourteen "bilateral clamps" with the external characteristics of diode pairs.

9-5 REFERENCES

1. L. Levine and W. Myers, "Timing: A Crucial Factor in LSI-MOS Main-Memory Design," *Electronics,* July 1975, pp. 107-111; J. Altnether, "High Speed Memory System Design Using 2147H," *Intel Application Note AP-74,* 1980.

2. Intel Inc., *MCS-85 User's Manual,* 1978, pp. 2-1–2-15.

3. Levine and Myers, 1975.

4. Levine and Myers, 1975; Altnether, 1980.

5. B. McCormick, "Use a General Procedure to Interface your 8085 or 8086 Processor to Memory," *Electronic Engineering Times,* April 2, 1979; also Intel *Article Reprint AR-85,* 1979.

6. Intel *MCS-85 User's Manual,* 1978.

7. Altnether, 1980.

8. Motorola Inc., "M6800 Microprocessor Applications Manual," *Motorola Microcomputer Applications Engineering*, 1975, pp. 4-48–4-54.

9. C.F.G. Delaney, *Electronics for the Physicist*, Penguin Books Ltd., 1969, pp. 188-191; I. Cult, D. Walton, and M. Davidson, *Digital Hardware Design*, The Macmillan Press Ltd., 1979, pp. 4-26.

10. J.B. Peatman, *Microcomputer-Based Design*, McGraw-Hill, 1977, pp. 300-303.

11. Altnether, 1980.

12. E.E. Davidson and R.D. Lane, "Diodes Damp Line Reflections Without Overlooking Logic," *Electronics*, February 19, 1976, pp. 123-127.

13. Davidson and Lane, 1976.

Making the
Microprocessor Work

10-1 INTRODUCTION

The purpose of this chapter is to discuss the analog circuitry required to make the microprocessor work. A common misconception is that all that has to be done is to apply + 5 volts and ground and the microprocessor will burst into life. However, without a reliable clock, a reset circuit, and appropriate power supply decoupling, the microprocessor is doomed to be willing but unable to function.

Hence, the core material in this chapter is devoted to an explanation of the various requirements associated with clock oscillator and reset circuits. Both circuit types invariably employ Schmitt trigger gate inputs to "clean up" slowly rising and falling edges. The following section explains the input characteristics of this special digital signal conditioning IC input.

10-2 SCHMITT TRIGGERS[1]

IC logic families normally require fast transitions between voltage levels to operate satisfactorily. If a signal level is changing slowly and a fast transition or edge is required, the Schmitt trigger is a useful interfacing device. This is because the output of a Schmitt triggered gate makes a rapid transition whenever the input voltage passes through a certain threshold voltage, irrespective of how slowly the input signal level may be changing with time. As a typical example, if the shape of a pulse has been corrupted by transmission over a line with a restricted bandwidth, then the pulse edges can be squared, and its correct voltage levels reestablished, by passing the pulse through a Schmitt trigger.

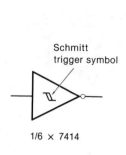

Schmitt trigger symbol

1/6 × 7414

(A) Circuit symbol.

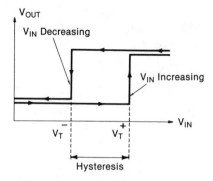

V_{OUT}

V_{IN} Decreasing

V_{IN} Increasing

V_{IN}

V_T^- V_T^+

Hysteresis

(B) Voltage transfer characteristics.

Fig. 10-1. Schmitt trigger input IC.

The circuit symbol and input/output voltage transfer characteristics of a typical Schmitt trigger input IC, the 7414 voltage inverter, are illustrated in Fig. 10-1. The transfer characteristic shows that a positive-going threshold voltage V_T^+ exists, corresponding to V_{IH}, as the input signal increases from below V_T^-. Since the Schmitt trigger input is connected to an inverting gate, the output makes a rapid high/low transition as V_{IN} passes through V_T^+. Similarly, a negative threshold voltage V_T^- exists, corresponding to V_{IL}, as the input signal level decreases from above V_T^+. The region between V_T^+ and V_T^-, in other words $V = V_T^+ - V_T^-$, is referred to as the *hysteresis* of the trigger. Fig. 10-2A shows that the established output state of the trigger is maintained even if the input signal level wanders around within the hysteresis region. This is because the signal must come from below V_T^- to above V_T^+ (or from above V_T^+ to below V_T^-) before an output transition will occur. Fig. 10-2A also shows the pulse-shaping effect of the trigger. As a consequence of its hysteresis, the trigger also exhibits excellent noise immunity and, as Fig. 10-2B illustrates, it is most effective in "cleaning-up" noisy signals.

Typical 7400 series integrated circuits that incorporate Schmitt trigger inputs include: the 74132 quad two-input NAND gate, the 7413 dual four-input NAND and the 7414 hex Schmitt trigger inverter. For these devices, values for V_T^+ and V_T^- lie within the ranges of 1.5–2.0 volts and 0.6–1.1 volts, respectively, with a guaranteed hysteresis range, ΔV, of 0.4 volt. In addition, monostables such as the 74121 employ a Schmitt trigger input which ensures jitter-free response to slowly varying input signals and also reduces the possibility of false triggering from extraneous noise.

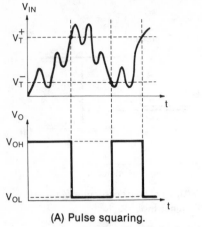

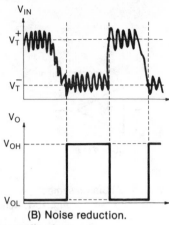

(A) Pulse squaring.   (B) Noise reduction.

Fig. 10-2. Schmitt trigger applications.

Apart from the application to pulse regeneration, another important application of Schmitt triggers is associated with the power-up reset circuit for a microprocessor.

10-3 RESET CIRCUITS[2]

A microprocessor typically incorporates a *reset input* which initializes the system by setting in the program counter a particular address from which the processor begins to execute instructions. This facility is required under several conditions:

- At initial system power-up.
- During microcomputer operation when a manual reset is required.
- Following a transient failure of the power supply.

The reset input operation can be enabled using either a *level-sensitive* signal, as in the Intel 8080 or 8085 series, or an *edge-sensitive* signal, as in the Motorola 6800 series. In the former case, the Schmitt trigger circuit is incorporated on-board the microprocessor chip, while in the latter case, an external Schmitt trigger is normally required.

10-3-1 Level-Sensitive Reset Inputs[3]

A typical circuit for driving a level-sensitive reset input that is asserted low is illustrated in Fig. 10-3. Fig. 10-4 shows a set of typical waveforms for the supply voltage and capacitor voltage and the consequent response of the output from the on-board Schmitt trigger ($\overline{\text{RESET}}$) for the following conditions: power-up, transient supply failure, and manual reset.

Consider first the initial power-up sequence. When the power supply is turned on, a finite time t_1 elapses before the supply voltage exceeds $V_{CC}(MIN)$. This delay is largely due to the time taken to charge the various capacitors within the power supply and distributed around the circuit boards. In addition, some microprocessors that operate from a single positive supply, such as the 8085, employ a substrate bias generator to increase their operating speed. This generator consists of an oscillator and a charge pump that develops a negative bias voltage (V_{ss}) of about -2 volts from the basic positive supply and applies it to the substrate. Hence, a further time delay of about 10 ms is required, while V_{ss} is established, before the microprocessor becomes operational. It is therefore necessary to ensure that, at initial power-up, the reset input ($\overline{RESET\ IN}$) is asserted low and remains in this state until all the correct power supply voltages have been established. Thus, for example, the Schmitt trigger input in Fig. 10-3 must be less than V_T^- when the trigger first becomes active so that the reset state is established, and then remain less than V_T^+ until all the supply voltages have stabilized. Once V_T^+ is exceeded, the reset state is no longer asserted and normal microprocessor operation can commence.

The required voltage sequence on the reset input ($\overline{RESET\ IN}$) is obtained by connecting the resistor and capacitor as in Fig. 10-3. At initial power-up, the capacitor is fully discharged so that $V_x = V_{\overline{RESET\ IN}} = 0$. Subsequently, the capacitor charges via the resistor according to the relationship:

$$V_x = V_{CC}\left[1 - \exp\left(-t/RC\right)\right] \qquad \text{(Eq. 10-1)}$$

To ensure that the reset state is established, it is essential that V_x be still less than V_T^- at time t_1. That is, when the Schmitt trigger becomes operational at time t_1, it must "see" a low

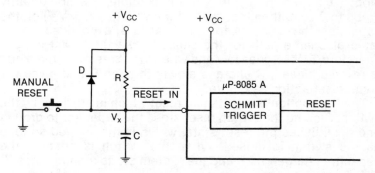

Fig. 10-3. Power-up reset circuit for a level-sensitive asserted-low input.

voltage. This condition is satisfied by making the time constant RC large compared with t_1. More precisely, if $t_1 \ll RC$ then Equation 10-1 simplifies to

$$V_x \approx V_{CC}\left(\frac{t}{RC}\right)$$ (Eq. 10-2)

so that the condition on RC becomes,

$$RC \geqslant t_1 \frac{V_{CC}}{V_T}$$ (Eq. 10-3)

For example, if $V_{CC} = 5$ volts and $V_T^- = 0.5$ volts then RC is $\sim 10t_1$. Since t_1 depends on the total capacitance in the power supply and around the system, and also on the bias generator, it is difficult to closely estimate its value. However, if we assume that it takes two cycles of the AC mains to establish the supply voltages and a further 10 ms for the bias generator (assuming the worst case where the Schmitt trigger does not become active until V_{ss} is established — Intel doesn't say!), then $t_1 \sim 50$ ms. Consequently, if $RC \sim 10t_1$, then values of $R \sim 500$ kΩ and $C \sim 1$ μF give $RC \sim 10t_1 = 0.5$ s. These provide a reasonable starting point. If the reset action is found to be unsatisfactory, then it may be necessary to increase the value of either R or C.

The reset state is maintained, as Fig. 10-4 shows, until V_x exceeds V_T^+ at a time t_2 whereupon the reset is disabled and normal microprocessor operation proceeds. If a typical value of 2 volts is chosen for V_T^+ and $V_{CC} = 5$ volts, then from Equation 10-3, $t_2 \sim 0.5$ RC. If a very large value for RC is employed, the time for which the reset is applied may be unacceptably long.

During a transient power failure, the contents of various microprocessor registers will become corrupted if V_{CC} drops below 4.75 volts, so an automatic reset is necessary to reliably restart the system. This action is achieved by means of the diode (D) shown in Fig. 10-3. If, for example, V_{CC} momentarily drops to 0 volts then, because of the voltage ($V_x \sim V_{CC}$) on the capacitor, the diode is forward biased and provides a very rapid discharge path for the capacitor via the power supply. Therefore, $\overline{RESET\,IN}$ goes low and when V_{CC} is restored, the diode is reverse biased; C charges slowly through R and gives the same reset action as before.

The final option is the manual reset which is provided by the switch. Closing the switch discharges the capacitor to ground and establishes the reset state, which is maintained so long as the switch is closed. When the switch is opened, the capacitor charges via R and the system starts running once V_T^+ is exceeded.

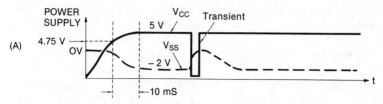

(A) Power supply and substate generator supply.

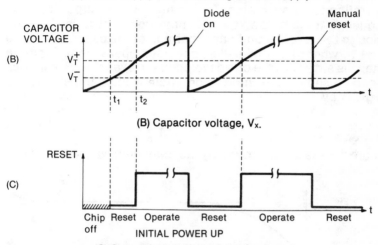

(B) Capacitor voltage, V_x.

(C) Output from internal Schmitt trigger.

Fig. 10-4. Voltage waveforms for the power-up reset circuit of Fig. 10-3.

10-3-2 Edge-Sensitive Reset Inputs[4]

A second group of microprocessors, such as the Motorola 6800 series, employs an edge-triggered reset input which initiates a reset on a rising (or falling) edge. A suitable circuit for implementing this function is shown in Fig. 10-5, where the resistor and capacitor have been interchanged (compared with

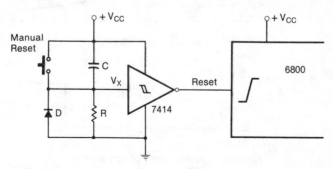

Fig. 10-5. Power-up reset circuit for a positive edge-sensitive reset.

Fig. 10-3) and an external inverting Schmitt trigger added. The waveforms in Fig. 10-6 show that, following initial power-on, the voltage across C is initially zero so that V_x follows V_{CC}. When the Schmitt trigger starts operating at time t_1, it "sees" the large positive voltage $V_{O_x} > V_T^+$ and its output goes low. As the capacitor charges, the voltage V_x falls and becomes less than V_T^- at time t_2. At this time, the output of the trigger goes high, causing the positive-going edge needed for the reset operation to be generated. To ensure that the output from the trigger is initially low, the RC time constant must be long enough to prevent significant charging of the capacitor before time t_1, when the trigger first becomes operational. From an analysis similar to the one developed for level-sensitive inputs, it can be shown that the RC condition needing to be satisfied is given by:

$$RC \geq t_1\left(\frac{V_{CC}}{V_{CC} - V_T^+} \right) \qquad \text{(Eq. 10-4)}$$

where V_{CC} is represented by its minimum value. Hence, if

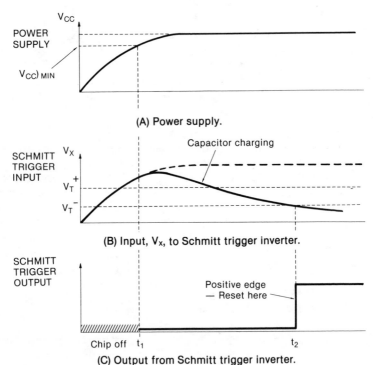

(A) Power supply.

(B) Input, V_x, to Schmitt trigger inverter.

(C) Output from Schmitt trigger inverter.

Fig. 10-6. Voltage waveforms for the power-up reset circuit of Fig. 10-5.

300

$V_{CC} = V_{CC}(MIN) = 4.75$ volts and $V_T^+ = 2.5$ volts, then from Equation 10-4, $RC \sim 2t_1$, where, as before, t_1 is governed by the constraints on the rise time of the power supply. Using the earlier estimate of 50 ms for t_1 leads to a value of RC of ~ 0.1 s, so that initial trial values of $R = 100$ kΩ and $C = 1$ μF would be suitable. In Fig. 10-5, the diode and manual switch perform the same functions as in the earlier level-sensitive circuit of Fig. 10-3.

A negative edge for reset purposes can be obtained by using the RC circuit from Fig. 10-3 in place of that used in Fig. 10-5. Similarly, an asserted high reset input can be generated by using the RC circuit of Fig. 10-5 in place of that shown in Fig. 10-3.

10-4 CLOCK OSCILLATORS

The microprocessor subsystem requires a master clock to make the system operate satisfactorily. The clock signal is produced by a square wave oscillator which may be either a nonlinear square wave oscillator or a linear oscillator followed by a suitable squaring network. For microcomputer applications, the most important class of linear oscillators is crystal stabilized. We therefore defer their discussion until some of the electrical and mechanical properties of crystals have been examined.

10-4-1 RC Nonlinear Oscillators[5]

Nonlinear oscillators usually employ some form of RC charging network and trigger circuit which either discharges the capacitor or charges it in the opposite direction when a certain threshold voltage is reached. The output from the trigger circuit provides the required square-wave clock signal.

Fig. 10-7 shows several circuits for RC nonlinear oscillators employing inverter gates as the active devices. Perhaps the simplest oscillator of this class is the one shown in Fig. 10-8. When this circuit is first turned on, the capacitor (C) is discharged so that V_i is low and V_o goes high. The capacitor then charges via the resistor (R) towards V_o with a time constant $T = RC$. When the capacitor voltage V_C crosses the upper threshold voltage V_T^+ of the Schmitt trigger, V_o goes low and the capacitor discharges via R towards 0 volts. When V_i reaches the lower threshold voltage V_T^-, the output goes high and C again charges. This cycle repeats indefinitely and therefore generates the required square wave clock signal at the output of the Schmitt trigger. For this simple circuit, the clock frequency is not precisely constant and the duty cycle is not

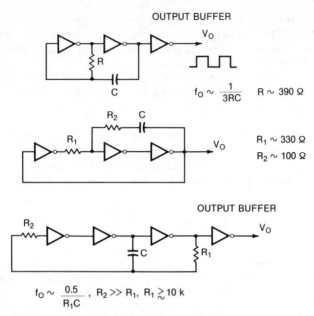

$$f_O \sim \frac{1}{3RC} \qquad R \sim 390\ \Omega$$

$$R_1 \sim 330\ \Omega$$
$$R_2 \sim 100\ \Omega$$

$$f_O \sim \frac{0.5}{R_1 C}\ , \quad R_2 \gg R_1,\ R_1 \gtrsim 10\ k$$

Fig. 10-7. Examples of nonlinear RC clock oscillators.

necessarily 50%. If a symmetric square wave is required, the inverter output can be connected to the clock input of an edge-triggered JK flip-flop wired in its toggle mode. The clock frequency will then be half that of the basic oscillator.

10-4-2 Crystals[6]

Certain crystals, of which quartz is the common example, exhibit a piezoelectric effect whereby mechanical deformation of the crystal generates a proportional potential difference across it. Conversely, if a potential difference is applied across a crystal in the X-direction, as illustrated in Fig. 10-9A, then elastic deformation or strain occurs in the Y-direction. These properties allow a crystal to be used as part of the feedback network for the linear oscillator illustrated in Fig. 10-10. If any small electrical disturbance is amplified and applied to the crystal, a small elastic wave is set up within it. The strain introduced into the crystal generates an increased piezoelectric voltage which is reapplied to the amplifier. Hence the positive feedback existing between the crystal and the amplifier can form the basis for a very useful oscillator.

The elastic waves traveling backwards and forwards through the crystal at a speed v and over a distance ℓ can set

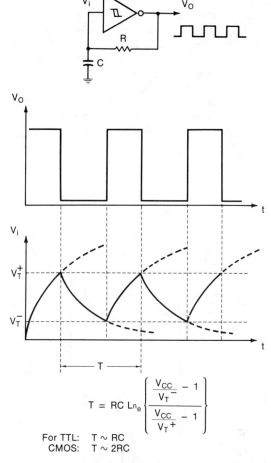

$$T = RC \, Ln_e \left\{ \frac{\dfrac{V_{CC}}{V_T^-} - 1}{\dfrac{V_{CC}}{V_T^+} - 1} \right\}$$

For TTL: $T \sim RC$
CMOS: $T \sim 2RC$

Fig. 10-8. Simple nonlinear RC clock oscillator employing a Schmitt trigger inverter.

up a standing wave pattern (see Fig. 10-9B) with a characteristic frequency f_n given by

$$f_n = n \frac{v}{2\ell} \qquad \text{(Eq. 10-5)}$$

where $n = 1, 2, 3$ depending on the mode of vibration.

As Equation 10-5 shows, the frequency f_n is determined by the properties of the crystal, and, in particular, by its length. Hence, crystals with different characteristic frequencies can be produced by cutting the crystals to the appropriate length. If the crystal is used in its *fundamental mode* with $n = 1$, then

303

values of f_n typically lie within the range from 100 kHz to 10 MHz. By slightly changing the internal geometry of the crystal, higher order harmonics or overtones can be excited, thus extending the useful frequency range of crystal oscillators. A third harmonic crystal ($n = 3$), for example, operates at three times the fundamental frequency. Typical crystal frequencies for microcomputer applications range from about 5 MHz to 27 MHz, although these frequencies are often divided to obtain the master clock frequency. The lower frequencies usually employ the fundamental mode, while frequencies greater than 10 MHz are generated using an overtone crystal. As an exam-

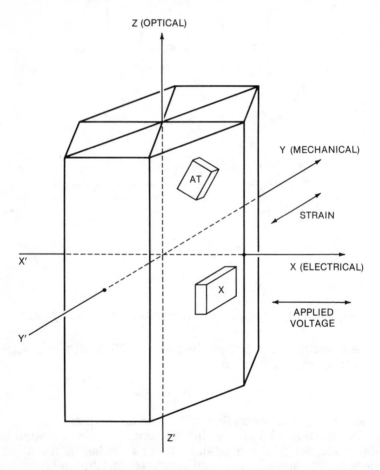

(A) Strain and voltage axes and typical crystal cuts.

Fig. 10-9.

ple, the Intel 8085A microprocessor can employ a crystal with a maximum frequency of 6.25 MHz which is divided by two internally to give the maximum microprocessor clock frequency of 3.125 MHz. Another commonly employed frequency is 6.144 MHz since this can be easily divided to give convenient baud rates. This can be seen by noting that 6.144 MHz is equivalent

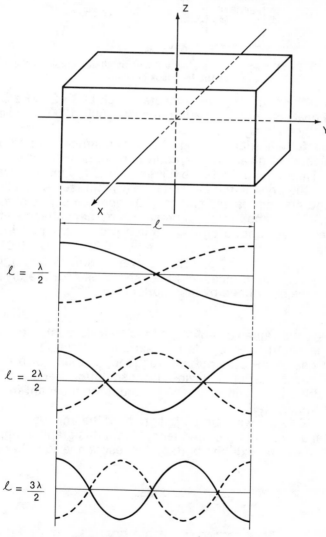

(B) Characterictic modes of vibration.

Quartz crystal.

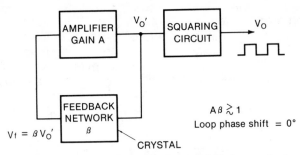

$V_f = \beta V_O'$

$A\beta \gtrsim 1$
Loop phase shift $= 0°$

Fig. 10-10. Block diagram of a simple linear oscillator employing a crystal as the feedback element.

to 3×2^{11} kHz which gives a master clock at 3×2^{11} kHz and a range of whole number baud rates (300, 600, 1200, and so on) simply by dividing by 2.

A useful electrical analog of the mechanical properties of the crystal is given by the equivalent circuit shown in Fig. 10-11. There, the inductance (L) represents the mechanical inertia of the crystal, the capacitance (C) represents its elasticity, and the series resistance (R_s) represents the damping losses. The capacitor C' represents the capacitance of the crystal holder and is typically much greater than C. Typical values for a 10-MHz crystal are: $L = 0.025$ H; $C = 0.01$ pF; $R_s = 20 \ \Omega$; and $C' = 10$ pF. The equivalent quality factor, Q, of the crystal, which measures the "sharpness" of the crystal's resonance, is defined by the relationship:

$$Q = 2\pi f L / R_s \qquad \text{(Eq. 10-6)}$$

Using the values given above for a 10-MHz crystal, the value of Q is about 80,000. It is this extremely large Q value that gives rise to the exceptional frequency stability of a crystal oscillator. For such a device, the oscillation frequency typically drifts by no more than 10 Hz about the resonant frequency of the crystal!

Fig. 10-12 shows a simplified graph of the impedance of the crystal as a function of frequency. From this graph, it appears that the crystal exhibits both series resonance (Z = 0) at a fre-

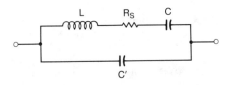

Fig. 10-11. Equivalent electrical circuit of a quartz crystal.

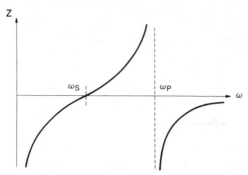

Fig. 10-12. Impedance diagram of a crystal showing series and parallel resonance.

quency f_s and parallel resonance ($Z = \infty$) at a frequency f_p, where f_s and f_p are given by:

$$f_s = \frac{1}{2\pi\sqrt{LC}}$$ (Eq. 10-7)

and

$$f_p = \frac{1}{2\pi\sqrt{L\left(\dfrac{CC'}{C + C'}\right)}}$$ (Eq. 10-8)

Since C' is much greater than C, f_p and f_s are almost the same, with a typical difference of about 0.03%. However, as we will see in the next section, the resonance mode (series or parallel) of the crystal is vitally important to the successful operation of crystal oscillator circuits.

10-4-3 Linear Crystal Oscillators[7]

For a linear oscillator, such as that shown in block form in Fig. 10-10, the loop gain $A\beta \geq 1$ and the phase shift around the loop must be zero. This implies that if the frequency-determining feedback element has zero phase shift at the required frequency, then a noninverting amplifier is required. Conversely, if the feedback element has a phase shift of 180°, then an inverting amplifier is needed.

When the crystal operates at its series resonant frequency, its impedance becomes a pure series resistance R_s with zero phase shift across the crystal. The amplifier or buffer used to complete a crystal oscillator must therefore have sufficient gain to overcome the losses due to R_s. It must also have an output which is in phase with the input to give a loop phase shift of zero. Having sufficient gain in the amplifier is particularly important to overtone crystal oscillators, since the

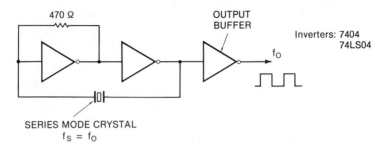

Fig. 10-13. Implementation of a linear oscillator using inverter gates and a series-mode crystal.

crystals tend to be thicker with correspondingly larger losses than equivalent fundamental crystals. A simple form of crystal oscillator employing a series mode crystal is illustrated in Fig. 10-13. The two inverters in the feedback loop have a net phase shift of zero, while the sharply tuned series resonance of the crystal gives the necessary zero phase shift only at its series resonant frequency.

When a crystal operates at its parallel resonant frequency, its impedance is almost purely inductive, apart from a small load capacitance C_L. The capacitor C_L represents the total capacitance seen across the crystal's terminals. It therefore includes the capacitance of the crystal holder, wiring capacitance and the input capacitance to the amplifier. Since any change in the reactance seen by the crystal alters its operating frequency and so causes frequency "pulling," the value of C_L should remain constant and be as small as possi-

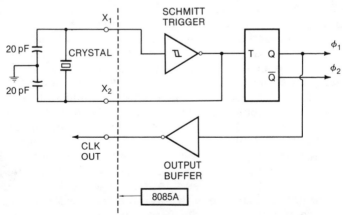

Fig. 10-14. Implementation of a microprocessor-based oscillator employing a parallel-mode crystal.

ble. This is achieved by firmly locating the crystal as close as possible to the amplifier to minimize the stray capacitance. In addition, because of the 180° phase shift between the ends of the crystal when it is operating at parallel resonance, an inverting amplifier is required to produce the loop phase shift of 360° needed to sustain oscillations.

A typical clock circuit requiring a parallel resonant crystal is shown in Fig. 10-14, illustrating the arrangement for the Intel 8085A microprocessor. The external crystal operates in its parallel mode and has a frequency of twice the required clock frequency. The two 20-pF capacitors ensure that the crystal operates at its fundamental frequency at power start-up by providing a bypass to ground for any higher order harmonics present. This precaution is particularly necessary for crystal frequencies of less than 4 MHz. The Schmitt trigger voltage inverter acts as the high gain inverting amplifier which provides the necessary positive feedback to maintain the oscillations. The output from the trigger toggles a flip-flop whose outputs generate the system clock signals Φ_1 and Φ_2 at half the crystal frequency. A buffered and inverted representation of the Φ_1 clock signal is available at the clock output pin (CLK) for driving any peripheral devices which must be slaved to the system clock.

When selecting a crystal for a microprocessor system clock:

- Check that the desired clock frequency lies within the range the microcomputer can handle.
- Check whether the crystal frequency is the same as the clock frequency or whether it needs to be some multiple of the clock frequency.
- Check whether a series mode or parallel mode crystal is required.
- For a series mode crystal, there is usually a specified maximum series resistance R_s which the crystal is permitted if the gain of the amplifier is to make up for the losses associated with R_s.
- For a parallel mode crystal, there is usually a specified maximum load capacitance C_L which is permitted across the crystal if significant frequency pulling is to be avoided.
- Check whether a fundamental mode or overtone crystal is employed. If the crystal operates in its fundamental mode, then small ($\sim$ 20 pF) bypass capacitors should be connected between each end of the crystal and ground to suppress the higher order harmonics.
- Often a small ($\sim$ 10 pF) capacitor is inserted in series

with the crystal to block any DC bias voltage, generated by the amplifier, from appearing across the crystal. If this is not done, then the permanent stress induced across the crystal by the DC voltage may lead to its long-term deterioration.

10-5 MISCELLANEOUS CONSIDERATIONS

10-5-1 Crosstalk[8]

Crosstalk is the unwanted coupling of signals from one line to another by inter-line capacitance or mutual inductance. Since the amount of coupling depends on the rate of change of a signal, crosstalk can be a major problem where fast pulses are concerned because of their very short rise and fall times, particularly with long lengths (~ 20 cm) of parallel lines. For this reason, long connections between logic gates should not be bundled, tied, or routed near each other. This is particularly important for clock inputs and the asynchronous set and clear lines to flip-flops, counters, and registers, because excessive coupling can lead to erratic counting induced by unwanted spikes picked up from adjacent lines. A potential source of crosstalk occurs when flat ribbon cable is used to transmit high-speed pulses. If this is necessary, one technique which can be adopted to minimize crosstalk is to use every second line for signals and to ground each intermediate line. In this way, the coupling occurs between signal lines and ground rather than between signal lines. A similar strategy can be adopted for a system backplane, where the clock pulse line is isolated from the data bus by the ground rail.

As we saw in Section 9-4, all lines carrying high-speed pulses should be properly terminated to prevent ringing. If this is not done, then the rapid signal changes associated with ringing can greatly contribute to crosstalk.

For signal lines other than clocks, where close coupling cannot be avoided, it is necessary to wait until disturbances induced following a transition on an adjacent line have died out before sampling the data on the line of interest. A reasonable time to wait, t_w, is twice the round-trip delay time t_d defined by Equation 9-21, i.e.,

$$t_w \geq 2t_d$$

where $\qquad t_d \geq t_r \text{ (or } t_f),$

whichever is the longer.

10-5-2 Decoupling Digital Circuits[9]

A significant potential source of undesirable coupling between integrated circuits occurs through the power supply rails shared by a large number of microprocessor subsystem ICs. This coupling is caused by the large, fast voltage spikes generated as gates turn on and off and flip-flops change state. As these switch, the rapid changes in current ($\Delta I/\Delta t$) and finite inductance L of the power supply rails induce large transient voltage spikes, V_I, according to the Equation:

$$V_I = L \frac{\Delta I}{\Delta t} \qquad \text{(Eq. 10-9)}$$

These may be transferred to data, clock pulse, or control lines through the crosstalk discussed earlier. It is thus important to isolate the transient effects on the power supply rails of the various ICs as they perform their switching operations. This is usually achieved by connecting a good quality capacitor between the power rail and ground at a point as close as practical to the IC package using very short leads. The capacitor provides a virtual short-circuit path to ground for any rapid transient voltage spikes and also acts as a local short-term storage device for maintaining a steady value for V_{CC} during the switching operation. Typical capacitor values range from 0.01–0.1 μF. As a rule of thumb, decoupling capacitors should be distributed as follows:

- One capacitor for each four small-scale integration TTL gates.
- One capacitor for each two medium-scale integration gates.
- One capacitor for each large-scale integration TTL gate.
- One capacitor for each monostable, flip-flop, driver, or line receiver. This last requirement is imposed because of the large rate of change of current associated with the rapid switching of these devices and the large voltage transients that can be induced.

In addition to the decoupling of individual ICs, each printed circuit card should be isolated from other cards by the addition of a 2–20 μF high quality tantalum capacitor between V_{CC} and ground where V_{CC} enters the card. As an alternative, on-card three-terminal voltage regulators can be employed as described in Section 11-5.

10-5-3 Grounds

Since all signals are eventually returned to ground, a good

low-resistance, low-inductance ground system is essential. This is particularly important when it is recalled that the noise margin for the low state of a gate is often less than the noise margin for its high state. Thus, for example, when laying out a printed circuit board (PCB) containing a large number of packages, the ground rail should be as wide as possible to minimize its resistance and inductance. In addition, ground loops either on the PCB or between boards should be avoided. That is, the good grounding procedures outlined in Section 4-5-1 should be adhered to within the microprocessor subsystem.

10-6 REFERENCES

1. D. Winkel and F. Prosser, *The Art of Digital Design,* Prentice-Hall, Inc., 1980, pp. 464–466.

2. J.B. Peatman, *Microcomputer-Based Design,* McGraw-Hill, Inc., 1977, pp. 102–104; Intel Corp., *MCS-80/85 Family User's Manual,* Intel Corp., Santa Clara, CA 95051, October 1979, p. 2-18.

3. Peatman, 1977, pp. 102–104.

4. W.I. Fletcher, *An Engineering Approach to Digital Design,* Prentice-Hall, 1980, Section 5-11.

5. "Crystals and Crystal Oscillators," *Marconi Instruments Applications Notes No. 40;* "Crystals: Specifications for Intel Components," *Intel Application Note Ap-35,* Intel Corp., Santa Clara, CA 95051.

6. *Intel Application Note Ap-35.*

7. Winkel and Prosser, 1980, pp. 481-482; Fairchild, Inc., *TTL Data Book,* Fairchild, 1978, p. 2-19.

8. Winkel and Prosser, 1980, p. 480; Fairchild, 1978, p. 2-24.

MODULE 3

THE POWER SUBSYSTEM

Linear Power Supplies

11-1 INTRODUCTION

Providing a stable, noise-free power supply is fundamentally important to the successful implementation of a microcomputer system. This chapter is devoted to the design and implementation of this most overlooked microcomputer subsystem. Typically, a small microcomputer-based instrument or control system will require:

- +5 volts at 2 to 3 amps for the microprocessor, RAM, ROM, and digital interface logic.
- ±12 volts at one amp for the EPROM (−12 V is used to provide −5 V and the serial communications circuits.
- ±15 volts at one amp for the analog interface circuits, including the operational amplifiers.

These voltages can be derived from suitable batteries, particularly for CMOS systems and for RAM backup. More commonly, they are derived from the AC mains by using a *power supply* to convert the AC to a smooth, stable source of DC.

Several broad classes of power supplies can be identified. The *constant voltage* power supply, which is the main subject of this chapter, maintains the output voltage constant as the load current varies. The *constant current* supply, on the other hand, maintains the output current constant while allowing the output voltage to vary. The *programmable* power supply is one in which the output voltage or current is controlled externally through the application of an appropriate analog or digital control signal. In addition to these broad classes of power supplies, various subclasses exist. These include supplies with positive and negative outputs, dual positive and negative supplies, supplies with variable outputs, and dual-tracking supplies. In the latter, the negative output is maintained at the same magnitude, but of opposite sign, to the variable positive output.

Since we are concerned with the power supply requirements of a microcomputer system, we will limit our discussion in this book to constant-voltage power supplies having either positive or negative outputs. Most of the principles introduced are applicable, however, to the design and implementation of other types of power supplies. The chapter deals mainly with the theoretical and practical design of power supplies. It should allow you to both understand and build power supplies to meet most of the situations you are likely to encounter in a microcomputer system. More specifically, in the sections that follow, we develop the complete designs for a ±15-volt, 1-amp supply, and also a +5-volt, 3-amp supply. If you don't want to do the job yourself but wish to purchase a complete commercial supply, Section 11-8 describes some of the things you should look for when making a selection.

11-2 IMPLEMENTATION

Fig. 11-1 shows the main functional blocks of a classical power supply along with the typical voltage waveforms observed at the output of each block. Four steps are needed to transform the alternating mains voltage of peak amplitude V_{pm} to a smooth, stable and constant DC voltage V_o, namely:

1. The mains voltage must be reduced to peak value V_{sm} using a *transformer* which also isolates the remaining power supply blocks and the microcomputer from the mains.
2. The sinusoidal mains voltage must be *rectified* to produce a unipolar, fluctuating voltage.
3. The fluctuations must be smoothed out or *filtered,* using, for the most part, an electrolytic capacitor as an energy storage device.
4. The smoothed voltage must be stabilized at the required value V_o over a specified range of load currents, I_o.

The output stabilization can be achieved in two entirely different ways, using either a linear element (a *linear regulator*) with high internal power dissipation or a switching element

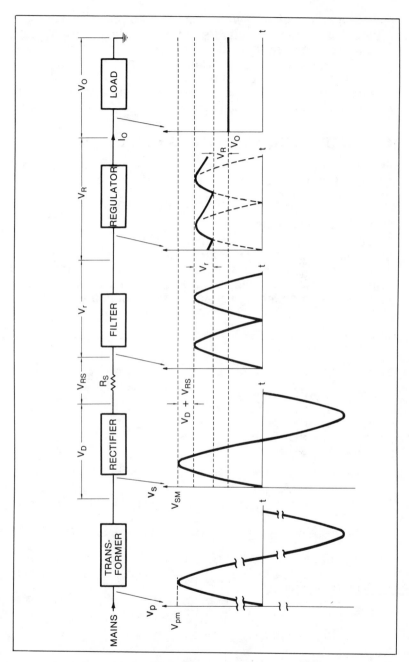

Fig. 11-1. Block diagram of a linear power supply.

317

(*switch-mode regulator*) with close to zero power dissipation. Although switching regulators are more efficient than linear regulators, they are more complex to design and construct. Hence, in the interest of providing a simple, practical power supply with the minimum of design effort, we will concentrate on linear supplies. The design and implementation of switch-mode supplies are discussed in Appendix B.

11-3 AN UNREGULATED POWER SUPPLY

In this section, we consider the design of a traditional unregulated power supply consisting of the transformer, rectifier, and filter blocks of Figure 11-1.

11-3-1 The Transformer

A basic transformer consists of two coils of wire, known as the *primary* and the *secondary,* wound on a laminated iron core as shown in Figure 11-2A. A changing current in the primary sets up a changing magnetic field in the core, which in turn induces a changing voltage in the secondary. If we con-

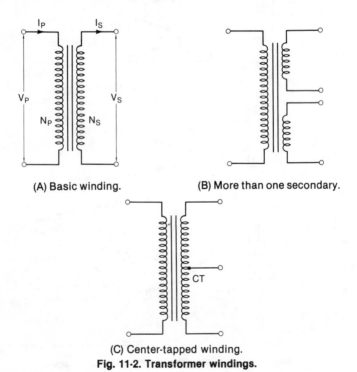

(A) Basic winding.   (B) More than one secondary.

(C) Center-tapped winding.

Fig. 11-2. Transformer windings.

sider an ideal (lossless) transformer, then it can be shown that the following relationships apply, linking the primary (p) and the secondary (s):

$$\frac{V_s}{V_p} = \frac{N_s}{N_p} \qquad \text{(Eq. 11-1)}$$

$$\frac{I_s}{I_p} = \frac{N_p}{N_s} \qquad \text{(Eq. 11-2)}$$

$$P_s = I_s V_s = I_p V_p = P_p \qquad \text{(Eq. 11-3)}$$

In these equations, V and I are the *root-mean-square (RMS) values* (0.707 peak) of the voltage and the current; P is the power and N is the number of turns in the coil. In this chapter we use the convention that uppercase letters represent DC or RMS values, while the addition of the subscript "m" indicates a peak or maximum value. Hence, for example, the peak values of I_s and V_s are written as I_{SM} and V_{SM}. The equations show that if the ratio of turns $N_s/N_p < 1$, then $V_s < V_p$ and we have a step-down transformer. However, if we make $N_s > N_p$, then $V_s > V_p$ and we have a step-up transformer. Equations 11-1 and 11-2 also show that the current ratio is the inverse of the voltage ratio. Hence for a step-down transformer, with $V_s < V_p$, the secondary current is greater than the primary. Equation 11-3 shows that in loss-free transformers, the power delivered to the primary is the same as the power delivered by the secondary. Real transformers, however, have some internal power dissipation, making $P_s < P_p$, but with typical efficiencies exceeding 90%, they are a close approximation to the ideal.

Fig. 11-2B illustrates a transformer with more than one secondary winding, and Fig. 11-2C shows a center-tap transformer in which an extra lead is brought out from a point midway along the secondary winding. All three configurations are used in different types of power supplies.

When rating a power transformer, manufacturers normally specify the RMS value of the secondary voltage for a nominal primary line voltage. Remembering that:

$$V_{PEAK} = \sqrt{2}\, V_{RMS}, \qquad \text{(Eq. 11-4)}$$

then when a manufacturer specifies a 10-volt transformer, it means that for a nominal line voltage of 115 volts RMS, the RMS value of the secondary voltage is 10 volts, while the peak value is 14 volts. Also, since the secondary voltage is usually specified at the maximum rated secondary current, the open circuit value of the secondary voltage can be somewhat higher than the specified value.

The selection of a suitable transformer depends on the following factors:

- The rectifier configuration.
- The secondary voltage rating.
- The secondary current.
- The power or VA rating.

The RMS secondary voltage rating (V_s) required for the transformer can be obtained by considering Fig. 11-1, from which it can be seen that:

$$V_s = \frac{1}{\sqrt{2}} V_{SM} = \frac{1}{\sqrt{2}} \ (V_o + V_R + V_r + V_{RS} + V_D) \ \frac{V_{NOM}}{V_{LOW}} \quad (Eq. \ 11\text{-}5)$$

where

V_{SM} is the peak secondary voltage of the transformer,
V_r is the peak-to-peak ripple voltage,
V_R is the minimum voltage drop across the regulator that is needed to keep it operating in its linear region, and is known as the *drop-out voltage,*
V_{RS} is the voltage drop across the surge current limiting resistor R_S,
V_D is the forward voltage drop across the diodes in the rectifier.

The last term (V_{NOM}/V_{LOW}) is included to take account of fluctuations in the line voltage from its nominal value. If the line drops to some lower value — for instance, when the load on the power station is increased — the secondary voltage may not be sufficient to keep all of the system blocks operating correctly. Thus we introduce this term to provide a safety factor. A sample calculation of V_s is given in Example 11-1.

EXAMPLE 11-1: TRANSFORMER SECONDARY VOLTAGE CALCULATION

Given: Required output $\quad\quad\quad\quad\quad V_o \quad = 15 \ V$
Regulator drop-out voltage $\quad V_R \quad = 2 \ V$
Filter ripple voltage $\quad\quad\quad V_r \quad = 2 \ V$
Surge resistor drop $\quad\quad\quad\, V_{RS} \ = 1.0 \ V$
Rectifier voltage drop $\quad\quad\, V_D \quad = 1.6 \ V$
Nominal mains line voltage $\quad V_{NOM} = 120 \ V$
Minimum mains line voltage $\quad V_{LOW} = 100 \ V$ (20% low)

From Equation 11-5, the required secondary voltage is:

$$V_s = \frac{1}{\sqrt{2}}(15 + 2 + 2.0 + 1.0 + 1.6)\frac{120}{100} = 18.3 \ V$$

Hence choose V_s = 18 volts.

If I_o is the maximum required DC output current and we assume that a capacitive filter (Section 11-3-3) is employed, then the required *RMS secondary current rating* I_s for the transformer depends on the type of rectifier (Section 11-3-2) as follows:

$$\text{Full-wave bridge rectifier: } I_s \approx 1.8 I_o$$
$$\text{Full-wave center-tapped rectifier: } I_s \approx 1.2 I_o \qquad \text{(Eq. 11-6)}$$

The total transformer specification is usually given in terms of its *VA rating*, which is a measure of the power handling capability of the transformer and which is defined as:

$$\text{VA rating} = V_{ST} \times I_s \qquad \text{(Eq. 11-7)}$$

where V_{ST} is the total RMS voltage across the secondary of the transformer. V_{ST} also depends on the type of rectifier, namely:

$$V_{ST} = V_s \text{ (bridge)}$$
$$V_{ST} = 2V_s \text{ (FWCT)} \qquad \text{(Eq. 11-8)}$$

A sample calculation of the VA rating of a transformer is shown in Example 11-2.

EXAMPLE 11-2: TRANSFORMER VA RATING

Given: RMS secondary voltage, $V_s = 18$ volts (from Example 11-1)
Maximum DC output current $I_o = 1.0$ amp
Filter type : Capacitive

Rectifier type:	*FWCT*	*Bridge*
From Equation 11-6,	$I_s = 1.2 \times 1 = 1.2$ A	$I_s = 1.8 \times 1 = 1.8$ A
From Equation 11-8,	$V_{ST} = 2 \times 18 = 36$ V	$V_{ST} = 1 \times 18 = 18$ V
From Equation 11-7,	VA $= 1.2 \times 36 = 43$ VA	VA $= 1.8 \times 18 = 36$ VA

Allowing for a safety margin, the VA rating for both rectifiers should be specified as 50 volt-amp.

The complete transformer specifications therefore become:

	V_p	V_s	I_s	VA
FWCT:	120 volts	18-0-18 volts	1.2 amp	50 volt-amp
Bridge:	120 volts	18 volts	1.8 amp	50 volt-amp

If a transformer with more than one secondary winding is used, then the secondary voltage specification may appear as, for example, V_s: 5 volt/7.5 volt/18 volt, while a center-tapped transformer may be designated as 15-0-15 volts.

11-3-2 The Rectifier

The rectifier converts the alternating secondary current to

an unsmoothed but unidirectional DC current. This function is almost invariably performed by one or more diodes arranged in various configurations. Fig. 11-3 shows three popular arrangements:

1. The full-wave center-tapped (FWCT) rectifier.
2. The full-wave bridge rectifier.
3. The tapped full-wave bridge for dual polarity supplies.

The operation of the *full-wave center-tapped (FWCT) rectifier* in Fig. 11-3A can be understood as follows. Suppose there is an alternating voltage across the secondary coil and that the center tap (CT) is at ground. On the first half-cycle,

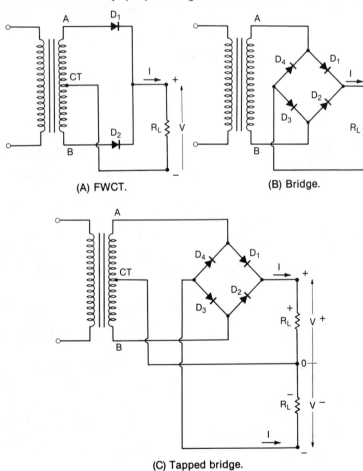

(A) FWCT.

(B) Bridge.

(C) Tapped bridge.

Fig. 11-3. Rectifier arrangements.

point A is positive and point B is negative. Diode D_1 is therefore turned on while diode D_2 is off. Current I_o flows through D_1 and the load R_L in the direction shown, returning via CT and point A. On the next half-cycle, A is negative and B is positive, so that D_2 is on while D_1 is off. Current now flows through D_2 and the load, again in the direction of I_o, and completes the loop via CT and point B. Hence the load current I_o always flows in the same direction. In addition, the maximum voltage appearing across the load is equal to that appearing between the center tap and one end of the secondary winding, that is, half the total peak secondary voltage.

A similar description can be developed for the *bridge rectifier* in Fig. 11-3B. Assuming that, during the first half-cycle, point A is positive with respect to B and that diodes D_1 and D_3 are on while D_2 and D_4 are off. Current therefore flows through the load in the direction shown, following the path A, D_1, R_L, D_3, B. On the next half-cycle, A is negative with respect to B, so that diodes D_2 and D_4 are on while D_1 and D_3 are off. The current now follows the path B, D_2, R_L, D_4, A, and thus again flows through the load in the same direction. For the bridge rectifier, the maximum voltage appearing across the load is equal to the peak voltage appearing across the secondary of the transformer.

Fig. 11-3C shows how a center-tapped transformer and bridge rectifier can be combined to produce a *dual complementary rectifier,* in other words, two identical outputs of opposite polarities sharing a common ground. This type of rectifier is extremely useful if we want a bipolar supply for, say, an operational amplifier requiring ±15 volts. This circuit can be regarded as a pair of back-to-back, full-wave, center-tapped rectifiers. Diodes D_1 and D_2 are the same as in Fig. 11-3A and provide the positive output, whereas D_3 and D_4 have been reversed to provide the negative output.

Design Points

When designing a rectifier, the following points should be noted:

1. A forward-biased diode has a voltage drop across it which is typically 0.7 volt, rising to about 1 volt for diodes operated at high currents. Hence, when determining the voltage rating, V_s, for the secondary of the transformer, 1 volt must be allowed for the voltage drop, V_D, across the rectifier when using the FWCT configuration. For the bridge configuration, 2 volts must be allowed since two diodes are on at any time.

2. If a large reverse bias is applied to a diode, then avalanche breakdown and possible damage to the diode can occur. The maximum allowable reverse voltage that avoids this situation is specified by the diode manufacturer and is represented by the symbol V_{RM}. In a rectifier circuit, diodes are subjected to a reverse bias voltage during those times when they are not conducting. The maximum value of this in-circuit voltage is known as the *peak inverse voltage* (PIV) and the PIV depends on the type of rectifier, as follows:

PIV — FWCT	: twice the peak secondary voltage between the CT and one side of the transformer (V_{SM})	
PIV — Bridge	: peak secondary voltage of the transformer (V_{SM})	(Eq. 11-9A)
PIV — Tapped Bridge	: same as for FWCT	

Hence the diodes selected should be such that:

V_{RM} (manufacturer's specs) > PIV (for the rectifier circuits)   (Eq. 11-9B)

However, since line transients may cause voltage spikes across the rectifier, it is usual to allow an extra factor of two in the voltage rating of V_{RM} as a safety margin when choosing suitable diodes.

3. Diode bridges are readily available in single packages designed for a wide range of currents and reverse voltages.

4. If a capacitive filter is used, the maximum current from the rectifier is two to three times the average load current, because the rectifier delivers the current to the capacitor in short bursts. On the other hand, for the full-wave rectifiers only half the diodes are on at any time. Hence, when determining the current rating for the diodes, the minimum requirement is to choose diodes capable of handling currents equal to the maximum load current. However, when the power supply is initially turned on, a current surge occurs as the filter capacitor charges from zero. For power diodes, the single-cycle surge current rating is typically ten times the average DC current. Allowing a good safety margin for surge currents, the diode current rating design criterion becomes:

Diode current rating (I_D) = 2 × maximum load current (I_o)   (Eq. 11-10)

5. In many cases the initial surge current is limited by placing a small resistance, R_s, between the rectifier and the capacitive filter. The maximum surge current occurs if, at switch-on, the transformer secondary voltage is at its max-

imum and the capacitor is fully discharged. Limiting the surge current to ten times the diode current rating, we get:

$$R_S = V_{SM}/20I_o \qquad \text{(Eq. 11-11)}$$

Under normal operating conditions, the voltage drop across R_S becomes

$$V_{RS} = I_oR_S, \qquad \text{(Eq. 11-12)}$$

and if R_S is employed, then this drop should be included in Equation 11-5. In some instances a thermistor may be preferred, because starting from cold its resistance is high and limits the surge current during the first cycle of operation. The heating produced after switch-on then reduces the resistance to a low value for steady-state operation.

6.   In a high-current supply delivering several amps, there is a possibility of significant power dissipation within the diodes and voltage drops along the wires. Consequently, large gauge wires of minimum length are required, and the diodes should be mounted on adequate heat sinks.

A sample calculation of the reverse voltage rating and forward current rating for the diodes in a bridge rectifier is given in Example 11-3, together with an estimate of the value of the surge-limiting resistor R_S.

EXAMPLE 11-3: DIODE SPECIFICATIONS AND SURFACE-LIMITING RESISTOR CALCULATION

Given:	Rectifier type :	*FWCT*	*Bridge*
	V_s :	18-0-18 volts	18 volts
	I_o :	1.0 amp	1.0 amp
Hence,	$V_{SM} = \sqrt{2} \times 18$:	26 volts	26 volts
From Equation 11-9,	PIV : $2 \times 26 = 52$ volts		26 volts
Allow,	$2 \times$ PIV $= V_{RM}$:	100 volts	50 volts
From Equation 11-10,I_D	: $2 \times 1.0 = 2$ amp		2 amp

Surge-limiting resistor R_S is the same for both rectifiers. Hence from Equation 11-11:

$$R_S = \frac{26}{1.0 \times 20} = 1.3 \text{ ohm}$$

Thus, choose $R_S = 1.0$ ohm, so that from Equation 11-12:

$$V_{RS} = 1.0 \times 1.0 = 1.0 \text{ volt}$$

11-3-3 The Filter

The purpose of the filter is to smooth the raw unidirectional voltage from the rectifier to give a quasi-constant DC output.

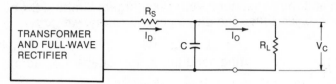

Fig. 11-4. Capacitive filter and load.

This is achieved by storing electrical energy so that it can be delivered to the load anytime insufficient power is supplied by the rectifier. Electrical energy can be stored either by inductors or capacitors or by various combinations of these components. In this book, we discuss only the capacitor, since large inductive chokes tend to be bulky, heavy, and expensive. Fig. 11-4 shows a simple capacitive filter connected to a full-wave rectifier. R_S is the surge-limiting resistor and R_L is the load.

Fig. 11-5 shows the output voltage from the filter as a function of time, along with the current I_D from the rectifier. The dotted curve represents the output that would be observed from the rectifier in the absence of the filter capacitor. At time t_A, the rectifier turns on and current I_D flows, supplying the load current I_o and charging the capacitor to its maximum value V_{MAX}. At time t_B, the rectifier turns off, but the load current is maintained by the partial discharge of the capacitor. The output voltage therefore drops by an amount V_r to its minimum value V_{MIN}, whereupon the process is repeated. The average output voltage V_{DC} lies halfway between V_{MAX} and V_{MIN} and is the voltage observed by a DC voltmeter placed across the output of the filter. From Fig. 11-1, the value of V_{MAX} is given by:

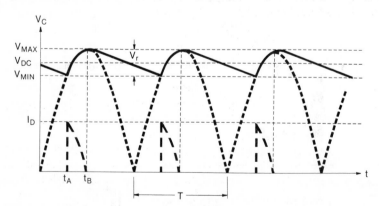

Fig. 11-5. Capacitive filter waveforms. Solid line: actual output. Dotted line: output without filter capactor. Dashed line: rectifier current.

$$V_{MAX} = V_{SM} - V_D. \qquad \text{(Eq. 11-13)}$$

If the surge limiting resistor R_S is employed then:

$$V_{MAX} = V_{SM} - V_D - V_{RS}. \qquad \text{(Eq. 11-14)}$$

Ripple

The magnitude of the ripple voltage, V_r, depends on the load current I_o and on the size of the capacitor. It can be estimated as follows.

Assume that the capacitor is initially charged to voltage V_{MAX}. It then partially discharges over a time T, which is equal to the period of the ripple voltage, while maintaining an average load current I_o. The charge lost by the capacitor is I_oT. When the capacitor is recharged by the rectifier (Fig. 11-5), the voltage increases by V_r so that the charge gained is CV_r. Equating the charge lost to the charge gained gives:

$$I_oT = CV_r \qquad \text{(Eq. 11-15)}$$

For a full-wave rectifier, T is equal to $1/f$, where f is twice the mains frequency or 120 Hz. Hence, for design purposes we can write from Equation 11-15:

$$CV = I_o/f = I_o/120 \qquad \text{(Eq. 11-16)}$$

It should be noted that Equation 11-16 is an approximation that is valid only if V_r is less than about 10% of V_{MAX}.

The relative magnitude of the ripple voltage is measured in terms of the *ripple factor,* r, which is defined as:

$$r = \frac{\text{RMS ripple voltage } (V_r\,\text{RMS})}{\text{average DC output } (V_{DC})} \qquad \text{(Eq. 11-17)}$$

Since $V_r(\text{RMS})$ is approximately $V_r/2\sqrt{3}$ and V_{DC} can be expressed as I_oR_L, the ripple factor becomes:

$$r = \frac{V_r(\text{RMS})}{I_oR_L} = \frac{I_o}{2\sqrt{3}fC} \times \frac{1}{I_oR_L}$$

$$r = \frac{1}{2\sqrt{3}f\,R_LC} \qquad \text{(Eq. 11-18)}$$

Thus a small ripple factor can be achieved by employing a large filter capacitor or a large load resistor, which in turn implies a small load current.

Note that, when choosing a capacitor, you need to ensure that its maximum allowable working voltage, V(working) or WV, is greater than the peak voltage from the rectifier, V_{MAX}. That is,

$$V(\text{working}) > V_{MAX} \qquad \text{(Eq. 11-19)}$$

In large electrolytic capacitors, internal heating caused by the finite resistance of the capacitor and the large charge/discharge currents can lead to problems. Manufacturers therefore usually specify a maximum permissible RMS ripple current that must not be exceeded. In high current applications, this ripple current rating may be a more significant parameter than the ripple voltage and may demand a larger capacitor to prevent excessive heating. For a capacitive filter, the RMS ripple current is about two to three times the value of I_o, so a capacitor must be chosen which has at least this ripple current rating. That is,

$$\text{Ripple current rating, } I_r(\text{RMS}) = 2.5I_o. \qquad \text{(Eq. 11-20)}$$

Since failure of the filter capacitor is the main reason for power supply faults, it is important not to skimp in this area. Example 11-4 illustrates the procedure for selecting a filter capacitor.

EXAMPLE 11-4: FILTER CAPACITOR CALCULATION

Given: Output voltage $V_o = 15$ volts
       Load current $I_o = 1.0$ amp

From Example 11-1, assume that an 18-volt transformer and bridge rectifier are employed.

From Equation 11-14, $V_{MAX} = 18\sqrt{2} - (2 \times 1.0) - 1.0 = 22.5$ volts

For Equation 11-16 to be valid, assume that:

$$\text{Ripple voltage } V_r \approx 10\% \ V_{MAX} = 2.0 \text{ volts}$$

From Equation 11-16, the required capacitor value is:

$$C = I_o/V_rf = \frac{1.0}{2 \times 120} \approx 4200 \ \mu F$$

Since the peak voltage across the capacitor, $V_{MAX} = 22.5$ volts, choose capacitor working voltage, WV $\sim$ 25 volts.

From Equation 11-20, RMS ripple current rating $= 2.5I_o = 2.5$ amp.

Minimum Output Voltage

As Fig. 11-1 shows, the regulator requires a minimum voltage drop V_R across it to operate correctly. This *drop-out voltage* has a typical value of 2–3 volts for commercial regulators. If V_o is the output voltage from the regulator, then the input to the regulator must always be greater than $V_o + V_R$.

Hence from Fig. 11-5, the value of V_{MIN} must always be such that:

$$V_{MIN} \geqslant V_o + V_R. \qquad \text{(Eq. 11-21)}$$

If V_{MIN} falls below this value, then the regulator loses control and the unregulated filter output breaks through to the load. Fig. 11-5 shows that

$$V_{MIN} = V_{MAX} - V_r = V_{MAX}\left(1 - \frac{V_r}{V_{MAX}}\right). \qquad \text{(Eq. 11-22)}$$

As this equation shows, in obtaining the required value of V_{MIN}, there is a trade-off between the value of V_{MAX}, determined principally by the value of V_{SM}, and the value of V_r, determined by the size of the filter capacitor. A reasonable compromise, and one that maintains the validity of Equation 11-16, is to settle for about 10% ripple by choosing $V_r/V_{MAX} = 0.1$. If this figure is adopted, then from Equation 11-22:

$$V_{MAX} = \frac{V_{MIN}}{(1 - V_r/V_{MAX})} = 1.1V_{MIN}. \qquad \text{(Eq. 11-23)}$$

Also,

$$V_r = \left(\frac{V_r}{V_{MAX}}\right)V_{MAX} = 0.1V_{MAX}. \qquad \text{(Eq. 11-24)}$$

Example 11-5 illustrates the procedure for establishing the required value of V_{MIN}.

EXAMPLE 11-5: ESTABLISHING THE VALUE OF V_{MIN}

Given:			
Output voltage	V_o	= 15	volts
Output current	I_o	= 1.0	amp
Regulator drop-out voltage	V_R	= 2.0	volts
Surge resistor voltage	V_{RS}	= 1.0	volt
Voltage drop across rectifier	V_D	= 1.6	volts
20% line variations	V_{NOM}/V_{LOW}	= 1.2	

From Equation 11-20:

$$V_{MIN} = 15 + 2 = 17 \text{ volts}$$

Assume $V_r/V_{MAX} = 0.1$. From Equation 11-23:

$$V_{MAX} = 1.1 \times 17 = 18.7 \text{ volts}$$
$$V_r = 0.1 \times 18.7 = 1.87 \text{ volts}$$

From Equation 11-16:

$$C = \frac{1.0}{120 \times 1.87} = 4500 \ \mu F$$

From Equation 11-5:

$$V_s = \frac{1}{\sqrt{2}}(1.2)\,[1.6 + 1.0 + 18.7] = 18.1 \text{ volts}$$

11-3-4 Fuses and Switches

On the primary side of the transformer, the power supply needs an on/off switch, an indicator lamp, and a fuse, as shown in Fig. 11-6. The switch is inserted in the active side of the mains, together with a suitable fuse. The fuse rating for the primary current may be determined as follows. From Equation 11-3,

$$\frac{I_p}{I_s} = \frac{V_s}{V_p} \qquad\qquad \text{(Eq. 11-25)}$$

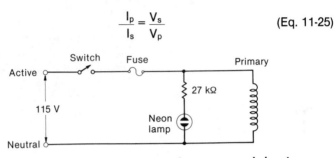

Fig. 11-6. Fuse and indicator lamp for power supply input.

Also, from Equations 11-6 and 11-7, the value of I_s depends on the type of rectifier employed. However, as a compromise set $I_s = 1.5I_o$, whence:

$$I_p = 1.5I_o\left(\frac{V_s}{V_p}\right) \qquad\qquad \text{(Eq. 11-26)}$$

If a slow-blowing fuse is employed to cover the initial surge at turn-on, then Equation 11-26 can be used to calculate the required fuse rating. In particular, if $V_p = 115$ volts, then

$$I_{fuse} \approx \frac{1}{75} I_o V_s. \qquad\qquad \text{(Eq. 11-27)}$$

Example 11-6 illustrates the procedure.

EXAMPLE 11-6: FUSE RATING

Given: $V_o = 15$ volts;
         $I_o = 1.0$ amp

From Example 11-5, $V_s = 18.1$ volts.

From Equation 11-26,

$$I_{fuse} = 1.5I_s\left(\frac{V_s}{V_p}\right) = 1.5 \times 1.0 \times \left(\frac{18.1}{115}\right) = 0.24 \text{ amp}$$

Hence a 250-mA fuse is appropriate.

A note on the mechanical details of construction. Great care should be taken to ensure that the mains power lead is well anchored to the chassis and that it is led through the chassis via a rubber grommet. The earth lead should also be in good electrical contact with the chassis.

11-4 REGULATORS: GENERAL PRINCIPLES

11-4-1 Introduction

In Section 11-3 we discussed the design of an unregulated power supply that produces a specified DC output. For many purposes, however, one could not accept the variation in output voltage from such a supply that would occur with changing load current or line voltage. This is particularly important in the +5-volt microcomputer supply, since most microprocessors and digital integrated circuits simply stop working if the 5% low voltage supply tolerance (4.75 V) is exceeded. In these circumstances, it is essential to place a voltage regulator between the filter and the load. In this section, we examine the general principles of linear voltage regulators and their practical implementation using integrated circuit technology.

Since monolithic regulators are both cheap and easy to use, a major change has occurred in the way power is distributed in a complex electronic system. At one time, the practice was to have a single large regulator and to distribute a regulated voltage to the various parts of the system. This sometimes led to unwanted noise pickup or voltage drops along the power rails. In addition, the various parts of the system were often coupled via the shared supply rails. In contrast, the current approach uses a single large *unregulated* power supply and distributes the raw, unregulated DC around the system. Small local "on-card" regulators are then employed wherever a particular regulated voltage is required. In this way, well-defined, well-regulated voltages are available where they are required, and the problems outlined above are avoided.

11-4-2 The Linear Regulator as a Control System

A regulator is basically a closed-loop control system in which negative feedback stabilizes the output voltage. The block diagram in Fig. 11-7 shows the main elements of a typical series-pass linear voltage regulator such as may be found, for example, in a monolithic three- or four-terminal regulator. In this system, the error amplifier compares a reference voltage V_{REF} with a fraction of the output voltage,

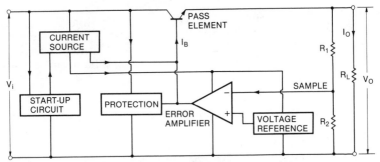

Fig. 11-7. Block diagram of a linear regulator.

which is derived from the sampling resistors R_1 and R_2. The amplifier output controls the input signal to the series-pass element through which the load current flows; hence it regulates the output voltage. Suppose, for example, that for some reason the output voltage rises. The sampled voltage also rises, and since the positive input to the amplifier is held at the reference voltage, a negative error signal results. This signal reduces the base current drive to the pass transistor, which in turn reduces the load current. The drop in current is such that the output voltage falls by an amount just sufficient to counter the initial increase. Thus negative feedback in the system has stabilized the output voltage.

To illustrate these ideas, let us consider the 723 precision voltage regulator, a versatile general-purpose building block available in IC form from many manufacturers. It consists of a series-pass transistor, an error amplifier, a temperature-compensated voltage reference, and a current-limiting protection circuit. Since each of the major circuit blocks is separately accessible, a wide range of circuits can be constructed by adding a few external components. A typical example is the positive regulator with an external pass transistor reproduced in Fig. 11-8. This is derived from the manufacturer's Application Notes[1] but has been redrawn to emphasize the close relationship between the general block diagram of Fig. 11-7 and the detailed implementation using the 723. An added feature of Fig. 11-8 is the crowbar overvoltage protection circuit formed by V_z, R_4, SCR1, and the fuse F_1. With the component values shown in Fig. 11-8, the circuit delivers +15 volts at currents of up to 1 amp.

11-4-3 System Blocks of a Linear Regulator

In this section, we discuss each of the system blocks of Fig. 11-7 in more detail, emphasizing particular points of design philosophy.

Sampling Network

The voltage sampling network consists of the resistors R_1 and R_2 and picks off a fraction V' of the output V_o, given by:

$$V' = V_o\left(\frac{R_2}{R_1 + R_2}\right) \qquad \text{(Eq. 11-28)}$$

As in any control system, the sample (V') should directly represent the quantity to be stabilized (V_o). Further, any sampling technique should disturb the system as little as possible. In this case, the total sampling resistance, $R_1 + R_2$, is made large compared with the load resistance, so that the current flowing through it is small compared with the load current.

Voltage Reference Source

A most important part of the system is an accurate voltage reference. This is because in any control system it is impossible to make the output more stable than the reference. Although the subject of voltage references is covered in detail in Chapter 12, we can note here that a zener diode, connected as shown in Fig. 11-9A, often makes an adequate reference

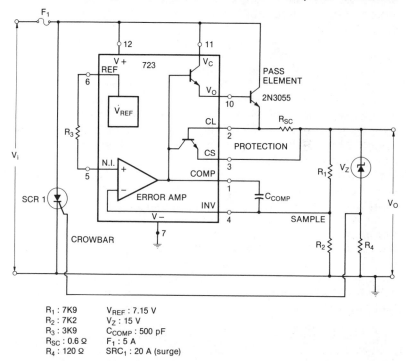

R_1 : 7K9	V_{REF} : 7.15 V
R_2 : 7K2	V_Z : 15 V
R_3 : 3K9	C_{COMP} : 500 pF
R_{SC} : 0.6 Ω	F_1 : 5 A
R_4 : 120 Ω	SRC_1 : 20 A (surge)

Fig. 11-8. A +15-volt, 1-amp power supply using a 723 precision regulator.

333

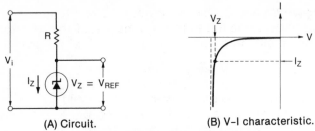

(A) Circuit.　　　　(B) V–I characteristic.

Fig. 11-9. Zener diode reference.

source. The zener diode is operated under reverse bias, and as Fig. 11-9B shows, avalanche breakdown occurs at a well-defined voltage V_z. Since the breakdown characteristic is not quite vertical, the zener current, I_z, should be held constant, and the output should be buffered by a voltage follower to reduce circuit loading.

Error Amplifier

The error amplifier is basically an operational amplifier with a very high open-loop gain. Assuming that $V' = V_{REF}$, it follows from Equation 11-28 that:

$$V_o = \left(1 + \frac{R_1}{R_2}\right) V_{REF} \qquad \text{(Eq. 11-29)}$$

This equation shows that a range of output voltages can be obtained by changing the ratio R_1/R_2 and that the minimum value of V_o ($= V_{REF}$) is obtained when $R_1 = 0$. Control of the output voltage can also be achieved by placing a voltage divider across the reference and applying a fraction of V_{REF} to the noninverting input. In this case, with V_o connected directly to the inverting input, the output becomes:

$$V_o = \left(\frac{R_2}{R_1 + R_2}\right) V_{REF} \qquad \text{(Eq. 11-30)}$$

Thus we have values of V_o which are always less than V_{REF}.

Series-Pass Element

This component is almost invariably a transistor or a combination of transistors. Since the total load current passes through the transistor and a substantial voltage drop may exist across it, the internal power dissipation can be considerable. In a monolithic regulator, virtually all of the power dissipation comes from the internal pass transistor. Hence, whether an IC regulator or an external pass transistor is employed, careful attention must be paid to the power dissipation and adequate heat sinking provided if required.

For an unregulated input V_i, output V_o, and load current I_o, the power dissipated in the pass element is given by:

$$P_D = I_o(V_i - V_o) \qquad \text{(Eq. 11-31)}$$

The minimum value of the potential difference $(V_i - V_o)$ is the *drop-out voltage,* V_R, and is usually about 2–3 volts. Thus, the minimum power dissipation becomes $P_{MIN} = I_o V_R$. In many cases, however, the power dissipation is much greater than this minimum value. Typical situations include:

- A large value of V_i.
- A variable output power supply operating at a low value of V_o.
- An output short circuit where $V_o = 0$, so that $(V_i - V_o)$ and I_o become very large. In this case, the power dissipation may cause damage if there is no form of current-limiting protection.

If a high-current, high-power transistor is used as the pass element, then because of its low current gain, the drive available from the operational amplifier may not be sufficient to supply the required base current. In this situation, a *Darlington pair* such as that shown in Fig. 11-10 solves the problem. Transistor Q1 has a high current gain, since it need only supply the base current for the power transistor Q2. The total current gain is essentially the product of the individual gains of Q1 and Q2. Darlington pairs can be constructed from individual transistors or are available in a single package from several manufacturers. As Fig. 11-8 shows, the driver transistor may be part of an IC regulator connected to an external power transistor.

Current Source

Fig. 11-7 shows that the blocks making up a regulator are operated from a constant current source. This is done to make

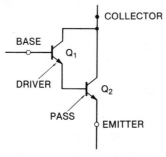

Fig. 11-10. Darlington pair connection.

the operation of the circuits insensitive to wide fluctuations in the input voltage and hence improves the stability of the input. Thus, for example, constant current operation of the zener diode in Fig. 11-9 improves the stability of V_z.

Start-Up Circuit

An easy way to construct a current source is to use the stable, regulated output voltage and a large resistor. However, since the output is zero when the supply is off, the current source may not start to function when the supply is first turned on. Hence, a start-up circuit operating from the unregulated input may be required to start the current source. Once started, the regulated output can take over and keep the system running.

11-4-4 Protection Circuits

Protection circuits are required to protect both the power supply and the microcomputer system from fault conditions and possible damage. Protection for the power supply includes: current limiting, safe operating area, and thermal overload protection. For the load, and in particular for the microprocessor subsystem's digital circuits, overvoltage protection is essential since digital circuits can tolerate only a small overvoltage without damage. Power supply protection is generally achieved by controlling the base current to the pass transistor and is usually incorporated as part of a monolithic regulator. The most common overvoltage condition occurs through failure of the pass transistor, which allows the unregulated input voltage to reach the load. Overvoltage protection must therefore be independent of the regulator itself and is most commonly provided by some form of external crowbar circuit.

Current Limiting

Fig. 11-11 illustrates a typical current-limiting circuit designed to provide short-circuit protection by starving the pass element of its base current drive. The circuit relies on the fact that

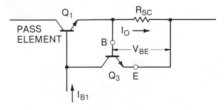

Fig. 11-11. Current-limiting circuit.

the base-emitter voltage, V_{BE}, of the limiting transistor Q3 needs to be greater than about 0.6 volt before Q3 turns on. In Fig. 11-11, V_{BE} is provided by the potential drop across the current sense resistor, R_{SC}, and is given by:

$$V_{BE} = V_{SENSE} = I_o R_{SC} \qquad \text{(Eq. 11-32)}$$

The value of R_{SC} is chosen so that, under normal conditions, V_{SENSE} is less than 0.6 volt, so that Q3 is off and the full drive current reaches the base of the pass transistor, Q1. However, if I_o exceeds its maximum allowable value, V_{SENSE} becomes greater than 0.6 volt, Q3 turns on, and the drive current flows through Q3 rather than reaching the base of Q1. The pass transistor therefore closes down, thus limiting the load current as illustrated in Fig. 11-12A. If an external pass transistor is employed to boost the current drive capability of a monolithic regulator, then a current-limiting circuit should always be included.

Foldback current limiting, an extension of the above ideas, ensures that the short-circuit current is much less than the maximum current at the rated output voltage. Fig. 11-12B sketches a typical foldback current characteristic. The main advantage of this arrangement is that it reduces the power dissipated by the pass transistor under short-circuit conditions.

Safe operating area (SOA) protection guards the regulator against excessive voltage differences between the input and the output. *Thermal overload protection* shuts down the regulator if the temperature of the regulator or the pass element becomes excessive.

Crowbar Protection

In this form of overvoltage protection, a fuse is made to blow, shutting down the system, if the output voltage exceeds some maximum allowable value. Such protection is strongly recommended in microcomputer systems, since a sudden

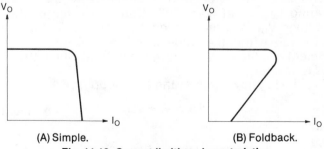

(A) Simple.　　　　　　　(B) Foldback.
Fig. 11-12. Current-limiting characteristics.

overvoltage condition on the power rails may cause considerable damage.

Fig. 11-13 illustrates a basic crowbar circuit in which a fuse, or circuit breaker, is placed in the active line to the regulator, together with a thyristor connected between the line and ground. The thyristor is normally turned off, but if the output becomes higher than some set point, the thyristor triggers, giving a virtual short circuit to ground. The thyristor therefore diverts all of the load current to ground until such time as the fuse blows, whereupon some form of manual reset becomes necessary.

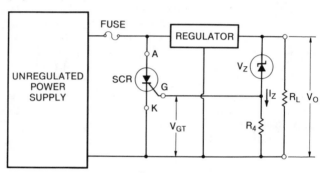

Fig. 11-13. Crowbar overvoltage protection circuit.

The simple trigger employed in Fig. 11-13 consists of a zener diode, with a breakdown voltage about 1 volt less than the required set-point voltage, and a resistor R_4. Under normal conditions the zener diode is not conducting; there is no current through R_4 and the gate of the thyristor is at ground. If an overvoltage condition occurs, the zener conducts and current I_Z flows through R_4, generating a sufficiently large gate voltage V_{GT} to trigger the thyristor. The design of this crowbar circuit consists of the following steps:

1. Choose a thyristor with a single-cycle surge current rating I_{surge} of at least $20I_o$. Note the value of the gate voltage V_{GT} required to trigger the device. Typical values of V_{GT} lie within the range $0.2 < V_{GT} < 1.0$ volt.
2. Select a value for V_{OM}, the value of V_o at which the circuit is to trigger.
3. Fig. 11-13 shows that at the trigger point:

$$V_{OM} = V_Z + V_{GT}$$ (Eq. 11-33)

and

$$V_{GT} = I_Z R_4$$ (Eq. 11-34)

4. From the data sheets, select a zener diode with the V_Z value closest to that required by Equation 11-33. Note the corresponding value of I_Z.
5. Use the values of I_Z and V_{GT} in Equation 11-34 to find the value of R_4.
6. Note that, as shown in Fig. 11-9, the value of V_Z depends on I_Z. Hence, some variation in V_{OM} can be obtained by changing the value of R_4. In particular, if R_4 increases, then the value of I_Z and hence that of V_Z decreases, thus decreasing V_{OM}.
7. Select a fuse or circuit breaker for insertion into the active lead to the regulator. It should have a current rating of $5-10I_o$. This sets the fuse current at a value somewhere between the normal ripple current of $2-3I_o$ and the maximum surge current of $20I_o$.

A typical crowbar design for a +15-volt supply is given in Example 11-7.

EXAMPLE 11-7: CROWBAR OVERVOLTAGE PROTECTION DESIGN

Given:
$$V_o = 15 \text{ volts}$$
$$I_o = 1.0 \text{ amp}$$

Thyristor selection:
$$I_{surge} = 20 \, I_o = 20 \text{ amps}$$
$$V_{GT} = 0.6 \text{ volt}$$

Select maximum output voltage $V_{OM} = 16$ volts.

From Equation 11-33:
$$V_Z = 16 - 0.6 = 15.4 \text{ volts}$$

Select a zener diode with $V_Z = 15$ volts at $I_Z = 5$ mA.

From Equation 11-34:
$$R_4 = \frac{0.6}{5 \times 10} = 120 \text{ ohms}$$

Select $I_{fuse} = 5I_o = 5 \times 1 = 5$ amps.

11-5 LINEAR REGULATORS: IMPLEMENTATION

When considering which type of regulator to use, many options exist depending on the particular application. The easiest option, and often the most convenient, is a monolithic three-terminal regulator. This regulator provides fixed, preset voltages and requires a minimum of external components. The simplest form of variable regulator is the monolithic four-terminal regulator. It is essentially the same as the three-terminal regulator, except that an extra terminal has been added to control the value of the output voltage. The 723 precision regulator introduced in Section 11-4-2 is a most versatile device, but it requires considerable external circuitry. The final option is to construct your own regulator by choosing the appropriate pass element, operational amplifier, and voltage reference. This option is needed only in specialized power supplies.

11-5-1 Three-Terminal Regulators

Three-terminal regulators are available with a wide variety of output voltages, load currents, and packages. A typical family of three-terminal regulators is the 78XX series, where the XX gives the output voltage rating. Their data sheets appear later in Fig. 11-20. These regulators are available with fixed outputs of 5, 6, 8, 10, 12, 15, 18, and 24 volts. They are mounted in TO-3 aluminum cans and, with a suitable heat sink, can deliver output currents of 1.5 amps.

The basic regulator connections are shown in Fig. 11-14. The manufacturer recommends using a 0.2-μF disc ceramic capacitor C_1 on the input to maintain stability if the regulator is located more than a few inches from the main filter capacitor. Although not strictly necessary, it is also recommended that the output be bypassed by capacitor C_2, a 0.1-μF disc ceramic to improve the transient response to sudden load changes. As indicated in Fig. 11-14, single-point grounding (see Section 4-5-1) should be used to maintain stability and noise immunity. Since the drop-out voltage for all the devices in this series is 2 volts, we must always maintain the input at a potential which is at least 2 volts higher than the output. Thus,

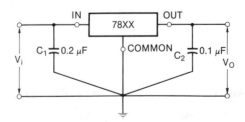

Fig. 11-14. Basic three-terminal regulator.

for example, if a 7805 is employed with $V_o = 5$ volts, then the value of V_{MIN} in Fig. 11-5 must be at least 7 volts.

Although intended primarily for fixed voltage applications, three-terminal regulators can be modified to give a variable output voltage or a constant current output as shown in Figs. 11-15A and B. Remembering that the fixed output voltage V_{REG} always appears between the output and the common terminal, it follows that in Fig. 11-15A,

$$V_o = V_{REG}(1 + R_2/R_1), \qquad \text{(Eq. 11-35)}$$

whereas in Fig. 11-15B,

$$I_L = V_{REG}/R. \qquad \text{(Eq. 11-36)}$$

Although these modified regulators work quite satisfactorily, there is some slight degradation of the specifications compared with the basic regulator. It should be noted that the nominal output voltage from a three-terminal regulator is only guaranteed to within 5%, so that, for example, the output of a 7805 may lie anywhere within the range of 4.8–5.2 volts. The circuit in Fig. 11-15 is therefore useful for trimming V_o to the required value.

If a negative output voltage is required, for example, to provide a −15-volt rail, then complementary families of negative three-terminal regulators are available with specifications similar to their positive counterparts. As an example, the previously discussed 78XX series is matched by a 79XX series of negative regulators.

A typical dual ±15-volt power supply employing a tapped bridge is shown in Fig. 11-16. Note in particular the polarity of the electrolytic filter capacitors. The reverse-biased diodes D_5 and D_6 are included to prevent a possible latch-up when the supply is first turned on. They should have a current rating of at least half the maximum load current. The component values

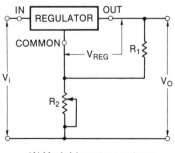

(A) Variable output voltage.

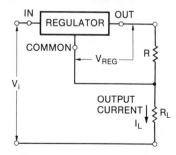

(B) Constant current supply.

Fig. 11-15. Three-terminal regulator applications.

shown should give a maximum current of about 1 amp on both the +15-volt and −15-volt rails. The design for the unregulated supply is taken from the examples given in Section 11-3.

11-5-2 Four-Terminal Regulators

The obvious disadvantage of a three-terminal regulator is that only certain fixed output voltages are available. In terms of the block diagram in Fig. 11-7, the solution is to bring the sampling resistors R_1 and R_2 off the chip, replace them by an external voltage divider, and make the inverting input of the operational amplifier available as a control terminal on the package. The 78XX and 79XX series have been modified in this way to give the 78G and 79G four-terminal positive and negative adjustable regulators.

The manufacturer's Application Notes[1] for these devices give many examples of different types of supplies, including high current, high voltage, tracking, and programmable supplies. Since most four-terminal regulators are derived from their three-terminal counterparts, their specifications are very similar.

The basic circuit for a four-terminal regulator is shown in Fig. 11-17. The control or reference voltage V_{CONT} appears between the control and common terminals. The resistors R_1 and R_2 pick off a fraction of the output voltage so that, as in Equation 11-29,

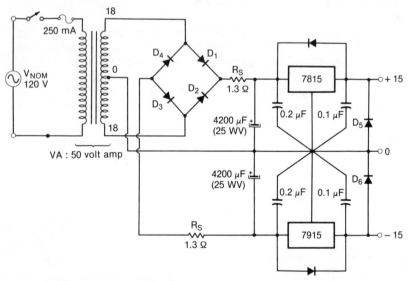

Fig. 11-16. Complete ±15-volt, 1-amp power supply.

$$V_o = (1 + R_1/R_2) V_{CONT} \qquad \text{(Eq. 11-37)}$$

For the 78G, $V_{CONT} = 5$ volts; for the 79G, $V_{CONT} = -2.2$ volts. Hence, knowing V_o and V_{CONT}, the value of R_1/R_2 follows from Equation 11-37. The data sheets recommended $I_2 = 1$ mA, so that for $V_{CONT} = 5$ volts, $R_2 = 5K$; and for $V_{CONT} = -2.2$ volts, $R_2 = 2.2K$. R_1 can then be found.

Fig. 11-17 also shows that bypass capacitors should be used on both input and output lines. The circuit for the 79G is virtually the same as in Fig. 11-17, except for the change in polarity and the change in values of C_1 and C_2 to 2 μF and 1 μF. Note that although C_1 and C_2 can sometimes be omitted for positive regulators, the manufacturer states that *they must always be employed with negative three- or four-terminal regulators.*

11-5-3 Selecting a Regulator

Selecting a suitable regulator from a manufacturer's available range of products usually involves the following steps:

1. Begin by specifying:

   - The required output voltage V_o.
   - The maximum output current I_o.
   - The mean unregulated input voltage V_i.

   The value of V_i is the average output voltage from the filter. That is, from Fig. 11-5,

   $$V_i = V_{DC} = V_{MAX} - \tfrac{1}{2}V_r. \qquad \text{(Eq. 11-38)}$$

   Note that sometimes the value of V_i will not be known until the preliminary design of the unregulated supply has been completed.

2. Select a regulator initially based on the values of V_o and I_o.

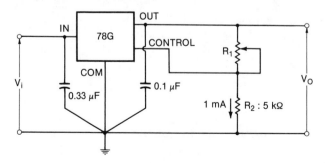

Fig. 11-17. Basic four-terminal regulator.

3. From Equation 11-31, calculate the power dissipation and choose a type and package with a power dissipation capability higher than this figure.
4. Since monolithic regulators have internal current-limiting and thermal overload protection circuits, a large value of P_D may cause the value of I_o to self-limit. For many monolithic regulators, this occurs if $(V_i - V_o) \geqslant$ 5–7 volts. Consult the data sheet of the selected regulator for a graph showing "maximum output current I_o versus voltage differential $(V_i - V_o)$" and determine I_o for your value of $(V_i - V_o)$. A typical set of these curves is reproduced in Fig. 11-18.
5. If the value of I_o from Step 4 is less than that required for your application, then several options exist:

  • Choose a regulator with a larger I_o.

Positive regulators

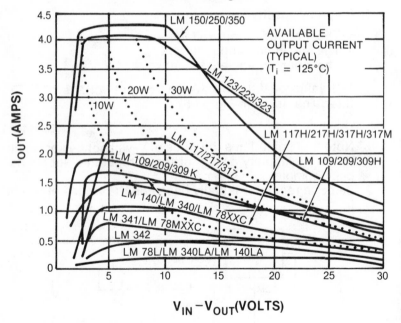

Max available output current at Tj = 125°C

Fig. 11-18. Maximum output current I_o versus voltage differential

- Reduce the value of V_i without, of course, making $V_i - V_o$ less than the dropout voltage.
- Use an external pass transistor as a current booster, including a current-limiting protection circuit.

11-6 SUMMARY OF POWER SUPPLY DESIGN PROCEDURES

In this section, we draw together the various design steps developed throughout the chapter. Following the procedure outlined below, you should be able to design a suitable power supply to meet most of your requirements. When faced with a design problem where the required output conditions are specified, the usual procedure is to start at the output and work backward toward the input, hence the order of the steps below.

Negative regulators

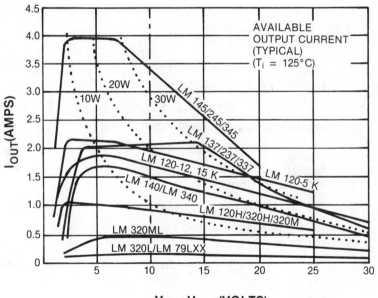

NOTE: PEAK OUTPUT CURRENTS FOR THE LM120H ARE APPROXIMATELY HALF THOSE OF THE LM120K.

$(V_i - V_o)$. (*Courtesy National Semiconductor*)

1. Write down the general specifications for the power supply output voltage V_o, the output current I_o, and the load and line regulation figures.
2. Decide on an overall configuration: regulator, filter, rectifier, and transformer.
3. Following the procedure outlined in Section 11-5-3, choose a suitable three- or four-terminal regulator to meet the specifications outlined in Step 1, and note the regulator's drop-out voltage V_R.
4. Determine V_{MIN} from:

$$V_{MIN} \geqslant V_o + V_R \qquad \text{(Eq. 11-21)}$$

5. Choose a value for V_r/V_{MAX}, where a value of 0.1 is typical.
6. Determine V_{MAX}, V_r, and V_i from:

$$V_{MAX} = V_{MIN}/(1 - V_r/V_{MAX}) \qquad \text{(Eq. 11-23)}$$

$$V_r = (V_r/V_{MAX})V_{MAX} \qquad \text{(Eq. 11-24)}$$

$$V_i = V_{MAX} - \tfrac{1}{2}V_r \qquad \text{(Eq. 11-38)}$$

Check the regulator power dissipation as in Section 11-5-3.
7. Specify the filter capacitor.
   a. Calculate the capacitance from:

$$C = I_o/120V_r \qquad \text{(Eq. 11-16)}$$

   b. Estimate the required working voltage from:

$$V(\text{working}) > V_{MAX} \qquad \text{(Eq. 11-19)}$$

   c. Specify the ripple current rating from:

$$I_r(\text{RMS}) = 2.5I_o \qquad \text{(Eq. 11-20)}$$

8. Calculate the value of the surge-limiting resistor, R_s.
   a. Calculate R_s from:

$$R_s = V_{MAX}/20I_o \qquad \text{(Eq. 11-11)}$$

   where it is assumed that $V_{SM} \approx V_{MAX}$.
   b. Determine V_{RS} from:

$$V_{RS} = I_o R_s \qquad \text{(Eq. 11-12)}$$

9. Specify the diodes.
   a. Specify the rectifier configuration.
   b. Specify the diode current rating as:

$$I_D = 2I_o. \qquad \text{(Eq. 11-10)}$$

   c. Determine the diode reverse voltage V_{RM} as:

$$V_{RM} > 2V_{SM} \text{ for FWCT and tapped bridge}$$
$$V_{RM} > V_{SM} \text{ for bridge} \qquad \text{(Eq. 11-9)}$$

d. Estimate the forward voltage drop, V_D, across the rectifier.

10. Outline transformer specifications.
    a. Specify the transformer configuration.
    b. Determine the RMS secondary voltage rating from:

$$V_s = \frac{1}{\sqrt{2}} (V_o + V_R + V_{RS} + V_r + V_D) \frac{V_{NOM}}{V_{LOW}} \qquad \text{(Eq. 11-5)}$$

assuming a 20% line voltage variation ($V_{NOM}/V_{LOW} = 1.2$).
    c. Calculate the RMS secondary current rating from:

$$\text{FWCT: } I_s = 2I_o; \quad \text{Bridge: } I_s = 1.8I_o \qquad \text{(Eq. 11-6)}$$

    d. Determine the transformer VA rating as:

$$V_{ST}I_s \qquad \text{(Eq. 11-7)}$$

$$\text{where } V_{ST} = 2V_s\text{(FWCT) or } V_{ST} = V_s\text{(bridge).} \qquad \text{(Eq. 11-8)}$$

11. Determine the fuse current rating from:

$$I_{fuse} = 1.5I_o(V_s/V_p) \qquad \text{(Eq. 11-26)}$$

12. Design an overvoltage protection circuit.
    a. Specify a maximum allowable output voltage V_{OM}.
    b. Select a thyristor, $I_{surge} = 20I_o$, and note V_{GT}.
    c. Determine $V_Z = V_{OM} - V_{GT}$. $\qquad$ (Eq. 11-33)
    d. Select a zener diode to give V_Z at a current I_Z.
    e. Determine $R_4 = V_{GT}/I_Z$. $\qquad$ (Eq. 11-34)
    f. Choose a fuse: $I_{fuse} = 5I_o$.

11-7 DESIGN EXAMPLE: 5-VOLT SUPPLY

In this section, we illustrate the principles developed in this chapter by designing a 5-volt, 3-amp power supply. The design for a 15-volt, 1-amp power supply is obtained by following through the examples given in the earlier sections. The circuit for a complete ±15-volt, 1-amp power supply was shown in Fig. 11-16. Following the procedure given in Section 11-6, we develop the design as follows:

Specifications
    Output voltage, V_o $\qquad$: +5.0 volts
    Maximum output current, I_o : 3.0 amps
    Regulator $\qquad$: Monolithic three-terminal
    Filter $\qquad$: Capacitive
    Rectifier $\qquad$: Bridge
    Protection $\qquad$: Crowbar overvoltage

Regulator Selection

Step 3: From general specifications $V_o = 5$ volts, $I_o = 3$ amps, $V_i = ?$
Initial selection: From Fig. 11-18, select LM123.

$V_R = 2$ volts

Proceed with Steps 4, 5, and 6 of the design procedure (below).

From Step 6:

$V_{MAX} = 8$ volts; $V_r = 0.8$ volt

$V_i = 8 - (0.5 \times 0.8) = 7.6$ volts   (Eq. 11-38)

$P_D = 3(7.6 - 5.0) \approx 8$ watts   (Eq. 11-31)

From LM123 data sheet, $(P_D)_{MAX} = 30$ watts.

From Fig. 11-18, with $V_i - V_o = 2.6$ watts, find $(I_o)_{MAX} = 4$ amps.

Since $P_D < (P_D)_{MAX}$ and $I_o < (I_o)_{MAX}$, the choice of LM123 is confirmed.

Determination of V_{MIN}, V_{MAX} and V_r

Step 4: $V_{MIN} = 5 + 2 = 7$ volts   (Eq. 11-21)

Step 5: $V_r/V_{MAX} = 0.1$ (assumed value)

Step 6: $V_{MAX} = \dfrac{7}{1 - 0.1} = 7.7 \approx 8$ volts   (Eq. 11-23)

$V_r = 0.1 \times 8 = 0.8$ volt   (Eq. 11-24)

Filter Capacitor

Step 7: $C = \dfrac{3.0}{120 \times 0.8} = 31,000\ \mu F$ (Eq. 11-16)

V(working) > 8.0 volts (10 volts preferred value)   (Eq. 11-19)

$I_r(RMS) = 2.5 \times 3 = 7.5$ amps   (Eq. 11-20)

Surge-Limiting Resistor

Step 8: $R_s = \dfrac{8}{20 \times 3} = 0.13$ ohm   (Eq. 11-11)

$V_{RS} = 3 \times 0.13 = 0.39$ volt   (Eq. 11-12)

Diode Specification

Step 9: $I_D = 2 \times 3 = 6$ amps   (Eq. 11-10)

PIV = 12 volts (See Step 10 for V_{SM}.)   (Eq. 11-9)

$$V_{RM} \geqslant 2 \times 12 = 24 \text{ volts}$$
$$V_D = 2 \times 1.0 = 2 \text{ volts}$$

Transformer Specification
Step 10: Single secondary winding.

$$V_s = \frac{1.2}{\sqrt{2}} (5 + 2 + 0.4 + 0.8 + 2) = 8.7 \text{ volts} \qquad \text{(Eq. 11-5)}$$

$$V_{SM} = \sqrt{2} \times 8.7 = 12.2 \text{ volts}$$

$$I_s = 1.8 \times 3 = 5.4 \text{ amps (for bridge)} \qquad \text{(Eq. 11-6)}$$

$$VA = 8.7 \times 5.4 = 47 \approx 50 \text{ volt-amp} \qquad \text{(Eq. 11-8)}$$

Fuse Calculation
Step 11: $I_{fuse} = \dfrac{1.5 \times 3 \times 8.7}{115} = 0.34 \text{ amp}$ \qquad (Eq. 11-26)

Overvoltage Protection
Step 12: V_{OM} = 6 volts (specified value)

     I_{surge} = $20 \times 3 = 60$ amps

     V_{GT} = 0.8 volt

     V_Z = $6 - 0.8 = 5.2$ volts

     Zener diode: $V_Z = 5.6$ volts at $I_Z = 5$ mA

     R_4 = $\dfrac{0.8}{5 \times 10^{-3}} = 140$ ohm

     I_{fuse} = $5 \times 3 = 15$ amps

The complete circuit design is shown in Fig. 11-19.

11-8 BUYING OR BUILDING: POWER SUPPLY EVALUATION

In this chapter, we tried to provide you with enough theory and practical detail so that you can understand and build your own power supply. However, in many cases you may prefer to buy a complete commercial one. The decision whether to buy or to build depends on a number of mostly personal factors. Some of these include:

- *Cost.* The cost of components for a homemade supply is about one-third the cost of the equivalent commercial supply.
- *Areas of competence or interest.* If you are interested mainly in the software aspects of a microcomputer system, then a commercial supply may be most attractive.

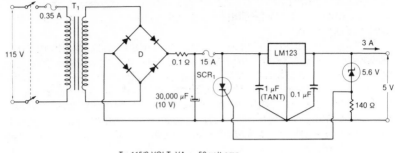

T₁: 115/9 VOLT, VA = 50 volt-amp
D: DIODE BRIDGE : I = 6 amp, $V_{RM} >$ 25 volts
SCR₁: $I_{SURGE} \geq$ 50 amp
REGULATOR: LM123, V_O = 5 volt $I_O \leq$ 3 amp

Fig. 11-19. Complete +5-volt, 3-amp power supply.

- *Time.* The time required to construct a power supply may be rather longer than that suggested by the comparative simplicity of the circuits. This is due largely to the amount of mechanical work required. Since the system must be able to handle large currents and possibly hazardous voltages, the metal work and wiring must be rugged and reliable.

- *Availability.* Sometimes a commercial power supply that meets your specifications may not be readily available on the market, in which case building may be the only option. On the other hand, the building option may be restricted by inaccessibility of suitable components.

Whichever option you choose, reading the specifications for a three-terminal regulator or for a complete supply will present you with a long string of parameters. These supply parameters include:

Output Voltage	Output Current
Output Voltage Range	Short Circuit Current Limit
Output Impedance	Quiescent Current
Line Regulation Figure	Ripple Factor
Load Regulation Figure	Ripple Rejection
Temperature Stability or "Tempco"	Line and Load Transient Response
Long-term Drift	Protection Circuits
Output Noise	

Although a number of these terms were introduced earlier in the chapter, it is worthwhile to consider some of the more important ones here.

The *load regulation figure* describes the ability of the power supply or regulator to maintain a constant voltage across its output terminals during changes in the output current I_o drawn by the load. The drop in the terminal voltage as I_o increases is due to the internal voltage drop across the *output impedance*, Z_o, of the supply. Hence, a low output impedance yields good load-regulating properties. As an example, the data sheet for the 78XX series in Fig. 11-20 gives:

$$Z_o \approx 0.017 \text{ ohm} \quad \text{and} \quad \Delta V_o \approx 15 \text{ mV} \quad \text{for} \quad 5 \text{ mA} < I_o < 1.5 \text{ amp}$$

The *line regulation figure* shows the variation in the output voltage occurring due to a change in the input voltage. For a complete power supply, the input voltage would normally be the AC line voltage; for a regulator, it is the input to the regulator itself. Again, from the data sheets for a 7805:

$$\Delta V_o = 3 \text{ mV} \quad \text{for} \quad 7 < V_i < 25 \text{ volts.}$$

The *ripple factor,* which was defined by Equation 11-17, measures the AC content of a nominally DC signal. The *ripple rejection* figure measures the ability of a system to reduce the amount of ripple at its output compared with the ripple at its input. A typical figure for the 78XX series is about 80 dB rejection. That is, given a 1.0-volt ripple signal at the input, the output ripple is about 10^{-4} volts.

The *temperature stability factor* or *temperature coefficient* ("tempco") indicates the change in output voltage with temperature. It has typical values of around -1 mV/°C for three-terminal regulators. Minimizing the temperature coefficient is one of the most important factors in producing the highly stable voltage reference sources that we discuss in Chapter 12.

The parameters described above will determine the likely accumulated change in output voltage, V_o, from the supply over a range of line, load, and temperature conditions. For a microcomputer system, the tightest power supply tolerance is ±5%. Thus, a satisfactory microcomputer power supply is one for which ΔV_o is less than 5%.

11-9 REFERENCES

1. *Fairchild Voltage Regulator Handbook,* 1978; *National Semiconductor Voltage Regulator Handbook.*

μA7800 SERIES

3-TERMINAL POSITIVE VOLTAGE REGULATORS
FAIRCHILD LINEAR INTEGRATED CIRCUITS

GENERAL DESCRIPTION — The μA7800 series of monolithic 3-Terminal Positive Voltage Regulators is constructed using the Fairchild Planar* epitaxial process. These regulators employ internal current limiting, thermal shutdown and safe area compensation, making them essentially indestructible. If adequate heat sinking is provided, they can deliver over 1 A output current. They are intended as fixed voltage regulators in a wide range of applications including local (on card) regulation for elimination of distribution problems associated with single point regulation. In addition to use as fixed voltage regulators, these devices can be used with external components to obtain adjustable output voltages and currents.

- OUTPUT CURRENT IN EXCESS OF 1 A
- NO EXTERNAL COMPONENTS
- INTERNAL THERMAL OVERLOAD PROTECTION
- INTERNAL SHORT CIRCUIT CURRENT LIMITING
- OUTPUT TRANSISTOR SAFE AREA COMPENSATION
- AVAILABLE IN THE TO-220 AND THE TO-3 PACKAGE
- OUTPUT VOLTAGES OF 5, 6, 8, 8.5, 12, 15, 18, AND 24 V

ABSOLUTE MAXIMUM RATINGS

Input Voltage (5 V through 18 V)	35 V
(24 V)	40 V
Internal Power Dissipation	Internally Limited
Storage Temperature Range	−65°C to +150°C
Operating Junction Temperature Range μA7800	−55°C to +150°C
μA7800C	0°C to +150°C
Lead Temperature (Soldering, 60 s time limit) TO-3 Package	300°C
(Soldering, 10 s time limit) TO-220 Package	230°C

CONNECTION DIAGRAMS
TO-220 PACKAGE
(SIDE VIEW)

OUTPUT
COMMON
INPUT

COMMON

TO-3 PACKAGE
(TOP VIEW)

COMMON (3)   OUTPUT

INPUT

ORDER INFORMATION

OUTPUT VOLTAGE	TYPE	PART NO.
5 V	μA7805C	μA7805UC
6 V	μA7806C	μA7806UC
8 V	μA7808C	μA7808UC
8.5 V	μA7885C	μA7885UC
12 V	μA7812C	μA7812UC
15 V	μA7815C	μA7815UC
18 V	μA7818C	μA7818UC
24 V	μA7824C	μA7824UC

ORDER INFORMATION

OUTPUT VOLTAGE	TYPE	PART NO.
5 V	μA7805	μA7805KM
6 V	μA7806	μA7806KM
8 V	μA7808	μA7808KM
8.5 V	μA7885	μA7885KM
12 V	μA7812	μA7812KM
15 V	μA7815	μA7815KM
18 V	μA7818	μA7818KM
24 V	μA7824	μA7824KM
5 V	μA7805C	μA7805KC
6 V	μA7806C	μA7806KC
8 V	μA7808C	μA7808KC
8.5 V	μA7885C	μA7885KC
12 V	μA7812C	μA7812KC
15 V	μA7815C	μA7815KC
18 V	μA7818C	μA7818KC
24 V	μA7824C	μA7824KC

*Planar is a patented Fairchild process.

Fig. 11-20. Data sheets for the 78XX

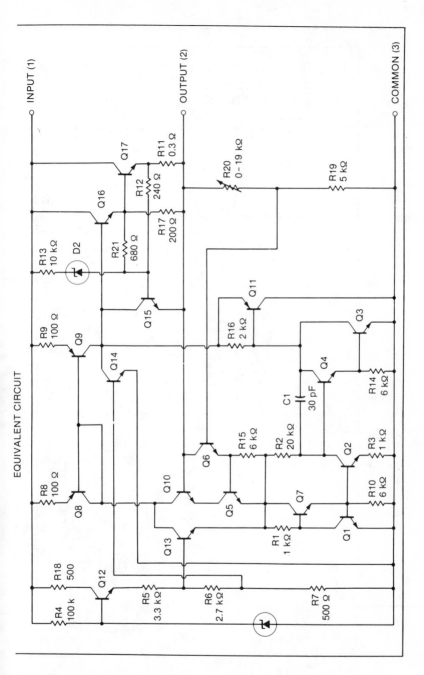

EQUIVALENT CIRCUIT

series of three-terminal regulators.

FAIRCHILD • μA7800 SERIES

μA7805

ELECTRICAL CHARACTERISTICS: V_{IN} = 10 V, I_{OUT} = 500 mA, $-55°C < T_j < 150°C$, C_{IN} T 0.33 μF, C_{OUT} = 0.1 μF, unless otherwise specified.

CHARACTERISTICS		CONDITIONS (Note 1)		MIN	TYP	MAX	UNITS
Output Voltage		T_J = 25°C		4.8	5.0	5.2	V
Line Regulation		T_J = 25°C	7 V < V_{IN} < 25 V		3	50	mV
			8 V < V_{IN} < 12 V		1	25	mV
Load Regulation		T_J = 25°C	5 mA < I_{OUT} < 1.5 A		15	100	mV
			250 mA < I_{OUT} < .750 mA		5	25	mV
Output Voltage		8.0 V < V_{IN} < 20 V 5 mA < I_{OUT} < 1.0 A P < 15 W		4.65		5.35	V
Quiescent Current		T_J = 25°C			4.2	6.0	mA
Quiescent Current Change	with line	8 V < V_{IN} < 25 V				0.8	mA
	with load	5 mA < I_{OUT} < 1.0 A				0.5	mA
Output Noise Voltage		T_A = 25°C, 10 Hz < f < 100 kHz			8	40	μV/V_{OUT}
Ripple Rejection		f = 120 Hz, 8 V < V_{IN} < 18 V		68	78		dB
Dropout Voltage		I_{OUT} = 1.0 A, T_J = 25°C			2.0	2.5	V
Output Resistance		f = 1 kHz			17		mΩ
Short Circuit Current		T_J = 25°C, V_{IN} = 35 V			0.75	1.2	A
Peak Output Current		T_J = 25°C		1.3	2.2	3.3	A
Average Temperature Coeficient of Output Voltage		I_{OUT} = 5 mA	$-55°C < T_J < +25°C$			0.4	mV/°C/
			$+25°C < T_J < +150°C$			0.3	V_{OUT}

Fig. 11-20 — cont. Data sheets for the

µA7815

ELECTRICAL CHARACTERISTICS: $V_{IN} = 23\,V$, $I_{OUT} = 500\,mA$, $-55°C < T_j < 150°C$, $C_{IN}\,T\,0.33\,\mu F$, $C_{OUT} = 0.1\,\mu F$, unless otherwise specified.

CHARACTERISTICS		CONDITIONS (Note 1)		MIN	TYP	MAX	UNITS
Output Voltage		$T_J = 25°C$		14.4	15.0	15.6	V
Line Regulation		$T_J = 25°C$	$17.5\,V < V_{IN} < 30\,V$		11	150	mV
			$20\,V < V_{IN} < 26\,V$		3	75	mV
Load Regulation		$T_J = 25°C$	$5\,mA < I_{OUT} < 1.5\,A$		12	150	mV
			$250\,mA < I_{OUT} < .750\,mA$		4	75	mV
Output Voltage		$18.5\,V < V_{IN} < 30\,V$ $5\,mA < I_{OUT} < 1.0\,A$ $P < 15\,W$		14.25		15.75	V
Quiescent Current		$T_J = 25°C$			4.4	6.0	mA
Quiescent Current Change	with line	$18.5\,V < V_{IN} < 30\,V$				0.8	mA
	with load	$5\,mA < I_{OUT} < 1.0\,A$				0.5	mA
Output Noise Voltage		$T_A = 25°C$, $10\,Hz < f < 100\,kHz$			8	40	$\mu V/V_{OUT}$
Ripple Rejection		$f = 120\,Hz$, $18.5\,V < V_{IN} < 28.5\,V$		60	70		dB
Dropout Voltage		$I_{OUT} = 1.0\,A$, $T_J = 25°C$			2.0	2.5	V
Output Resistance		$f = 1\,kHz$			19		mΩ
Short Circuit Current		$T_J = 25°C$, $V_{IN} = 35\,V$			0.75		A
Peak Output Current		$T_J = 25°C$		1.3	2.2	3.3	A
Average Temperature Coeficient of Output Voltage		$I_{OUT} = 5\,mA$	$-55°C < T_J < +25°C$			0.4	mV/°C/
			$+25°C < T_J < +150°C$			0.3	V_{OUT}

AC CHARACTERISTICS $T_A = 0°C$ to $70°C$, $V_{CC} = 5V \pm 5\%$, unless otherwise noted.

78XX series of three-terminal regulators.

Voltage References

12-1 INTRODUCTION

A *voltage reference* may be defined as a stable, precisely known voltage source used for purposes of comparison. The need for such a reference source was introduced in the preceding chapters, and three main application areas were identified:

- Power supplies.
- Analog-to-digital converters.
- Signal conditioning circuits.

These are illustrated in Fig. 12-1. Voltage references are also needed for digital-to-analog converters, which are not discussed in detail in this book.

Of the three applications discussed here, the power supply places the least stringent demands on the performance of its voltage reference. This is because most integrated circuits in microcomputer systems can tolerate at least a ±5% variation in their supply voltages. Thus, the voltage reference determining the regulation of the power supply may vary by up to 5% without affecting the operation of the microcomputer system ICs. The performance of the voltage reference for an analog-to-digital converter (ADC), however, directly determines its accuracy and repeatability and hence the accuracy and repeatability of the binary code that is input to the microprocessor. A stable voltage reference is also required in the analog signal conditioning line, particularly for offsetting. In this case, the accuracy and repeatability of the conditioned signal (as a representation of the physical variable) depends directly on the accuracy and stability of the reference used to provide the offset.

The *stability* of a voltage reference is normally its most important property, since referencing relies on measurement comparisons made at different times, sometimes over an extended period. Clearly, for two measurements of the same value to provide the same code for input to the microprocessor, then the two reference voltages — one providing an offset in the analog signal conditioning line, the other to the ADC — together must change by less than the resolution of the ADC. Table 12-1 recalls the figures for the resolution of an ADC (given earlier in Table 2-2) to illustrate the requirements that these figures impose on the stability of the voltage reference sources. The table shows, for example, that in a 10-bit system, the total accumulated error arising from a lack of stability in

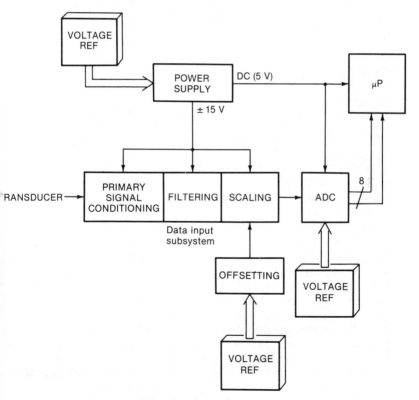

Fig. 12-1. Location of voltage references in microcomputer systems.

357

Table 12-1. Voltage Reference Requirements Imposed by System Resolution

ADC Bits	Resolution (%)	Max Reference Change (%)	Max Reference Change (mV/V)	S_t for $\Delta T = 10°C$ (%/°C)
8	0.4	0.4	4	0.04
10	0.1	0.1	1	0.01
12	0.025	0.025	0.25	0.0025
16	0.0015	0.0015	0.015	0.00015

the reference voltage sources for the offset signal conditioning circuit and for the ADC must be less than 0.1% if the full
resolution of the system is to be realized.

The main specifications governing the stability of a voltage
reference source include:

- Temperature coefficient or "tempco," S_t (mV/°C or %/°C).
- Long-term stability (μV/month or μV or %).
- Noise (μV/(Hz)$^{1/2}$).
- Load regulation or output impedance (see Section 11-8).
- Line regulation (see Section 11-8).

Of these specifications, the temperature coefficient and the
long-term stability are the most critical, since various
measures can be adopted to minimize the effects of the other
parameters. Load and line regulation can be controlled, if
necessary, by proper buffering of the reference device and by
the use of a preregulator, respectively; noise can be minimized
by a suitable low-pass filter. To illustrate the significance of
the temperature coefficient S_t, Table 12-1 shows the maximum
allowable value of S_t for ADCs of increasing resolution, assuming a 10°C change in temperature. The 10°C change is typical
of what could be expected in an unairconditioned situation
and well illustrates the importance of this insidious environmental effect.

If the absolute value of the measured voltage is also important, then the *precision* to which the value of the reference
voltage is known must also be better than the resolution of the
ADC. The parameter that specifies the precision of the voltage
reference is its *output voltage tolerance*. This is the maximum
deviation in output voltage that can be expected from identical
voltage references. It is usually defined at a specific
temperature and input voltage.

12-2 MODERN VOLTAGE REFERENCE SOURCES

In modern electronics, only two physical effects are commonly
used to provide reference voltages, namely, *avalanche* or

358

zener breakdown and the *band-gap effect.* These effects, and the devices and/or circuits that make use of these effects, are described below.

12-2-1 Zener Diodes

The so-called *zener diode* has been in use for some time now as a voltage reference. Fig. 12-2 shows the circuit symbol and the current/voltage (I/V) characteristic of a typical zener diode. When forward-biased, and with low values of applied voltage in the reverse direction, the device behaves like a normal diode. However, once the applied reverse voltage reaches the zener voltage, V_z, conduction occurs and a reverse current, I_z, flows. This reverse breakdown phenomenon is characteristic of a zener diode and is due to one of two effects within the semiconductor material: avalanche breakdown or zener breakdown.[1] Avalanche breakdown occurs predominantly in lightly doped diodes where $V_z > 6$ volts; the zener breakdown effect occurs in heavily doped diodes where $V_z < 6$ volts.

Because the slope, $\Delta I_z / \Delta V_z$, of the zener characteristic in the reverse breakdown region is so great, the voltage across the diode, V_z, is nearly constant for large variations in the reverse

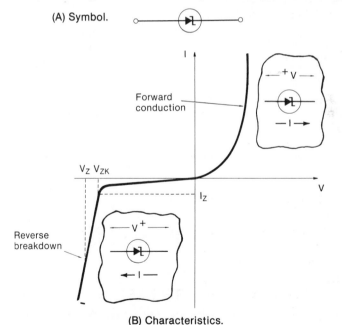

(A) Symbol.

(B) Characteristics.
Fig. 12-2. The zener diode.

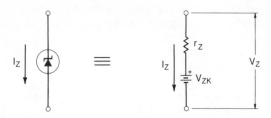

Fig. 12-3. Equivalent circuit for zener diode.

current, provided that I_z is greater than I_{ZK}. Hence, the reverse breakdown voltage, V_z, which is set when the diode is fabricated, can be used as a reference voltage.

If a zener diode is used in this way, then it may be conveniently represented by the equivalent circuit shown in Fig. 12-3. In this circuit r_z, the *slope resistance* or *dynamic resistance,* is simply $\Delta V_z / \Delta I_z$ and is a quantitative measure of the steepness of the reverse breakdown section of the zener's I/V characteristic. From this equivalent circuit, V_z may be expressed as:

$$V_z = V_{ZK} + r_z I_z \qquad \text{(Eq. 12-1)}$$

This equation shows clearly that a *small value of r_z* is needed for V_z to be approximately constant, and that r_z is an important indicator of the quality of a zener as a voltage reference. Fig. 12-4 shows the reverse voltage section of the I/V characteristics for the BZY88 series of zener diodes from

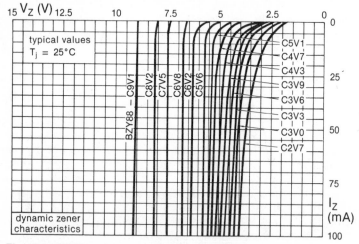

Fig. 12-4. BZY88 series zener diode reverse characteristics. (*Courtesy N. V. Philips Gloeilampenfabrieken*)

Philips. It illustrates the very steep slopes, and therefore the small r_z values (about 2–40 Ω), which are possible at moderate (20-mA) reverse currents I_z. This can be seen quantitatively in Fig. 12-5, which shows the reduction in r_z with increasing reverse current.

V_z also has a temperature dependence, typically about 0.1% per degree Celsius. However, below about $V_z = 6$ V, the temperature coefficient, S_t, is negative (i.e., V_z decreases as the temperature increases), whereas above $V_z = 6$ V, the temperature coefficient is positive. Very small temperature coefficients are possible, then, for diodes with $V_z \sim 6$ V, as can be seen in Table 12-2 for the BZY88 series of zeners. In addition, by combining zener diodes of opposite temperature coefficients in series with each other, the temperature coefficient of the total combination can be made very small. Thus, for example, while a 10-volt zener has an S_t of 7.3 mV/K, a 4.7-volt and a 5.6-volt zener in series with each other have a total breakdown voltage of 10.3 volts and a value of $S_t = -0.85 + 1.0 = +0.15$ mV/K.

Noise has traditionally been regarded as one of the greatest problems faced when using the zener diode as a voltage reference. Since the device depends on the passage of current across a junction, it generates shot noise (see Section 4-3-1) in addition to the noise generated by the breakdown process itself. Typically, a voltage reference zener diode (e.g., the BZY88 series from Philips) will produce about 1 μV rms of noise over a measurement bandwidth of 500 Hz for a reverse current, I_z, of about 5 mA. This amount of noise, being less than a 0.0001% variation on a 5-V reference (less than the resolution of even a 16-bit ADC), is simply not a problem in microcomputer systems. However, particularly noisy zeners can be quieted very simply by connecting a capacitor in parallel to reduce their bandwidth. Since we are interested only in the steady-state or DC value of the reference, large capacitor values of up to 1 μF will most effectively reduce the bandwidth of the voltage reference toward the ideal of zero. The noise properties of zener diodes, including their long-term stability, can also be improved at the fabrication stage by placing the breakdown site below the surface of the semiconductor, where it is shielded from surface effects.[2] The improved — and more expensive — device is known as a *buried zener.* This type of zener is currently being built into monolithic ADCs such as the Analog Devices AD570 shown in Fig. 12-6. Here, the functional block in the lower left region of the diagram shows that a buried zener is used as an on-chip voltage reference.

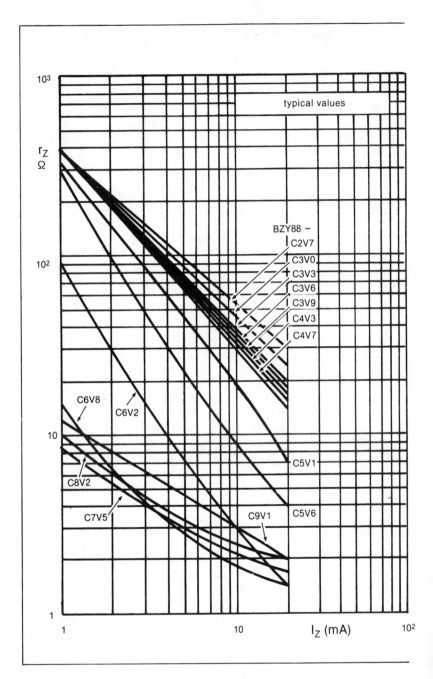

Fig. 12-5. Variation of r_z with I_z for the BZY88 series of

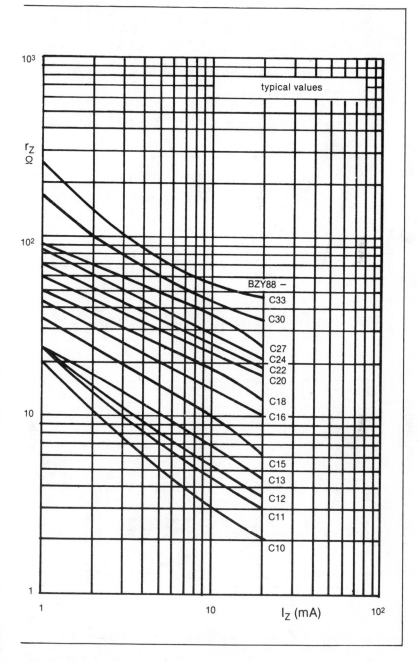

zener diodes. (*Courtesy N. V. Philips Gloeilampenfabrieken*)

Table 12-2. Characteristics of the BZY88 Series of Zener Diodes

BZY88-...	Working Voltage Vz at Iz = 20 mA min.	nom.	max.		Temperature Coefficient Sz at Iz = 20 mA min.	typ.	max.		Typical Noise Voltage* Iz = 1 mA	Iz = 5 mA
C2V7	3.0	3.25	3.5	>	-3.5	-2.4	-0.6	mV/°C	22	12 µV RMS
C3V0	3.3	3.6	3.9	>	-3.5	-2.5	-0.6	mV/°C	20	11 µV RMS
C3V3	3.5	4	4.2	>	-3.3	-2.4	-0.5	mV/°C	19	10 µV RMS
C3V6	3.9	4.2	4.4	>	-2.5	-1.55	-0.5	mV/°C	18	9 µV RMS
C3V9	4.2	4.45	4.65	>	-2.4	-1.55	-0.5	mV/°C	16	8 µV RMS
C4V3	4.45	4.7	4.95	>	-2.0	-1.5	-0.5	mV/°C	15	8 µV RMS
C4V7	4.9	5.1	5.3	>	-1.5	-0.85	0	mV/°C	14	7 µV RMS
C5V1	5.1	5.35	5.7	>	-1.5	-0.8	0	mV/°C	13	8 µV RMS
C5V6	5.45	5.75	6.1	>	-1.0	0	+3.0	mV/°C	13	9 µV RMS
C6V2	5.95	6.4	6.7	>	+1.0	+2.2	+4.0	mV/°C	14	10 µV RMS
C6V8	6.6	6.9	7.25	>	+2.8	+3.2	+3.8	mV/°C	25	15 µV RMS
C7V5	7.2	7.65	7.95	>	+2.5	+4.2	+5.9	mV/°C	33	20 µV RMS
C8V2	7.9	8.4	8.75	>	+4.0	+5.0	+6.0	mV/°C	55	28 µV RMS
C9V1	8.7	9.4	9.7	>	+5.0	+6.0	+7.0	mV/°C	79	35 µV RMS
C10	9.5	10.1	10.8	>	+7.0	+7.3	+7.5	mV/°C	87	43 µV RMS
C11	10.5	11.1	11.8	>	+8.5	+9.1	+9.5	mV/°C	92	48 µV RMS
C12	11.6	12.2	12.8	>	+8.9	+9.6	+10.3	mV/°C	100	50 µV RMS
C13	12.6	13.2	14.3	>	+11	+11.5	+12.5	mV/°C	110	52 µV RMS
C15	14.1	15.3	15.9	>	+12	+13.5	+14.5	mV/°C	120	54 µV RMS
C16	15.6	16.3	17.4	>	+13	+14	+15	mV/°C	135	56 µV RMS
C18	17.2	18.4	19.6	>	+15	+16	+18	mV/°C	160	58 µV RMS
C20	19.3	20.5	21.9	>	+17.5	+18.5	+20.5	mV/°C	210	60 µV RMS
C22	21.3	22.6	24.1	>	+19	+20.5	+22.5	mV/°C	255	62 µV RMS
C24	23.3	24.7	26.7	>	+20	+23	+25	mV/°C	290	65 µV RMS
C27	25.8	28.1	30.1	>	+23	+25.5	+28	mV/°C	320	69 µV RMS
C30	29.0	31.3	33.4	>	+25	+28	+32	mV/°C	350	73 µV RMS
C33	32.0	34.5	36.6	>	+27	+30	+38	mV/°C	380	78 µV RMS

*Noise voltage measured using a bandwidth ±3 dB of 10 Hz to 50 kHz.

12-2-2 Band-Gap Effect

The second of the two modern voltage reference sources is commonly found in integrated circuit voltage references and is known as a *band-gap* reference. This device uses the base-emitter voltage, V_{BE}, of a transistor. For a silicon transistor at room temperature (300 K), this is typically 0.6 volt. However, we saw in Section 3-3-2 that V_{BE} is temperature-dependent and is thus used as the basis of temperature transducers such as the AD590 and the LM335. V_{BE} has, in fact, a *negative* temperature coefficient, S_t, of 2 mV/K and can be expressed in general as:

$$V_{BE} = 1.2 - S_t T \qquad \text{(Eq. 12-2)}$$

Hence, V_{BE} itself cannot be used as a voltage reference source, and effective temperature compensation must be employed to remove the temperature-dependence illustrated in Equation 12-2. This is done by adding to a V_{BE} a temperature-dependent voltage, V_1, with a *positive* temperature coefficient *a,* to produce a reference voltage, V_{REF}, which has a very low temperature coefficient. That is:

$$V_{REF} = V_{BE} + V_1, \qquad \text{(Eq. 12-3)}$$

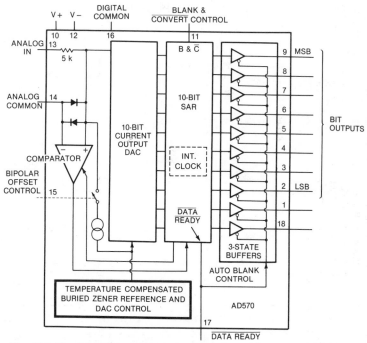

Fig. 12-6. The AD570 monolithic ADC. (*Courtesy Analog Devices Inc.***)**

where $V_1 = aT$, so that from Equation 12-2,

$$V_{REF} = (1.2 - S_tT) + aT. \qquad \text{(Eq. 12-4)}$$

The value of a is now adjusted to have the same value as S_t, so that the temperature-dependent terms cancel each other and

$$V_{REF} = 1.2 \text{ volts} \qquad \text{(Eq. 12-5)}$$

This figure of 1.2 volts is the difference in potential between the top of the valence band and the bottom of the conduction band in silicon.[3] It is known as the *band-gap voltage,* V_G, and provides the name and nominal output voltage for this class of voltage reference sources.

The temperature compensation voltage $V_1 = aT$ is usually obtained by using a monolithic pair of transistors, operating at different current densities J_1 and J_2, to develop a predictable and controllable voltage, ΔV_{BE}, of the form:

$$\Delta V_{BE} = \frac{kT}{q} \ln\left(\frac{J_1}{J_2}\right) \qquad \text{(Eq. 12-6)}$$

where $J_1/J_2 > 1$ so that ΔV_{BE} has a positive temperature coefficient.[4]

A typical circuit employing this principle is shown in Fig. 12-7, where:

$$V_{REF} = V_{BE1} + V_1, \qquad \text{(Eq. 12-7)}$$

$$V_1 = (I_1 + I_2)R_1 \approx 2I_2R_1, \qquad \text{(Eq. 12-8)}$$

since $I_1 \approx I_2$, and

$$I_2 = \Delta V_{BE}/R_2. \qquad \text{(Eq. 12-9)}$$

Substituting Equations 12-8, 12-9, and 12-6 into Equation 12-7 gives:

$$V_{REF} = V_{BE1} + \left[2\,\frac{R_1}{R_2}\frac{k}{q}\ln\left(\frac{J_1}{J_2}\right)\right]T, \qquad \text{(Eq. 12-10)}$$

or, using Equation 12-2 for V_{BE1},

$$V_{REF} = 1.2 - S_tT + \left[2\,\frac{R_1}{R_2}\frac{k}{q}\ln\left(\frac{J_1}{J_2}\right)\right]T. \qquad \text{(Eq. 12-11)}$$

If the value of R_1/R_2 is adjusted so that:

$$2\,\frac{R_1}{R_2}\frac{k}{q}\ln\left(\frac{J_1}{J_2}\right) = S_t, \qquad \text{(Eq. 12-12)}$$

then $V_{REF} = 1.2$ volts with an almost zero temperature coefficient.

Although this type of voltage reference is less noisy than

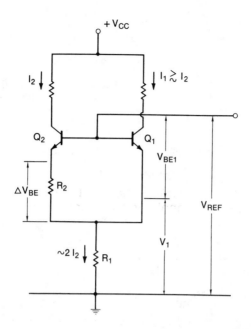

Fig. 12-7. Schematic circuit for band-gap voltage reference.

the zener diode and has better long-term stability, its voltage tolerance is more difficult to control at the manufacturing stage because of the need to adjust R_1, R_2, J_1 and J_2. The residual temperature coefficient, after trimming R_1/R_2, is also normally higher than for zeners.

Practical monolithic band-gap references usually incorporate an output buffer stage, possibly with gain, so that reference voltages of other than 1.2 volts are available. These devices are discussed in greater detail in Section 12-4.

12-3 DISCRETE COMPONENT VOLTAGE REFERENCE CIRCUITS

The characteristics of the zener diode, which were discussed in Section 12-2-1 and illustrated in Fig. 12-4 for the BZY88 series, indicate that a zener must be operated at constant current to obtain a constant voltage. This is normally achieved by connecting the zener in series with a current-limiting resistor, R_{CL}, across the power supply lines, as shown in Fig. 12-8. The value of this resistor can be calculated by selecting a moderate zener current such that:

$$I_z < I_{zMAX} = P_{tot}/V_z \qquad \text{(Eq. 12-13)}$$

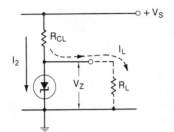

Fig. 12-8. Basic zener diode reference circuit.

where P_{tot} is the maximum power dissipation of the zener; and by applying the following equation:

$$R_{CL} = \frac{V_s - V_z}{I_z} \qquad \text{(Eq. 12-14)}$$

A stability problem arises, however, if any load is connected in parallel with the zener: this reduces the reverse current flowing through the zener and changes its voltage. To maintain a constant zener voltage even if the load on the voltage reference circuit changes, a buffering circuit, such as that shown in Fig. 12-9, is necessary. In this circuit, a voltage follower has been used to provide good buffering between the zener and the load. Because the temperature coefficient of the BZY88 series of zeners is lowest for a breakdown voltage of about 5.5 V (see Table 12-2), a 5.6-V zener (C5V6) has been used. The value for the current-limiting resistor was determined by selecting a 20-mA zener current and by applying Equation 12-14. Note that P_{tot} for the BZY88 series is 400 mW. This means, for Equation 12-13, that I_{zMAX} is 71 mA, which is very much greater than the selected zener current. The zener circuit is followed by a resistive voltage divider to obtain a 5-V reference. If a variable reference voltage is required, or a fine

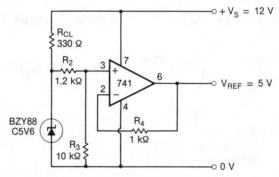

Fig. 12-9. Buffered 5-V voltage reference.

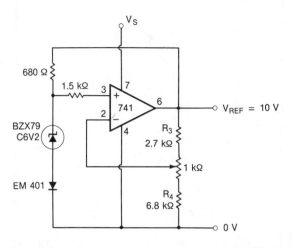

Fig. 12-10. Buffered and temperature-compensated 10-V reference.

adjustment to compensate for the tolerance of the resistors, R_1 can be replaced by a potentiometer.

An improvement on this circuit is shown in Fig. 12-10. Here the zener diode is driven from the reference voltage, rather than from the power supply, to obtain greater constancy of the output voltage. Note that the zener has been connected in series with a silicon diode to improve the temperature coefficient of the voltage reference. At 5 mA, the zener shown has a temperature coefficient of +2.3 mV/°C, while the EM401 has a temperature coefficient of −2.2 mV/°C. This gives the combination a net temperature coefficient of +0.1 mV/°C, or 0.0015%/°C. The voltage follower circuit is used with gain so that a 10-V reference voltage can be obtained from the 6.8 V (6.2 + 0.6) appearing across the two diodes in series. This circuit has good stability and a low temperature coefficient. Its low cost may make it preferable, in low budget applications, to the IC voltage references described in the following section.

12-4 INTEGRATED CIRCUIT VOLTAGE REFERENCE CIRCUITS

12-4-1 Zener-Based Devices

Fig. 12-10 illustrated how a zener diode can be provided with temperature compensation and buffering *externally.* To simplify circuit construction, it is possible to purchase integrated circuit (IC) packages in which zener diodes and their temperature compensation and buffering are fabricated on the

Table 12-3. Summary of Voltage References

Device	Voltage (volts)	Precision (%)	S_t(%/°C) (typical)	Long-term Stability (%)	r_z (Ω)	Line Regulation	Load Regulation
LM329	6.9	5	0.0006–0.005	0.002	1	—	—
LM399	6.9	2	0.0003	0.002	0.5	—	—
LM313 (AD589)	1.22	5 (or better)	0.01	N.A.	0.3	—	—
LM336	2.5	4 or 2	0.001	0.002	0.4	—	10 mV (0.4%) (ΔI = 10 mA)
AD580	2.5	1–3	0.001	0.01	—	3 mV (0.1%) 4.5 ≤ V_{in} ≤ 7	
AD581	10	0.05–0.3	0.001	0.0025	—	1 mV (0.01%) 13 ≤ V_{in} ≤ 15	0.2 mV/mA
LM10	0.2–40 Adjustable	N.A.	0.002	N.A.	—	0.01%/V	0.01%
Three-terminal regulator	Various	2	0.01	0.1–1	0.01–0.1	—	—
Buffered zener (Fig. 10-9)	Adjustable	5	0.02	N.A.	10^{-3}	—	—
Buffered and compensated zener (Fig. 10-10)	Adjustable	5	0.0015	N.A.	10^{-3}	—	—

N.A.: Not Available

same silicon chip. Here are two examples of such devices, available from National Semiconductor Corporation.

The *LM329* is a two-terminal device that can be used exactly as if it were a zener diode, but with improved performance. As can be seen from Table 12-3, the LM329 has a much lower dynamic resistance, a much lower temperature coefficient, and a better long-term stability. It produces 6.9 V and so can be used as a direct substitute for the zener diode plus rectifier diode shown in Fig. 12-10, although the circuit recommended by National Semiconductor is a little different.[5] A typical application of the LM329 in a signal conditioning situation is shown in Fig. 3-23 and repeated in Fig. 12-11 for convenience. Here the LM329 is used to provide an offset voltage for the LM335 temperature sensor (Section 3-3-2) so that the 10-mV/K output of the LM335 can be converted into a 10-mV/°C signal. To obtain a better apparent temperature coefficient from an active zener such as the LM329, it is necessary to stabilize the temperature of the silicon chip.

The *LM399* is a four-terminal device which has a temperature stabilization circuit alongside an actively buffered and compensated zener on the same silicon chip. The temperature stabilization circuit is connected to the power rails independently of the active reference zener. Thus the zener may be used in the same way as an ordinary zener. The performance of the LM399 (see Table 12-3) is similar to that of

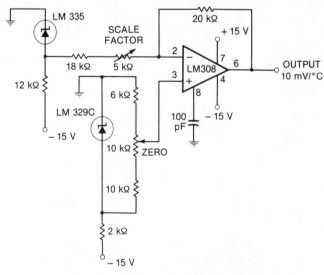

Fig. 12-11. Ground-referred Celsius thermometer.

371

the LM329, except for an improved initial tolerance and a guaranteed temperature coefficient of 0.0001% per °C.

12-4-2 Band-Gap Devices

The *LM313* from National Semiconductor Corporation and the *AD589* from Analog Devices, Inc., are inexpensive (less than $3 in 1981) voltage references that use the band-gap effect described in Section 12-2-2. These two-terminal devices can be used as if they were zener diodes having a breakdown voltage of 1.22 V and a low dynamic impedance. The AD589 is claimed to be better than the LM313, but performance figures were not available to the authors at the time of this writing.

The *LM336* is a three-terminal device whose third terminal is provided for fine adjustment of the output voltage. It can be used without the third terminal and connected in the same way as a zener diode having a breakdown voltage of 2.5 V and a low dynamic impedance. Fig. 12-12 shows how the third terminal is used to trim the "breakdown" voltage and minimize the temperature coefficient.

The *AD580* and *AD581* from Analog Devices, Inc., also have three terminals. However, the terminals have different functions from those of the LM336, as can be seen from the functional diagram in Fig. 12-13. V_{in} for the AD580 can vary from 4.5 to 30 V while providing a V_{out} of 2.5 V $\pm1\%$ at up to 10 mA. For the AD 581, V_{in} can vary from 12 to 40 V to give a V_{out} of 10 V ±5 mV at up to 10 mA. Because of their configuration, the "dynamic resistance" is not an appropriate parameter to quote. Instead the "line regulation" and "load regulation" (see Section 11-8 for a discussion of these terms) are each quoted for the AD580 as 10 mV over its operating range. An example of the use of the AD580 is shown in Fig. 12-14, where it provides a

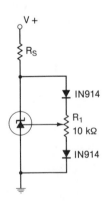

Fig. 12-12. A 2.5-V reference with minimum temperature coefficient.

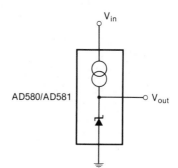

Fig. 12-13. Configuration of the AD580 and the AD581.

2.5-V offset to convert the 2.5-V to 12.5-V output of an IC pressure transducer (see Section 3-3-1) to the range of 0–10 V.

The *LM10,* shown in Fig. 12-15, is a very useful and inexpensive (about $4) device containing a band-gap voltage reference circuit, an adjustable buffer for this circuit, and an independent OA in a single IC package. The manufacturer suggests numerous applications and stresses its usefulness in portable equipment, since it can operate with supply voltages in the range of 1.1–40 V while drawing only 270 μA.[6] The application circuit, which is of prime interest in this chapter, is shown in Fig. 12-16, where it can be seen that only two resistors are needed with the LM10 to produce a well buffered and compensated 10-V reference source. An additional op amp is often needed with any of the IC voltage references to *scale* their output voltage to the required value. The LM10 is therefore particularly attractive, since it provides the op amp internally. This reduces the component count and, with it, the complexity and cost of circuit construction. Note that a discrete component, zener-based voltage reference such as that shown in Fig. 12-10 requires seven components, compared with three for the LM10 equivalent.

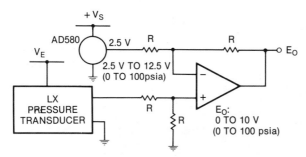

Fig. 12-14. Offsetting semiconductor pressure transducer output.

373

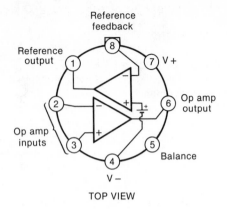

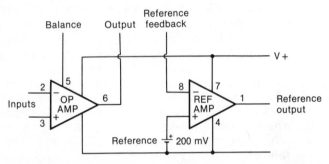

Fig. 12-15. Connection and functional diagrams of the National Semiconductor LM10. (*Courtesy National Semiconductor Corp.*)

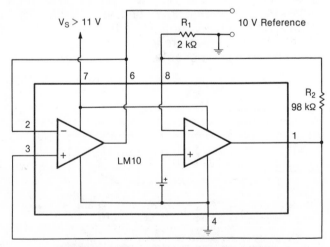

Fig.12-16. A 10-V reference using the LM10.

12-5 THREE-TERMINAL VOLTAGE REGULATORS

A possibility that should not be ignored when looking for a voltage reference is the use of a three-terminal regulator such as those mentioned in Section 11-5-1. The long-term stability of the output voltage will not be as good as for some of the IC voltage references mentioned in Section 12-4, but the three-terminal regulator is generally less expensive. When used as a reference source, the three-terminal regulator will only be expected to deliver about 10 mA, so it does not need a heat sink. For such low output currents, a low temperature coefficient (0.01%/°C) and a low output impedance can be expected, providing a performance similar to some of the voltage references mentioned earlier.

12-6 CHOOSING A VOLTAGE REFERENCE CIRCUIT

Before the information in this chapter can be used to select a circuit for a voltage reference, we need to decide what is required of the reference source in terms of its:

- Voltage
- Precision
- Short-term stability
- Long-term stability

Once these specifications have been defined, they can be used, one at a time, to narrow the choice of useable circuits by comparing Table 12-3 with Table 12-1. A final decision can then be made on the basis of cost and/or convenience. To simplify the elimination process, the specifications should be considered in this order: (1) precision, (2) long-term stability, (3) short-term stability; and (4) voltage.

1. *Precision*

If the *absolute value* of the reference voltage is important, then, from Table 12-3, only the AD581 is precise enough, as supplied "off the shelf," to ensure that any deviation of its actual voltage from its nominal voltage will be less than the resolution of even an 8-bit analog-to-digital conversion. The AD581 has, in fact, sufficient precision for a 10-bit conversion, but all the other circuits mentioned in this chapter will need local calibration, as described in Chapter 7.

2. *Long-term stability*

If long-term stability is important, then the long-term changes in the output voltage of three-terminal voltage regulators of from 0.1% to 1% make them unsuitable for anything but possibly 8-bit resolution, where the required stability (and therefore, the resolution) is 0.4%. The remaining voltage reference sources listed in Table 10-3 are suitable, in this respect, for up to 12-bit conversions, having long-term stabilities of better than 0.025%.

3. *Short-term stability*

Short-term changes in the output voltage of a voltage reference source can occur for three reasons, namely:

- A change in the supply voltage (V_s) to the reference.
- A change in the resistance of the load driven by the reference.
- A change in ambient temperature.

Of these, the first two problems should not be important in microcomputer systems, because their reference sources are usually operated from a well-regulated supply and with constant loads. Where line regulation and load regulation figures are quoted for devices in Table 12-3, you can see that those devices should be adequate for up to 12-bit conversions when operated from a well-regulated supply. An exception is the AD580, which would need variations in its output current to be limited to less than 0.5 mA.

Devices characterized by a value of r_z can be described, under operating conditions, by Fig. 12-8 and Equation 12-1. Thus, suppose a 5-V reference (V_z) suffers a change in operating current (ΔI_z) of 1 mA due to either a change in V_s or a change in I_L. In this case, the upper limit of r_z is 20 Ω for an 8-bit ADC, 5 Ω for a 10-bit ADC, and 1 Ω for a 12-bit ADC. The 1 mA is likely to be a conservative estimate of the change in I_z for a reference used in any of the situations shown in Fig. 12-1. For example, if the 5-V reference is operated from a V_s of 10 V, there will be 5 V across R_{CL}. A 5% change in V_s will produce about a 10% change in the voltage across R_{CL} and, consequently, a 10% change in I_z. If I_z is 10 mA (a reasonable value), ΔI_z becomes 1 mA. Alternatively, if an extra 5 kΩ load is placed in parallel with R_L, I_L will increase by 1 mA, reducing I_z by 1 mA. Hence, any of the circuits quoted in Table 12-3 should be adequate for up to 12-bit ADCs, although an unbuffered zener diode is likely to be unsuitable for even an 8-bit ADC.

A change in ambient temperature remains the most likely problem affecting the short-term stability of a voltage reference. We have already suggested 10°C as a typical temperature change and have tabulated, in Table 12-1, the maximum allowable "tempco" (S_t) on this basis. By directly comparing the S_t values in Table 12-1 with those of Table 12-3, we can now select possible devices (or eliminate some) as follows:

12-bit ADC: The uncompensated zener diode (as used in Fig. 12-9), the three-terminal voltage regulator, and the LM313 and AD589 can be eliminated, as can some versions of the LM329. The performance of the remaining devices should be just adequate for a 10°C change in ambient temperature. But if a larger temperature range is likely, then only the LM399 and the better versions of the LM329 will be adequate.

10-bit ADC: The uncompensated zener diode can be eliminated from consideration, but the LM313 and AD589 may be just good enough, as may a three-terminal voltage regulator, if it has not already been eliminated on the grounds of inadequate long-term stability. The performance of the remaining devices should be satisfactory.

8-bit ADC: All of the voltage references mentioned in this chapter should have a sufficiently small tempco for applications requiring only 8-bit system resolution, with the proviso that if an uncompensated zener diode is used (as in Fig. 12-9) then V_z must lie between 5 and 6 V.

4. *Voltage*

Although the voltage required from the voltage reference at first appears to be its most important property, we believe that this parameter should be considered last in the selection process. This is because it can be adjusted if necessary by a scal¼ ing circuit (Section 5-6) which, apart from its buffering action, affects only convenience and cost. Hence, we prefer to consider first the more important electrical requirements already described and then to make a final selection from the remaining options based on cost and convenience.

Once this stage is reached, it is evident that only three of the IC references mentioned in this chapter have output voltages such that they are likely to be used on their own without scaling circuits: the LM336 (2.5 V), the AD580 (2.5 V), and the AD581 (10 V). Although these are probably the most expensive devices mentioned, their convenience as single-component voltage references may well make one of them the best choice if the required voltage is either 2.5 or 10 V. For other values of required voltage, a suitable three-terminal regulator may be available, if that choice has not already been ruled out on the basis of inadequate short- or long-term stability.

If scaling becomes necessary, there is not much difference in convenience (as measured, for instance, by component count) between adding a scaling circuit to one of the IC voltage references or compensating and buffering a zener diode as in Fig. 12-10. There is, however, a substantial difference in cost; components for the zener diode option cost about $1 at 1982 prices. An option with much to recommend it is the LM10, with its built-in op amp. It can produce any required voltage in the range of 200 mV to nearly 40 V with the addition of only two resistors. For the circuit configuration shown in Fig. 12-16, the output voltage is determined by the ratio of R_1 to R_2 according to the equation:

$$V_{REF} = 0.2 \times \frac{R_1 + R_2}{R_1} \qquad \text{(Eq. 12-15)}$$

The component cost for this option should be less than $5 at 1981 prices.

12-7 RECOMMENDATIONS

The simplest and least expensive voltage reference is a three-terminal voltage regulator, but this is likely to have insufficient short- or long-term stability for system resolutions of more than eight bits.

For applications where total component cost is more important than component count, the zener circuit of Fig. 12-10 (or similar) is recommended. It should be adequate in systems requiring up to 12-bit resolution.

For applications where simplicity is important, the LM10 is a highly recommended, cost effective solution, though in special cases the LM336, AD580, or AD581 may be preferred.

When high resolution is required in a location with temperatures varying over 10°C, the LM399 will need to be used, or possibly some versions of the LM329.

12-8 REFERENCES

1. J. Millman and C.C. Halkias, *Integrated Electronics,* International Student Edition, McGraw-Hill Kogakusha Ltd., 1972, pp. 74–75.

2. National Semiconductor Corp., *Voltage Regulator Handbook,* p. 9-5.

3. Millman and Halkias, 1972, pp. 14 et seq.

4. Analog Devices Inc., *Data Acquisition Components and Subsystems,* 1980, p. 7-7; National Semiconductor Corp., *Voltage Regulator Handbook.*

5. National Semiconductor Corp., *Linear Databook,* p. 2-24.

6. National Semiconductor Corp., *Linear Databook,* pp. 3-55–3-61.

APPENDICES

appendix

a

Additional Transducers

The volume of printed material on transducers is enormous. In Chapter 3, we mentioned the material we thought most likely to be of practical value to users of microcomputer systems. This appendix reports on transducers that use less common effects than those described earlier and that use effects already described, but for the purpose of sensing other physical variables. This appendix also includes methods for sensing some of the physical variables not mentioned in Chapter 3.

A-1 MECHANICAL EFFECT TRANSDUCERS

A-1-1 Measuring Displacement

The need to measure displacement has spawned a great variety of measurement techniques and devices. Two of the most straightforward types of devices were mentioned in Chapter 3. Here are a few more.

Capacitive Devices

The capacitance, C, of an electrical capacitor can be expressed as:

$$C \propto \frac{A}{d} \qquad \text{(Eq. A-1)}$$

where A is the area of its plates and d is their separation. Fig. A-1A schematizes the *variable separation* capacitive displacement transducer. From Equation A-1, it can be seen that the output from this device is nonlinear. As a result, its range is

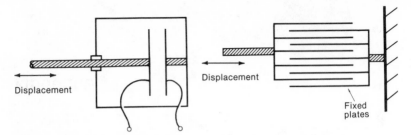

Fig. A-1. Variable capacitance displacement transducer.

very limited. The *variable area* transducer, shown in Fig. A-1B, has the advantage that its capacitance varies linearly with displacement, hence its range is potentially larger. Either device needs to be incorporated into an AC bridge circuit to obtain an electrical output. This circuit is often built into the transducer housing of commercially available transducers. A variable area capacitor, similar in construction to the rotary tuning capacitor of an AM radio, can also be used to provide a voltage output that varies linearly with angular displacement.

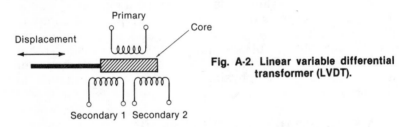

Fig. A-2. Linear variable differential transformer (LVDT).

Inductive Devices

The linear variable differential transformer (LVDT) is very popular as a displacement sensor in industry. It consists of a transformer, which has one primary and two secondary coils (Fig. A-2), and a moveable core. The position of the core determines the mutual inductance between the primary and each of

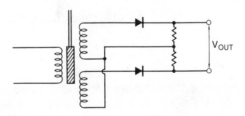

Fig. A-3. Obtaining a DC output from the LVDT.

the secondaries. As the core moves, the output of one of the secondaries decreases as a result of reduced magnetic coupling to the primary. Meanwhile, the output of the other secondary increases. Although AC current must be used to excite the primary, it is possible, using the simple circuit shown in Fig. A-3, to obtain a DC output voltage whose sign specifies the direction of the displacement. By carefully matching the secondaries of the LVDT, it is possible to get a resolution of about 1 μm. Models with ranges of up to 10 cm are available. Compared to the potentiometer (Section 3-2-2) the LVDT is not as sensitive to mechanical vibrations, wear, shock, and other adverse environmental conditions. This ruggedness and improved resolution make the extra electronic complexity of the LVDT worthwhile in many situations.

A sensor with a slightly simpler construction is the variable inductance transducer shown in Fig. A-4. It has many of the advantages of the LVDT and is cheaper, having only one coil compared with the LVDT's three, which includes carefully matched secondaries. Normally, however, it is included in the tank circuit of an oscillator, so that when the core changes position, the oscillator frequency changes via the change in coil inductance. Because of the required electronics and the frequency output, the inductance transducer is less popular than the more expensive LVDT.

Piezoelectric Crystal

The piezoelectric crystal, described earlier in Section 3-2-1, gets its output from the distortion of the crystal. This distortion may result from a displacement, so the piezoelectric transducer is just as often considered to be a displacement transducer as a force transducer. The allowable displacements are small, even when the crystal is mounted as a beam subject to bending, as in the crystal microphone shown

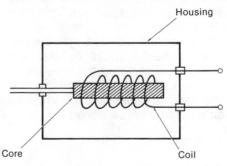

Fig. A-4. Variable inductance displacement transducer.

schematically in Fig. A-5. But the voltage output is large, which explains the former popularity of these crystals in microphones and phonograph pickups. The nonlinearity of their output has proved to be a sufficient disadvantage to outweigh their advantages of robust construction and high output voltage. This has reduced their popularity relative to capacitive and magnetic methods.

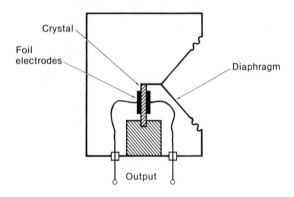

Fig. A-5. Crystal microphone.

Magneto-resistance Devices

An element that changes its resistance according to the strength of the local magnetic field is described as *magneto-resistive.* Such an element can form the basis of a position measuring system in much the same way as a Hall effect device (Section 3-2-2). The Unimeasure-80 displacement transducer from Unimeasure Inc., for example, consists of a fixed magneto-resistive element and a permanent magnet mounted on the mechanical input shaft.[1] As the shaft moves, there is a change in the magnetic field strength at the magneto-resistive element; the resistance of the element is then a measure of shaft displacement. This instrument has an advantage over the strain-gauge method of displacement measurement (see Section 3-2-1) in that the resistance of the element can be measured on an ordinary multimeter. The manufacturer claims a resolution of better than 1 μm if a 3½-digit multimeter is used. Various adaptors allow the basic transducer to be used to measure pressure, force, and similar physical variables that can be derived from a displacement measurement.

Encoders

Position information can be obtained directly in digital form.

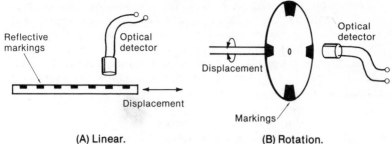

(A) Linear.   (B) Rotation.

Fig. A-6. Simple position encoders.

To do this, a scale of either optical or magnetic markings is attached to the object whose displacement is to be measured or to a shaft attached to that object. The scale, consisting of evenly spaced bars of reflective paint, moves past an optical detector as shown in Fig. A-6. The pulses from the optical detector are counted to provide a measure of the displacement of the object. This is a particularly simple and useful method for measuring the amount of unidirectional rotation or displacement of a shaft.

If the position information needed should not depend on counting from a known reference position, then a position encoding scale can be attached to the object. Examples are shown in Fig. A-7. They are four-bit encoders that require four optical detectors, one to register each bit. Clearly, more bits

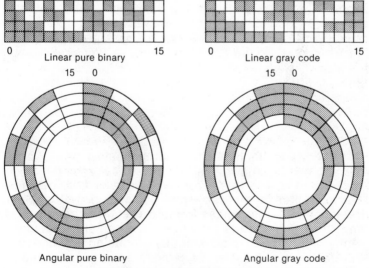

Fig. A-7. Four-bit encoder scales.

must be added if increased resolution is required. Gray code is often preferred to a pure binary code in this application, because only one bit changes at a time as the object moves from one resolvable position to the next.

Although optical methods of position encoding are very common, the same end can be achieved magnetically. Magnetic encoding methods, we believe, are likely to become progressively more popular because of the ready availability of Hall effect switches and the better reliability of magnetic methods over optical methods in harsh environments.

A-1-2 Measuring Acceleration

Accelerometers rely on detecting, or compensating for, the force exerted on a carefully suspended mass when the transducer is accelerated along a given axis. An accelerometer that uses a piezoelectric load cell to detect the force is shown in Fig. A-8. In this force detection type of accelerometer, a suspension guides the mass so that it may move along only one axis. A fixed load cell measures the force, and therefore the acceleration, of the mass along this axis. Frequently, the load cell is a piezoelectric crystal, but an arrangement of strain gauges bonded to a support is sometimes used.

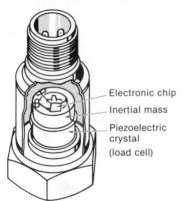

Electronic chip

Inertial mass

Piezoelectric
crystal
(load cell)

Fig. A-8. Piezoelectric accelerometer.
(*Courtesy BBN Instrument Co.*)

A type of accelerometer that compensates for the force of acceleration is known as a *servoaccelerometer* and is diagrammed in Fig. A-9. This system uses a displacement detector (often of the capacitive type) to detect any small movement of the test mass from its specified reference position. This information is used to energize an electromagnet to exactly nullify the displacement by producing a force that accelerates the test mass at the same rate as the unit containing it. The system is inherently capable of great accuracy but is

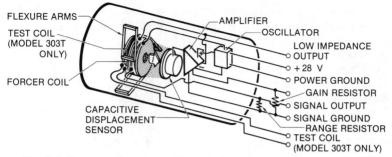

Fig. A-9. Servoaccelerometer. (*Courtesy Sunstrand Data Control, Inc.*)

expensive to construct. The electronics necessary to actuate the servo mechanism are normally contained within the transducer housing and give a very linear output ranging typically over ±5 V. Acceleration ranges vary from 0.5 g to 60 g, with resolution down to 1 μg.

A-1-3 Measuring Velocity

A fairly obvious and frequently used method for determining the velocity of an object is to differentiate the output of a displacement transducer. This is accomplished quite simply in either the analog or the digital domain. The pulse-counting methods used to record shaft position (Fig. A-10A) lend themselves to this treatment; the velocity information comes directly from the pulse rate. On the other hand, tacho-generators produce an electrical voltage that is directly pro-portional to the angular velocity, ω, of the shaft. They are small and can produce a DC or an AC output. By attaching a wheel of known radius, r, to the shaft and placing the wheel in contact with a moving surface (Fig. A-10B), the linear velocity, v, of that

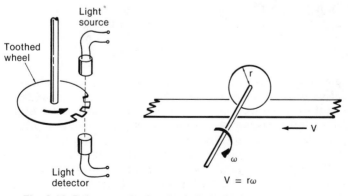

Fig. A-10. Pulse-counting methods for velocity measurement.

389

surface can be measured. This is a convenient method for measuring the speed of a conveyor belt, for example.

The principle of magnetic induction that provides the tachogenerator voltage may also be used to detect linear velocities over short distances, using the sort of arrangement shown in Fig. A-11. The output voltage of the pickup coil is proportional to the rate of change of the magnetic flux within it, and this in turn depends on the approach velocity of the magnet. This is the operating principle behind magnetic pickups on phonographs and moving coil microphones. It is what transforms the velocity of the stylus, in the first case, or of the diaphragm, in the second case, into a voltage.

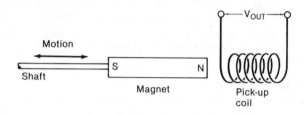

Fig. A-11. Inductive velocity detector.

A-2 FLUID TRANSDUCERS

A-2-1 Measuring Pressure

Pirani Gauge

Vacuum pressures between 1 Torr and 10^{-3} Torr (1 Torr = 1 mm of Hg) are often measured using a Pirani gauge. This gauge consists of a resistive element within the vacuum under observation, this element being heated by a current passing through it. The thermal conductivity of the low-pressure gas determines the equilibrium temperature of the resistive element, hence its resistance. Since gas conductivity is determined largely by its pressure, the resistance of the element is a measure of the gas pressure. Thermistors, whose resistance varies greatly with temperature, are commonly used as the resistive element, although the older hot-wire resistance elements still abound. To allow for the effect of changes in ambient temperature, a compensating thermistor is mounted close to the measuring thermistor, but external to the vacuum system, as in Fig. A-12. The two thermistors are then wired in adjacent arms of a Wheatstone bridge.

Ambient temperature variations can be better compensated for, and the upper end of the measurement range substantially

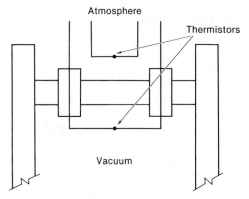

Fig. A-12. Pirani gauge.

extended, by incorporating the two thermistors in separate Wheatstone bridges. The bridge voltages are then controlled to run the thermistors at constant resistance, as shown in Fig. A-13. The amplifiers A1 and A2 provide enough current to their respective bridges to keep the bridges balanced. This ensures that the thermistors operate at constant resistance. A3 is configured as a difference amplifier to measure the difference between two bridge voltages. V_o is a measure of the pressure at the sensing thermistor.

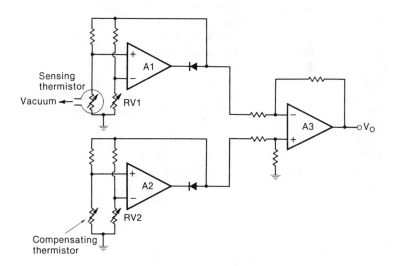

Fig. A-13. Electronics for Pirani gauge.

A-2-2 Measuring Temperature

Resistance Thermometer (RTD)

The resistance of a metal wire increases with temperature in an approximately linear form and is given by:

$$R_{T2} = R_{T1} [1 + \alpha (T2 - T1)] \qquad \text{(Eq. A-2)}$$

Platinum, in particular, exhibits close to linear behavior and is thus very popular, although its value of α ($3.9 \times 10^{-3}/°C$) is only average compared with other metals. However, platinum can be obtained in close to pure form, has good mechanical and electrical stability, and resists contamination. This has made possible the construction of platinum sensing elements with good reproducibility and extremely low drift with age, properties which have led to the adoption of the laboratory platinum resistance thermometer as the world standard for temperature measurement in the range of −270 to +660°C. The industrial version of the platinum RTD performs at close to laboratory standards and is rugged enough to withstand harsh environments and temperatures of up to 1000°C.

The sensing element of an RTD typically consists of a length of platinum wire, of resistance 100 Ω, wound on a ceramic former and encapsulated in a stainless steel sheath. The diameter of the sheath is usually one quarter inch or less, and the response time of the element varies from a few seconds to a few tens of seconds depending on the size of the element and the nature of its environment. A recent development is the platinum thin film detector, consisting of a thin film of platinum deposited on a ceramic substrate. The smaller sensing element of this type of RTD provides much shorter response times (fractions of a second), while its accuracy is claimed to equal that of conventional wire-wound elements. Omega Engineering, Inc., manufactures a range of both wire-wound and thin film platinum RTDs.[2]

Table A-1 shows the resistance of a 100-Ω platinum RTD varies with temperature. This change of resistance can be

Table A-1. Platinum RTD Response

Temp °C	Resistance Ω	Temp °C	Resistance Ω
−200	18.53	+400	247.06
−100	60.20	+500	280.93
0	100.00	+600	313.65
+100	138.50	+700	345.21
+200	175.84	+800	375.671
+300	212.03		

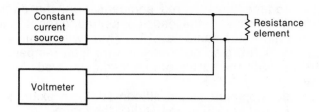

Fig. A-14. Four-wire resistance measurement.

measured directly using the circuit arrangement in Fig. A-14. Four leads are used to exclude the voltage drop across the current-carrying leads (which may be quite long) from the measurement. Using a high-resistance voltmeter minimizes the current flowing in the voltmeter leads and the consequent error voltage. The voltmeter can now be calibrated to read temperature directly. More accurate measurement systems incorporate the RTD into a Wheatstone bridge, whose out-of-balance voltage is then a measure of temperature. Three common configurations are shown in Fig. A-15. The two-lead connection in Fig. A-15A is simple but has the lead resistance included with the RTD resistance. This potential disadvantage will not matter if the lead temperature is constant, since we are looking for resistance changes. However, any change in the temperature of the leads will cause a change in the lead resistance. This can be compensated for by including a pair of dummy leads in another arm of the bridge as shown in Fig.

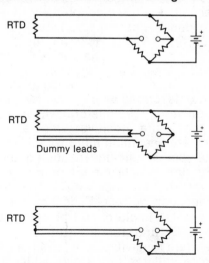

Fig. A-15. Bridge methods for measuring RTD resistance.

A-15B. To produce the required compensation, the dummy leads must be identical to the leads connected to the RTD and must be laid along the same path. The three-wire connection shown in Fig. A-15C also compensates for lead temperature variations, but with the saving of one lead compared with the arrangement of Fig. A-15B.

A recent development is the silicon RTD, an example of which is the KTY10 from Siemens. Unlike the thermistor, which is described next, the silicon RTD has an approximately linear temperature dependence over the temperature range of −50°C to +150°C with an α of $7.5 \times 10^{-3}/°C$. This results in a resistance change of about 1 kΩ from a nominal 2 kΩ at 25°C to over 3 kΩ at 100°C. The KTY10 comes in a plastic case similar to the TO-92 transistor package and has a thermal time constant of 4 seconds when used in oil. Its linearity can be improved by inserting a resistor in series with it so that, over certain temperature ranges, the absolute error can be kept below 1% (see Section 6-7-1).

Thermistor

Thermistors are made from semiconductor material, and their temperature changes greatly with temperature. They can be made very small to ensure a rapid reaction to a changing environment. Time constants of less than 4 seconds in still air, or less than 0.5 second in a moving fluid, are possible. They can also be encapsulated to make them extremely rugged for operation in harsh surroundings. These advantages of robustness and high sensitivity, often coupled with low cost, make the thermistor an ideal temperature transducer in the temperature range of −100°C to +300°C. However, the disadvantage of this device is that its resistance changes exponentially, rather than linearly, with temperature, as shown in Fig. A-16. Most thermistors show a decrease in resistance as the temperature increases; they are described as *negative temperature coefficient* (NTC) thermistors. Thermistors whose resistance increases with temperature, positive temperature coefficient (PTC) thermistors, are becoming more widely available.

It is possible to approximate linearization of the response of a thermistor with the simple circuit of Fig. A-17, where a resistance R_L is inserted in series with an NTC thermistor, R_T. A temperature-dependent voltage, E_T, is then measured across R_L. Unfortunately, this simple circuit produces a linear relationship between E_T and temperature only over a very restricted temperature range (typically less than 40°C), and R_L must be chosen to suit the range over which the linear re-

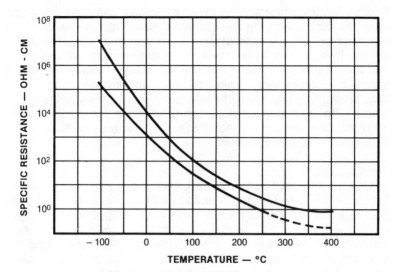

Fig. A-16. Thermistor characteristics.

sponse is required (see Section 6-7-1). For more rigorous applications, thermistor–resistor networks that produce a linearized response are commercially available.

When experimenting with thermistors as temperature measuring devices, it is necessary to minimize the current flowing through the thermistor to avoid self-heating. The amount by which the thermistor temperature rises above its surroundings due to this effect varies according to the size and construction of the device. As a rough guide, the temperature rise is typically 1°C/mW. Hence, to retain accuracy of better than 1°C, the current in a 10-kΩ thermistor must be restricted to less than 1 mA.

The negative temperature coefficient of most thermistors poses an additional problem, known as *thermal runaway,* which has potentially catastrophic consequences. To illustrate this effect, consider that a thermistor is connected across a constant voltage source so that the current flowing through the thermistor is a measure of temperature. Any in-

Fig. A-17. Approximate linearization of thermistor response.

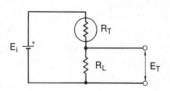

crease in the temperature of the thermistor will produce a corresponding increase in the current flowing through it, hence a further rise in its temperature due to self-heating. Stability is normally achieved by a more rapid distribution of heat from the thermistor to its surroundings at the higher temperature. In some circumstances, however, the temperature of the thermistor will continue to increase until the thermistor destroys itself. The inclusion of a series resistor to limit the current available is a simple precaution that will protect the thermistor from this kind of catastrophe.

Noncontact Methods

One of the traditional noncontact methods of measuring temperature is to focus the radiation from the body of interest onto a blackened disc. Its temperature change is then gauged using a thermopile, which is simply a number of thermocouples connected in series. This has been the basis for some commercially available instruments such as the Leeds and Northrup Rayotube detector, which reads temperature differences of 200–5000°F and has an output of approximately 24 mV at 1260°C. The response of the detector is surprisingly quick, with a time constant of 0.015 second.

Pyroelectric substances are now being used in place of the blackened disc and thermopile. A pyroelectric substance shows a temperature-dependent electrical polarization which is normally set during the manufacturing process. When used as the dielectric in a capacitor, the pyroelectric substance will produce a change in charge on the electrodes of the capacitor as its temperature changes. Mullard, Plessey, and Eltec all manufacture temperature detectors from thin slices of ceramic pyroelectric material. The detectors are mounted in a TO-5 type of encapsulation, together with a JFET for impedance matching. The equivalent circuit of the Mullard devices is shown in Fig. A-18.

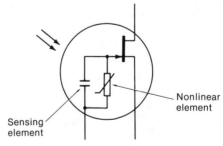

Sensing element

Nonlinear element

Fig. A-18. Pyroelectric detector.

The radiation transmission characteristics of the window in the encapsulation can be chosen to suit the application. One of the major uses for this kind of detector is in intruder alarms. Since radiation from the body at room temperature peaks at around 10 μm, the window is often chosen to make the detector insensitive to the near infrared rays and to sunlight. The arrangement of an intruder alarm is shown in Fig. A-19, where a mirror is used as the focusing device rather than a more expensive infrared transmitting lens.

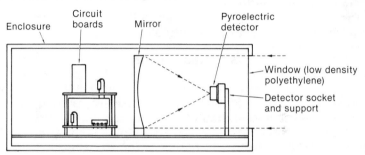

Fig. A-19. Pyroelectric intruder alarm.

The plastic polyvinylidene fluoride (PVDF), generally employed as a transparent wrapping film, can also be used as a pyroelectric substance. Electrodes are made by evaporating aluminum onto the film. However, devices made from this material seem to be at the laboratory stage as yet and are not commercially available.

A-2-3 Level Sensing

Capacitance Method

For insulating liquids, an arrangement such as the one depicted in Fig. 3-25 can be used. In this case, the measured quantity is the capacitance between the electrodes rather than the conductance. A convenient configuration for the electrodes is a pair of concentric cylinders which are open at the bottom. The liquid partially fills the space between the two cylinders and increases the capacitance of the probe as the liquid level rises. An AC method (as in Section A-1-1) is needed to measure the capacitance of the probe, and calibration is needed for each fluid used.

Thermal Method

This discrete level sensor makes use of the change in heat dissipation from a self-heated resistive device. A thermistor is normally the most convenient device to use because of its large temperature coefficient of resistance. It is operated at high currents so that the self-heating effect is significant. When the liquid level reaches the thermistor, the rate of heat conduction away from the thermistor will increase substantially and the temperature of the thermistor will drop, with a corresponding change in resistance. This method is quite popular for use with cryogenic fluids.

Pressure Sensor Method

The pressure in a fluid is related to its height, h, above the point of measurement by the formula:

$$P = P_o + \rho gh \qquad \text{(Eq. A-3)}$$

where P_o is the pressure at the surface of the fluid (normally atmospheric), ρ is the density of the fluid, and g is the acceleration due to gravity. If a pressure transducer reading gauge pressure is mounted at the bottom of a tank, as in Fig. A-20, it will provide a measure of depth for a liquid of known density. If the transducer is always to be used with the same liquid, its output can be calibrated in terms of depth rather than pressure units.

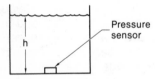

Fig. A-20. Depth measurement using pressure sensor.

Sonic Echo Method

In this method a sound pulse is transmitted and a measure is made of the time required for its echo to return from the surface being sensed. The sound may be transmitted from the bottom of a vessel, so that the elapsed time is directly proportional to the depth of the liquid. Or, the sound may be projected from above a surface, so that the elapsed time is directly proportional to the distance of the level being sensed below the transducer. This second approach is a noncontact method and is particularly useful when corrosive or otherwise harmful liquids are being used. This method can also be used when a solid level is being sensed.

Polaroid markets a relatively inexpensive ultrasonic ranging kit that can sense the presence of objects within the range of 0.9 to 35 ft. A microcomputer-controlled scanning ranging system that uses this kit has been described.[3] It can be used in simplified form, without the scanning facility, to find the range of an interface along a fixed direction.

A-2-4 Measurement of Flow

There are a variety of mechanical methods for measuring flow rate.[4] Most of these place some kind of obstruction within the flow to be measured and then measure the displacement of the obstruction. Or they measure its rate of rotation if a turbine or a nutating disc, for example, is used. An electrical signal can then be obtained by attaching one of the displacement or rotational velocity sensing transducers discussed earlier. However, we prefer to discuss here methods that are more direct and that avoid moving parts.

Pressure Difference Methods

(a) *Pitot Tube.* When there is a fluid flow past the Pitot tube, as shown in Fig. A-21, the pressure, P_b, at the impact hole is higher than the pressure, P_a, at the static hole by an amount that is directly proportional to the square of the fluid velocity, i.e.,

$$v^2 = K(P_b - P_a) \qquad \text{(Eq. A-4)}$$

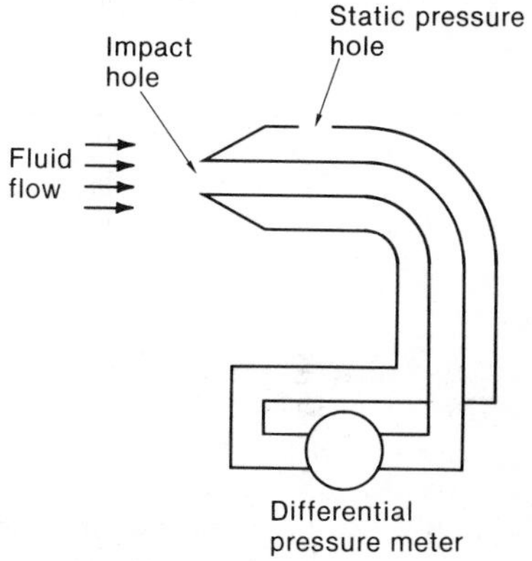

Fig. A-21. Pitot tube flowmeter.

In the formula, K is a constant that is dependent only on the fluid density. Hence, an integrated circuit pressure sensor of the type discussed in Chapter 3 (Section 3-3-1) can be used in the differential configuration to derive an electrical signal that is proportional to the square of the velocity of the fluid. Taking the square root of this signal (see Section 6-6) provides a voltage which is proportional to the fluid velocity.

This method is insensitive at low fluid velocities, due to the low pressure differentials generated across the Pitot tube. An air speed of 50 ft/sec (16 ms⁻¹), for example, sets up a pressure difference of only about 0.04 psi (0.28 kPa). A water speed of 5

399

ft/sec ($\sim$ 1.6 ms⁻¹) sets up a pressure difference of about 0.4 psi. However, misalignment of the Pitot tube head relative to the fluid flow is not as critical as might be expected. Even a 20° misalignment will lead to only about 2% error in determining the velocity.

(*b*) *Venturi Tube.* When fluid flows along a constricted tube, as shown in Fig. A-22, the pressure, P_a, upstream of the constriction will be higher than the pressure, P_b, at the constriction. The pressure difference is proportional to the square of the fluid velocity upstream of the constriction according to the equation:

$$P_a - P_b = K(V_a^2 - V_b^2)\left[\left(\frac{A_a}{A_b}\right)^2 - 1\right] \qquad \text{(Eq. A-5)}$$

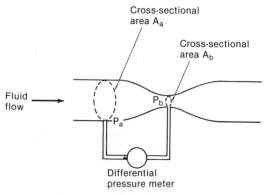

Fig. A-22. Venturi effect flowmeter.

where K is a constant that again depends on the density of the fluid. As for the Pitot tube, an IC differential pressure transducer can be used to provide the velocity-dependent electrical signal. In principle, this method is much more sensitive than the Pitot tube, but at the expense of severely obstructing the fluid flow and wasting some of the head pressure. In practice, the constriction is not normally smooth, as in Fig. A-22, but is achieved by inserting an "orifice plate" for which there are standard specifications covering the siting of the pressure measurement tubes and the geometry of the plate.[5]

Electromagnetic Induction

The electromagnetic induction method of flow measurement places no obstruction in the path of the fluid flow. It produces a direct electrical output and bears some resemblance to the Hall effect discussed in Section 3-2-2. If a magnetic field is applied across the direction of flow of a conductive fluid, then a voltage, V, will appear across that fluid at right angles to both the direction of flow and the applied magnetic field, as shown in Fig. A-23.

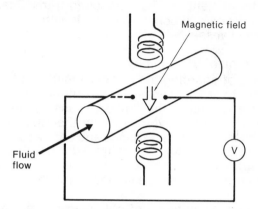

Fig. A-23. Electromagnetic induction flowmeter.

The size of this output voltage is given by:

$$V = Blv \qquad \text{(Eq. A-6)}$$

where B is the magnitude of the magnetic field in tesla (10^4 gauss), l is the distance between the sensing electrodes in meters, and v is the velocity of the fluid in ms^{-1}. Although Equation A-6 does not explicitly involve the conductivity of the fluid, the method is not very successful if the conductivity, σ, of the fluid is less than 10^{-5} Ω^{-1} cm^{-1}. In addition, the voltage measuring equipment must have a high input impedance, especially for low values of σ.

This sensor has the particular advantage that it is unaffected by changes in viscosity, density, temperature, and consistency of the fluid; even turbulent flow will not affect its output. The inclusion of suspended solids in the fluid, such as in the feed to paper mills, is also no problem.

Doppler Shift

When either a source or a detector of sound moves with respect to the medium in which the sound is propagating, an apparent frequency shift occurs. The measurement of fluid flow rate using this phenomenon requires a complete measurement system and so will not be discussed in detail in this appendix, which is concerned with transducers per se. Suffice it to say that such instruments have been used in medicine for

401

some years; they have measured blood flow with ultrasonics in much the same way that traffic police measure automobile velocity with microwave radar. Recent developments in IC technology have resulted in a total system that is small enough to be implanted. The ultrasound transducer, a 3-mm square lead titanate zirconate crystal, is sutured against the side of a blood vessel.[6]

A-2-5 Measurement of Humidity

Some ways of adapting the classical methods for humidity measurement to produce an electrical output are obvious. Two examples are replacing the liquid-in-glass thermometers of the "wet and dry bulb" hygrometer by thermistors, and coupling an animal hair, which expands and contracts with changing humidity, to a displacement transducer.[7] Similarly, dew point measurements may be automated by optical sensing of droplet formation on a surface cooled by the thermoelectric effect.[8]

Of more interest, in terms of obtaining a direct output and simple operation, are hygroscopic sensors. Some substances, such as phosphorous pentoxide, lithium chloride, calcium chloride, and zinc chloride, absorb moisture from the air and change their conductivity. This enables a resistance measurement to provide a reading of atmospheric humidity. The sensitive element is designed to maximize its surface area and therefore the speed and sensitivity with which it responds to atmospheric changes. Unfortunately, these devices also tend to be very sensitive to temperature and therefore must be used with care.

Ion exchange materials, such as sulphonated polystyrene, can also be used to produce electrical output in the form of a resistance change. A capacitance change is also possible and may be preferable in some circumstances, because a small change in moisture content of the material can lead to a large change in its dielectric constant.

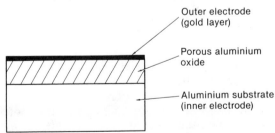

Fig. A-24. Aluminum oxide humidity sensor.

Another transducer that can sense humidity as either a resistance value or a capacitance value uses a porous coating of aluminum oxide on an aluminum substrate as shown in Fig. A-24. Moisture in the air permeates the pores in the aluminum oxide, reducing the resistance of the layer and increasing its dielectric constant. The behavior of a typical transducer is shown in Fig. A-25. As the figure indicates, the resistance change property is best at low humidity, whereas the capacitance change is better at high humidity.

A-2-6 Anemometry

The traditional method of measuring windspeed, the rotating cup anemometer, produces an electrical output via a tachogenerator and will not be discussed here. However, it is worth noting that a low-cost version has been described that makes use of a single-bit optical shaft encoder (Section A-1-1) and a ratemeter (Section 6-3-3) in place of the tachogenerator.[9] Of greater interest to the electronics enthusiast may be an inexpensive fully electronic instrument, with no moving parts, which is based on the "hot-wire" anemometer.

The operating principle of the hot-wire anemometer is very similar to that of the Pirani gauge: an electrically heated element loses heat at a rate which is determined by its surroundings. In the case of the Pirani gauge, the degree of vacuum is important. For the anemometer, the wind speed past the element determines the cooling rate. A simple way of using this effect is to drive a resistor from a constant voltage or a constant current source and then to measure its resistance. The

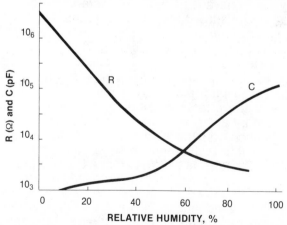

Fig. A-25. Characteristics of aluminum oxide humidity sensor.
(*From A. J. Diefenderfer*)

403

resistance will depend on the temperature attained and therefore on the wind speed.

A better approach is to run the probe at constant temperature and to measure the power variation required to keep the temperature constant. Fig. A-26 shows how this can be done by incorporating the sensing resistor in a Wheatstone bridge. Amplifier A1 detects any out-of-balance condition in the Wheatstone bridge and corrects this by providing more or less current (via R1) to the probe, thereby heating or cooling it. Amplifier A2 is configured as a differential amplifier to amplify the voltage across R1 as a measurement of wind speed. The output voltage, E_o, then needs to be processed through linearizing and offsetting circuitry.

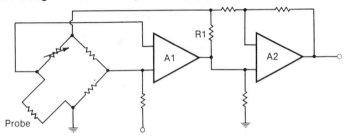

Fig. A-26. Constant temperature hot-wire anemometry.

Running the probe at constant temperature has a great advantage: the response of the system is not limited to the thermal response time of the probe but can be considerably faster. This may be irrelevant in ordinary meteorological measurements, but it will allow turbulence effects to be detected, for example, in wind tunnel studies. Full details of an application of this method have been described by Stellema.[10]

A further variation is to use a transistor as the sensor with the temperature dependence of the base-emitter voltage, V_{BE}, being the important property. A bead type transistor is suitable, and the effects of ambient temperature variations can be offset by using a second transistor of the same type which is shielded from the wind. One of the simpler circuits for implementing this technique, which is still accurate enough for many applications, is shown in Fig. A-27. T_1 is the wind sensor and T_2 is used to correct for the ambient temperature variations. The transistors are run at essentially constant current to eliminate the dependence of V_{BE} on the emitter current.

The op amp adjusts the collector voltage of the sensor transistor T_1 and therefore its power dissipation to keep T_1 at a constant temperature above ambient (as sensed by T_2). The

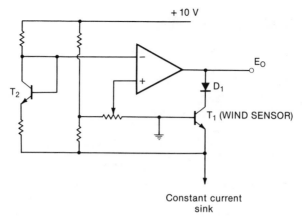

+ 10 V

E_O

D_1

T_2

T_1 (WIND SENSOR)

Constant current
sink

Fig. A-27. Transistor anemometry.

diode D_1 is present to provide an approximate V_{BE} drop. Thus the voltage measured at the op amp output (relative to earth) is approximately equal to V_{CE} of the sensor transistor T_1. Full details of this method are described by MacHattie.[11]

A-3 RADIATION TRANSDUCERS

A-3-1 Measurement of Light

Light-Dependent Resistor (LDR)

When light falls on a semiconductor, the photon energy may be sufficient to promote valence electrons into the conduction band. The resulting increase in the number of charge carriers increases the conductivity of the semiconductor, so that a block of semiconductor material can be used as a light-dependent resistor. The most popular material for the manufacture of LDRs is cadmium sulphide (CdS) because its spectral response curve, peaking in the green, approximates that of the human eye. Because of this and its low cost, small size, and low power consumption, the LDR finds extensive use in camera light meters. However, the nonlinear relationship of resistance to light intensity, evident in Fig. A-28, together with the temperature sensitivity and "memory" of LDRs makes them less popular for other light measurements. On the other hand, the large change in resistance between the "light" and "no light" conditions (typically from 100 Ω to 1 MΩ) makes the device useful in switching or chopping applications.

The temperature dependence of the LDR (up to 0.5% of the "light" resistance per °C) can be reduced by incorporating two of them into a Wheatstone bridge arrangement so that one is

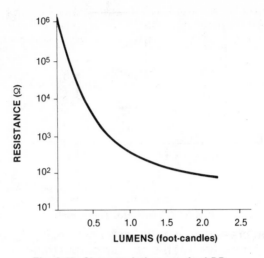

Fig. A-28. Characteristic curve for LDR.

shielded from the light for temperature compensation as shown in Fig. A-29. However, there is nothing that can be done about the "memory" effect, wherein exposure to strong light can affect measurements taken several hours later.

Photovoltaic Cells

The photodiode and phototransistor can be used as photovoltaic cells, as indicated in Fig. 3-28, in that a voltage can be developed across the device when it is illuminated. However, the name is normally used for cells more specifically designed for power conversion (solar cells) or cells which are capable of driving a meter (light meter) without assistance. Nevertheless, the operating principle of these devices is the same: the incident radiation creates electron-hole pairs in a semiconductor near a junction, and charge separation occurs as the minority

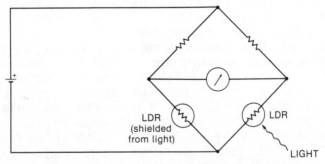

Fig. A-29. Temperature compensation for LDR.

carriers thus created are swept across the junction under the effect of the barrier potential. The difference lies in the internal resistance of the device when it is regarded as a voltage generator.

The voltage generated by a photovoltaic cell is dependent on the band gap of the material. A silicon photocell develops around 0.6 V; a gallium arsenic (GaAs) cell develops around 0.9 V under open-circuit conditions. The short-circuit current developed in a photovoltaic cell is linearly related to the intensity of the light falling on the device. However, the linear dependence of output current on illumination intensity is disturbed if the resistance of the measuring device is too high. Measuring the current output of the cell directly with a microammeter provides a simple light measuring system, but it leads to a fatigue effect as the output will drop over a period of time under constant illumination. So that the results are more reproducible, the output voltage needs to be measured with a high impedance device.

A-4 BIBLIOGRAPHY

Acceleration
   Morris, H.M., "What Users Do Wrong with Accelerometers." *Control Engineering,* March 1979, p. 66.

Velocity
   Morris, H.M., "Rotary Tachometers Dominate the Velocity Sensing Market." *Control Engineering,* December 1978, p. 37.

   Morris, H.M., "The Many Roads to Measuring Speed Are Increasingly Digital." *Control Engineering,* March 1980, p. 57.

Temperature
   Tavener, J., "Platinum Resistance Elements: A Guide to Performance." *Control and Instrumentation,* September 1979, p. 95.

   Byatt, D.W.G., "Plastic film sensors." *Electronics Industry,* September 1979, p. 21.

   Dance, B., "Infra-red Pyroelectric Detectors." *Australian Electronics Engineering,* September 1980, p. 61.

Level
   Border, J.A., "Pointers to Progress in Ultrasonic Level Detection." *Control and Instrumentation,* September 1979, p. 71.

Flow
   Hall, J., "Solving Tough Flow Monitoring Problems." *Instruments and Control Systems,* February 1980, p. 41.

Bailey, S.J., "Trade-offs Complicate Decisions in Selecting Flowmeters." *Control Engineering,* April 1980, p. 75.

Morris, H.M., "Ultrasonic Flowmeter Uses Wide Beam Technique to Measure Flow." *Control Engineering,* July 1980, p. 99.

Humidity
Bailey, S.J., "Moisture Sensors 1980: On-line Roles Increase." *Control Engineering,* September 1980, p. 112.

A-5 REFERENCES

1. Unimeasure Inc., 909 Williamson Loop, Grants Pass, OR 97526.

2. Omega Engineering, Inc., One Omega Drive, Box 4047, Stamford, CT 06907.

3. S. Ciarcia, "Home in on the Range!" *Byte,* November, 1980, p. 32.

4. P.J. O'Higgins, *Basic Instrumentation,* McGraw Hill, 1966; R.P. Hunter, *Automated Process Control Systems,* Prentice-Hall, 1978.

5. O'Higgins, 1966.

6. News Scope, "IC Flowmeter Measures Blood in Two Directions," *Electronic Design,* January 18, 1978, *2,* p. 19.

7. Hunter, 1978.

8. A.J. Diefenderfer, *Principles of Electronic Instrumentation,* W.B. Saunders, 1972.

9. J. Clarke, "Wind Speed Indicator," *Electronics Australia,* October 1981, p. 50.

10. L. Stellema, "A Constant Temperature Hot-Wire Anemometer," *Australian Electronics Engineering,* August 1979, p. 14.

11. L.E. MacHattie, "The Transistor as an Anemometer," *Journal of Physics E: Scientific Instruments,* 1979, *12,* p. 754.

The Theory and Design of Switch-Mode Power Supplies

B-1 INTRODUCTION

Chapter 11 described in some detail the design and construction of classical power supplies based on the use of linear voltage regulators. The appendix outlines an alternative approach which employs on/off switching of a current to control the output voltage. Because of its high efficiency, this technique is rapidly growing in popularity. However, until the recent introduction of dedicated integrated circuits, the switching approach was confined to specialized applications because the necessary control system is so complex.

Two basic approaches to the application of switching techniques have evolved. First, switching principles have been applied to a voltage regulator. This application is referred to as a *switch-mode regulator* (see Fig. B-1A). It replaces a conventional linear regulator but still requires the traditional transformer, rectifier, and smoothing capacitor considered in Chapter 11. A second, more radical approach is shown in Fig. B-1B. This involves directly rectifying and smoothing the AC mains and then chopping the resulting unregulated DC voltage at a high frequency ($\sim$ 20 kHz) using a pair of switching transistors. This approach forms the basis of a *direct-off-line, switch-mode* power supply.

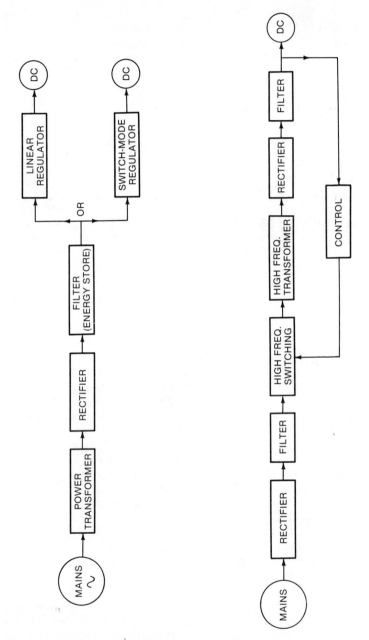

(A) Classical power supply employing linear or switch-mode regulation.

(B) Direct-off-line switch-mode power supply.

Fig. B-1. Switching techniques.

In this appendix, we first consider the general principles for obtaining a controlled DC output voltage from an unregulated DC voltage source, using current switching, and show that step-up, step-down and inverting configurations are possible. We then apply these principles to practical switch-mode regulators and finally to a direct-off-line switch-mode power supply.

B-2 GENERAL PRINCIPLES OF SWITCH-MODE VOLTAGE REGULATION

B-2-1 Step-Down Regulator

Fig. B-2 shows the main elements of a step-down regulator. Q1 is a high speed switching transistor driven by *pulse-width-modulated* (PWM) pulses at frequencies that typically lie between 10 and 100 kHz. Since Q1 is either cut off or in saturation, its power dissipation is very small and the overall efficiency of the regulator is high. V_i is an unregulated DC input voltage and V_o is the regulated output. D is a freewheeling or catching diode and is used to provide a continuous current path for the inductance, L, during those times when Q1 is off.

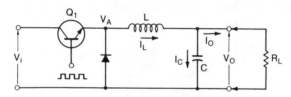

Fig. B-2. Basic step-down switch-mode regulator.

To understand the operation of the circuit, suppose that at time t = 0 the transistor, Q1, is turned on (Fig. B-3A). Neglecting the small voltage drop across Q1, the voltage V_A at the input to the inductor is essentially the same as the input voltage V_i. The basic relationship for the voltage across an inductance is:

$$V = L \, dI/dt \qquad \text{(Eq. B-1)}$$

It follows that, with an almost constant difference of $V_i - V_o$ across L, the current, I_L, through the inductance increases linearly with time according to the formula:

$$I_L = \frac{Kt}{t_i} + I_1 \text{ for } o < t < t_1, \qquad \text{(Eq. B-2)}$$

where

$$K = (V_i - V_o)t_1/L, \qquad \text{(Eq. B-3)}$$

and I_1 is the initial current through the inductance. The form of this graph, together with the values of I_1 and K, is illustrated in Fig. B-3B. Note that K also represents the difference between the maximum and minimum values of I_L. If I_o is the almost constant load current and I_c is the current through the capacitor, then:

$$I_L = I_c + I_o \qquad \text{(Eq. B-4)}$$

When Q1 turns on at $t = 0$, $I_L < I_o$ so that the capacitor continues discharging to supply the required proportion of I_o. The output voltage V_o therefore falls to a value V_{MIN} at a time t_{MIN}. At this time, I_L has increased sufficiently to become greater than I_o, the capacitor begins to charge, and the output voltage V_o starts to rise.

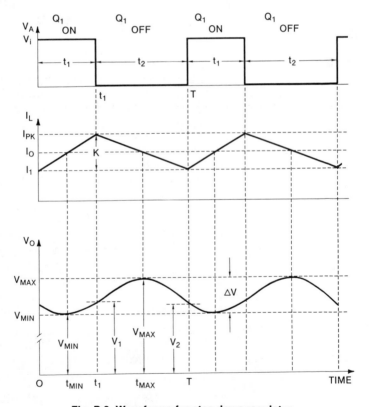

Fig. B-3. Waveforms for step-down regulator.

412

At time t_1, Q1 turns off, the current I_L has a maximum value I_{PK}, and the output reaches V_1. Since the current through the inductance cannot change instantaneously, the freewheeling diode D turns on, reducing the voltage V_A to zero. (This assumes that the small forward drop across D is neglected.) The voltage across L is now $-V_o$, and I_L follows the equation:

$$I_L = \frac{-V_o}{L}(t - t_1) + I_{PK}, \quad \text{for } t_1 < t < T \qquad \text{(Eq. B-5)}$$

At time T, $I_L = I_1$, and with $I_{PK} = I_1 + K$, we obtain:

$$I_1 = \frac{-V_o}{L}(T - t_1) + I_1 + K. \qquad \text{(Eq. B-6)}$$

Hence, using the definition for K given in Equation B-3,

$$\frac{V_o}{L}(T - t_1) = K = \frac{(V_i - V_o)}{L}t_1. \qquad \text{(Eq. B-7)}$$

Rearranging this expression gives:

$$\frac{V_o}{V_i} = \frac{t_1}{T}. \qquad \text{(Eq. B-8)}$$

This last result shows that, because the duty cycle $t_1/T < 1$, then $V_o/V_i < 1$, giving a step-down regulator. Also, the output voltage V_o is directly proportional to the duty cycle. Hence, the duty cycle of the PWM pulses applied to the base of Q1 can be used to control the output voltage.

At time t_1, the current I_L is still greater than I_o so that the capacitor (C) continues to charge to a maximum value V_{MAX} at a time t_{MAX}. For $t > t_{MAX}$, $I_L < I_o$ and C discharges. V_o therefore falls to a value V_2 at a time T equal to the period of the pulse train, whereupon the cycle starts again.

The difference between the voltage V_1 at turn-off and V_2 at turn-on, $V_1 - V_2$, is known as the *hysteresis* of the regulator. The ripple voltage ΔV is the difference $V_{MAX} - V_{MIN}$. The increase in V_o from V_1 to V_{MAX} and the decrease from V_2 to V_{MIN} is known as *overshoot* and is due to I_L differing from I_o at thetimes when switching takes place. Excessive overshoot is sometimes a problem in switching regulators, but it can be reduced by increasing L and decreasing C while maintaining a constant value for the product LC.

An expression for ΔV can be derived as follows. The mean load current I_o is given by:

$$I_o = V_o/R_L, \qquad \text{(Eq. B-9)}$$

where $V_o = V_i (t_1/T)$. It can also be expressed as the mean value of I_1 and I_{PK}, from which:

$$I_{PK} = I_o + K/2. \qquad \text{(Eq. B-10)}$$

The peak-to-peak value of the ripple ΔV can be found by noting that between t_{MIN} and t_{MAX}, the charge added to the capacitor is:

$$Q = C \, \Delta V. \qquad \text{(Eq. B-11)}$$

If we assume that $t_{MAX} - t_{MIN} = T/2$ and that the average current charging the capacitor during this time is:

$$\overline{I}_c = \tfrac{1}{2}(I_{PK} + I_o) - I_o = K/4, \qquad \text{(Eq. B-12)}$$

then

$$Q = C\Delta V = \overline{I}_c T/2 = KT/8. \qquad \text{(Eq. B-13)}$$

Hence, substituting the expression for K gives:

$$\Delta V = \frac{T^2}{8LC} V_i \left(1 - \frac{V_o}{V_i} \right). \qquad \text{(Eq. B-14)}$$

When designing a circuit of this type, we can assume that the values of V_i, V_o, I_o and T are specified. With this information, we can calculate the on-time t_1 from Equation B-8. The value of L is then chosen using Equation B-3 so that the change in the inductive current, K, is less than 20% of the load current I_o. Finally, the value of C is calculated to satisfy the ripple (Equation B-14) specification.

Note that this circuit generates considerable noise on its input side because of the switching transients, although the output is fairly quiet. Attention therefore needs to be paid to the installation of low-pass filters on the input lines to suppress electromagnetic interference (EMI). Careful mechanical design and shielding are also required to suppress radiated radio-frequency interference (RFI). Finally, specially designed fast-switching diodes and pass transistors are essential. Low-frequency power transistors and diodes quickly overheat if used in high-speed switching applications.

B-2-2 Step-up Regulator
Fig. B-4 illustrates the basic configuration of components required to produce a step-up regulator. The analysis of this circuit is similar to that developed for the step-down regulator. Thus at $t = 0$, assume that Q1 turns on, so that $V_A = 0$. The voltage V_i appears across the inductance, L, and the current through the inductance, I_L increases linearly with time, so that:

$$I_L = I_1 + (V_i/L)t \quad \text{for } 0 < t < t_1, \qquad \text{(Eq. B-15)}$$

where I_1 is the current flowing at $t = 0$.

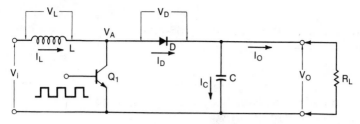

Fig. B-4. Basic step-up switch-mode regulator.

Since $V_A = 0$ and $V_o \neq 0$, the diode D is under reverse bias and all of I_L flows through Q1. At time $t = t_1$, I_L reaches a peak value I_{PK} and Q1 turns off. Hence:

$$I_{PK} = I_1 + (V_i/L)t_1 \qquad \text{(Eq. B-16)}$$

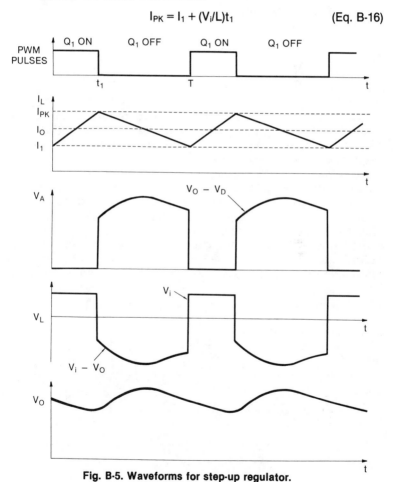

Fig. B-5. Waveforms for step-up regulator.

415

I_L as a function of time is illustrated in Fig. B-5. When Q1 turns off, I_L cannot change instantaneously, so the diode D turns on to provide a current path for I_L. Voltage V_A rises to the output voltage V_o, except for the small forward voltage drop across the diode. Also, the voltage $V_A = V_o$ must be greater than the input voltage V_i if the correct polarity is to be maintained across the inductance. This is because I_L, flowing through D to the load, decreases linearly with time. Thus,

$$I_L = I_{PK} - \left(\frac{V_o - V_i}{L}\right)(T - t_1) \qquad \text{(Eq. B-17)}$$

for $t_1 < t < T$. At time T, the period of the pulse train, $I_L = I_1$ and Q1 turns on. Hence at $t = T$,

$$I_{PK} - \left(\frac{V_o - V_i}{L}\right)(T - t_1) = I_1. \qquad \text{(Eq. B-18)}$$

Therefore, from Equations B-16 and B-18,

$$\frac{V_o}{V_i} = \frac{T}{T - t_1} = \frac{T}{t_{OFF}}. \qquad \text{(Eq. B-19)}$$

Since $T > t_{OFF}$, $V_o > V_i$ and a step-up regulator is obtained with an output voltage greater than the input. Note that the increase in voltage stems primarily from the voltage polarity developed across the inductance as the current through it increases and decreases. Since the flow of current from the inductance to the load occurs only intermittently when Q1 is off, the capacitor C is required to smooth out the fluctuations in the output voltage. The output waveform is also sketched in Fig. B-5.

It is useful to consider an energy argument to show the step-up action of this circuit. For an ideal regulator with zero internal power dissipation, the input power should equal the output power so that:

$$V_i I_i = V_o I_o \qquad \text{(Eq. B-20)}$$

The input current I_i is the same as the current I_L. It is always present because I_L can flow either through Q1 or the load. $I_i = I_L$ is therefore true for the whole period T, and the total energy delivered to the regulator during T is $I_L V_i T$. However, the output current through the diode to the load flows only when Q1 is off and delivers energy $V_o I_L t_{OFF}$. Hence in the absence of losses:

$$V_i I_L T = V_o I_L t_{OFF}$$

or

$$\frac{V_o}{V_i} = \frac{T}{t_{OFF}}$$ (Eq. B-21)

Since the input current is continuous and the diode current is intermittent, only a small amount of electrical noise is developed in the input line, while the output noise is quite large.

B-2-3 The Inverting Regulator

The third configuration, shown in Fig. B-6, produces an output which is of opposite polarity to the input and whose magnitude is governed by the ratio t_{ON}/t_{OFF}. The operation of this circuit may be seen as follows. If Q1 is turned on at $t = 0$, then V_A rises to V_i, D is reverse biased, and I_L increases linearly with time to a peak value I_{PK} at a time t_1 when Q1 turns off. Thus:

$$I_{PK} = (V_i/L)t_1 + I_1, \quad \text{for } 0 < t < t_1.$$ (Eq. B-22)

Since I_L cannot change instantaneously, D turns on when Q1 turns off, and I_L continues to flow in the direction shown while decreasing linearly with time. To achieve this, the voltage V_A must go negative, taking on the value $- V_o$. Thus:

$$I_L = I_{PK} - (V_o/L) (t - t_1) \quad \text{for } t_1 < t < T.$$ (Eq. B-23)

At time $t = T$, $I_L = I_1$ and:

$$I_{PK} = (V_o/L) (T - t_1) + I_1 = (V_i/L)t_1 + I_1.$$ (Eq. B-24)

Hence, from Equations B-22 and B-24:

$$V_o/V_i = t_1/(T - t_1) = t_{ON}/t_{OFF}.$$ (Eq. B-25)

This last result shows that the magnitude of V_o depends on the ratio of the on-time to the off-time and that it is possible to have an output which is either greater than or less than the input. The direction of current flow in the output loop is governed by the diode, which ensures that the output voltage is negative.

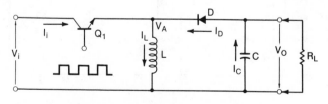

Fig. B-6. Basic inverting switch-mode regulator.

Since the current flow is intermittent in both the input loop and the output loop, electrical noise is generated at both the input and the output.

B-3 PRACTICAL SWITCH-MODE REGULATOR CIRCUITS

The previous section examined the theory of the three basic switching regulator circuits. This section describes the practical implementation of this theory. We assume that a dc voltage source, V_i, is available. This may be the output from a conventional unregulated power supply, from a battery, or from an already smoothed and regulated source such as a 5-volt supply. The switch-mode regulator is then employed either to directly replace a conventional linear regulator, or to produce a regulated output which may be either lower or higher or inverted compared with the input. Practical switch-mode regulators can be classified as *free-running* (self-oscillating) or *driven* regulators, depending on the source of the signal applied to the switching transistor. We now examine each of these types in more detail.

B-3-1 Free-Running Regulator

Fig. B-7 shows the circuit of a typical self-oscillating switching regulator with an output V_o. The basic step-down configuration of Section B-2-1 has been modified by the addition of a reference source and a comparator which has built-in hysteresis provided by the positive feedback and by resistors R_1 and R_f.

If Q1 is on, the output V_o rises, and since the voltage V^+ is initially greater than V_o, the output from the comparator is positive and provides the base current needed to keep Q1 on. Neglecting the drop across Q1, the voltage V_A is equal to the

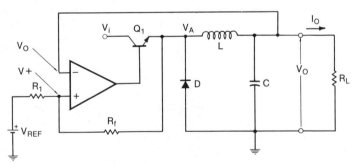

Fig. B-7. Free-running switch-mode regulator.

input voltage V_i. At time t_1, the output has risen to the value V_1 which is sufficient to make $V_o > V^+$. The comparator therefore changes state, sending its output negative. This turns off Q1. The value of V_1 at which this transition takes place can be found by calculating the value of V^+ due to the voltage divider action of R_1 and R_f on V_{REF}, and of R_f and R_1 on V_A (= V_i). The result of this calculation is that:

$$V^+ = V_1 = \frac{V_{REF} R_f + V_i R_1}{R_1 + R_f}. \qquad \text{(Eq. B-26)}$$

With Q1 turned off, V_o starts to fall until at time T it reaches a value $V_2 < V^+$. The comparator therefore changes state, sending its output positive. This turns on Q1. The value of V_2 can be found by noting that while Q1 is off, the diode D is on and V_A is approximately zero. Thus, from Equation B-26, and with $V_A = 0$:

$$V^+ = V_2 = \frac{V_{REF} R_f}{R_1 + R_f}. \qquad \text{(Eq. B-27)}$$

By suitable choice of V_{REF}, R_f, and R_1, the voltages V_1 and V_2 and the hysteresis $V_1 - V_2$ can be determined. If we assume that the required output is the mean of V_1 and V_2, then:

$$V_o = \frac{V_{REF} R_f + \frac{1}{2} V_i R_1}{R_1 + R_f}, \qquad \text{(Eq. B-28)}$$

and the hysteresis

$$\Delta V = \frac{V_i R_1}{R_1 + R_f}. \qquad \text{(Eq. B-29)}$$

Usually the minimum hysteresis is governed by the required input-switching voltage of the comparator, while increasing the hysteresis leads to increased output ripple and lower frequencies. A sample calculation is shown in Example B-1.

In practical applications, it is often convenient to use the reference voltage and differential amplifier of a monolithic integrated circuit such as the 723 precision voltage regulator. An external switching transistor is usually employed and the necessary positive feedback added around the amplifier. Fig. B-8, derived from the application notes for the 723, illustrates a practical self-excited regulator.[1] In this circuit, which is designed to deliver 2 amps at 5 volts, R_1 and R_2 divide the 7-volt reference to give a nominal 5-volt reference at the noninverting terminals; R_3 and R_4 provide the positive feedback required for the hysteresis in the circuit. Q1 and Q2 are a pair of high-speed switching transistors connected as a Darlington pair and driven by the internal power transistor of the 723. When constructing this circuit, the final value for the capacitor C_2 is obtained by trial and error. The recommended 1.2-mH (millihenry) inductance can be constructed from about forty turns of No. 20 enameled copper wire wound over a ferrite core.

EXAMPLE B-1: DESIGN OF A FREE-RUNNING REGULATOR

Given a comparator for which we require $\Delta V = 30$ mV, $V_i = 30$ volts, $V_o = 5$ volts, and $V_{REF} = 5$ volts, determine suitable values for R_1 and R_f.

From Equation B-29:

$$30 \times 10^{-3} = \frac{30R_1}{R_1 + R_f}$$

Thus, $R_f \approx 10^{-3} R_1$, and with $R_1 = 1$ kΩ, $R_f = 1$ MΩ.

From Equation B-28:

$$V_o = \frac{V_{REF} \times 10^3 R_1 + 15R_1}{R_1 + 10^3 R_1}$$

Thus, $V_o \approx V_{REF} = 5$ volts.

These results show that to achieve the required condition, $R_f \gg R_1$, $\Delta V \approx V_i (R_1/R_f)$ and $V_o \approx V_{REF}$.

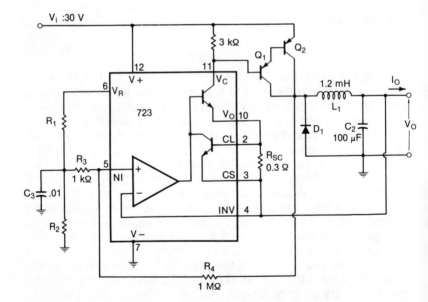

Fig. B-8. Implementation of free-running switch-mode regulator using a 723 precision voltage regulator.

B-3-2 Driven Regulators

In the last few years, a number of manufacturers have developed monolithic switching regulator ICs that incorporate the various control and switching elements required to produce a complete regulator with the minimum of external components. Typical elements include reference sources, comparators, oscillators, modulators, and power switching circuits. Review articles have appeared covering the theory and applications of these devices.[2] Here we will concentrate on the Fairchild μA78S40 universal switching regulator subsystem because of its great versatility and its extensive documentation.[3]

The major functional blocks and the pin configuration for the μA78S40 are shown in Fig. B-9. The current-controlled oscillator has an off-time which is determined by an external timing capacitor C_t, an internally fixed duty cycle of 8:1 and a current-limiting circuit I_{PK} that senses the current through the switching transistor, Q1, via an external resistor R_{sc} (see Fig. B-10). A 1.3-volt temperature-compensated reference source is included and is normally connected to the noninverting input of the high-gain differential comparator. The inverting input is usually supplied by a sample of the output voltage to be controlled. The output from the comparator is combined with the output from the oscillator in an AND gate and therefore turns off the switching transistor when the sample output voltage becomes greater than the reference. The timing capacitor then keeps the oscillator off for a time t_{OFF}, during which the output falls sufficiently for the comparator to change state. Thus, when the oscillator next goes high, the comparator output is also high and the transistor turns on. The IC also contains a switching transistor and diode, each capable of carrying 1.5 amps and withstanding up to 40 volts. The uncommitted high-gain operational amplifier has a 150-mA drive capacity and is useful when there is a need for series-pass regulation or for feedback control in some switching regulator applications.

Fig. B-10 illustrates one application of the μA78S40 as a step-down regulator giving a 5-volt output at 500 mA from a 25-volt source. To design such a regulator, the following steps should be followed.

1. If we assume that I_1 in Fig. B-3 is zero, then the required peak current $I_{PK} = 2I_o$. Hence, if $I_o = 0.5$ amp, then $I_{PK} = 1.0$ amp.
2. The current-limiting resistor, R_{sc}, is given by:

$$R_{sc} = V_{SENSE}/I_{PK} \qquad \text{(Eq. B-30)}$$

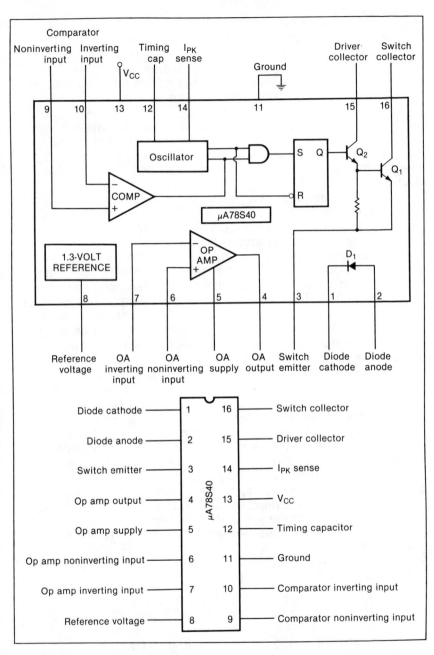

Fig. B-9. Block diagram showing major functions of Fairchild µA78S40 universal switching regulator subsystem.

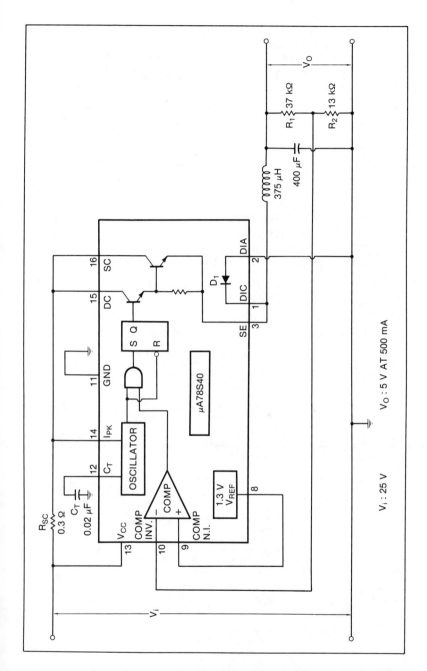

Fig. B-10. Implementation of a driven step-down regulator using the μZ78S40.

423

3. For the μA78S40, $V_{SENSE} = 0.33$ volt, so that with $I_{PK} = 1.0$ amp, $R_{sc} = 0.33\ \Omega$.

4. From Equation B-8, taking into account the saturation voltage V_s across Q1 and the forward drop V_D across D_1, the ratio t_{ON}/t_{OFF} becomes:

$$\frac{t_{ON}}{t_{OFF}} = \frac{V_o + V_D}{V_i - V_o - V_s} \qquad \text{(Eq. B-31)}$$

For the μA78S40, $V_D = 1.25$ volts and $V_s = 1.3$ volts. Hence, with $V_o = 5$ volts and $V_i = 25$ volts:

$$\frac{t_{ON}}{t_{OFF}} = \frac{5 + 1.25}{25 - 5 - 1.3}$$

The manufacturer recommends that both t_{ON} and t_{OFF} should be greater than 10 μs. Hence, if we choose $t_{ON} = 20$ μs, the required value of $t_{OFF} = 60$ μs.

5. The required value of the timing capacitor C_T is given by:

$$C_T(\mu F) = 45 \times 10^{-5}\, t_{OFF}(\mu s) \qquad \text{(Eq. B-32)}$$

Thus $C_T = 45 \times 10^{-5} \times 60 = 0.025\ \mu F$.

6. Rearranging Equations B-3 and B-8, with $K = I_{PK}$, and taking into account the diode voltage drop gives:

$$L = \frac{V_i - V_o - V_s}{I_{PK}} \times t_{ON} \qquad \text{(Eq. B-33)}$$

Hence,

$$L = \frac{(25 - 5 - 1.3)20 \times 10^{-6}}{1.0} = 375\ \mu H.$$

7. The output capacitor C determines the amount of ripple. Thus from Equation B-13,

$$C = \frac{I_{PK}T}{8\Delta V} \qquad \text{(Eq. B-34)}$$

where $T = t_{ON} + t_{OFF}$. In the present example, if we assume that $\Delta V = 25$ mV then:

$$C = \frac{1.0(20 + 60) \times 10^{-6}}{8 \times 25 \times 10^{-3}} = 400\ \mu F.$$

8. The resistive voltage divider R_1, R_2 samples the output voltage for comparison with V_{REF} of 1.3 volts. Thus:

$$V_{REF} = V_o \left(\frac{R_2}{R_1 + R_2} \right)$$

If $R_1 + R_2$ is chosen to be 50 kΩ then,

$$R_2 = 50K \times \frac{1.3}{5.0} = 13 \text{ k}\Omega$$

and

$$R_1 = 37 \text{ k}\Omega.$$

The component values given in Fig. B-10 are essentially the same as those recommended by Fairchild.

9. The efficiency η of a step-down regulator is given by:

$$\eta = \left(\frac{V_i - V_s + V_D}{V_i} \right) \left(\frac{V_o}{V_o + V_D} \right) \% \qquad \text{(Eq. B-35)}$$

In the present example,

$$\eta = \left(\frac{25 - 1.3 + 1.25}{25} \right) \left(\frac{5}{5 + 1.25} \right) = 80\%$$

The Fairchild application notes for the μA78S40 list the design formulae and give examples for the common step-up, step-down and inverting regulators; as well as discussing a number of more sophisticated applications.[4]

B-4 DIRECT-OFF-LINE SWITCH-MODE POWER SUPPLY

As described in Chapter 11, the purpose of a power supply is to transform the AC mains voltage to a smooth, stable DC voltage. To accomplish this transformation, several steps are needed:

- The output voltage is either increased or decreased and is isolated from the mains.
- The mains voltage is rectified to give unidirectional current flow.
- An energy storage device smoothes out fluctuations in the output.
- Some form of closed-loop control stabilizes or regulates the output voltage.

In many respects the classical power supplies discussed in Chapter 11 perform these operations in a most unsatisfactory way, as the following points show:

- The first step is nearly always provided by a transformer, which is often the most bulky, heavy, and expensive part of a power supply. However, all three of these undesirable features can be reduced if the operating frequency of the transformer is increased.

- Energy storage is usually performed by a capacitor. The size of a capacitor depends on the stored charge $Q = CV$, where C is the capacitance and V is the voltage to which the capacitor is charged. The stored energy $E = \frac{1}{2}CV^2$, so it is advantageous to operate the main storage capacitor at as high a voltage as possible. In addition, high-frequency charging of the capacitor is desirable, since the capacitor is "topped-up" more often and this improves the capacitor's smoothing action.
- Regulation is more efficiently implemented using the switching principles outlined in the earlier parts of this appendix, rather than using linear regulators with their high internal power dissipation.

The ideas outlined above have led to the evolution of the direct-off-line switch-mode power supply. This is illustrated in block form in Fig. B-11 and incorporates the switching principles outlined earlier in Section B-2. The AC line is filtered by an EMI filter to remove transients and to keep interference generated by the supply from reaching the mains supply line. The line voltage is rectified by the diodes D1–D4 and smoothed by the capacitor C_1, which typically has 150 volts across it. The switching transistors Q1 and Q2 and capacitors C_2 and C_3 form a bridge inverter feeding the high frequency power transformer T_1. The transistors are turned on alternately at a frequency which is typically about 40 kHz and with an on-off time set by the control circuit. The secondary voltage from T_1 is full-wave rectified by diodes D5 and D6 and smoothed by the LC filter formed by L_1 and C_4. Note that the use of inductors as filter elements becomes attractive at the high switching frequencies employed.

The control circuit shown in Fig. B-11 uses closed-loop control to provide a stable, well-regulated output voltage. The output voltage is regulated by sampling the output voltage and comparing it with a reference value in the error amplifier, V-amp. The error signal is then used as the modulating signal applied to the input of a pulse-width modulator. The output from the modulator drives the bases of the switching transistors via the isolating pulse transformer T_2. As shown in the previous section, variations in the mark/space ratio are used to control the output voltage. Control of the output current is obtained by sampling the current from the inverter using the current transformer T_3. The rectified signal from T_3 is compared with a suitable reference in the error amplifier I-amp, whose output is also applied to the modulator. The control signals for various protection circuits can also be applied to the

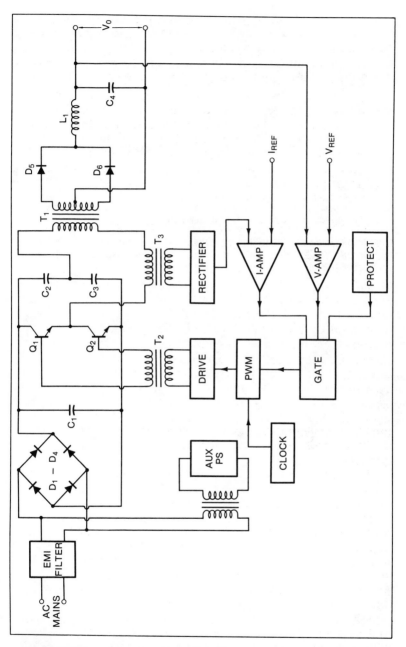

Fig. B-11. Block diagram showing the main elements of a direct-off-line switch-mode power supply.

modulator to close down the system if required. The circuit blocks making up the control system are often powered by a subsidiary linear power supply connected directly to the mains. Overvoltage protection can be obtained by closing down this power supply and thus the whole control system.

B-5 REFERENCES

1. Fairchild, Inc., "µA723 Precision Voltage Regulator Data Sheets and Applications," *Fairchild Voltage Regulator Handbook,* 1979, pp. 7-110–7-116.

2. B. Dance, "Switching Regulator Devices," *Electronics Industry,* June 1979, pp. 23–30.

3. T. Valches, "µA78S40 Switching Voltage Regulator Applications," *Fairchild Application Note 344,* December 1978.

4. Fairchild, Inc., "µA78S40 Universal Switching Regulator Application Notes," *Fairchild Voltage Regulator Handbook,* 1978; pp. 3-55–3-61, data sheets pp. 7-128–7-132.

Digital IC Voltage and Current Specifications: Definitions

C-1 VOLTAGES

V_H   *Input HIGH Voltage* — The range of input voltages that represents a high in the system. $V_{IH}(min)$ is the guaranteed input-high threshold. For 7400 series:

$$V_{IH} = 2V(min) \qquad\qquad (4.75 \leqslant V_{cc} \leqslant 5.25)$$

V_{IL}   *Input LOW Voltage* — The range of input voltages which represent a low in the system. $V_{IL}(max)$ is the guaranteed input low threshold for the device. For 7400 series:

$$V_{IL} = 0.8\ V(max) \qquad\qquad (4.75 \leqslant V_{cc} \leqslant 5.25)$$

$V_{OH}(min)$ *Output HIGH Voltage* — The minimum voltage at an output terminal for a specified output current, I_{OH}, and at the minimum value of V_{cc}. For 7400 series:

$$V_{OH}(min) = 2.4\ V \qquad\qquad (I_{OH} = 400\ \mu A)$$
$$\phantom{V_{OH}(min)} = 3.4\ V\ typically \qquad (V_{IL} = 0.8\ V)$$
$$\phantom{V_{OH}(min) = 3.4\ V\ typ} (V_{cc} = 4.75\ V)$$

V$_{OL}$(max) *Output LOW Voltage* — The minimum voltage at an output for a specified output current, I$_{OH}$, and the minimum value of V$_{cc}$. For 7400 series:

$$V_{OL}(max) = 0.4 \text{ V} \qquad\qquad (I_{OL} = 16 \text{ mA})$$
$$= 0.2 \text{ V typically} \qquad\quad (V_{cc} = 4.75 \text{ V})$$
$$(V_{IH} = 2 \text{ V})$$

C-2 CURRENTS

I$_{IH}$ *Input HIGH Current* — The current flowing *into* an input when a specified high voltage is applied. For 7400 series:

$$I_{IH} = 40 \, \mu A(max) \qquad\qquad (V_{IN} = 2.4 \text{ V}, V_{cc} = 5.5 \text{ V})$$

I$_{IL}$ *Input LOW Current* — The current flowing out of an input when a specified low voltage is applied. For 7400 series:

$$I_{IL} = -1.6 \text{ mA(max)} \qquad\qquad (V_{IN} = 0.4 \text{ V}, V_{cc} = 5.5 \text{ V})$$

I$_{OH}$ *Output HIGH Current* — The current flowing out of an output when the output is in its high state. For 7400 series:

$$I_{OH} = -400 \, \mu A(max) \qquad\qquad (V_{OUT} > 2.4 \text{ V}, V_{cc} = 5 \text{ V})$$

I$_{OL}$ *Output LOW Current* — The current flowing into an output when the output is in its low state. For 7400 series:

$$I_{OL} = 16 \text{ mA(max)} \qquad\qquad (V_{OUT} < 0.4 \text{ V}, V_{cc} = 5 \text{ V})$$

Index